Hedges,
Ditches
and Dreams

Also by Alastair Ashford-Brown
Songs of Sorrow and Joy
Nets in the Wind

Also Available from Bardic Press

Gnostic Tendencies
Andrew Phillip Smith
Pages From a Welsh Cunning Man's Book
Andrew Phillip Smith
The Four Branches of the Mabinogi
Will Parker
Voices of Gnosticism
Other Voices of Gnosticism
Miguel Conner
*The Gnostic: A Journal of Gnosticism, Western Esotericism
and Spirituality 1–6*
Spirit Possession and the Origins of Christianity
Stevan Davies
Revolt of the Widows
Stevan Davies
The Gospel of Thomas and Christian Wisdom
Stevan Davies

Visit our website at www.bardicpress.com
email us at bardicpress@gmail.com

Hedges, Ditches and Dreams

Tales From the Flames of Youth

Alastair Ashford-Brown

Bardic Press

The author age 17

Cover painting 'The Guiding Self' © 2023 Alastair Ashford-Brown
Printed on acid-free paper
Published by Bardic Press
(Check website for mailing address)
http://www.bardicpress.com

ISBN 978-1-906834-47-0

Contents

To my mother and father who gave me life.

You must fulfill the way that is in you.

Carl Jung

Chapter 1
Paris in the Springtime

The best way to get to know a city (just as it's, eventually, the best way to get to know oneself) is first of all to get lost in it – set out without maps, venture down those dark alleys, tread where angels dread your treading; that was how I'd got to know Paris.

Not long arrived here, eighteen and green as the first shoot of spring, I've been up at the Sacré Coeur watching the sun set and the lights going on all over the city and am now coming down the hill and find myself in a street full of bars with women leaning in the doorways. They don't have much clothing on, in fact some of them have barely any clothing at all; perhaps I should avert my eyes and turn back the way I've come – after all, I've set out on this great journey to seek romance and adventure, not to fall into the pitfalls of sin. I try to turn back but there's one little chink in my armour, one impediment to my resolve to remain the virtuous knight on a quest I see myself as, and I'm totally disarmed by the urge to see more and to walk further down this street. This shameful desire has me firmly in its grip. My will almost defeated, I resolve to tie myself to the mast as Odysseus had done and observe, merely observe, those alluring sirens and resist their enticements and to stride with unbending will, what I have left of one, to the far end of the street and safely leave it, getting as far away as I can and putting the whole thing behind me and out of mind. A hot flush is coming over me as I begin my absurd march, which is more like that of a lamb on trembling legs proceeding to its slaughter. Stiffening my resolve I've made it almost to the end of the street and am passing the very last of these evil-looking dens, when one of these alluring creatures beckons me – oh my god she's well endowed under that flimsy bit of lace and I should be crying out immediately, 'Tie me tighter, men,' but I don't, I am lost.

'*Tu viens, chéri?*'

'Er . . . *bonsoir, madame* . . . ' I stammer, my voice trembling.

'*Tu veux . . . ?*' and she smacks her lips as though in a kiss – she really is quite brazen.

'*Je veux du lait* . . . ' I say, as though reduced to a helpless infant.

'*Du lait?*' she asks, astonished, '*alors*, I have meelk . . . ' at which she pulls a huge, milk-laden breast from her blouse, squeezes the nipple from which a couple of drops dribble, saying, 'I have meelk, *viens chéri.*'

Hypnotized by those mammaries I follow her into the dark interior of the bar, where loathsome-looking specimens have their hands all over the sirens languishing there, and through to the far end of the saloon and into a curtained cubicle where there's a small table with enough room for one person on either side of it; motioning me to sit down, she's saying, 'We drink champagne now . . . .' '*Non, Non,*' I say, alarmed – champagne costs a fortune – 'Only a hundred francs . . . ' she purrs, '*Non, non,* I just want milk.' She takes her breasts out and lays them on the table, 'we'll drink milk with the champagne – my milk is warm . . . ' they wobble on the table like jellies and I'm delirious with desire, 'touch them,' she says and my hand, beyond the dictates of my will, now starts reaching towards them and will surely seal my fate as I lose all control and bury my face between those heavenly orbs, when the curtain is drawn aside and a waiter appears with a bottle of champagne on ice, '*Non, Non,*' I cry as he begins to open it, with the woman saying, '*ouvre, ouvre!*' and I, absolutely panic-struck, crying, '*Non, non, n'ouvre pas* . . . ' so loudly that another man appears at the opening in the curtain, a big fellow, gorilla-like, who growls, 'Is there a problem in here?'

'I . . . I . . . don't want champagne. I only wanted to drink some milk . . . ' I stammer. He glares at me, 'Milk? Milk? You are in here and you want milk, my friend, you think this is a dairy? You think

this babe is a cow and you want to milk her tits? *Ho Ho, mon cher ami, tu veux du lait? Viens avec moi,'* and, with my tail between my legs, he delivers me from the clutches of the temptress, whose face has turned sour as curdled milk, and up to the counter where he slams down a glass of milk in front of me, roaring with laughter and saying, '*Pour le bébé*, on ze house.'

You've caught me at an embarassing moment but now that I'm back safely on the street let me introduce myself; I'm known as 'Lala' to family and friends, an odd name for a bloke but I've learnt to live with it. It was my sister, Wendy, who christened me thus, unable at the time of my birth, one mid-winter night, to pronounce my proper one, Alastair. She was two years old and pointing at me said, with absolute conviction, 'Lala' and it stuck forevermore. Perhaps that's what made me unable to take anything seriously as I would have done had I been called Alastair – an altogether more serious-sounding name. Perhaps the name suits my appearance and I some-times think we grow to look like the name we're called. I'm long and lanky with a giraffe neck and a very prominent Adam's apple (when I swallow it looks like the lift in a ten storey building, hurtling to the top, where it rings an imaginary bell, and dashes down again.) My lips are rather thick, my eyes somewhat slit, I have a shock of reddish hair upon which, at the moment, a pork pie hat sits, an affectation perhaps, though not a very sophisticated one. A foolish grin betrays my excruciating naivety about the world which makes me a sitting duck for the wolves who prowl the city streets. I write poetry, mainly on the subject of love of which I know nothing as yet – and so they're basically about unrequited love and the adoration of girls from afar.

So here I am in Paris, staying with my brother Ashley and his girl-friend Inês, both struggling artists who eke out a living in a gar-ret at number sixteen rue Bézout, near Alésia. I sleep in the atelier amongst the paints and canvases. In the evenings it's open house to all manner of Bohemians and artists, the table's laden with wine and food and the air turns thick with the smoke of *Gauloises*. There are painters, writers, musicians and anarchists – a poster from May '68 with a student hurling a rock at a cordon of police hangs in promi-nence on the wall. New to this world, I fancy myself a poet but, in the eyes of others, am but a gawky boy from the countryside with this naïve, rather ridiculous grin, puffing at a pipe and sporting this pork pie hat which, in the evenings, hangs on a peg behind the door slowly getting cured by the smoke. I am lucky to have this refuge after a day's peregrinations in the streets. I recount to my hosts the little incidents of my forays as we sit in the early evening over a bottle of wine – cheap rot-gut wine for which I'm acquiring quite a taste – and amuse them by my reactions to this most brazen of cities. I confess to them that I could easily be led astray, like the night I returned late – I hadn't really been sitting at a café reading a book, that was a lie. My tongue is loosening up with this wine and I begin to tell them what I've just been telling you.

'And so you were saved from the beauty by the beast,' says my brother chuckling, 'here, have a glass of wine – on the house.'

'But what, what, has brought you here again?' you exclaim as you espy me descending the steps of the *Sacré Coeur* and turning down the very same street in which the scenario – which scared the pants off me – took place the other evening. And this time I have the money for that bottle of champagne . . . you see exactly what's coming next – the cunning-faced fellow who's been drinking in the bars down here all day and has spent his dough is making his way up the street that I am on the way down. You are, you tell me, going to have to be on your toes.

'*Mon ami* . . . ' – here we go, he's greeted you, how can you not return his greeting without being thoroughly impolite? On the side of his face, lit up by the lights of a bar, you see a scar which runs from his mouth to his ear – he must be a cutthroat – you haven't yet been given that invaluable bit of advice by the Gypsies, 'don't be afraid of the geezer with the scar on his face, but watch out for the one who put it there.'

He's saying something with a smile you don't trust; that's because it's not a smile, it's a leer. What does he want, what is he asking for? *Du fric? Des sous? Du pez? Argent!* – you learnt that word at school – yes, he wants money, what are you going to do about it? just stand there blushing and trembling, telling him you haven't got any? Come on, he's not going to buy that. His eyes which have been darting over you since the moment you collided with him have already located the pocket you keep it in: and he's going to get as much of it off you as he can. Shout at him to go away—you don't want to give him anything, but you hand him a franc, just to keep him quiet . . . a franc? 'Pah,' he spits, what's a measly franc going to get him? he isn't very happy about your lack of generosity—you outrage him with your franc. After all, he asked you nicely, remember? Called you *'mon ami'* and said *'s'il vous plaît'* but you've tried his patience and now he's turning nasty—you want to run like buggery but you're frozen with fear: his hand has slipped like lightning into your pocket and he's up the street and out of sight before you can say Jack Robinson. No use standing there looking aggrieved—your moral indignation's not going to bring him back, saying, 'I'm frightfully sorry, old chap—here's your money back.' Your indignation's a joke to him: in fact I wouldn't be surprised if he wasn't at the end of the alley doubled up with mirth at the sight of you trembling with impotent rage. Actually old bean, you ought to be grateful to him: he's taught you a valuable lesson—cheap at the price, what, a hundred francs in all? Oh, plus the one you gave him . . . You have some more in the bank—next time you won't.

I, gawky boy from countryside, am out of my depth. I fling my pork pie hat on the ground and trample on it.

So how was it I'd got here—what had preceded this first sojourn in Paris, the first city I'd ventured alone into? Why was I so gawky, so naïve, so wet behind the ears?

Well, after my expulsion from Marlborough I was at a complete loss as to what to do with my life. I hung around at home a few months, listless and despondent. I thank my stars I had such patient and understanding parents—for I must have been a trial to them as well as being an utter failure in the eyes of the world. And then I decided to go in search of a post as a shepherd. My mother had always spoken to us of the wonderful life shepherds lead, always up in the hills with their flocks—it was to his shepherd that her father would always listen when he needed any advice about the farm, the livestock, the tilling of the fields—because, as my grandfather would say, 'he has all the wisdom of the winds and the earth.'

To lead that life, far from the business of the world, appealed to me very deeply—I could wander lonely as a cloud and converse with the winds, which came from afar, from who knows where, and from all directions, with the animals, the birds and the trees, I could sing under the stars and compose to the moon. 'What a great idea,' my mother had exclaimed as I announced my plans—though my poor father looked rather more reserved about it, and though he never said anything to discourage me, he must have thought, 'All that money spent on his education, and he's off to become a shepherd.' Most people set off for the city, with its streets of gold and glittering lights to find their fortune, but I set off for Exmoor, with its flocks of sheep and glittering stars.

It wasn't long before I found myself employed on a farm near South Molton. The farm house, where I was given a room, was in the middle of nowhere, reached by a lonely road which wound over the moor. The reality turned out to be very different from the dream. Although there was a flock of five hundred woolly ewes to watch over it was to be by no means the idle, idyllic life I'd imagined it to be. I was put to hard physical labour from dawn to dusk under the vigilant eye of the farmer, an irascible fellow, a drunkard, who worked me to the bone on the thousand and one tasks that needed doing about the farm. He'd get around on his horse and come across me loafing behind a hedge, smoking my pipe, away from the biting wind. Coming upon me thus, his fury knew no bounds and he'd let loose a volley of the vilest cussing and swearing my tender ears had ever heard, bringing to an abrupt halt my flights of poetry. Poetry was my all consuming passion; I wanted to hymn to nature, who so moved me, and give voice to the feelings she aroused in me. Nature, it seemed to me, was an intelligent, all-embracing being, of which I was a part but from which I was separated and to which, with all my heart and soul, I wished to reunite; but I would have to go out into the world awhile to burn, to learn, so that I could to my roots, enriched, return. I'd first have to fight, to struggle, to overcome so much in myself before I could get back to myself.

My boss, was not a bad man—he was an unhappy man; he'd been a jockey, had had a bad fall and was virtually paralyzed in one leg, which he dragged along as he walked. He'd taken to gin for solace and gin, of all liquor, is the one which makes one's misery bearable, almost a joy. He'd go right up like a blazing streak of fire in which he gallopped around the hills like a demon possessed, and then he'd come crashing down, in the evening usually, when he, myself and his wife would be sitting at supper, he'd burst into floods of remorseful tears, apologising to me for his fit of temper in the field in the morning and begging me not to take it to heart – I was doing a good job on the farm, he'd say and I was not to assume that he was ungrateful – 'But when I see you stretched out on the bank in the sun, over behind a hedge, hiding from me, and letting the sheep wander where they will, it . . . it . . . cnrages me. You have all night to sleep – the daytime's for working. Time is money. But please forgive me – I don't mean to be hard – I'm very fond of you . . . In fact, if you leave . . . ' he'd break down weeping, leaving me in a state of nervous bewilderment. His wife would watch on coldly, silently.

'Time is money,' that was the first time I'd heard that awful expression: if that was all time was then I'd be happy to relinquish my time here on earth. And talking of money, I was not exactly making a fortune here, just two pounds ten shillings a week, but that didn't worry me: on Sundays, my one day off, I'd walk to South Molton and with my wages I could buy a pint of beer and a tin of tobacco for my pipe – that was enough for me. It was not very much, for sure, but I was employed as a trainee shepherd and I got my board and keep. So I needed for nothing really and as long as I could afford a pint of beer on Sundays and a tin of tobacco to keep my pipe going for the week, I was more than happy.

It was not the idyllic life I had envisioned but nor was it the time of nothing but miserable toil and loneliness. I learnt many things, from cutting and laying hedges, to building stone walls, from rounding up a flock of sheep, to driving a tractor and harrowing a field, to wielding a chainsaw. A thousand and one things I learnt and, when left alone to get on with them, I was happy at my work – that is, when my fingers and toes weren't numb with cold from the icy wind which cut like a knife up the valley and when I could put Syra out of my mind. And there were moments of great beauty up there in the lonely moors – the wind whistling through the grasses and the hedgerows and the sky traversed by fleecy white or black storm clouds, ever shifting and fleeting above the windswept khaki landscape, which patches of sunlight would illumine like a tapestry.

My best friend there was the sheepdog, Maggie, a highly-strung, highly intelligent collie, with whom I'd spend hours talking to and comforting in her box of straw outside. She was a trembling bag of nerves, cursed at and sworn at all day long by Andy whom she had to accompany on his demonic flights. She was highly skilled in her work with the flock but, to him, she could never do anything right and would be constantly cowering under the lash of his crop. She and I would talk to each other and it was to her pricked up listening ears I'd spill out my heart and the story of Syra, the girl I had fallen madly in love with when I worked in the riding stables near Topsham, in the summer and who filled all my dreams. First love cuts the deepest, they say, and when one dismal morning in January the dream. I'd been up on the hill and saw the red postman's van winding up the road to the farmhouse. All on tenterhooks for one of her secret letters – she hadn't written for over two weeks, which worried me – I sneaked down and retrieved a letter from the porch. It was written in an unfamiliar hand but addressed to me and postmarked Topsham – it must be from her, who else could it be? – and, slipping it into my pocket, raced, heart pounding in my chest, back up the hill where I tore it open, my heart sinking like a distressed ship on the ocean as I read, 'It was a New Year's party, I was a little tipsy with champagne and fell down the stairs . . . at the bottom a boy picked me up and kissed me – I'm sorry Alastair . . . '

I flung myself down on the hillside and pummeled the earth with my fists. And whose was the unfamiliar hand? In a P.S. she'd written, 'I fell off my horse and sprained my wrist, a friend has written this letter for me.' I wondered about that, and whether it was true, but it took a long time for the penny to drop. Perhaps it was this crisis on the hill which set the course of my life and I resolved from then on to wander, to escape from the world and heal the pain.

The first spring flowers began to push through the icy earth as the days began to draw out and the evenings get longer and longer. The ewes began to drop their lambs and we were with the flock

night and day—helping the little bundles out when the mother had difficulty, then watching her lick the jelly-like afterbirth off them in which they had slipped out, and seeing them climb, trembling, onto their spindly legs, all bewildered in the sudden world. Spring was here, and with it a shimmering in my blood. Birth was all around, new growth, life. Buds were breaking, flowers were turning their fresh bright faces to the sun which was pouring forth its warmth, the birds were full-throated with song and all the hillsides were singing with streams. The whole earth was coming to life and the scents and sounds which travelled along the winds intoxicated me.

'The road . . . I'll take to the road!' I suddenly exclaimed to myself. The long winding road which leads forever towards the horizon, towards the sky. No one to tell me what to do—only my heart will do that, it will steer me, set my course—it knows the way. I'll set out and seek romance and adventure. Who knows what tomorrow will bring—who cares? I'll wander into the blue and nourish my soul, and make of my life a tale I will one day write in a book.

Chapter 2
The Road Beneath my Feet

Everything I need I have upon my back—a sleeping bag, a change of clothes, a toothbrush, some soap, a penknife, a book and in my pocket a little precious money. How lovely these days of my youth, the hedgerows ablaze with flowers and the sweet May air intoxicating. I'm off to seek romance and adventure, to follow my heart wherever it may lead.

There's no shortage of fruit lining the roads: cherries a-plenty hanging from trees which sag under the weight of them. But I can't live on fruit alone—a man needs bread. Money's running out and I'm facing, for the first time in my life, the prospect of being absolutely penniless. I'm going to have to devise a means of pepping up my finances. I remember my French master at Marlborough telling me one could live on ten shillings a day in France—I'm going to live on a lot less than that. I've never really had to think about money before, having grown up in a little village without shops, where there was no call for it. And besides, my mother had always said, 'a gentleman shouldn't have to think about money,' and so I never did, for my mother was always right.

Perhaps I can sell cherries. I laugh at the sheer audacity of the idea of nicking them from the orchards and selling them at the side of the road. What else could I do? Be a shoeshine boy—buy shoe polish and brushes and polish the footwear of the citizens of the towns I pass through. I like that idea—maybe I'll have a crack at it. Let's see, what else could I do to keep the wolf from the door? And I start making a list in my head of all the possible and sometimes outrageous things I could do to conjure up the wherewithal for survival on the road. I am by nature impractical but necessity will make me resourceful. Rationing myself to cheese and a loaf of bread, I'm little more than skin and bone. But I'm free and that's the main thing: free from the tyranny of senseless work. And what about the bottles discarded in the bins along the roads – aren't they worth something? – I mean, don't they have some kind of a price on their heads? Yes they do, ranging from five centimes to thirty – bingo, I'll fill my belly.

A strange thing happened to me on my way south. I was already down in Provence, some fifty kilometres north of Montpéllier, to which I was heading. Evening was falling and the kindly young man who had taken me the last twenty kilometres or so in his *Deux Chevaux* was turning left and so he dropped me off in the middle of the ripening wheat fields which bordered the road. I was hungry and would have sorely liked to come to a village to buy something to eat but I decided to forego my hunger as darkness was falling. I'd been on the road since early morning, and these corn fields looked inviting. I stepped off the road and through the almost waist-high, ripening wheat, and, dog-tired, flopped down and immediately fell into a deep sleep from which I was startled awake by something rushing over the whole length of my body, like a huge dog or some other beast, or some terrible wind which had the wheat waving wildly and, waking with a start, saw an arm, thrust over the tops of the wheat stalks holding a book, a huge leather-bound tome just above my heart; I screeched in fear and it vanished. What was in the book I'll never know; why I was being shown it, I'll never know. If only I hadn't panicked, if only I'd let the hand turn the pages for me to read – perhaps it held the key to my life, perhaps therein was written a secret for which I'd been singled out. I felt as Parzifal must have felt when he failed to ask the Fisher King the all-important question, 'Who does the Grail serve?' – when the candlelit procession passed by at the Grail castle, and it would consequently take years of questing and hardship to at last find the answer.

I first set eyes on the Mediterranean at Agde, reaching the beach along a sandy path bordered by plantations of bamboo that wavered and whispered in the fresh, cool, liquid wind from the sea. I make

this beach my first home by this sea on which I'll spend so much of my life and which will truly become home to me. I make myself a little shelter from bamboo to keep out of the midday sun in these days which are hotter than any I have ever known. I plunge into the crystal blue, sparkling, sea which is still invigoratingly cool, it being just the beginning of summer. I lie in rock pools in water warm from the sun, and in the evenings I wander into the town, sit on the terrace of a café and fall in love with the women who pass by in their evening dresses – their skin dark and exotic and the air scented with perfume on their passing. All this impels me to express my feelings, the ecstasy of these moments and my first days of wandering and the utter, total, freedom they bring with them. I take out a notebook and start writing:

> On your passing
> in the evening
> scented, sultry and mysterious
> as the moon
> which is beaming –
> with a glance, you unaware
> make a heart dance

And I return to my encampment with a baguette, some Camembert and a bottle of wine, and in that bottle is a poem and I write it on a page, a poem to the moon, no less, and I sing it to the sea and tell the stars of all the secret longing which grips me. Where does this longing come from? is it a memory of things from a time unknown, a time when I was one, not divided as I am now and seemingly cut off from the innermost core of myself, a time when there was no 'other', this 'otherness', this estrangement I feel when a woman walks by and the pain that gives rise to?

If Egypt is an image of the whole cosmos, as Thoth maintains, then what am I? Buried under the sands of the Sahara are marvels we cannot begin to imagine; buried beneath my surface mind it must be somewhat similar. How to remove the sand? Trying to use the mind as a spade would be futile, and besides it would employ every trick in the book to deceive me, to throw me off the track – it does not want to dispel the illusion it has created to obscure the reality that lies beyond it. To turn the mind upside down and inside out would be a start in the right direction and by which one could drive the sky through the sand and turn the grains into crystals. As long as one abandoned logic this could very easily be done – but then one also needs the key – the key which is everywhere but we don't see it – until we suddenly do.

The waves are crashing on the shore, moving horizontally across the bay. What would happen if the sea sprung a leak and the water all drained away, where would it go, and what would be exposed on the sea bed? Rocks, crevasses, caves, rotting hulls of wrecks, monsters. Would, over time, plants grow, trees, rivers start to run? Would birds sing where previously only the silent fishes had swum? And what other forms of life would emerge, brought to life from nothing and animated by the light and air? Mermaids perhaps would dispense with their tail-fins and grow legs, their pudenda suddenly sprouting thick tufts of hair . . . And where would the sea have gone, would it have gushed down into the hollow centre of the earth or would it have leaked out into outer space and dispersed, or even re-formed itself somewhere in the solar system or beyond so that somewhere out there a sea afloat among the stars which would eventually become the matrix of a new world, all manner of life generated in its swirling depths and then again, what if this sea was in fact the mind and it had drained away into the unconscious and we were being chased around by those monsters that lurk there: Minotaurs, sirens, many-headed desires . . . and then on the foam Aphrodite comes ashore, wells up into consciousness, and everything starts all over again.

Not being used to the ferocity of the Mediterranean sun I'm beginning to get terribly sunburnt and I wonder what to do to protect my fair northern skin from its glare. One day I get talking to some young people on the beach and ask them how they manage to keep from burning, lying out in the midday sun as they are. 'Well, we're used to it,' they tell me, 'and we use olive oil with a little lemon juice to stop the skin from drying out.' In town that evening I buy a bottle of olive oil and a couple of lemons which the following morning I plaster all over my face and body and then lie out in the sun.

After a while I begin to sizzle like a fried fish and my whole body turns scarlet and breaks out in blisters. I won't be trying that again.

Combing the beaches in the evenings, the tourists all gone home, their litter left behind them, I always get enough for a meal, a bottle of wine, a packet of cigarettes. Whilst cleaning up the beaches and re-cycling glass I'm providing fuel for the vehicle in which I live and move and have my being. Nothing that I've learnt at school can be compared with what I'm learning now (though I did learn that you can live on ten shillings a day in France, which is proving to be true.) In fact, my real schooling is only just beginning: I'm learning to become intelligent about down-to-earth things, like filling my belly, for instance: and about people, people of the everyday world. I'm learning (though tottering like an infant at the outset) to stand on my feet in the world into which I've walked: how not to be hood-winked by every Tom, Dick and Harry that crosses my path (though I will be in due course.) And I'm learning about myself, of whom I'm as ignorant as I am about others. I have a long, long, way to go but 'a journey of a thousand miles begins beneath ones feet'—and these are the first steps.

And so I drift along the coast, the translucent Côte d'Azur, tasting for the first time the life, the 'carefree life', of a tramp. I'm surviving and I'm alive. Surviving means to get oneself, in whatever way one can, from one day to another—being alive means to taste every moment of those days, with relish and with wonder. I meet others, young and old, who, for a thousand and one reasons are on the road—some by choice, most by circumstance. Tramps, thieves, jugglers, fire-eaters, musicians, dice-throwers, pimps, card-sharps, acrobats, prostitutes, murderers, deserters, madmen, poets—they're all here, down at street level, lining the path I'm taking—each with his story, each with his bottle, each with his dream.

No longer do I turn tail and run when coming upon the underworld community hanging around the fountain in the squares of every city in France. I'm less aloof now and it's invariably this motley gaggle that gives me my first welcome upon arriving in a strange town. Hailed as I cross the square, 'Hey, *copain*,' I'm handed a bottle, offered some bread and informed about the town: soup kitchens, Red Cross offices, where one can doss down for the night in comparative safety (meaning out of the eyes of the law), what the citizens are like – friendly or hostile – how the police behave, and so forth, the sort of things one doesn't go to the tourist information offices to enquire about. Like a little theatre – a side-show – a town within a town this stage in the square is animated day and night by its gesticulating actors acting their pieces, sometimes comic, mostly tragic. Periodically the cops arrive and drag everyone away to a de-lousing station and then deposit them on the road, some miles out of town. A day or two and everyone's back again. Such is life on La Cannebière, that teeming artery of the city of Marseille. Arriving one evening, flat broke, hungry, I'm glad of that familiar, 'Hey, *Copain,*' with which a ragged assembly around a bench have greeted me. On going over to them I'm offered a bottle from which I drink. Amongst them is a German fellow who introduces himself as Jurgen. He's stout, jovial-looking, with a mop of unkempt hair and a beard, 'And zis is my dog, Volf, hey Volf,' he calls out to a lean, lively-looking, Alsatian burrowing in a dustbin nearby, '*Volf, komm!*'

'Volf and I make good business' – he tells me, ruffling the dog's head affectionately. 'Ven every day ve are begging togezzer he, by obligation, must not fat become – understand, ja? Ze people are seeing fat dog zen zey are unbelieving he is hungry – unbelieving zat is not goot for business, no goot for begging.' Ha, yes, I understand. Jurgen asks for food for his dog – 'Ze people are better liking dogs zan people: zey give ze money for ze dog, not for me – so I can much eat and get fat – but not Volf: he must by obligation stay tin. Drink, mein freund.'

He hands me the bottle of Kronenbourg beer from which he's drinking.

'Danke,'

'You are begging too?'

'Oh NO!'

'Zen, how you are money-making?'

'Empty bottles.'

'Empty bottles,' he fairly explodes with laughter. 'Ho, mein freund, you won't find ze empty bottle for ten kilometres around here. Every man is looking for ze empty bottle. You must beg. You never beg?' He tilts his shaggy, bearded, head on one side and looks at me, 'Ja, you not know how – I teach you: Vatch,' Calling his dog Wolf to him, he sets off along the Cannebière, going up to everyone he passes. He points at Wolf, who's become quiet and subdued looking, and then I see money being given to this wily, jolly, German chap. Everyone he approaches gives him something, as far as I can see, and in just a few minutes he's back, his pockets absolutely choc-a-bloc and an enormous grin upon his face.

'It's easy, *mein freund*. Now you are trying – and zen ve haf a lethal (I presume he means little) drink togezzer, ja?'

But it's the hardest thing in the world for me: it goes against everything I've been brought up to believe in; it goes painfully against my pride: I? I? sink to that? No. Never!' But I do – I have to – and it does me the world of good.

Jurgen, as my first teacher of *la manche* – literally, 'the sleeve' – looks pleased with me when I arrive back after my first foray along the Cannebière with a fistful of francs, enough for a 'lethal drink'.

And so I have a new skill up my sleeve, under my hat, so to speak. It might stand me in good stead when my back is up against the wall – as it will be.

Jürgen had been some kind of debt collector in Germany. He'd had to go around and get money off people who wouldn't pay their debts – sometimes by using force. He doesn't look the type to get nasty, he seems far too easy-going and benevolent for that. There had been good money in the job and usually people paid up immediately when he turned up on their doorstep, for he'd assume a threatening manner. But then one day he was sent along to this young woman's house. She had a child, no work and a lot of debts. There was no way she could pay. His job demanded that he become threatening with her and so he got her up against the wall, emptied her pockets of every damned *pfennig* she had in them, turned the house upside down for anything she might have concealed and told her he'd be back for the rest of what she owed, and owned, the next day – so she'd better beg, steal or borrow because he wasn't playing around.

The next day he returned to her house with the money he'd taken from her plus all that she'd need to pay off her debts. He begged her forgiveness for his violence of the day before, which she, weeping hysterically, gave. He quit his job and took to the road.

'Zis is ze life more applicable to my nature,' he said, 'and still I am living like a collectioner of ze debts but I am not obliged to be angry ven ze people zey are not giving ze money.'

Chapter 3

The Girls from Calais

I come to a little harbour town called Cassis. The sea, crystal blue, is enclosed in a circular bay, fishing boats bobbing alongside the quay upon which nets are spread. The June sun is hot and it's good to spend the days on the beach, reading and bathing, and at night to sleep out along the cliffs under the brilliant stars. The days are drifting by effortlessly. My needs are few and I've devised the means of attaining them. I'm young and everything's new and fresh. It doesn't matter that time is drifting by – the days are sufficient unto themselves, each one of them bringing something new, from which I glean a little wisdom, a little poetry, perhaps.

One night, sitting alone along the cliffs, watching the moonlight on the sea, two girls are suddenly at my side, saying, '*Salut!*' They sit down beside me and a shiver runs through me at the closeness of their bodies. Girls are still unknown to me, are still just dreams.

I can see them clearly in the moonlight – they're beautiful, in that very French way. Sisters from Calais, they're spending their summer holidays with their parents, here in Cassis.

'We were passing, we saw you, you looked like you were making poems to the moon – were you?' asks the elder one, whose name's Brigitte and whose corn-coloured hair flows over her shoulders and down her back like a water fall.

'Yes, I was.' She's looking at me so piercingly a thrill rushes through me, a panic.

'Do you write poetry?' she asks

'Yes, I try to; real poems are very difficult to write.'

'You must be inspired, huh? What inspires you apart from the moon?'

'Oh, the sea, the stars, the smell of the pines trees.'

'And girls?' her eyes piercing into mine, 'do girls inspire you?'

'Oh yes,' I say – I want to say, 'you inspire me – I would write a thousand poems as we lay together beneath the moon,' but instead I look down at the ground, unable to bear the intensity of my feelings and, after a few moments silence, the girls get up saying they'd better be getting back; their parents will be worried about them.

'*Bonne nuit, poète*. We could meet tomorrow, if you like.'

'*Ah oui.*'

We arrange to meet in the harbour, beneath the beacon, at noon. We can spend the day together on the beach.

Whoopee! I dance and leap and cart-wheel beneath the very moon. Lying awake, looking up at the stars, I'm praying fervently to God that everything will go well tomorrow and, by nightfall, Brigitte and I will be in one another's arms. I'm praying fervently to God – for what will be the last time.

The clock has struck noon, I'm nervously smoking a cigarette – all of a sudden they're at my side, '*Bonjour.*'

We set off to the beach. Walking between them, I begin to feel awkward and gangling and tongue-tied. The longing I've nurtured overnight is choking me, making me unnatural, tense. In broad daylight I've lost that aura of being a poet composing to the moon – in broad daylight I'm a blithering idiot who can hardly compose a sentence to this girl, for whom I tremble in every fibre of my being, without stuttering and blushing.

> Something stands between me and my nature
> for I reach for your hand but hesitate
> your false movement's unnerved me
> and the moment is fled–
> forever now I'll agonise
> how it might have been otherwise
> and to what sweet fate it might have led.

I turn to her sister, Anne, saying, 'It's hot already.'

'Yes, it's hot on the Mediterranean.'

'Much hotter than in the north.'

'Yes, of course it is,' and with that she closes the conversation.

Coming to a spot on the beach that's quite secluded, the girls lay out towels on the stones and we sit down. They strip off to the bikinis they have on underneath. With the proximity of their nearly naked, voluptuous, bodies and the scent of their fresh sweat, I begin to get aroused, visibly – oh horror! I try, by a stupendous application of will, to reverse the process before it becomes evident to them, betraying the nature of the thoughts I'm entertaining – oh shame! – but the situation is beyond the dictates of the will – in fact quite out of control and, grabbing my note book from my rucksack, I roll over quickly onto my stomach and make pretence of writing.

'You're inspired?' asks Brigitte – at which she dashes into the sea. Anne follows her and I, slowly recovering my dignity, come after them.

There's a cool, handsome-looking, guy in the water with whom Brigitte begins to play, splashing water over him. Laughingly, he splashes her back. How I envy the ease with which they interact with one another.

The picnic the girls produce is sumptuous – bread and cheese, olives, tomatoes, cucumber, yoghurt, apples and juicy, fresh peaches. But how ill-at-ease I am with them now as we sit here on the towels eating. This isn't at all how the day should be going. Where's the magic of the night before? Why's it always nothing but dreams when it comes to girls? Why can I sing so sweetly of them in my poems but when it comes to talking to them in real life I'm a tongue-tied twit?

And now the handsome, brawny guy is coming out of the sea and Brigitte's calling to him to join us. ('No, Go away!' I want to scream.) He's here, drying his sun-tanned body with Brigitte's towel, accepting an apple she's handing to him and sitting down next to her; he's got her laughing and smiling with his witty talk, and his cool glances are bringing her closer and closer to him and further and further from me. The food has stuck in my throat. A chasm of emptiness has opened within me and my whole being is plunging into it, along with my faith and my hopes and my dreams.

I get up, slinging my knapsack over my shoulder, my voice shaking, 'I have to go now.'

'You've been inspired?' asks she, whose corn-coloured locks are being pleated by her Romeo's hands.

'Yes.'

'Alors, bon chance, au revoir.'

Night has fallen. I'm sprawled on the steps of a doorway with a bottle, with tears of rage – rage against God to whom I'd prayed, with all my heart, and now I curse, with venom, with spittle, with fist:

'O God, cruel Creator, I beseeched you, begged you with all my being and now you do this to me.'

Poor old God. He'd set everything up for me to give me the chance to make what I could of it and it was I who had bungled it, not him, and here I am shouting at him in a blind, drunken, fury. No wonder there will be times when he'll turn a deaf ear to me in my darkest hours when crying up to him for deliverance.

I slumber drunkenly, brokenly, on the beach. This morning, hung over, sad, ashamed at the anger and loss of command the drink caused in me, I take the road to Nice.

I feel so crushed and battered by the experience of yesterday. Why is it that I become so knotted up inside whenever I'm in the company of girls? Am I afraid of them? Will I ever be able to be at ease with them? I ponder these things as I trudge along the road. I begin to glimpse what I reckon to be at the root of the problem – it's what they evoke in me: these desires, this intense yearning which gives rise to the turmoil in what seems like the very depths of my soul. And these desires and yearnings well up from me and clutch at her, whoever she might be, who has had the power to call them up – along with the feeling that I shall never, ever, be able to attain this which is so strange to me, so mysterious, as though she were the mystery of mysteries.

Yes, it must be something like that. I'm kicking a stone along the road, am beginning to feel better. The fresh wind blowing off the sea is reviving me, bringing me back to my senses. And this kind of 'thinking things out' as I call it, clarifies my mind and stills the turbulence in my heart. I see myself as a poet, pure and noble, too high-minded to acknowledge the darker side of myself, the animal in which all manner of desires crouch. But an animal is noble too, and graceful when it's allowed free expression – but I keep the doors of its cage firmly shut, afraid to acknowledge it as though it were some kind of Minotaur, so that it becomes like a creature kept in darkness: savage and emaciated. It would tear its captor to shreds if it could burst from its captivity, if it could bolt from its dungeon – as it surely will.

Tramping along the coast, gathering bottles as I go, I arrive in Nice. Selling the bottles I buy wine, cheese, a baguette and sup on a bench on the promenade. The sun dips into the sea in the west and the stars, one by one, peep out in the pink twilight. Aglow with wine I stroll into town. The houses, the yellow colours of Italy, retain the sun's light and warmth. I sit on some steps and soak up the atmosphere of the place. Young couples pass, arm in arm, cooing to one another. The tapping of a blind man's stick on the cobbled street is getting closer. I watch him as he passes, with his dark glasses and his sure unfaltering steps seeming to know every twist and turn and stone. What a strange, dark world. And yet perhaps he's filled with a glowing interior light which we, always distracted by things outside us, are blind to. Perhaps he's already seen what we are seeing now, taken what he'd needed from it, and now's turned his gaze inward.

Another man, briskly pacing along the street, espies me and makes in my direction. He's expensively dressed, about fifty I'd say.

'*Bonsoir.*' he says cheerily.

'*Bonsoir.*'

'*Anglais?*'

'*Oui.*'

'You look thin. Would you like to come and have something to eat with me?'

'Er . . . '

'Come on – I invite you. A growing boy like you must eat.' His tone is insistent.

'Well, it's very kind of you to offer,' I say, getting up. What does he want? I ask myself as we walk side by side along the street.

'Here it is fun to eat,' he says as we arrive in a small street full of restaurants. They are all places that make this strange stuff called socca, a kind of grilled cornflour, similar to polenta, which is absolutely delicious. We sit at a long table, on a bench, eating this, with wine poured from earthenware jugs. I'm glad of the food and wine, very glad, but I'm uneasy about the fellow who's treating me – his conversation's continually drifting towards matters of sex:

'Do you like women?' he asks me.

'Yes.'

'What do you feel when you see a beautiful woman?'

'Well I . . . '

'You feel desire?'

'Yes', I blush.

'Excited?'

'Er, yes.'

'And when she touches you, excited?'

'Well, yes,' I say, blushing.

His hand's now settled on my leg under the table. What can I do now? I can't push it off, that would be rude of me.

'Do you think there's a *toilette* here?' I ask with sudden inspiration.

'Of course – inside.'

When I come back I sit down on the other side of the table. He resumes his questioning, getting to the point now.

'Do you like men?'

'Well, er, what d'you . . . ?'

'Do you like to make love with them? I mean . . . '

'No.'

'Have you tried?' he probes.

'No, I haven't.'

'Then how do you know you wouldn't like it?' he leers at me, reaching out to stroke my hand which is clutching my wine glass. I withdraw it.

'Because I feel no desire for men.'

'It's a pity. I could teach you to like it and then you could enjoy sex with women *and* men. You'll have double the fun – think of it.'

'It doesn't interest me.' I say firmly – I realise I have to be bold now, not worry any more about offending him. It isn't kindness that's moved him to buy me a meal, it's self-interest. I get up to go.

'I'll pay you,' he blurts out as one last attempt.

'No, thank you,' and slinging my sack over my shoulder, I head off towards the beach.

'Oi!' I shout at the owner of the hand that's worming its way down my sleeping bag, and lash out at him so that he lies squirming on the stones a few feet from me.

'I just wanted to play with you. You like?'

'No I don't like – *piss off!*' He'd been after my passport and any-thing else I keep down my sleeping-bag, and upon which he'd nearly had his hand. He slinks away into the night.

I learn that there's a gang of North Africans who go along the beaches robbing people every night.

'And if it isn't the Arabs bothering you it's the police,' Louis-le-Grand tells me, 'So be careful. Best to find somewhere other than the beach if you want your nights to be restful.'

'Louis-le-Grand?' Who's he? well, that's what he calls him-self – others, his fellow *clochards*, call him Louis-le-sans-jambe (leg-less Louis) owing to the fact that one of his legs is missing. 'Run into any trouble in this town,' he says to me, in a fatherly fashion, 'and you just mention my name – that you're a *copain* of Louis-le-Grand.'

Well, I'll try it perhaps, but what if I get tangled up with the po-lice or some Arabs or some thugs from the Foreign Legion – is it re-ally going to swing things in my favour if I announce that I'm a mate of Louis-le-Grand? I think not. But I forgive him for his delusions of grandeur because, although his brain seems somewhat knocked askew (by the wine, no doubt), his heart's in the right place and he really does seem to be concerned about my welfare, as though I was his *protégé*, and he my mentor. Always hailing me if he sees me passing, he asks me how things are going, offers me a drink from his precious bottle, *un mégot* (a 'dog-end') – from his tobacco tin, and if he happens to wheedle out of me that I'm 'broke', he'll slip me a franc or two.

'You're a young lad, you've a lot to learn,' he says, 'but you're learning.'

And I *am* learning: every day which passes is packed with people and events from which I can glean something. Everyone and everything are teachers of something or other to me – yes, even the Arab on the beach even he was teaching me something, to be on my guard.

Louis-le-sans-jambe has a novel way of capitalizing on his legless state: the stump of wood with a boot on it which replaces the original limb he leaves on the pavement outside a café where he's drinking, with a note pinned to it:

> The owner of this cumbersome stump, 'Louis-le-Grand', war veteran and heroic patriot, can be located in this café in need of a drink.

It works apparently; people hunt him out, pay for a drink at the bar and leave him a little something for later on. He's a wily old fellow for sure.

'If you play your cards right,' he winks, 'you'll have no cause to complain of hunger or thirst in Nice.'

I certainly lack for neither food nor drink. Apart from the bottles which provide me with the necessary income for the little luxuries like cigarettes and wine, I get a plentiful supply of fruit from the market each morning – fruit the vendors throw out if it has the slightest blemish, like a bruise or is a little over-ripe, like the masses of bananas I gleefully stuff down my gullet.

And there's that soup kitchen which Louis-le-Grand told me about – *le Fourneau Economique*. It's found at the top of a little flight of steps on the rue de Choeur and run by the 'good sisters' of the church. As the hour strides towards noon, the little square outside its inviting doors fills up with us who are living rough around

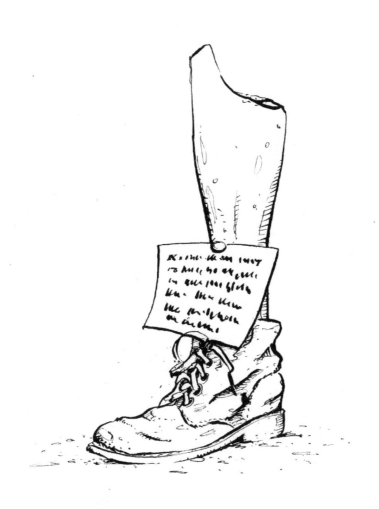

town. And, dead on noon, as the bell in the clock tower strikes the hour, the bolt's slid back and a grey-clad, white-faced, nun cries, '*Allez!*' – the signal for us to rush into the cool, dark, interior and line up at the counter where, for a mere franc, one is doled out a large bowl of chick-peas and handed a hunk of bread. Jugs of water are on the tables to wash it down with, wine being strictly forbidden by the nuns who oversee us though they know full well that a bottle of rouge is concealed under the coat of every rogue that sits at those long tables, and that it will be just a matter of time before a bottle's spotted, being lifted to the lips of an adept giving way to indiscretion in his zeal to slake his thirst, and emitting a long, glugging, sound like a drain overflowing, and then the hushed and holy atmosphere of the refectory will be shattered by the shriek of a furious *bonne soeur*,

'*Pas du vin ici, monsieur.*'

'Ah, beg pardon, *ma soeur*, beg pardon, but it's not wine. No, honest, it's cherryade.'

'You're lying monsieur.'

'No Sister' I'm not lying – I never lie.'

'*Allez!*'

Everyone has fun at these little repartees, including the nuns who, though they try to maintain a demeanour of no-nonsense severity, are indulgent with us, treating us as their flock whose souls they might eventually save by way of our bellies. Fat chance of that.

Inebriated by the grape one starry evening I'm strolling through *le vieux quartier* when I hear the hesitant strumming of a guitar coming from somewhere up ahead of me in a narrow alley. Getting closer I can make out the figure of a girl, sitting in the shadows of a door-step playing a guitar. She looks up at me, like an animal crouched in the near darkness, a look of defiance in her eyes

'*Assis toi,*' she says, making a space beside her, '*bois,*', she offers me a bottle. I do as she bids and she goes on playing, not very well – she only knows a few chords around which she's trying to weave a tune – but her absorption in this modest rendition's indescribably beautiful. Bent over the instrument, her lips pouted, her greasy, straggly, black hair falling over her face, her occasional mutter of '*merde,*' as she plays a note false. On an impulse I lean towards her and, taking her swarthy face in my hands, lift it towards me and kiss her brow. Letting her guitar slip noiselessly to the pavement, she puts her arms around my neck and shows me how to kiss without restraint.

We go hand in hand down to the beach, she walking without flinching over the stones in her bare feet. As we sit down she pulls a little lump of hash from her pocket and starts to roll a joint. I watch her with a kind of silent joy, watch her brown fingers deftly manipulating the papers, the tobacco, the hashish, in the wind which every moment threatens to blow it all out of her hand. I notice the three points tattooed in the hollow between her index finger and her thumb – she's probably been in prison. There's an intriguing blend of sadness and determination about her as though her life's been one of struggle and sorrow. Without knowing why I have the certainty that she's grown up an orphan.

There's no need to speak – we're at ease with one another. Something flows between us too deep for talk. I'm filled with a joy which has no need of words. The night is full of stars, the only sound is that of the waves breaking at our feet. She finishes her skilful work with a neat twist at the end of the *petard* and hands it to me with the faintest of smiles,

'*Tiens . . . fume,*' and she offers it to me as though it was a gift of love.

She lays her head in my lap as we smoke and gazes up at me, 'Your face looks as though it's looking down from the stars,' she whispers, 'perhaps you are of the stars and I am of the earth.' I look down at her, at her swarthy skin the colour of russet earth. Perhaps she's right.

'We're sprung from the stars and sown in the earth,' I say.

'Yes, sow me,' and she pulls me down to earth and soothes the unhappy beast within me.

When I awake she's gone. She must have crept away quieter than a thief. The only thing that remains of her is the flower that had adorned the neck of her guitar; she's laid it by my head. I search all over town for her – the streets, the cafés, the beaches – but in vain, and I constantly return, with sadness and longing, to the doorstep in the alley where I'd found her playing her lost chords.

Summer's winding down. The great heat has abated and there's a sudden chill in the air in the evenings. The cafés are closing up and there's a feeling of emptiness along the seafront. It's nearing the end of September and the season's on the change. Autumn's here and a feeling of melancholy pervades my being. Waking one morning on the beach, to a grey sky and a gusty wind which has stirred the sea up to a black broth topped with white-crested waves, I resolve to leave Nice and make for Bordeaux where I've heard that work in the vineyards is abundant and will begin any time now. Good money's to be made and one is fed and watered like a king. I need a good feed-up and some money in my pocket.

And so I wave goodbye to Nice. I'll miss the life here, my daily life which has fallen into an easy routine. Bathing in the early morn-ing and walking along the Promenade des Anglais basking in the morning sun. Reading a book or writing a poem and smoking as I sit over coffee in a café. Ambling through the cool, winding streets and courtyards of the *Vieille Ville*, to the kitchen of the good sis-ters, having a swig of a flagon and *un mégot* with Louis-the-legless and the others and then, bloated with chick-peas, sprawling on the beach for the afternoon, until it's time to procure the first alembic of rouge, and idling along to the promenade with it and toasting the setting sun: 'Thank-you Sun, for another day on earth.'

> The stars glimmer
> the moon glides
> the waves glitter
> So much wine I've drunk this evening
> it's got the heavens reeling
> round my turning head and heart

Chapter 4
The Knife Thrower

How good it is to be on the road again. I stride out with the renewed vigour that autumn brings after the languid, sultry days of summer. The leaves, turned golden in the trees, are beginning to shake loose in the winds. The smell of wood-smoke drifts along the valleys from the chimneys of red-roofed houses in the villages I pass through. The Earth, who has been labouring all summer long under the sun, is offering up her fruits, most of which have been gathered, leaving stubble fields – like the stubble on my chin which is slowly becoming a beard, albeit it a very scanty one – over which a chill mist settles in the evenings and it's cold now sleeping out in the night. The skies are streaked with ribbons, grey, brown, mauve, pink and sometimes black and laden with rain over the crests of the distant Alps. Coming to Avignon, with its broken bridge jutting out into the river, I sing as I approach the portals of this ancient city that old song:

> *Sur le pont d'Avignon*
> *On y danse tout en rond . . .*
> *On y danse, on y danse tout en rond.*

City full of towers, colonnades and squares, all the stuff of mediaeval romance, pageantry, intrigue and murder. The main square's alive with young people sitting around in groups, drinking, singing and playing guitars. It seems a very merry place and, procuring a bottle of wine I wade into the square to join the merry-makers.

Darkness has fallen and a fire-eater's caught everyone's attention who, stripped to the waist and with a shaved head, is taking a mouthful of spirit and, to the roll and crescendo of a drum, leans backwards whilst inhaling a lungful of air and then with a leap forward, holding a lighted torch to his mouth, expels a pillar of fire, high above our heads. 'Ooooh,' goes the crowd.

'*Impressionant*, huh?' a fellow standing at my side has spoken. I turn to him, '*Oui, c'est formidable.*' We get talking. I share with him what remains of my bottle and then we set off in the direction of a bar where, he says, all the young people gather in the evenings. It's a lively place, filled with smoke and so full it's bursting out of its doorways onto the street. There are some musicians at the tables with a couple of guitars and a concertina.

'Avignon's a lively place at this time of the year, when the grape picking begins,' my companion says. He's French, with a pale face, piercing eyes and a pointed beard – he looks like someone who's trying to look like a magician.

'I am a knife thrower – at least, I'm learning to be. I need practice, actually, before I can say with any confidence that I'm a knife thrower.'

'A knife thrower? that's an interesting occupation, I've never met a knife thrower before.'

'Yes, I suppose it's in the same category as a fire eater,' he says, 'many of these old things are dying out in France. There's probably no more than a handful of knife throwers left in the whole country, and they're all Gypsies.'

'Gypsies,' I exclaim with excitement, 'are there many Gypsies in France?'

'Many Gypsies? France is full of them. Haven't you seen any on the move in their caravans?'

'No.'

'Well, you'll come across them soon enough because they're all around the South of France at this time of the year, for the *vendange*, especially around Bordeaux.' Then I'm heading for the right place.

I've had such dreams about the Gypsies, those colourful outlaws roaming the world, living their mysterious, adventurous lives in the wide-open spaces. They passed through our village when I was a child, in their gaily-painted caravans and set up a tiny (it seemed huge at the time) circus tent in a field nearby. Our mother took us to see the performance with its flying acrobats, clowns, horses, monkeys and its uproarious music and its glistening, glittering lights. They cast a spell one summer night under the blazing stars. In the morning they were gone, leaving me touched with a strange magic and with a longing to climb into their magical wagons.

'Have you met any?' I ask naïvely.

'Oh, you bump into them all over the place, they're everywhere, in the bars, in the markets, anywhere there's commerce or entertainment. But you can't get close to them, in fact, you want to avoid them.'

I want him to talk more on the subject but he doesn't seem very interested; he obviously doesn't know much more about them than what he's already told me, and apart from that he obviously doesn't like them one bit. He suddenly produces his throwing knives from his breast pocket – slender, glistening blades with ivory handles inlaid with stones. He puts them down on the table in front of me.

'Actually, I bought these from a Gypsy,' he says, 'he charged me an extortionate price, but they're the real thing. You won't find better anywhere.'

I handle them, reverently. Yes, I can just see a Gypsy hurling these like flashes of lightning through the air and striking the heart of a rival in love. Maybe these actual knives had been the implements of such dramas.

'Are they old?' I ask.

'So the Gypsy told me. If one can ever believe a Gypsy.'

'Ah, the very instruments for slicing the salami,' a drunkard has espied the knives and is lurching over towards our table with this fickle remark about the knives. This doesn't go down at all well with Pierre, my companion, who scoops them up off the table and back into his pocket out of sight and out of reach of the offensive fellow who gets the message and staggers off to annoy the company at the next table.

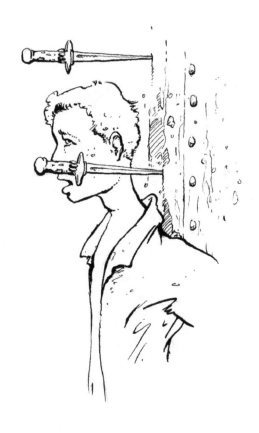

'I need practice, as I said,' Pierre begins, 'but I can't always find people to practice on.'

'Why not?' I ask.

'They think I'm going to miss all the time. You're not afraid, are you?'

'Er . . . no, no not at all.'

'Well, maybe we can practise together?'

'Yes, but . . . '

'Come on,' says Pierre and he's already heading for the street – no backing out of it now.

'So you stand against this door with your arms spread out as though on a cross. Yes, perfect, just like that,' he's saying excitedly, no doubt hardly believing his luck at finding someone naive enough for him to practice on.

I haven't deliberately done anything as foolish as this since my shepherding days when Andy bet me a pound I wouldn't keep a ferret up my trousers for a minute. It was at a little party at Christmastime when he'd had his friends around and they'd managed to get me quite drunk and so I took him on – after all a quid was a bit of money in those days, nearly half my week's wages in fact. The ferret raced around inside my trouser legs as Andy held his watch and watched the seconds go by and his friends, guffawing, cheered me on, 'Go on boy! Go on!' they encouraged, in their deep west country accents, although I think they were a little concerned about where this was going to go. The ferret spared me and I won the money but I might have lost something worth a great deal more than that. I'd never do something as stupid as that again, once bitten twice shy and all that, but here I am, spreadeagled against this heavy, oak door up a side street in Avignon with a half-drunken amateur about to outline my by-now-decidedly-trembling body with knives. He takes them out of his pocket and tests them for their balance, getting a feel for them in his hands.

'Ready?' he asks, looking up.

'I'm ready,' I choke, wishing I was anywhere but here now.

'*Allez*, here goes,' and lifting his right hand to the level of his ear he hurls the knife through the air. With a thud it sticks in the wood two or three inches to the left of my neck. It buzzes for a moment as it trembles violently. Crikey!

'Ready?'

'Y . . . yes,' I brace myself again. This time the knife strikes just above my head – this is not a joke.

'I . . . I want to stop now,' but already he's aiming the third knife, 'Ready?' there's an almost maniacal look in his eyes as he sizes up his target and the third one flashes through the air, and with a loud clatter, strikes a nail in the door and bounces off onto the pavement.

'*Merde!*' cries Pierre as he rushes to retrieve it and examine his precious blade for damage. I take advantage of the situation and get out of the doorway. I'm shaking like a leaf, and glad that I'm not having to check myself for damage.

Chapter 5
The Gypsies

A few days of tramping and hitch-hiking have brought me to the village of St. Emilion. Row upon row of heavily-laden vines cover the gently-sloping countryside. Every here and there groups of pickers can be seen, their voices ringing clearly through the sharp morning air.

Leaves scattering beneath my feet, I approach a château by way of an avenue of sycamore trees. Before me is a thick timber door upon which I knock and, whilst waiting, look about me at the flagstone yard in which chickens are picking about in straw, just like the yard at home. A peacock's strutting around, putting up its fan of feathers and staring at me with its thousand inlaid eyes. It sees a tall, red-faced fellow with a long neck, topped by a mop of unkempt hair and wrapped in a great-coat, donated by the Red Cross in Montpéllier. On unsocked feet it sees a pair of sandals held together by little more than blind faith and on his back a bundle of meagre belongings. Haughtily it sizes me up, no doubt coming to the conclusion that I'm some kind of tramp. I stare back at it: Well sod you, you puffed up ninny. The door creaks open.

'*Oui, monsieur, je peux vous aider?*' an old woman, dressed in black, stands before me.

'*Je cherche du travail, madame.*'

'*Travail monsieur, couper les raisins?*'

'*Oui madame,*'

'*Alors, suivez-moi, monsieur.*'

I follow her through a long hall-way and into a kitchen which smells of fresh bread and other delicious things and logs are smouldering in a huge great fireplace imbuing everything with the pleasant smell of wood smoke. Some women are busy preparing food and filling jugs with wine from huge casks. This looks like the place to be. They look up at me, smiling, '*Allemand? Anglais?*' they enquire, 'you looking for work? *Tenez*!'

One of them has put a glass in my hand and is filling it with ruby-coloured wine. Ah, what a delicious feeling of warmth as I drink it down. They seem glad to have this little interruption in their morning's work and start chatting and asking me questions: how I got here, what do I think of France, am I married – to which I pointedly reply 'no' as I look into the eyes of a pretty scullery maid – ever hopeful – and meanwhile my glass keeps being replenished, so that by the time the *patron* appears, whom the old lady had set off to find, I'm half cut and would gladly have stayed in that warm kitchen in the company of these congenial women all day.

When the *patron* does appear, a kindly grey-haired old fellow, he looks me up and down curiously, 'Have you done this kind of work before?' he asks,

'No, but I worked on a farm, I was a shepherd.'

He smiles at my eagerness, 'Follow me,' and as we make our way out towards the vineyard he tells me a little about the place, that it's the Château Ausone, the oldest and most prestigious of all the vineyards at St. Émilion, founded by the Roman governor and poet Ausonius. We go towards one of the groups of pickers I'd seen from the road. 'You can start here,' he says, handing me a *panier* and a pair of secateurs. 'They'll show you what to do,' and he turns back towards the château, leaving me to fend for myself among the Gypsies.

They're suddenly all around me, laughing, calling to one another in a strange language, not a word of which I understand. My arrival in their midst seems to be a veritable entertainment of the first degree – I feel awkward, totally at sea. I don't know what to say, nor how to act; I blush, stammer, am at a complete loss, but I'm somewhat fortified with the wine. I've never encountered people that have so thoroughly disarmed me, so artfully pulled the ground from under my feet. How they raise the heavens with laughter at the way

I speak French, at the way I stand before them like a puppet whose mechanics no longer work, its strings collapsing one by one around it.

Order's called by a fine-looking, fatherly fellow with a flowing moustache and hunter's cap, its peak pulled down low across his brow, against the glare of the sun. Beneath it I see penetrating eyes sizing me up. He puts me picking on a row with one of the girls who shows me what to do. It's easy enough; the most difficult thing's the continual bending down—the vines are low and we have to work fast in order to keep pace with the others.

My partner, on her knees, moves along the other side of the row from me and every now and then I catch a glimpse through the leaves of her lovely face; she looks like Flora in a painting by Boticelli. Fascinated, I watch her hands deftly sever clusters of grapes from the vines; they know their work, they're quick and intelligent, like her eyes. Her hair's tawny and it flows along her neck, a neck as slender as a marble column. I'm slow at first and she has to work doubly fast for we're beginning to lag behind. But I begin to pick up her pace and we fall into an easy rhythm, exchanging glances and smiles whenever our faces meet through the tangle of vines. Something somersaults in the pit of my stomach at a chance brush of her hand. Her name's Peloupé and she's one of the daughters of Nehri, the fellow who'd called order and put me picking with her.

'Who are the others here? Are they your brothers and sisters?' I ask looking around at the other thirty or so Romanies amongst the vines, 'I mean, are some of them your brothers and sisters?'

'Yes, some of them—the others are cousins.' Gypsies are all brothers, sisters and cousins for they're all of the same blood, the same vine, as it were.

A shrill, exquisitely-pitched, voice rises up in song and hovers above the vineyard like a lark for a few moments, sending a shiver of rapture down my spine before it breaks up in a clatter of laughter.

'That's my sister, Nina,' says Peloupé. 'When she's not cussing or giggling she's singing.'

She points out other sisters to me: Chella and Kikina, who are working on the row next to ours. Kikina's only seven and Chella nine but they're as fast as anyone. Her younger brother, Bébé, is the one that's always making a noise and a nuisance of himself over there – that's why they call him Bébé. Her older brothers, Dzingo and Madjini, patrolling the terraces with big baskets strapped to their backs, are dark and look rather menacing. They're *porteurs* who carry all the grapes up to the vats at the end of the rows.

'You're not French?' I query naïvely. She glares at me as though I had insulted her, '*Non*.'

'Then?'

'*Romanichels*.' and then she thrusts her hand through the vines and gently slaps me as though to wake me up, 'We are Gypsies,' and she clicks her fingers in a kind of hypnotic rhythm.

'Where are you from?'

'*De partout, de partout*, from everywhere, *gadjo*,' she looks at me and laughs. She's funny she keeps saying things half to me and half to herself – she seems to be very amused by me and makes me feel rather foolish. But somehow I think she likes me asking her questions, and so I go on, cautiously, trying to sound casual and not like I'm prying.

'Gypsies . . . do you travel in caravans?'

'Yes, look, over there,' she says, standing up and pointing over towards a small cluster of caravans, drawn up in a circle in the distance.

'Ah – how wonderful!'

Throughout the morning I glance over towards the caravans from the midst of which a thin stream of smoke's winding up into the blue sky. 'A real Gypsy encampment,' I keep thinking.

'What's the language you speak when you speak with the others?' I ask Peloupé.

'It's our language, *Manouche*. You understand nothing, huh?' she laughs. 'I'll teach you.'

She starts pointing to things and naming them, '*Bowlapen* – sky; *cheklo* – bird; *o kum* – sun; *mooi* – mouth; *mé* – me, pointing at herself; *toot* – you, pointing at me – *camootoot!* – I love you!' she giggles, I blush. She holds her hand up and counts on her fingers, '*Yek, dooi, trin, shtar, punch*.'

She has me repeat the words she's taught me in front of the others. This brings even greater hoots of laughter than when I speak French.

'Now say this,' they say and have me repeating things after them, of which I have no idea of the meaning, but which brings forth such raucous merriment that I'm left in no doubt as to the absurdity of the things I repeat parrot fashion.

I'm getting used, as the days go by, to their high-spirited bantering and am learning not to remain an object of ridicule any longer than is necessary. Their teasing keeps me on my toes, demanding that I parry their jibes. They're showing me a new way to see and, little by little, they're teaching me how to speak. I, a non-Gypsy, a *gadjo*, a clodhopper, am learning their language.

The work is arduous, the hours long; from dawn till dusk we're stooped over the endless rows of vines. The clicking of secateurs, the ripping of leaves, laughter, curses, songs, rise up above the fields.

At mid-morning there's a break. Hampers are produced and out of them come loaves, still hot from the ovens, cart-wheels of brie and camembert, salami, olives, wine. How heavenly to bask a while in the sun, munching a sandwich and sipping a glass of cool Bordeaux in the morning sunshine.

'*I sap! I sap!*' a little urchin's come upon a snake in the vines, he's running to tell us. Madjini grabs the bread knife and leaps at the viper, quick as a flash and holds its wriggling, decapitated body up above his head for all of us to see. It's black against the sun. At noon a cry goes up, '*La soupe! la soupe!*' – We down tools and race for the château where long wooden tables are laden with victuals. *Food.* Ravenous, we dive into great cauldrons of lentils and slurp vessels of wine; and then we lie stretched out on the grass savouring the precious moments of rest. The boys teach me how to spar with sticks, how to play splits with knives, and a game of skill and profit with stones. The girls teach me how to make crowns from vine leaves. Back at work we alleviate the tedium of the afternoons by waging war with juicy bunches of grapes which we hurl at one another over the tops of the vines. Sometimes things get so out of hand that Nehri has to call order, for he's responsible for the work in progress and a certain number of vats must reach the cellars by the end of the day. The boss of the château rarely shows his face in the vineyard – a wise move on his part for a Gypsy hasn't the slightest respect for a *gadjo* and resents being ordered about by one. Nehri spends most of the time up at the end of the rows supervising the filling of vats and the transport of them to the cellars. He surveys us with a weather eye. Sometimes I look up and see him gazing into the distance, all the essence of the Romany concentrated in his being. He seems far away – on who knows what road – but nothing about him ever seems to sleep. At other times he rummages around in the hedgerows with his stick looking for *neegli* – hedgehogs – a Gypsy's favourite dish.

I've been spending my evenings at the château, where I have a room, supping in the kitchen with the old estate workers who busy themselves in the cellars all day crushing the grapes and whose blue tunics are pungent with the fumes of the new vintage. I am with the workers, and the women who run the kitchen (alas, not the young scullery maid who only seems to work during the day) and who spoil me with tasty tit-bits and the best wine from the cellars; but I long to be with the Gypsies around their fire. They, to my dismay, don't have supper with us at the château. Coming after work to the kitchens to fetch cauldrons of lentils and meat, flagons of wine and loaves of bread, they take them back to their encampment, the en-campment to which I wander as closely as I dare after dark, to get a glimpse of these mysterious people around their fire. Nevertheless, I enjoy these evenings in the kitchens with the great log fire burning in the grate, the high ceiling with its ancient timbers, the sturdy wooden table, the cauldrons, the steaming kettles, the cat that nestles on the mantelpiece, the faded picture hanging above it with its mountain scene with rushing torrents and conifers, the strident ticking of a grandfather clock, the hissing and sputtering of logs as they smoulder and flare up suddenly, sending a shower of sparks up the chimney. And as for the company with whom I sup, the old cellar workers all attired in their blue boiler suits who are kindly enough and seem quite animated to have a young man in their company, and wanting to know of course about where I come from, whether I am a student, what do I think of France and, although I sometimes find it difficult to understand their heavy dialects, I glean a lot of information about the area.

One of them, who's obviously a bit of a historian, is intrigued when I recount the incident in the cornfield and the hand holding the book and he starts to tell me about the Cathars. The jist of what he told me was as follows: that the majority of the population of the Languedoc and Provence were practising what the Church saw as a heretical cult, but which the people felt was closer to the simple lives they led. Practically the whole population had abandoned the Church of Rome, which they saw as corrupt and out of touch, and had embraced Catharism, which seemed much closer to Christ's teachings. However, the Church was not going to tolerate this for long and after an incident or two with the church authorities the Pope raised a crusade against them and soon the fields of the whole region were soaked in the blood of men, women and children. Those who managed to escape fled to the castle of Montségur in the Pyrenees which was then besieged by the crusaders. They held out for many months, during which time, legend has it, they managed to smuggle out the legendary Cathar treasure, which was purported to be enormous and which no one really knows what it actually was and to this day it remains a mystery as to where it went. Some say it wasn't material, some say it was the Holy Grail itself. And some have even suggested it was a holy child. In March 1244 just after Easter, at Montségur, they finally surrendered and all were burnt on the fires the crusaders had prepared for them at the bottom of the mountain. It's reported that they sang as they walked into the flames. I find all this very interesting and old Jeannot is pleased to be able to show off his knowledge of such things.

I tentatively ask them about the Gypsies; 'Ah les Gitans.' (The French call all Gypsies 'Gitans', even though they're a completely different tribe from the *Manouches*) and a dark look comes over them. 'They come here every year,' they tell me, 'they work well, keep themselves to themselves, not really a problem . . . but Gypsies are Gypsies, have to keep an eye on them . . . one hears stories, you see . . .'

He can see that I'm interested and he goes on, 'One of their tricks is to pick up young foreigners, usually students, who've come look-

ing for work on the *vendange*, they turn up at a château with him or her claiming he's one of their company so that he goes onto their payroll – well, at the end of the picking of course they go off with his wages. It happened down the road at the Château Bel Aire some years ago; the police got involved but they couldn't track the Gypsies down . . . can't trust 'em see . . . pretty girls amongst them, though,' and they all snigger.

'*La soupe! La soupe!*' The sun's gone down, the cry's gone up. It's the end of the day and I'm helping Nehri with the vats, heaving them up onto the trailer of the tractor. '*Mishto, mishto,*' he smiles at me as we slide the final one up beside the others and the last load of the day is towed away to the cellars. And then, again in Romanês, '*Hup lonshi yuk erat i pies mawl,*' Come to the fire tonight and drink wine – the invitation I've so ardently longed for.

Dogs bark, chickens squawk, urchins run around, kicking up the dust with their bare feet and crying, '*Gadjo! Gadjo! Gadjo!*' A din indeed as I come into the circle of caravans and I'm motioned to a beer-crate by the fire drawn up for me to sit on. Peloupé brings me a cup and pours me wine. A warm glow spreads through me and I look up at the faces, all of whose eyes are upon me, and say, '*C'est magique.*'

Truly, a dream, cherished since childhood, has come true – I've been brought to the Gypsy fire. Five caravans are drawn up in a circle around this central hearth, 'like the planets around the sun,' I muse, 'and up above us the moon.'

Nehri's caravan is a metallic silver and blue. It's lit by gaslight and through the lace-curtained windows it glitters like a palace. A large woman, wearing several layers of skirts and huge golden earrings, emerges from the doorway bringing a bowl and spoon for me and saying, '*Jarla,*' – she's Nehri's wife, Pita. Food arrives from the château – the château which will see little of me from now on. Nehri winks cheerily at me as I tuck into the broth, '*Latchi zummin,*' he says. Yes, it's good soup alright but I'm hardly aware of it, so greedily am I drinking in everything around me. In a circle of light we're on a moving, shifting stage. I listen to the strange tongue, the hissing and crackling of the fire. The firelight dances with the shadows on the leaves of the trees which encircle us, on the caravans, and over the faces in which thousands and thousands of nights like this one are written. Who are they? Why are they forever wandering? Is some special destiny theirs? Perhaps the earth demands an eternally nomadic people, restless as quicksilver, inventive as Vulcan, to run like a bloodstream through her, a procession of riot and colour and unrestrained song.

I come every night to the fire now – they expect me to. Nehri I've begun to call '*Tatta*', like his children do, it means daddy in their language – and we joke that I've been adopted, that I'm his new son. And, though I say we joke about it, the gesture is significant, 'You were meant to be a Romany,' he says to me.

They ask me a thousand and one questions: about England, which road do you take to go there? Over the sea! Is it a big sea? Are there ships which go there? Is it hot or cold there? Is there a moon? Are there cars and televisions? Are there *Manouches* on the roads in England? Their curiosity comes from the fact that they've never had any contact with England, it's just a name to them, it could be anywhere in the world. Now, about Spain or Italy or Germany they can tell you anything you want to know – they've travelled the length and breadth of these lands but England, well, it might as well be at the ends of the earth and totally undiscovered. But from asking questions, questions which sometimes seem absurd – ones that enquire after the very colour of the earth, they begin to build a picture of the land from which I come.

The picking's over. The last of the grapes have been severed from the vines by our industrious hands. A jubilant roar bursts from us as we come to the end of the last back-breaking lines. We can straighten up our backs and keep them straight – what untellable relief. We leap over the vines, we hurl bunches of grapes, we roll on the earth, spring in the air and we laugh. At the caravans a fire, stacked high with old vine stumps, is roaring and crackling. Sparks are belching out in torrents to paste the twilit sky with stars. The walls of the château across the vineyard still retain the glow of the sun which has sunk behind the slopes and is sending up the curtains of night.

It's exquisite to be standing here at the fire, the sweat of labour drying and evaporating into the air. I drink a cup of wine, smoke a cigarette and let the warmth of the fire soak into me. The evening's already chilly and there's mist on my breath. I find myself alone in my thoughts: what now? Where will I be this time tomorrow? I really don't know where I'm going and don't really want to think about it. It looks very much like we're going to be bidding farewell. They'll be away somewhere, off and away to who knows where with their gay tinkling laughter and their free lilting songs. They'll have touched me with their strange magic, put a spell on me and kindled a fire in my soul, so that things can never be the same again. I feel unutterably sad all of a sudden – is this the closest I'll ever get to these people, to work with them awhile to share their fire and their wine for what would be just a brief moment on their endless migrations – could I ever really penetrate deeper than just the surface of their mysterious lives – could I ever really *know* them? These people are the only ones who have ever made sense to me; they remember how to live, they possess a secret, and abundance beyond measure.

Tatta's calling me to come over, '*Hup kaï!*'

He's round at the side of his caravan and has filled a basin with hot water. Handing me a bar of soap and a towel, he says, 'Have a good wash – work's finished – be *shookar* now,' Stripped to the waist I'm shaving. I catch sight of Peloupé in the mirror – she's looking over at me from where she's standing by the fire. Steaming pots of food and flagons of wine are arriving from the château. Chella and Nana, Sylvia and Magdala, Zunda and Kikina are lugging the cauldrons along between them. Little Loli's staggering beneath a pile of freshly baked loaves. A Mercedes pulls up – it's Djanko, Tatta's brother, and his wife, Carla. Working a nearby vineyard they were here the other evening when I'd heard of Carla's childhood in a German concentration camp, 'At the outbreak of war we were travelling in the Black Forest – *O Dével*, we should have known better than to be in Germany at that time. Everywhere we saw bad things happening, heard of bad things happening – they were getting the Jews, you see. Then they came for us, the *Zigeuner*. They came in the middle of the night, three trucks, one full of soldiers, two empty ones to put us in, they had loud motorbikes and big, vicious, dogs swarming all over the camp and into the caravans – ah *Dével, Dével!* – there was screaming and the shouting of an officer and the soldiers hitting us and putting us into the trucks.'

I could feel a sort of intangible fear shimmering through the assembled company as she spoke, as though this was an ancestral terror they all know, 'I was six years old and was forced to work eighteen hours a day on a crust of bread and a bowl of thin soup. My bones were sticking through my skin. We worked in the fields in the snow with no shoes. The guards hit us if we cried. Day after day, night after night – we saw no end. A Gypsy will survive where others won't, but plenty of us died too.'

She clenched her cigarette in her knuckles – there was a haunted, deeply intelligent, look about her eyes; just as there was about her daughter's, Touroute, who's here with them tonight standing, quietly composed, looking into the fire; sixteen, dressed in black, and exquisitely beautiful. I could imagine the German death squads singling her out for 'special treatment' before killing her.

Headlights flash along the tracks through the vineyard. Cars are pulling up at the encampment and *Roms and Romlis, chavi and chaïa*, are stepping out of them and gathering around the fire. They hail from all over, the length and breadth of the land, from far and wide: Pau, Paris, Marseille, Limoges, Aix-en-Provence, Montpéllier, Poitiers, Toulouse, Strasbourg, Nantes, St. Jean de Luz, Carcasonne, Lyon, Narbonne, Biarritz, Bayonne, les Hautes Garonnes . . . from afar and scattered, from everywhere, from nowhere . . .

> As though a bugle'd blared a gong'd boomed
> I remember!
> Caravans on the white roads
> fires – stars – on the plains
> and my dark brothers and sisters
> looming up before me
> arms outstretched
> to tell me
> I'm home
> with them for whom home is nowhere

and everywhere –
I hear again the song
the call to life
that stirs up my soul like a Gypsy fire
the fire that I knew in the flames of my youth
as a girl who swirls like smoke
patters the rhythm with her feet on the turf . . .

I'm awoken by the sounds of camp being broken up: engines being tested, spluttering and stalling, hammering, shouting, squawking, barking, cussing, singing.

I leap from the tent to which, tottering with wine, I'd been steered by Bebé, laughing at my side, saying, 'The château's a million miles away and your legs will not take you there tonight – this tent's nearer.'

At the fire Peloupé hands me a bowl of coffee and a chunk of bread, *'Kaï jas kudīvis?'* she asks – Where are you going today?

'Jinoga,' I reply, and I really don't know.

Tatta's hitching up the van; he calls me over, asks if I can help him align the trailing gear, 'We're leaving for Pau today,' he says. I've heard all about the encampment at Pau where they spend the winters – it's a great big place full of *Manouches*. How I'd love to go there.

'It's a pity,' I begin. Tatta must have detected a note of sadness in my voice for he looks up at me and says, 'Are you sad that we're leaving?'

'Yes.'

'Then come with us.'

'Can I?' unable to believe my ears, '*Can* I, Tatta?'

'Yes, you can,' he's beaming at my display of unbounded joy, 'Go and get your things, get your pay: we're leaving soon.'

I run to the château.

'Alors, my English friend – you are now going back to England to spend ze winter, huh?' smiles the *patron* handing me a fat envelope bulging with crisp bank notes, my well-earned pay.

'Non, monsieur, I'm leaving with the Gypsies.'

'*What . . . ?*' he leaps from his seat in horror, 'they'll take you five kilometres down the road, knock you on the head and take all the money I'm giving you now.'

'I don't believe that, monsieur.'

'You don't believe that?'

'No.'

'Do you know these people, do you know what they're like? they're . . . '

'They're my friends.'

'Your friends? How can they be your friends? You don't know them. They're dangerous, they're thieves, they'll trick you, you'll see.'

'I don't believe that, monsieur, and I'm going with them.'

'Then you're a fool.'

'I shall always be a fool!'

I turn on my heels and slam the door behind me. The caravans are pulled up outside, their engines running.

'Jump in,' call my friends – and off we go.

'I shall always be a fool!'

My own words ring in my head as I'm crushed in the back of the citroën van between children and dogs. But isn't that what life's about – to be a fool, to dare, to risk everything? I'm not sure what's before me now as we bump and rattle down the avenue and take the road for Pau. I cannot deny that the *patron*'s words have sown some fear in me, but I don't want to believe what he said; I want to trust what I feel, it's so important that I do, and if I'm wrong about the Gypsies and they do trick and rob me, well, at least I'll have found out for myself. My heart's beating fast. I'm on the road with the great wanderers of the earth – you see, dreams do come true, you just have to work at them with your whole being. Thirteen of us are aboard, Tatta at the wheel, Pita up beside him, Nato on her lap from whose head she's picking fleas. The rest of us are in the back, I squashed between Tonino and Chella. We wend our way south through picturesque landscapes and remote villages, the gaily-coloured, blue and silver caravan trailing along behind us. We're in a convoy of three.

Suddenly we pull up at a crossroads, 'Can you read?' asks Tatta, turning to me.

'Yes.'

'What does the signpost say?' I climb up to the front of the van and peer out of the window, 'Toulouse.'

'That's the *latchi drom*, the right road,' says Tatta, slamming the vehicle into gear. 'Stay up here in the front, you'll see the Pyrenees soon.' And before long the gigantic ranges loom up on the western horizon. We drive towards them and then turn south. We're in Basque Country and the people in the villages from whom Tatta asks directions have a strange accent, even I can notice it. It seems almost another language they're speaking, almost another country here. We pull up in one of the village squares to buy bread from a *boulangerie*. It's strange the way people look at us, I detect a mixture of curiosity and fear – watch your pockets, lock your doors, the Gypsies are passing through. An old, benevolent-looking fellow wearing a beret and carrying a stick has been besieged by the smaller children and is handing them coins. The girls, like splashes of colour in the stone square, are filling containers with water at the fountain, giggling as they put on a little show for the old men lining the bench, lifting their skirts, clapping their hands and tapping their feet on the flagstones, '*Olé!*' The women are coming out of the boulangerie, laden with long loaves, and Nato's stuffing a handful of sweets into his mouth before he's caught with them. We jump back into the vehicles as a sonorous bell strikes the hour.

The sun has begun its plummet towards the earth and soon will vanish behind the mountains. That hint of melancholy which comes towards the evening has begun to pervade me, together with a sense of insecurity, uncertainty – do I know where I'm going, or why? Things take on a different light when the day draws to an end. I'm alone in my thoughts – in fact I feel quite alone and, suddenly, lonely. The sky's turned from blue to pink and now it's darkening. We pull off the road, come to a halt. We're in a wild and desolate landscape, a deep river runs away under a bridge. This is the hour, the setting, in which to cosh me over the head. 'We stop here, tonight,' Tatta tells me as we get out of the van. The caravans are drawn up in a circle and a fire, kindled in their midst, is flaring up with showers of sparks to join the stars looking down on us.

'Come and look for wood with me,' says Tonino, tugging my arm.

'Alright,' I laugh, happy now and we race off to a near-by copse to look for sticks before it's too dark. The birds are nesting in the trees. Tonino pulls a catapult from his pocket along with some round, smooth, stones, '*Deek!*' he says, 'Look!' and he stretches his lethal weapon, aiming it into the branches, the stone rips through the leaves.

'*Deek!*' he says taking aim again – this time there's a squawk, a shriek and a little bird falls onto the ground, dead. Tonino rushes to it and picks it up, puts it in his pocket. We hear some voices a little way off in the wood, the snapping of twigs underfoot, whispers and giggling. '*Sshhh,*' says Tonino putting his finger to his lips, a mischievous glint in his eye, 'follow me, quick,' and he proceeds stealthily in the direction of the voices – not quite sure whether I should, I tag along behind him. We arrive 'just too late'. Sylvia and Carmen who'd come to the wood to 'make pee pee' are pulling their skirts up and, upon seeing the rascally Tonino peering at them through the undergrowth, are hissing, '*Jovek! Jovek!*' – 'Go away, go away!'

We come back to the fire with armfuls of wood. Sylvia steps over to Tonino and starts to twist his ear, '*Aaaiee,*' he cries, dropping his load. '*Na, na, maw pen* – Never again, never again.'

'Good,' she says, letting him go and smiling at me, 'Tonino's always thinking of *minche*, little Gypsy!'

There are some twenty-six of us here around the fire. There's Darko and Mungi's family, they were with us at the château; and the other caravan belongs to Sinto and Zina, who joined up with us last night – they can't be more than sixteen years old and they have a baby so young it hardly seems to have its eyes open. It's like a little foetal bundle in Zina's lap, its face is dark and curiously lined like an old man's, and is staring around with a look of puzzled wonder at this sudden world.

I'm handed a steaming bowl of soup, some bread and some wine. '*Boot latcho mawl*' Tatta says as he hands it to me – and yes, it really is good, very good, wine, a barrel of the finest wine produced here which the *patron* has gifted to him. It feels good as it imparts a glowing warmth to every fibre of my body and being. Tonino's grilling his *cheklo* over the flames, fending off Nato who's trying to steal it. He's putting it inside a piece of bread and is eating it, bones, head and all.

And now there's some excitement. Madjini, who's been absent, is coming out of the darkness holding, triumphantly, a *neeglo* curled up in a ball in his hands. He's been rummaging around the hedgerows with a dog and has come up with the prize he was seeking. Putting it on the ground, the dog snapping and barking at it, he draws his stick along its underside and starts rubbing the hedgehog's belly which makes it uncurl and with a quick movement he's brought the heavy stick down on its head and killed it outright, at least it was quick. Now he's putting a thin stick into its bloody mouth and pushing it right through its body so that it comes out of the other end. He puts it on the fire, revolving it, until all the spikes have burnt off and, when he pulls it out it's a black, charred, ball. With his knife he opens it up, guts it and puts it on the grill. Soon an appetising smell is everywhere and eager faces watching as it spits and sizzles. Madjini's looking at it covetously but he knows full well that everyone's going to get a taste. 'It tastes better than chicken, better than anything you can imagine,' he tells me. Madjini's very similar to Dzingo: dark, swarthy, with eyes wide-apart and a head like an arrow. At first I'd found them menacing, had been somewhat intimidated by their looks and their manner – but that was before I got to know them, before they took to me like brothers. 'If anyone gives you shit, let us know,' they'd said to me. No empty words for one night, back at the château, we'd gone down to the village of St. Émilion, a few of us, to the brasserie in the square. I honestly don't remember who'd started it, for I'd been drinking hard like everyone else, but I found myself in a dispute with an obnoxious French fellow, nearly coming to blows, when Dzingo and Madjini, leaping over the tables were at my antagonist's throat and choking the life out of him, 'Leave him alone in future,' they hissed as they left him to stagger, half dead, out of the café.

Dzingo's fetched his guitar now from the caravan and sings, an old Romany love song:

> *Tigini chaï amunsa*
> *Ano zenelo vesh*
> *Rodarmungi o fraisili*
> *Chorlin an taw baïa*
> *Imun i poori geiga*
> *Mit trin zeiti pré . . .*

> Little girl follow me
> To the green wood
> We'll pick strawberries
> And hide them down your blouse
> I have an old violin
> With three strings on it . . .

The sky is immense. Now and then a shooting star blazes a trail across a minute portion of the firmament. On the western horizon the Pyrenees rise up in towering blackness.

'Tomorrow, Pau,' I think as I look up from where I lie in my sleeping-bag beside the fire. I pat the breast pocket of my coat folded under my head. 'Still there.'

My fingers feel the bulging envelope full of money.

Chapter 6

The Great Encampment at Pau

In a wood, a handful of miles from Pau, is a walled compound, known by the *gadjos* as the *Camp des Nomades*. Some sixty or seventy caravans are within, a veritable Gypsy citadel. I'm to have the ground pulled from my feet once again as I step down from the van and set foot in this big encampment for the first time. Standing awkwardly amidst the multitude that's gathered round I let Tatta explain who the *gadjo* is before them. The hostile looks about me begin to thaw.

'They thought you were a spy,' he tells me later.

'A spy? But I'm far too gullible and guileless for that.'

'That's what I told them,' says Tatta. We laugh.

As the days go by I find myself being more and more accepted, if not yet as a *prāl* (brother) at least as a *mal* (friend), and a traveller like themselves; I'm welcomed at the various fires throughout the encampment and invited into the *kampinas* which are cosy and glitter like palaces. Tatta's fixed me up with an old Citroën van for a home. There's a wide bed and a stove which I have roaring merrily on nights when I feel like being solitary. I roast chestnuts, write poems or my diary, add to my list of Romany words. But most evenings I'm at the fires, fascinated by the faces, the stories, the constant dramas enacted around them. I listen to the strange tongue, watch the quick, graceful movements. It's an ever-animated, shifting, kaleidoscopic, stage, trodden by vibrant players and lit by flashing flames.

Here comes Djanko: he's had a fight with a *gadjo* in town and now he's going through it blow by blow. Djina, who stands quietly by the fire, is in love with him and her eyes anxiously follow his every move. She doesn't know whether he won, as he claims, or whether he ran. He's back, that's all she cares about. She'd like to clean those bleeding knuckles for him. He's probably been messing about with a *gadjine* in town – that's why he's got into a fight again. He'd better watch out or he'll find himself hitched up to one – that'll sober him up. 'Oh why won't he look at me?' she sighs.

Here comes Chico: he comes with the news that there's been a break-in at the offices of a supermarket in town. People are putting it about that it's the Gypsies' doing. So there's bound to be a visit from the *Gendarmes*. A woman curses, putting all damnation on the head of the *gadjo* who gives rise to such slanderous rumours; one of her sons is languishing in jail because of one of these accusations. Pita's searching through little Nato's hair for fleas. He's standing there with nothing but a vest on, his thumb in his mouth, looking around him with wide eyes. He looks at me for a long time – he still cannot understand who I am or where I come from. Manni throws an armful of dry tinder on the fire, it flares up with flames and sparks and the monkey, sitting on Sandor's shoulder, screeches. The sparks melt like stars. Some caravans are arriving, pulling up on the other side of the compound. The wail of a clarinet and a drum beat.

'It's Mirko! Mirko! – he's out!' Out of prison and he's on the move again. Kikina rushes over calling 'Zelda, Zelda!' She's told me all about Zelda, her best friend, who rides horses bare-back in a circus near Paris. Mirko's hat's tilted at a jaunty angle over his eye. He wears a magnificent pair of baggy trousers tucked into American army boots. He arrives with much ceremony at the fire and a hero's welcome – he gave the police a run for their money. His daughter Zelda's come to the fire with Kikina. She has jet black hair, huge earrings and a face so pointed it seems like it's been streamlined by so much dashing around the circus ring. She sees me, *'Kūn o gadjo?'* she asks Kikina;

'He's our friend.'

I've become a kind of human fairground machine. All the children and little urchins line up, or rather, swarm around me for a swing round. That is, I take their hands in mine and whirl them round, flying sometimes higher than myself who am like a crane with my long legs and neck and with my extended arms I'm like the octopus, that exhilarating fairground ride with its long tentacles that whooshes you up towards the sky and swivels you round in its revolving chairs so that your stomach does delightful somersaults and then hurtles you down at breakneck speed and up again above the rooftops and up towards the stars and you cannot help but shout and whoop with ecstatic cries. And such are the children who cannot get enough and after a while I have to call a halt for my head is spinning and dizzy.

I'm awoken by a terrible volley of oaths, of cursing and shrieking. I leap out of bed to see what's happening. It's a woman the other side of the encampment screaming blue murder and, from what I can understand, it's her daughter she's treating to all manner of insults, calling her a filthy slut, a whore, a hussy – and that she'll knock the living daylights out of her if she gets hold of her.

'What's going on Tatta?' sitting calmly at the fireside he motions me to sit down, to be quiet – he's listening.

The women of the camp have gathered round the hysterical mother. Dogs are barking, chickens squawking, scattering before the barefoot urchins running about kicking up their usual din. What commotion! And sitting in the midst of it, Tatta, serene, listening – listening to the lament of the screaming woman.

'Mungi's married,' he says. All unseen, all unheard, a Gypsy wedding's taken place, proceeding according to custom.

In the middle of the night, as pre-arranged by the lovers, the young man steals up to the caravan where his sweetheart is lying awake, listening. He taps, infinitely quietly, on the window and she, who's been waiting breathlessly for this signal, tip-toes out from amidst her sleeping family and runs off with her suitor into the night. In the depths of a wood or on the slope of a hill, they give themselves to one another and knit their hearts together in a bond that will not be severed even at death. They're husband and wife – *Rom* and *Romli* – now and, when they return to the camp on the morrow they'll be greeted as such.

'But why all that shouting and screaming, Tatta?'

'It's always like that – the mother's sad to lose her daughter, so she curses her daughter who's the cause of her sadness.

'But the terrible things she was calling her.'

'Ach! Those are only words.'

'Peasant, Blondin,' Manni always calls me 'Blondin' – well, anyone would look blonde in comparison to him – he's as dark and as crafty as Caliban. He's a bully too, he loves to make me squirm, and he's good at doing it – like now. I'm cleaning up some metals with him and I've gone and busted the hammer head, 'You peasant Blondin – I'll use your head for a hammer now, it's thick and dense enough – *gadjo!*' But for all this, I can't help liking him – liking him because he'll never make any pretense to be nice; he relishes the discomfort he affords me, especially in front of others and above all in front of the girls – but, despite himself, he'll suddenly ruffle my hair, perhaps at a point where he's nearly reduced me to tears, and affectionately say, '*Gadjo*, Blondin.'

His wife, poor young thing, looks the unhappiest woman in the encampment – her face is always black and blue and her eyes swollen from crying. But he does pay me whenever I work on the metals with him and from him I've learnt a lot about this craft – I can see a bit of Vulcan in him as he sweats and curses, darkly, over obstinate iron, lead, copper or aluminium which will not break or yield under his powerful blows. 'This, Blondin, this copper stuff – *cupro* we call it – is worth a thousand times more than this common grey stuff – but it has to be "clean", Blondin, that is, not one tiniest piece of inferior metal must be stuck to it – so clean it up good – and you may have noticed, yes, even you, Blondin, that lead is heavier than aluminium so you have to have a lot more aluminium than lead to make up the same weight.'

He does most of his work in a copse, some way from the encampment, to which he drags or rolls his engines, refrigerators, boilers, his disused components, chassis and electrical wiring. A fire smoulders on which he melts lead, burns the plastic off copper wiring, lights his cigarettes and over which he roasts a chicken or a hedgehog.

Most of the time, though, I work for Tatta. Going out with Dzingo and Madjini in the lorry we drive around the villages, calling in at the farms and asking for any old iron. Sometimes we strike it rich and sometimes we come back empty-handed. Some of the ways we come by what we are after entail a certain amount of cunning, of daring – and there are times when we have to scarper, pretty damned quick.

There are still a handful in the encampment who look upon me with suspicion. One old crone, for instance, is convinced I'm a spy and starts cussing and hissing every time she sets eyes on me. Tatta's warned me to be on my guard with some of those about the compound and to avoid going near certain fires.

But now I've strayed over to one of those he warned me about. You see, I saw Magdala here, standing alone – and I like Magdala and I know she likes me – and she smiled at me as I passed but, as I approached, she turned and disappeared into one of the surrounding *kampinas*. And now, instead of her, I find myself in the company of two surly fellows looking daggers at me. One of them steps over to me, stabs me in the stomach with his finger and hisses, 'I'm gonna get you.'

The blood drains from me, the pit of my stomach jolts in a spasm of fear, 'W-why . . . what have I . . . '

'I don't like your mug,' he snarls, 'tomorrow morning, be here. We'll go out behind the wall.'

'Alright – I'll be here,' I say, trying to look as mean as him – inside, I'm shaking like a leaf. Christ! – how on earth am I going to stand up to a Gypsy? I'll not last a second, not stand a chance in hell. But I'm not going to back down, I'll be here, I'll be here alright.

The night's interminable – tossing and turning I dread the arrival of the morning. I'll be like a lamb to the slaughter. I know how Gypsies fight – there are no Queensbury rules with them. A kick in the balls, a smack in the face, quick as a flash and I'll be finished. I could tell Tatta first thing in the morning, or Dzingo and Madjini – they'd help me out. But, no, I've got myself into this, I must get myself out.

I'm by the smouldering fire, it's the appointed hour. With trembling fingers I take out a cigarette, put it to my lips, am about to light it when I see my aggressor and his accomplice approaching. I'm gonna need all the puff I can get. I put the cigarette back in my pocket. Staring into the embers of the fire neither of them looks at me. They may spring at me: I brace myself, glaring at my opponent as fiercely as I can. He takes a cigarette from his pocket, lights it, takes a couple of puffs, tosses it into the fire, 'Forget it,' he growls, and turns away. My body, which he'd have mashed to pulp, has turned to jelly as I make my way through the encampment to Tatta's fire.

I have no more trouble in the camp at Pau. I can wander freely, anywhere. Unwittingly that fellow set up something which worked very much in my favour. If it had come to combat I'd have lost but, as it's turned out, I've won, won the respect of the whole encampment.

I'm soon to see that Gypsy skill and ferocity in fighting. It's the month of May; there's an open-air ball in a square in town. A score or more of us from the camp have come along. A rock 'n' roll band's playing on the stage. A contingent of *parachutistes* – hated paratroopers – are present. It's a hot night, balmy, intoxicating, blood-enfevering. My companions are not pleased to see the swaggering squaddies with their shaven heads on the dance floor – not pleased at all. It'll only take a spark.

In a flash, the square's a battleground. The Gypsies, who've drawn coshes and belts loaded with lead, are trashing the military who've been taken by surprise. I realise, to my horror, that I'm going to have to step into the bloody fray and fight alongside my companions; not to do so would be unthinkable: I fancy myself as a *Romano pral*, do I not? Then I must fight like one. I'm about to take the plunge when a terrified paratrooper streaks past me, with Dzingo and a couple of others on his heels in hot pursuit, 'Come on, help us get this geezer,' and I join them in hounding the solitary soldier who's bolting, white faced, down an alley which leads out of the square. What luck – I can honourably flee the field. The quarry's put up against a wall and, one by one, turns taken to batter him senseless. Teeth crunch, blood spurts. 'Your turn now,' they turn to me who am next in line to have a crack at him, 'oh, I think he's had enough, don't you?' Nothing could have me beat this boy any more – I feel sick – he's crumpled up and whimpering.

'You're right. he's finished. let's go.'

Back at the square the fighting's over; the 'parachutistes' have fled and the Gypsies are gathered, victorious, on the field of battle. Back at the camp it's reported that I fought valiantly at their side, 'like one of us, a good fighter.'

I awake, the sun streaming through the window onto my face. I have an idea, a plot, to prove myself as smart as a *Rom*, to show I'm not just a clodhopping *gadjo*, that I can set up a little enterprise of my own and make money. What I'll do is this: I'll go to Pau, buy a bucket, some ice, some concentrated lemon squash and set up a little stall at the market. There are bound to be some shoppers and marketeers who'll be glad to quench their thirst with my ice-cool product which I'll sell at the unbeatably low price of a franc. I leap out of bed and out to the fire to tell Tatta my scheme.

'Impeccable plan. But you'd better hurry, it's a long walk to Pau, *latchi bok*, good luck,' he calls after me as I stride out onto the road, 'Good luck.'

The sun's already high and beating down upon my bonce.

Buying the equipment has taken longer than I anticipated and now noon's striking as I arrive, hot and sweating, at the market place. I quickly assemble my stall on a couple of packing cases, and start calling out, '*Limonade! Limonade! Un franc le verre!*' But, dammit, everyone's gone home, the whole place is deserted. My cry echoes around the nearly empty square. I throw the lemonade out and trudge up the hill: Christ – they're going to think I'm a *gadjo* now.

Arriving at the cathedral, which commands the heights of the city, I fling myself down on the grass and stare up at the glaring metallic sky. The day's become sultry, torpid – not a bird sings. I'm sticky, the grass is itching and my heart is beating against my temples. I'm deflated, my whole enterprise came to nothing, I kick myself for starting off so late. Next time I must start off at dawn. A bird starts singing, or rather, it's more like speaking, 'Look, look, look,' it clatters urgently on a branch above my head, I open my eyes and see what I hadn't noticed before. I'm surrounded by flowers, flowers of all kinds and colours. Finding some string and silver paper in the nearby dustbins I make little bouquets and now I'm standing at a corner calling out: '*Des fleurs, des fleurs, un franc le bouquet.*'

Jubilantly I return to camp my pockets jingling with coins

So now, whenever Tatta doesn't need me to help with the metals, I go into Pau to ply my new trade. I have to be careful not to raise suspicion by going too often to the gardens around the Cathedral and so I'm constantly on the lookout for new places to filch flowers from. There's the park, of course, and the hedgerows on the way into town from which I get most beautiful wild flowers and then, one day in the late summer when, due to the scorching heat flowers are getting scarce, I pass a cemetery. There are bound to be flowers on the graves and there certainly are, ready-made bouquets and all, albeit a bit wilted. But what's this? A grave's been dug up and at the bottom's an old coffin made of solid lead, worth a small fortune. Looking to see that no one's about I jump down into the hole. Christ, there are human bones in the coffin. I hesitate a moment or two, but no time for superstition or sentimentality. I tip out the bones, bend and compress the lead into a manageable lump, heave it up to the surface. It's heavy this block – I'll have to rip it in half and make two journeys. Now, one lump hidden in the undergrowth, the other on my shoulder, I leap over the wall and make for the scrap metal merchant. Forty-seven francs! Back for second half – there'll be no need to sell flowers today, ha! ha! I can have a drink instead.

'Where'd you get that?' Chavo's pulling out of the scrap merchant just as I'm arriving with this second lump on my shoulder. He looks surprised, and not a little impressed, to see me, staggering out of the blue, panting beneath the weight of such a find. But, when I tell him it's an old coffin, he gasps, *'Mooli!'* – Ghosts! – and he puts his foot down roaring away in his lorry as fast as he can. It's the Gypsy terror of the dead. Well, I hope these francs I'm getting in exchange for it don't haunt me. I'm getting another thirty-five of them. That makes, let me think, forty-seven plus thirty-five. That makes eighty-two hoot'n toot'n francs. I'm rich, folks, I'm rich!

I ask Dzingo about the tattoos which most of the Gypsies have on their arms, hands and faces. They are simple and obviously made by themselves or their friends. Some of them are little figurines like the depiction of the saint with a halo above his head, but many are just dots in various combinations like a secret code – the single blue dot on the high cheekbone, for example, they call the 'third eye' which is supposed to see round corners and give warning of the approach of a *glisto*, a cop – it doesn't always work – the origins of which are no doubt a talisman to ward off the 'evil eye'. Four dots forming a square with a fifth in the middle is a sign of imprisonment and three dots forming a triangle mean, 'I shit on the police.' Many of them have the figure 13, the departmental number of Marseille from where they hail.

I ask him how they make them, 'I will show you,' he says and goes into his caravan bringing back a little pot of Indian ink and some needles. He takes two needles and fastens them tightly to-gether with a couple of inches of thread.

'I'll make you one,' he says, 'of what, and where do you want it?'

'The single point, on my face,' and he sets to work. He dips the needles into the ink pot and it comes out with a blob of ink between the needle heads – it's painful as he stabs my flesh, drawing a fair amount of blood as he does so.

'There, now you have it,' he says, after a while, wiping away the blood, 'it is there forever and you will never forget us, your friends, the *Manouches*. Now you can make your own,' and he leaves me with the ink and the needles.

First I make a primitive image of the saint which Dzingo calls '*La signe de voyou*', 'the sign of the vagabond', and the protector of travellers and thieves, just as Hermes, Mercury, was to the Greeks. I wipe away the blood and, lo and behold, there is my first self-made tattoo. I then put the number '64' next to it – the number of Pau, and also the number of hexagrams in the *I Ching*, the Chinese divi-natory method of foretelling the future. And finally I make a cross with four dots in its corners which has always seemed a mystical sign to me, probably Indian in origin. All of these are on my left arm as my left hand would not have the dexterity to make any on my right. When I show them off to Tatta later this evening he smiles: 'Now you will have the luck of the Gypsy.'

'Now we just sit back and wait,' whispers Tatta.

We're concealed behind a bush; in the clearing before us is a song bird in a cage and next to it a branch covered in very sticky glue.

'Listen how she's singing: The males can't resist it. Look, one approaching, Shhh . . . ' he puts his finger to his lips. It's making cautious hops from branch to branch on the tree near-by, looking to left and right of it, nervously, like birds do. It's brightly coloured, like the female in the cage.

'A beauty,' breathes Tatta. '*Hup kai an taw tiginni romli,*' – Come to your little wife,' he whispers encouragingly. From her cage she's singing her heart out in full-throated song to her suitor in the tree and he, enchanted, is swooping down in the impassioned flight which will seal his fate.

'Got him,' says Tatta, triumphantly. 'He's got himself a wife and will fly no more. Now, you've seen another Gypsy trick,' As we pick our way through the wood towards the camp. I tell Tatta the road's calling to me again, the old restlessness is in my blood. Tatta and his family will not be travelling until the end of the summer. He's managed to get a deal with a *gadjo* who's disposing of tons of metal which means '*boot lovi*' – 'tons of money' – for Tatta.

'We'll miss you,' he says 'but a Romany's life's full of farewells so we don't get sad when someone leaves on a journey. For we know that it's only a matter of time before fate has our paths cross once more. Now, if you're passing through Marseille visit my brother, Djanko, and take him my greetings. You'll find him at the encampment at Mirabeau – I'll tell you how to get there.'

I've arisen early, packed my rucksack, slung it over my shoulder and stroll over to the fire. Pita's brought me some coffee and a hunk of bread to dunk in it. Dzingo's just got up and when he sees me with an air of departure all about me he comes straight over wishing

me a *latchi drom*, a good road, and saying, 'Don't forget us and don't forget to come back.'

Kikina and Loli rush up to me for a final swing round and, seeing this, swarms of other urchins converge on me from all over the camp for a throw and twirl in the air. They're swarming all round me as I reach the road and strike out for Marseille.

The Mirabeau encampment's a mountain range of scrap iron – piles of metal and car chassis as far as the eye can see and, in the valleys, so to speak, are the caravans, shacks and fires. Djanko and his family welcome me warmly, bringing out food and wine and giving me a place to sleep with the children in an old railway carriage. I know some of the other Gypsy families here – ones that have passed through Pau or were at the picking in St. Émilion. And to my delight, here's Touroute again! She takes me into her caravan and shows me her photographs. Here she is, seven years old, on a beach at Biarritz. Here she's riding bareback on a horse in the Camargue. This is a picture of Tatta and Pita, and this is Dzingo, the little urchin with the shaved head and catapult, at their side, 'and you see,' she says, 'still the same blue-and-silver *kampina* they have now.'

Here's a big fire with musicians around it, a girl dancing. 'Les Saintes-Maries-de-la-Mer,' she says, 'it's fun there,' but her face, lit up in a smile, becomes suddenly overcast as she turns the page. 'My brother – shot by the police. They say it was a mistake, but it's wasn't. They chased him all over Marseille and shot him in cold blood. You see now why I always wear black, I will always wear black, I cannot forget him. You see we were so close he and I.'

She's got up, is standing in the doorway. 'You understand these sorts of things, I think. That's why I've shown you my photographs, why I've told you of my brother. I keep this suffering to myself, but to you I wanted to speak.'

Djanko offers me some work for a few days. He has some lorries to break up. It'll be hard graft but he'll pay me for my pains. With mallets, crowbars and axes we set about smashing and ripping iron and metal. Sparks, jagged splinters, fly like shrapnel – we wear goggles and thick gloves. Four of us are at it: myself and Djanko, his son Pingas and a cousin, Toppo. Toppo's only half *Manouche*—his mother's a *barescri*. The *barescri* are basket makers and, though they're not of Gypsy blood, they and the *Manouches* live peaceably alongside one another. Toppo has wide-apart green eyes and freckles—he's always laughing. He shows me how to carve wooden figures with a pen-knife.

'Now stick,' he says to me, holding up a piece of wood, 'now man, from stick to man in just three minutes. You try!'

'Stick still stick,' he says laughingly after several minutes of my hacking unskilfully at the wood. 'Watch, like this,' and he shows me how simple it can be.

'Your forefathers have been making these sorts of things for centuries—it's in your blood.'

'Yes,' he laughs. He takes me to his caravan—one of the biggest I've ever seen. *'Bari kampina, huh,'*—yes, a big caravan—*'maw dat, maw dai'*—he introduces me to his father and his mother. A tiny man with a laughing face like his son, grasps my hand.

'My father's known as the *Géant du Nord,'* says Toppo, 'because of his height.'

'Because of my two wives and the enormous caravan I have to have to house them,' jokes the Giant. A big, jovial-looking woman, similar to the one Toppo's introduced as his mother, is coming down, the steps of the caravan, 'I married two sisters of the *barescri* tribe of Lyon—God have mercy on my soul,' he winks, 'and look at the pitiable size they've reduced me to with their constant nagging.'

Toppo shows me his collection of sculptures, carved from all kinds of wood—pine, ash, sycamore, chestnut, oak, willow, beech, some so intricately chiselled they're monuments to detail; others sparse, with the merest outline for form, unscratched surface for face. These latter, like the figures from the pre-Hellenic Cyclades, are the ones that seize my attention. I look at Toppo, 'They're incredible,' I breathe.

'Which one do you like best?'

'That one,' I point, without hesitation, at a standing figure, flat-faced, looking up at the stars.

'Then it's yours,' and he puts it in my palm and closes my hand over it.

'*Hup, hup! Deek, deek!*' children rushing are calling me, 'La cirque, la cirque!'

We run to the road at the confines of the encampment. Some caravans and wagons are newly pulled up: there's a monkey, a bear and a wild pig in a cage.

'*Kel, kel,*' sing the urchins to the bear, 'Dance, dance,' and the bear sways from one foot to the other in a clumsy, drunken lurch. They throw stones at its feet and a man jumps from a caravan shouting, '*Jovek, jovek,*' they run away. To me he lifts his hat and bows, '*Cirque de Budapest, pral.*'

Chapter 7

Spain

I was passing through one of the many abandoned villages one comes across here on the plains, evacuated by their inhabitants at the time of the civil war when bands of soldiers and mercenaries were marauding and terrorising the people in rural areas, so that villages were deserted as the inhabitants fled to the relative safety of the cities.

I'd arrived in one of these desolate places in the late afternoon, the wind blowing through the shells of crumbling stone cottages and whistling through corrugated iron roofs, most of which had collapsed into the dwellings along with the beams which supported them. It was eerie, with here and there an old shop front: a baker with the still discernible *Panaderia* written above the door, a café which must once have been the centre of the village, with tables outside under the now sprawling, overgrown trees beneath which labourers from the fields would have sought shade from the scorching midday sun. Today the sky was overcast with a cold wind blowing down from the mountains which formed a backdrop to this desolate scene. Coming upon a well I peered cautiously down its deep shaft to be greeted by the pitiful eyes of a dog staring up at me and letting out a heart-wrenching whine. It was floating on a large piece of polystyrene foam which it must have somehow managed to heave itself up onto. I could not leave it there. But how on earth was I to get the poor soul out? At some distance down the hill there was a busy main road on which a policeman was directing traffic – he must be able to help, I thought, and so set off as fast as I could down the stony, pot-holed track to where it joined the road at the bottom. The policeman watched me with some suspicion as I approached him waving my hands to him. *'Pero'*, I said coming up to him, *'pero in pozo—ayuda me, por favor,'* in my basic Spanish I told him there was a dog in a well and please help me get it out. He shrugged his shoulders disinterestedly and went on with his futile directing of traffic which paid him little attention anyway and just drove like Spaniards always do. Fuck him, I said to myself and hurried back up the hill to the village which I'd determined not to leave until I could somehow manage, by hook or by crook, to get that poor wee creature out of that horrid dark well. I started searching around all the houses for some kind of rope with which I could make a lasso and somehow haul it up. After a while I came upon a long electric cable and made a loop in the end which I then lowered down to where the dog was. But try as I might, I just could not get it to catch any part of the dog. I was in total despair, the dog looking up with pitiful eyes and whining ever more brokenly when suddenly, out of nowhere, a *Gitano* appeared and, peering down the well and immediately understanding the situation, took the cable from me and with true Gypsy deftness caught the dog by the hind legs and hoiked it up to the surface. The dear creature yelped with joy, looked at us with gratitude and ran off into the evening.

How miraculous that tall, noble-looking Gypsy with his wide-rimmed hat appearing just when he did. It was as though the universe had conspired to have him pass just at that moment—he took his leave clasping my hand in his which was strong and bony, flashing a smile of gold teeth, *'Suerte, amigo, vai con Dios,'* and he vanished into the twilight.

Night was falling. I didn't fancy spending it there. It was eerie as the shadows crept up and every sound the wind made in the ruins of the houses made me shudder; who knows what might have happened there which had led the settlement to be abandoned—it could have been very unpleasant, bloody and nasty. Civil wars are the

worst of all wars and I thought of some of Hemingway's descriptions of massacres which took place in little villages like this. No, I was not going to stick around there tonight, there could be any number of disembodied spirits prowling around, and even if there weren't, my imagination would conjure them up. There were lights on down in the valley some four or five miles away, must be a little town. Perhaps I could get a bite to eat and a drop of wine to wash it down with – and the thought of that had me leaping up from an old wall upon which I'd been sitting and shouldering my rucksack.

It was a steep, stony road down into the valley and in the dark, moonless night I had to feel every step beneath me as the road had not been maintained and in places rocks and large stones were strewn across it, just waiting for me to stumble over. It had become little more than a track which joined the main road in the valley and it must have been after midnight by the time I reached the town. Everything was closed up, no chance of anything to eat. Dammit, I was starving – a hunk of bread and cheese with a drop of wine would have been just the thing after this long march. Shutters all pulled down over the shop fronts and bodegas and not a soul or sign of life anywhere to be seen. Nothing for it but to find a place to sleep – sleep puts hunger out of mind. I came upon a building site just off the square which was easy to get into. In the dark I felt my way to the unfinished staircase and I had to watch every step for it was open on one side and was strewn with bags of cement which I had to make sure I didn't trip up on in the dark. I gingerly made my way up to the top floor, the fourth. With just enough light from a street lamp down below I was able to gather up some empty cement sacks and lay them on the cold concrete floor under my sleeping bag.

What bliss, as I snuggle in out of the cold March wind and drift off, falling into a sleep as deep as the well on the hill. But just as the little dog was hauled up to the surface by a cable I am jerked up from this blissful state by the sound of voices and a light flashing on me from the from the roof of the house across the street. Someone must have seen me entering the building or heard me scrabbling around gathering cement sacks. There's whispering and the powerful torch beam remains fixed on me. And then I hear the sound of heavy boots crunching on the stairs and the next thing two *Guardia Civil* brutes standing over me, pistols drawn and barking, '*Levanta tus manos!*'

I put my hands up and then, with gun to my head, am handcuffed and led out onto the street and marched to the police station. Once there, I'm searched and have my passport confiscated from me before being taken to a cell, with a board and a thin mattress which pass for a bed, and a hole in the floor to shit and piss in – not so savoury and rats could emerge from it – I shudder at the thought – but at least I'm out of the wind. My head hits the pillow and I sleep 'the sleep of the just' – an expression I once read on a bottle of Chinese tonic – a deep, deep sleep, and so oblivious to everything a whole family of rats could scurry over me and I'd be none the wiser.

Well, they've obviously sussed I'm not a Basque terrorist and this morning finds me on the road to Valencia, musing merrily that perhaps the cops had saved me from the people in the building opposite, who were really terrorists and had insisted, at the point of a gun, I come along to the safety of the police station. Coming down onto the coastal plains the road is bordered on either side by orange groves, miles upon miles upon miles of them. I will always think of white houses, blue sea and oranges when I think of Valencia.

I'm aboard the night boat to Ibiza. It's a fine old boat with a rough wooden deck and wooden upholstered interior. Even though the evening's chilly most of us are sitting out on deck where a group of young Spaniards are singing to the accompaniment of a guitar. I sleep out under the stars with the roll of the ship rocking me like a baby in its cradle.

We put into port just as the sun's climbing up the eastern sky. Stepping ashore I'm taken aside by the police who detain me for an hour or so whilst they check my papers and I fear they're going to send me back upon finding that I have no money. But, to my pleasant surprise they release me and, on leaving the harbour, I turn left along the coast, knowing not where I'm going for I have no map. Now my kingdom for a cup of coffee, and my kingdom is all I'm able to give as I don't have a bean. But what are these shining things that greet me glistening and winking at the side of the road? They're coins of course, infused with the warmth of the sun and Franco's head has never looked so pleasant; they're imbued in their metallic cores with the power to conjure up coffee and cigarettes. Pesetas from heaven, no less – thirty eight of them. I put them safely in my pocket and continue on my way.

After some time a city rises up ahead of me in the form of high-rise, Benidorm-style hotels. Yuk, this ain't what I picture Ibiza town to look like. And that's because it's not Ibiza but the hideous city of San Antonio I'm now walking into. Never mind, right now I'm going to grab a coffee and a pack of fags and I can think about how to get out of here later.

Ah, bliss, a long, delicious café con leche, piping hot, and now I'm leaning back smoking a cigarette, at peace with the world, or would be were it not for a fellow heading towards my table, English by the looks of things and clearly drunk. I can't really send him away when he asks if he can join me, though it would, seeing how things are going to turn out, be better to do so.

'Yer English, aren't yer?' he says, as though to be English is the only credential one needs to be pally with someone, and, upon my confirming that I indeed am, he starts out on the unhappy story of his life, pitiable it is really, his misfortunes, all of his own doing and a trail of destruction in his booze-sodden wake. He's from Sheffield, has been here some months spending the last of his earnings, having walked out of his job at a steel factory, 'stacking, loading, pissing about,' and out of his marriage – not walked, fucked off out of it, he says, 'Fucking bitch, couldn't have a drink without her going fucking ballistic – and that made me violent sometimes, can yer blame me?' I'm getting the picture.

'Listen pal, I'm renting a room here, got two beds, if you need a place to stay, won't cost yer nothing,' and he persuades me, against my better judgement, to take him up on the offer.

It hasn't taken me long to realise that he's as broke as I am. He seems to have enough for his bottles of gin but starts on about not having anything for food, hinting, at first, that I might do something about it, and then getting more forceful, 'I'm fuckin' providing you with a place to sleep, 'bout time you did something in return.'

So much for his 'won't cost yer nothin'', but I need to feed myself too and so I steal some cheese from a small supermarket on the corner and beg some bread from a bakery, at the expense of contemptuous looks and head bowed in shame.

'Nice one,' says he, seizing on it like a hungry dog. And so this becomes my job, my payment, every day. Except for the occasional crack through which one gets a glimpse of something nastier, Paul's quite affable most of the time – as long, that is, that he has drink.

In the evenings we go to a discotheque which we get into for free and where we 'mine-sweep' for drinks, that is we swipe other people's drinks – mainly Bacardi and cokes – when they go up on the dance floor, and we manage to get drunk.

Tonight, this fourth night, he's been in a queer mood and leaving the disco early says, with something like a growl, 'See yer,' I stay on for a couple of hours, having got into the swing of things and am on the floor dancing, ever fancying my luck with the mainly English girls with whom I don't stand a chance in hell.

When I get back to the pension, Paul, steaming drunk, greets me at the door, 'Get out of here,' he snarls.

'What d'you mean?'

'I've had enough of yer with yer stealing and begging.'

'What the . . . ?'

He grabs an empty bottle, smashes it and lunges at me with the jagged glass, 'Get yer things and get the fuck out of here!'

The town of Ibiza is a whole different kettle of fish; truly a lovely town and as picturesque and charming as I've heard it described. It's a strange mix of hippies and the jet set. Laid-back and Bohemian, it invites you to laze in its ubiquitous cafés and bars that line its winding cobbled alleys that circumvent its turquoise bay. My flower trade thrives and the evenings find me sitting on the main drag making up the little bouquets from the flowers I've gathered from my daily saunter into the surrounding countryside and which are abundant at this time of year. I make enough to fill my belly and to wet my whistle every night – so all's well with the world.

Every Thursday there's a little hippy market which is set up a few miles along the coast in a clearing in a pine forest which slopes down gently to the sea. I went out there last week with my new-found friend Michel, who hails from France and who travels regularly to India, bringing back silk clothing and tapestries which he sells on the streets and in markets such as this. It's a congenial place and I pondered the possibilities of selling something here – not flowers, of course, the place was full of wild flowers, it would be coals to Newcastle. It was swelteringly hot and I could see that some form of thirst quencher would be the thing. I mulled it over and came up with an idea.

And now, this Thursday I was up betimes and headed for the market in town where I purchased two large watermelons and took the bus out here, a thirty minute ride. The melons are cool and, as long as I keep them out of the sun, they should remain that way for a while. By the time I arrive it's getting hot and there are already a lot of people and so I waste no time in cutting the melons into slices and immediately start to sell them – and they sell like hot cakes. It could be said that I've been doing a roaring trade so that by now, at the very hottest part of the day, my pockets heavy with coins and both the melons gone, I'm sitting in the cool of the pine forest on the trunk of a fallen tree. With the searing heat and the constant, hypnotic clack of the *cicadas* I think I'm falling into some kind of revery but nay, this is no revery, this girl really is dancing towards me out of nowhere singing and, upon seeing me, comes up saying, 'I'm flying, I have wings, do you want to fly?'

'Oh yes . . . yes I do,' whereupon she places something in my palm, '*window panes*, you'll fly and see things through a magic window,' and away she flies.

I'm dropping the tab right here on the spot in the shade of the pines, and what better company could I wish for than these lovely trees, whispering in the breeze coming off the sea. It takes a while for anything to happen I've been told, Michel's told me that – that's ok, I have time. It does take a while but then it kicks in and I enter into a strange world – the pines have come alive, their tall trunks are swaying and their branches are reaching down like arms which want to lift me up into the sky. From the market a little way off there's the sound of drumming and a flute – I must go there – an invisible cord is pulling me and here in the circle the drum beats in the pit of my stomach and I'm undulating, a snake uncoiling through my body in waves of ecstasy; my body's dancing all by itself and with everyone and everything as if we were all part of one great living organism.

Darkness is falling, I'd better get back into town, I must find the bus . . . It's not easy buying the ticket, the coins don't make any sense to me and the driver gives me a suspicious look which makes me anxious. Once we arrive in town I go into a tobacconist to buy some cigarettes, why I don't know, I don't feel like smoking, force of habit perhaps, habit habit too much habit, but habit makes me feel safe, reassures me that I am who I think I am. The fan on the ceiling turns round and round in slow motion, making a strange whirring and clicking sound. The man behind the counter has a strange look, as though he has wooden shutters over his eyes, another man is watching me saying 'tut tut' in time with the fan . . . I run out of the shop, I don't know what's happening, I must find Michel. He's there, thank god, in his usual place with his stand. He knows immediately what's going on with me, 'Come on,' he says, 'we'll go somewhere quiet,' and he leads me to a little white-walled bar down by the harbour where artists, writers and hippies hang out. The atmosphere is peaceful and my friend reassures me everything is going how it should and there's nothing to be afraid of. Santana's *Caravanserai* is playing and the music takes me on a strange journey – I'm in a desert and camels are moving across the walls, the white walls are like a screen on which a magic lantern show is thrown. I hear crickets and feel I'm ascending on the electric waves of a guitar. I fall into a strange and delightful revery for an unknown length of time impossible to measure as it contracts and expands as in a dream. It might be an eternity, it might be just a second. The comforting presence of Michel has dispelled the anxiety, the panic, that was triggered by the fan in the tobacconist and has given me the courage to interact without fear and with my whole being in this Alice-in-Wonderland world I find myself in. It seems more real than anything I've ever known; how come I didn't know of it before – or did I? It seems like something I'd forgotten about, somewhere that was always there, behind the screens, as it were. I feel as though I've come home.

I turn to my friend and thank him, he's patiently been sitting beside me all the time I've been on these fabulous voyages of the mind, and I tell him I want to go out into the night and be alone again.

'Just remember, any fears you might have are only in the mind, even if you feel threatened by some people, they have no power over you, they are not real–and most people are well-intentioned anyway, although they are fast asleep. At the moment you are more awake than you've ever been, try to connect with everything you feel around you, everything you see, and store it up inside you–for you will fall asleep again, but a door has been opened.'

I ponder his words as I wander away and find myself out on a cliff path. Overhead and all around the rim of the sea the stars are joined by threads of light as though the earth and everything on it were caught in a great net. He was right, Omar Khayyam, when he wrote:

> We are the puppets
> and the firmament is the puppet master
> for a while we act upon this stage
> then we go back into the box of oblivion . . .

Am I the shadow of my shadow, or am I the one that's thrown it? Time has dematerialised I think . . . no, I don't think I . . . why do I say 'I'? because I don't know who I am if I don't say 'I' . . . yes you do . . . no I don't . . . melt into the word, it's ice and you're melting into it . . . melt, it's ice and it's melting . . . oh yes, I'm not who I thought I was–I'm a river now, drifting along, drifting along, back to my mother the sea, into the silence from which my thoughts flow . . . so silly to think I was ever anything but this, yet all this time I've been like some frozen 'I' stuck like an icicle outside the window panes–window panes ha ha ha!–and each drop a lifetime, lifetimes and lifetimes of millions of years fixed and coagulated . . . a stalactite . . . rigid–and now I'm a river as I was all along . . . and the stars are reaching down to me, as to Orpheus when he floated by, and the stars in this womb we call night are conjoined in a web of light. 'I' has melted and I am all this . . . I contain multitudes, and am contained by them.

I've been profoundly changed by that experience and see how up until now I've only lived on the surface, as it were, of myself which I've experienced as a distinctly separate entity from everything around me. But now I've had a glimpse of many layers of myself which lie beneath the surface and I've had the ecstatic realisation that at the very root, the uttermost depth of the well of my being, I am connected to all beings, to all things, not separate at all, but actually one with them. I was one with the stars that night which I'd seen joined by threads of light as though they were a great, all-enveloping net of which I was a part, along with the sea, the earth beneath my feet, the breeze which bathed my face, the crickets whose sound filled the night with their insistent clicking which seemed to be relaying some urgent message as they knitted a pattern over the earth, and the fire flies in amongst the undergrowth flashing like the stars up above.

Everything was a part of everything else, vibrating, pulsating with the bloodstream of the energy which flows through life. Everything was in communion and I was a part of it as vital as a thread in some vast, glorious, carpet from the Orient. Although I shall surely sink back into the ordinary consensual reality, seeming myself to be isolated, separated, from everything again and getting caught up in the things of life, the dramas of the emotions, the false perceptions, life with all its deceptions – yes, although I'll fall back into all this, and be torn to shreds, that glimpse into the depths of my being and the world, with all the veils torn away, will remain with me always deep inside, even when the events of life will seem to bury it, and will one day grow into the universe itself.

Not long after this, when, sitting on the street selling flowers, a girl comes up and starts talking to me. She's a slim brunette, seventeen or eighteen years old, from Salamanca. Her name is Meji and she wants to practise her English as she's going to university this coming autumn. We take a walk along the shore where we find ourselves in each other's arms. It's her last night in Ibiza, she's taking the boat back to the mainland tomorrow evening.

'Come to Salamanca,' she says, 'I will be waiting for you.'

Chapter 8
The Road to Salamanca

Strolling along, happy about being on my feet and on the move again, I'm out on the road heading north from Valencia. All of a sudden a car pulls up alongside me and a head protrudes from the window, '*Donde vas, amigo?*' and, upon my answering Salamanca, he opens the back door for me to jump in. I find myself in the back seat of a dilapidated Mercedes behind two rather sinister-looking fellows of about my age. They're pallid as corpses and have jerky, uncoordinated movements about them. The emaciated driver has his foot down on the pedal and at breakneck speed is negotiating this narrow, twisting road, from time to time slamming his fist down on the horn and breaking into into a volley of abuse – '*Puta madre!*', '*Ijo de puta!*' – every time he swerves to avoid another vehicle, sometimes by just a hair's breadth. His companion keeps turning to me, talking excitedly, almost manically, with perspiration gleaming on his forehead and his ghoulish sunken cheeks.

After a while we pull into the side of the road and a syringe is produced, along with a teaspoon and some white grains. Then I watch the sick procedure: the searching for veins, the tourniquets, the shooting up the arm. '*Tu quieres?*' they ask, turning to me and proffering the loaded syringe.

'Non gracias. . . ' I say, recoiling, and then more forcefully, '*Non gracias!*' as they try to insist.

We drive on for a few more miles into the interior and halt in a squalid, poverty-stricken street in a mountain village where my two companions signal for me to follow them into a dark sports bar; they pay me a beer and do a deal with someone at the counter where they examine a little package and slip it into a pocket. Back on the road one of them rolls a joint and offers it to me – I don't refuse, though the situation I'm in rings all my alarm bells for I know the effect hashish can have on me when I find myself in situations over which I have no control. I take a couple of puffs and immediately regret it – this stuff is absolute dynamite and the unease I've already been experiencing escalates into near panic. Who are these guys, why did they pick me up and where are they leading me? I catch the driver looking at me in the mirror as the other turns around, gabbling to me in a tongue which I no longer recognise. The driving's getting more erratic and faster, faster, faster. . . fear and nausea are rising in the pit of my stomach and then *BANG* – a tyre's blown and we're swerving uncontrollably over the road and straight at another car hurtling towards us at breakneck speed – this is it, I'm going to meet my death – how stupid a way to die!

God knows how, but the other car misses us, its horn wailing in terror as it streaks by. It's as though fate's had a change of mind, deemed it unnecessary we die and we jerk and shudder to a halt on the verge. The three of us, all shaken up, change the wheel and continue, carefully now, on our way. I've warmed to my companions by the time they drop me off in the centre of a small town, I think the shared experience of horror has knitted our souls together in some way, we all thought we were going to die.

'*Adios. amigo, vai con Dios. . . !*' they say as I get out of the car. It's the middle of the afternoon, the heat almost unbearable and the streets deserted, everyone in their houses with the blinds drawn down. I sit on a bench by the fountain in the square in the shade of a spreading pine tree. The splashing of water in the stone basin of the fountain soothes me and the paranoia I'd felt after those couple of puffs of the joint and what ensued turns into a lucid dreamlike state as the square shimmers in the afternoon heat. A man appears with a donkey that drinks thirstily at the fountain. He is of a considerable age, thin and wiry, burnished by the sun, a face sculptured by the elements, a black beret sitting upon his small head and on his feet a pair of faded red slippers in which he shuffles along. He hasn't noticed me sitting here in the deep shade of the tree and I call over to him,

'*Buenas dias, Señor . . .* ' I want to know where I am, the name of this town, '*como se llamas este pueblo?*' But either he hasn't understood my question, or he simply doesn't know himself, which is unlikely, he just shrugs his shoulders, saying, '*Vai con dios,*' as he resumes his journey with his donkey, both of them seeming to float over the square in the shimmering haze.

The clock on the bell tower of the little church at the north end of the square strikes the hour, five o'clock, awaking me from the slumber into which I'd fallen. People are emerging from their houses and beginning to populate the arcades which line the square, moving around leisurely and filling the cafés under the arcades. A taxi driver is filling a bucket from the fountain and dousing his over-heated, dusty vehicle with it. Women come with children who splash each other with the cool, crystal water. The square, which in the midday heat seemed to be unworldly, devoid of life, as though it were frozen in time, is suddenly bustling, and the fountain the focus, the hub round which everything turns. The children stare at me, giggling, and a little girl comes up to me and gives me a bag of pistachios which her mother has produced from her basket. Evening's falling and shadows lengthening. I take my note book out and jot down a rough sketch which I'll make into a poem:

> It's as though everything had sprung up around it
> its insistent, ceaseless, voice
> commanding all this masonry –
> the red-roofed, white-walled houses
> the little church of Santa Maria
> with its bell and its tower –
> into position as Amphion's lyre
> had done at Thebes and here
> on this sun-parched plain you can see
> how water had that power

It flows from an iron spout into a rough-hewn
bowl of stone in which the sky floats and two steps
lead up, well-worn;
from early morning women come and go
their chatter shrill above the water tumbling into buckets
It's the hub round which the whole town turns
where men and donkeys halt and taxi drivers douse
their over-heated cars –
where nervous little birds flitting round its rim
drink and preen their feathers –
and where the hours, forever pressing on
turn round and round but never touch it.
It's here the girl with heavy heart
sits awhile alone to tell
of her love and all the sorrows sown by it
and where in the hush of noon a traveller
putting down his pack will let
the murmur of the water weave about his mind and get
glimpses of the soul who weeps for his return.
It's as though everything was ever flowing from its depths
the red-roofed, white-walled houses
the children's cries, the mothers' calls
the shadows lengthening round the square
the hour that's striking from the tower . . .

Spain is such an immense, exotic, almost primeval country. I
trudge long miles of twisting roads, through sun-parched, barren
terrain, over dried up river beds, deep gorges, and in the middle of
nowhere I come upon Roman aqueducts, their huge vaulted arches striding across valleys, and upon crumbling fortresses, amongst
whose ruins I seek shade, and giant-sized lizards emerge from cracks
in the walls and piles of stones to stare at me with unblinking eyes.
To escape the unrelenting heat of the sun I'll often while away whole
afternoons in the shade of a rock or a solitary tree. I live on figs and
little else, they are abundant at this time of year and their spreading branches with their wide, deep green, leaves provide a cooling
canopy.

How small I feel amidst such immense stretches of earth and rock running up to the blue sierras which tower into the metallic skies. Eagles and vultures circle and soar above me and, at night, under the dome of crystalline stars, drunk with sunlight and solitude, I pray – I don't know to whom nor for what – but I pray, sometimes just to get me safely through the night, for I'm not without fear as I lie there alone in all this immensity. Dogs howl in the hills as I snuggle up in my sleeping bag to keep warm as the nights are cold.

I had a strange encounter which to this day I don't know if it was real or just a dream – I mean, a waking dream – most probably something in between; I was eating, as I said, little else but figs and the sun was playing tricks in my head. I arose from a hillside and went down the rough track to the little red-roofed village below and into a café called the Cantina Don Quijote. The interior was warm and so steamy it seemed as though a mist filled the place and I sat at a table and had a piping hot *café con leche* brought to me and smoked a cigarette. I became aware of another presence at the table, one that gradually seemed to materialise from the smoke and steam and as though through a veil of time. He was reading a book and seemed wrapped in thought. Suddenly looking up he said, 'It's your book'.

'What d'you mean?' I asked, astonished.

'It's *Hedges, Ditches and Dreams*, your book', he said, showing me the cover. It was a painting of a small figure trudging along a road in a mountainous landscape, with a rucksack on his back and a stick, and rising out of him was what appeared to be the outline of a giant replica of himself, towering above him, head in the stars and striding out with a long staff. There was my name, there was the title I'd long intended it to have. But how could this be, how on earth could this be? He looked at me, with the wryest of smiles on his face, which had now completely materialised, and was that of a young man about my age, 'So you're the character I'm reading about, I'm glad to meet you in the flesh.'

He seemed amused and was sizing me up with eyes which seemed to be able to see straight through me. 'It's a good tale,' he went on, 'but there are some things you've left out, you'll have to include them next time – without them you won't really be able to get to where you want to go, you'll only get so far.'

I knew what he was talking about: those things I'd never been able to face in myself.

For a moment or two I was a little downcast, feeling the truth of what he was saying, but he snapped me out of it, saying, 'Those things can come later, with age, what you've written so far is true and is nothing less than the account of a young man on a quest – the only quest worth undertaking.'

At these words I perked up and exclaimed, 'So there *has* been some purpose to my life, it has been a quest, I've been lost and so erring, my whole life, sometimes, devoid of meaning but you can see my path. Has the book really been published? I mean . . . I mean, *how*? I haven't written it yet.'

My new friend looked at me, again with a wry smile, 'Time goes backwards and forwards, you only see it going one way. You have written it, but not yet.'

Now there was a riddle if ever I heard one. Question: What has been written that has not yet been written? Answer: my book. I'd been planning the writing of it ever since I'd first set out on the road, that of course was like making a cake without the ingredients, the ingredients in this case being experience; and had long had the title, *Hedges, Ditches and Dreams,* just as it was on the book he was holding in his hands – it was to be the story of my life, but I hadn't lived my life yet, it all stretched out before me waiting for me to step into it and make it happen so I kept saying to myself, 'Wait until it's all fully formed inside you, digested, distilled – you're in the thick of it now, can't see the wood for the trees . . . ' and I might never have emerged from that dense wood and left only numerous notebooks with, jottings and rantings and wine stained verses, the pieces of a jigsaw puzzle which wouldn't fit together and nothing remotely coherent would I have written about my sojourn here on earth, I'd have fizzled out, not having accomplished what I came here to do.

We strode over the plains together for most of that day. I plied him with endless questions about the book – for he knew far more than I did about it – he was actually reading it! He made some interesting observations, foremost being there was something behind the narrative I couldn't quite break through to; he knew what it was but when I pressed him to tell me he said it would have to reveal itself to me, which it would one day, and he wasn't permitted to tell me. I wondered what he meant by 'permitted'. We were sitting in the lea of a rock, watching ants carting away the crumbs falling from the bread I was eating; he, he told me, wasn't hungry; 'You see', he laughed, looking round, 'I eat all this.' – it was a strange thing to say and I didn't quite understand. The ants were busy pushing and lifting boulders of bread and carting them off to a crevice in the rock. 'Not much different to humans, impelled by something they never question,' he said.

We sang songs as we strolled along, impromptu songs and poems sprang to our lips. We laughed wildly, uproariously at . . . at everything and nothing!

From time to time we'd stop and I'd ask him to read a chapter from my book, things I hadn't written yet and I realised that he could dictate to me as I wrote it down, that I could crib from my own future writings. I pulled out my notebook and my pen but dammit, I was out of ink! I'd have to remember it and write it down later. A whole chapter lay before me now as I wrote it into my memory. But I can't remember a thing about it now, not even a trace.

Sitting on the crest of a hill, looking out over the sierras and watching the sun go down behind them, I asked him a burning question, the answer to which I needed to know: when and where was I going to write the book.

'Near the Labyrinth', he replied, 'when the time is right.' And he was gone.

Salamanca, rising up out of the plains with its earth-red walls and towers shimmering in the sun. Crossing an ancient stone bridge I feel the presence of centuries of turbulent history and as I enter the city gates I fancy a fanfare of trumpets greeting my arrival and the king's daughter has espied me from the tower.

When I find Meji, living with an old aunt in the suburbs, she shows me all the little 'bodegas' where we drink the rough, potent, wine of the region and where *Gitanos* clap their hands and sing and make guitars cry as only Gypsies can. We cry too, at times, when the wine gets a grip on us and the song works its way into our hearts. We walk the streets, hand in hand, kissing in the shadows. And by the river-side with a last, long embrace, that makes time and the river stop, we say goodnight – she melting into the shadows and I laying down to sleep.

Chapter 9
Don Lamb of Venice

Bella fiore! Cento lire un mazzo di fiori!'

Crying out my wares in the towns and cities I'm making my way across Italy. I arrive in Ventimiglia, agog at the beauty of the old city, built like a pack of cards climbing the side of a hill overlooking the sea. I wind along its twisting alleys and up and down its narrow steps, my hand raised in salute to whomever I pass saying, '*Buon giorno, buona sera,*' I set up my flower selling business in the main shopping street, calling out in the minimal Italian I know, '*Bella fiore! Cento lire un mazzo di fiori!*'

Here in the verdant north there's an abundance of flowers which I gather and sell in the high streets for a hundred lire the bouquet. Hey presto – I fill my belly and with bottles of cool white vino to slake my thirst and fire me up I swing out along the roads singing arias in an invented Italian, nearly every word ending with 'o'. I work my way down the coast. At San Remo I meet up with some young communists who take me along to an open-air festival where we drink Russian beer and listen to Milva singing and where a girl, beautiful as a goddess, her hair lit up by the moon for a moment, takes my hand, saying something I don't understand but which makes me tremble and melt with desire before she's whisked away by another boy and onto the dance floor.

> Your swirling skirt, blue as heaven
> and your body beneath it white, milk white

–which writhes, which floats
on the waves of music flooding the floor –
disquiet me utterly
this summer night in Italy

The moon sails over the sea
the accordion swells
as do your breasts

And your corn-coloured hair
braided in a crown around your head
pours like water falls to your waist
where his hands laid lightly on your hips
Steer and glide you through the night
to my desolation and your delight

Genoa is enchanting, a maze of streets and houses climbing in card-like fashion up the hill, like Ventimiglia. I amble along the streets in the evenings with a bottle of wine, singing as I go and stop breathless with wonder at places which open out onto the moonlit sea.

Turning inland and skirting Milan I'm crossing a bridge which spans a dried-up river when I espy some tents pitched a little way down the river bed. Gypsies! My heart misses a beat and I climb down the side of the bridge. Two youths look up and watch my approach from the bonnet of a clapped-out car.

'*Jarla,*' I hail them.

They ignore my greeting and stare at me.

'*Inglesi?*' asks one of them.

'*Si,*'

'*Vieni qua,* help us with this engine,' I understand him to be saying, 'get underneath. I'll take your rucksack.' ('Be careful,' Tatta had warned, 'there are some of us who'll try to trick you, to rob you . . . ')

I'm under the car – what on earth am I doing here? – all of a sudden I'm wriggling out and diving into the tent where I find the fellow with my passport in his hand.

'*Démun,*' I shout, 'give it to me,' I snatch it from his hand, grab my belongings and flee – stones whistle past my ear as I do so. *Gadjo, Blondin!*

I *was* a *gadjo* there, but I'll tell you something that happened a while back when still in France. I'd arrived in Aix-en-Provence just as evening was falling and was strolling along a backstreet when everything told me trouble was heading straight for me. Tatta had warned me about the *Gitans,* 'They're aggressive,' he'd said, 'more than we are, be wary of them.' I took a deep breath and braced myself and then they were upon me, '*J'aime pas ta gueule,*' snarled one of them, jabbing me in the stomach with his finger, '*moi non plus . . .*' joined the other, shoving me. There was no way out of this, no point in running, I wouldn't have got far. No point in crying for help, no one would come. They were going to kick my head in, it was just a matter of a few formalities like telling me they didn't like my face, that I was a piece of shit, and then they'd start. But they were, after all, Gypsies and I knew they'd be superstitious and if I threw all the weight of my fear at them and pierced their eyes with mine I just might be able to turn things around . . . it was a long shot, but it was my only chance.

'Do you believe in black magic?' I asked, glaring at them.

'What'ya mean, black magic?' they snarled,

'I mean, black magic, *magie noire* . . . I can see your mother now – she's just climbing the steps into your caravan . . . '

'What'ya mean?'

'I can see your mother and with one movement of my hand I can make her fall and break her neck,' and I was now slightly closing my eyes as though seeing things from afar.

'What ya fuckin' talkin' about?' I could see they were enraged – how dare I speak of their mother, but they were clearly alarmed.

'One movement of my hand . . . ' and I started to move my right hand towards my left, 'and as soon as my hands touch – your mother will *DIE!*' and I shouted, with all the fury I could muster, into their faces. '*Non! Non!*' they screamed, 'don't do it, we are your friends . . . you are our friend, let us shake your hand – we are friends!'

To my utter amazement and untellable relief, I'd swung it! They'd shrunk to nothing before my eyes and were completely at my mercy. Just a few moments ago they'd been about to bash my head in and now the whole situation had been turned around. We shook hands and they slinked away; and, although I was still trembling, I was flushed with the triumph a warrior might feel on the field of battle and my fear had turned into a feeling of indomitable power.

I'm leaning from the window of a steam train as we glide over the lagoon to Venice – Venice which rises up like a dream from the water. I'm not sure it's not a dream as I descend the station steps to a waterfront teeming with little boats and a bridge arcing over it like a rainbow.

'It could be the bridge that links heaven and earth,' I think, en-raptured, 'with the blessed passing to and fro over it. Well, perhaps not so blessed,' I muse, leaning over its parapet, smoking a cigarette, and listening to the jarring accents of American tourists as they pass by in droves. 'Gee,' I hear one of them say, 'we liked Paris so much we stayed there a whole week-end. Guess we'll stay here a couple of days too.'

I take my shoes off to feel the warm flagstones beneath my feet and wander around the labyrinth of alleys, through the little squares and over bridges big and small. Everywhere the lapping of water against the ancient walls. Towers rise up from the waterfronts, sono-rous bells strike and clang and peal and priests in flowing garments rush by. Gondolas glide under the bridges, with their cargoes of tourists, steered by slick gondoliers in boaters and striped shirts who sing of *amore*. I dream like everyone else when I lean over a bridge in the evening, tipsy with wine, I listen to snatches of song drifting over water and my thoughts drift to San Remo and that girl on the dance floor.

Lamb's a Londoner, a happy go-lucky trickster. He's made his way down to Venice after nine months in Munich mugging busi-nessmen.

'I just pick pockets now,' he tells me. 'I'm not violent by nature, it's just that stickin' those fat businessmen up against a wall with a

knife after they came pissed and staggerin' out of the beer houses was the easiest thing to do – kid's play it was. I had no scruples: businessmen are robbin' us – hard fuckers they are and all cheatin' on their wives, in the strip joints, in their hotel rooms, and all on their expense accounts – but I'd 'ave 'em squealin', a kind of 'rough justice' I called it.'

We're in St. Mark's square, sitting on the steps of the little tower where many sit in the evening, listening to the violins playing on the café terraces. We're sharing a bottle of wine. Two American girls sit down on the step below us – they're pretty – perhaps we'll get to know each other, but then I see Lamb's hand in the handbag of one of them, 'You can't,' I breathe . . .

'I can and I 'ave,' says he, slipping something into his breast pocket. 'Comin'?'

'I . . . I . . .'

'Come on,' and he pulls me by the sleeve towards one of the alleys that leads out of the square. There's nearly a hundred dollars in the purse. I accept the meal in the swish restaurant Lamb offers me. 'You've earned it as my accomplice,' he says and the pizza I'm tucking into sticks in my throat.

However much Lamb tries to persuade me, promising to teach me all the tricks of the trade, I cannot bring myself to picking pockets. It just seems so sneaky to me – even mugging seems more honest (though I'm definitely not going to try my hand at that!) I agree with him that most people can afford to be relieved of the contents of their pockets ' 'cause they've got more in the bank' but I just can't bring myself to taking things off another's person like that. And yet I wouldn't have any scruples about robbing the bank where they've got the rest of their loot – that's different altogether, like stealing from super-markets: I can do that alright.

'It's a shame,' says my Cockney pal, 'we could've worked together, as a team – we'd make millions with all the tourists about.'

I like Lamb. I met him whilst drinking a coffee in the station canteen. He'd been hanging around the bookstall eyeing up the tourists arriving on the trains. I saw him go up to several girls, trying to chat them up, I suppose, in order to relieve them of their worldly riches.

He wasn't having much luck, getting rebuffed all the time and, after a while he headed towards the canteen for some refreshment. He made straight for my table with his cup of tea.

'English?' he asked.

'Yeah.'

'Can I join yer?'

That's when I heard all about his 'business'.

'It's a cinch in Venice – but there's all the 'Eyeties' on the game and they're good. There's a bit of a mafia and they don't much like me doin' what they're doin'. I have to watch out 'cause they're kind of territorial, if you know what I mean. I'm only around the station in the morning 'cause in the afternoon and the evenin' they're all around here, flocks of 'em, waiting for the trains to come in and they don't like to see *me* 'angin' around waitin' for the trains to come in,' he laughed, he's often laughing, I like that about him – and, it may sound strange, but I like his openness and his honesty; plus, he's generous to a 't' with his pals,

'Have another coffee, and a cake or somefin', on me,' and he went up to the counter and came back with a tray full of croissants, cakes and frothing cappuccinos.

'It's a good life here, I live well,' he smiled. 'I keep out of the way of the mafia and no one bothers me, not even the police. I make my livin' quietly you see. I live in a little hotel in the Lido, my own private bathroom, a view over the lagoon – yeah, mate, it's the life of a millionaire, well, almost – compared to the life I was livin' in London it is – in a squat in Hackney with a lot of down and outs and junkies, Jesus, I wouldn't go back there if you paid me. Where are you sleepin', mate?' I told him I usually picked a different spot every night: by the sides of the canals, on the steps of a church, anywhere.

'Just make sure yer hide yerself well,' he advised me, 'these 'Eyeties' are in full operation at night. They'll get everyfin' away from yer and then slash your feet through your sleeping bag so that you can't run after them. Yeah, they don't play around.' A train was pulling in, 'That's the ten forty-five from Milan,' said Lamb getting up. 'I never miss this one – catch you about.'

No, for all his tempting promise of riches and 'the good life' I'm not going to become his accomplice. I'll ply my own trade, humble as it may be. Not finding any parks in Venice, and therefore no flowers, I go to the flower market to see if I can find any thrown away from which I can assemble some bouquets. An old lady at one of the stalls sees me scrabbling about in the boxes and asks me what I'm looking for.

'Old flowers?' she looks bemused, smiles, 'Come in the evening – six o'clock – and I'll give you all the flowers you want.'

And so at night, with an abundance of flowers of all varieties, I hawk my wares around the cafés and restaurants, or sit on the bridges and sell them to young lovers as they pass me, wrapped in love with one another. No, Lamb, I'm sorry, but nothing could induce me to pick their pockets.

It's kind of incongruous to come across a Cockney in Venice: something of London always hovers about him like an aura; though he doesn't look altogether un-Italian as he slouches against a wall whistling at the girls, what with his small, wiry stature and his greased-back, jet-black hair. No, he doesn't look out of place: it's when he opens his mouth,

'Blimey, mate' he says to me, 'talkin' about accents, you've got a right toff's one there – where were yer – Oxford or somefin'?'

'No I never got that far,'

'What, some kind of posh school then?'

'Yes, posh, probably sums it up,' I laugh, 'Marlborough, you won't have heard of it, you'd probably think it was the cigarettes. I got kicked out.'

'Yer did, did yer?' says Lamb cocking up his ear, interested. 'What was that for, spending all the time in the pub?' and he casts a wry smile at the bottle raised to my lips.

'No, I was never caught in the pub – those of us in the know would only drink in the ones that had a secret room which the masters knew nothing about; it was lots of other little misdemeanours, like being caught out of bounds, being late for prep, missing the curfew in the evening – ha, I even got caned once for writing '*Frog-*

gery' on my French exercise book, The final thing was cutting the bell rope.'

'Ha, that sounds like an enterprisin' thing to do – what happened, you upset the timetable? – tell me about it.'

'Well, you see, there was this big bell which hung above the roof of one of the buildings, the Porter's Lodge, where the porter lived. He used to ring the bell. First thing in the morning to get us all up out of bed . . . '

'It was a boardin' school?'

'Yes.'

'Girls sleeping there too?'

'A few.'

'A few, blimey, what did you do, share 'em round?'

'Well, no – no, not exactly.'

'Posh girls I s'pose they were, with frightfully rich daddies.'

'Yes, I suppose they were,' I laugh, Lamb putting on a hoity-toity accent is even more amusing than he means it to be.

'So, yer stopped the bell ringin'. Blimey, wish I'd been there to see the stink that caused. Go on, tell me how you did it.'

'Well, it was one night in the summer term. I climbed out of my dormitory window with a knife and over the rooftops in my pyjamas and cut the rope which the porter pulled on down below. In the morning the bell didn't ring so no one got up. The servants were in the dining-hall waiting to dollop up breakfast – they waited all morning and all the lessons were late. I was proud of the havoc I'd caused; I'd put a spoke in the works.'

'What 'appened then – an interview with the auforities?'

'Yes, a short interview and that was the end of my school career.'

'Well done, mate, I'm proud of yer too. Bet your old man wasn't proud of yer, though, was he?'

'I think it gave him some concern for my future – but then he'd already given up on my doing anything serious in life, my reports increasingly showed him there was really no hope.'

'Well you wouldn't be 'ere if yer'd gone on studyin' and learnin', would yer? I dunno where you'd be but yer wouldn't be 'ere – sittin' in the sun in Venice, danglin' your feet in the lagoon, drinkin' a nice cool bottle of wine with the likes of me, a guttersnipe.'

'You're right; my real schooling began when I left school and took to a life of wandering, can't beat it, the best university there is. And others I bump into on the road who all unwittingly have something to teach me, they're in a way my profs, such as you Lamb, philosopher, professor – "professor of the pocket picked" – Don Lamb P.P., M.A. (hons.) Venice Academy – for tuition in the art of attaining the good life with dexterous fingers and guile.'

'Don Lamb,' he chuckles, 'I like that – Don Lamb,' he takes a pull on the bottle, 'Yer know we're from different worlds – but now we're in the same boat, equals, no pretensions, not tryin' to prove nuffin' to one anuvver – livin' from day to day, sharin' a bottle of wine, not too bovvered about tomorrow . . . under normal circumstances we'd hate each other – I mean you'd look down on me and I'd try to get the money out of your pocket in whatever way I could,' he looks at me, grinning, 'that's 'ow it'd be, and don't tell me it wouldn't.'

'You're right, I suppose it would.'

'But, as it is, we're mates – 'cause what we are is what we are right now – two 'uman bein's bein' open wiv one anuvver – sharin' a bottle of wine and enjoyin' the same sunshine. Cigarette?'

'Thanks.'

'I was at a right dump of a school – the rats could read better than ever what we learnt, the extent of my literacy was learnt from the graffiti on the shit house walls – no Latin or Greek there, nuffin' very philosophical beyond "I fucked your sister up against the wall" or "I'll show you mine if you show me yours." I got thrown out too, yer see I was always fightin'. I was small, you see, so I got picked on and I had to fight back – that's one thing I learnt at school, to fight, no Queensbury rules, nah, a kick in the bollocks to start and then go on to kick 'im in the 'ead when he's on the floor and the better I got at it the more I enjoyed it – but I'm not like that now, I only get rough with those fuckin' bloated business men who won't 'and over their fat wallets. Not shockin' yer, am I pal?' He looks a little coyly at me as though he might have revealed too many shameful details of his past.

'No,' I laugh, 'carry on.'

'Well then I got this girl in the family way, just fourteen she was, and 'er dad was mad at me when 'e found out – I think 'e'd have killed me if 'e'd got his hands around me neck. So, I disappeared, left me 'ome and all – I didn't have much of an 'ome: my old man was always 'inside' and my mum a fuckin' alcoholic. I was just fifteen and out on the streets – well, that's when I started to learn about how to look after meself. Never went short of a few bob. Started doin' burglaries, got caught, eighteen months in borstal – what a university that was, blimey what didn't I learn in there. Peddled drugs around Piccadilly, got caught, more 'time', and so it went on. One day I'd 'ad enough of London and came abroad. Amsterdam, Paris, Munich, now 'ere. Yer know, I like Venice – it brings out somefin' in me which I never knew was there – a kind of appreciation of beauty. I've never seen a city like this one: look around, it's like a paintin'. Sometimes I go in the churches around 'ere and look at the old paintin's in 'em – I never looked at a paintin' in me life – it was all fuckin' art to me, nuffin' to do wiv life. but now I . . . Shit, I'm gabblin'. Gimme a swig – you know, sometimes I sit for hours in those churches, in silence, and think about life – I never thought about it before, I mean beyond survivin', beyond gettin' rich some day.'

I'm leaving Venice the way I came, gliding over the lagoon in a steam train. The walls and towers are sinking back into the water. As is the figure of Lamb waving farewell on the platform.

'Watch yerself, mate – remember, they've got a kind of communist regime over there in Yugoslavia. I don't think the coppers'll like you sellin' flowers, it'll smack of capitalist enterprise to them. You should 'ave let me teach yer how to pick pockets. Anyway, look after yerself, mate. I'll miss yer for those chats we've 'ad over them bottles of vino. 'Ere, take this,' and just as the train starts to jerk into motion he thrusts a couple of thousand lira into my hand.

As we pull into Mestre the station clock reads ten forty-four. I smile – Lamb'll be getting ready to greet the ten forty-five now, bless him.

Chapter 10

Schooldays

I'm going to interrupt the narrative and give a fuller account of my schooldays than the brief outline I gave Lamb, for they were, after all, very formative years that, to a great extent, determined the direction my life was to take – though, having said that, my life would have taken the same direction with or without them for if one has a destiny, rather than just fate, it will play itself out whatever the circumstances.

I was sent away to boarding school at the age of nine, to a huge and spooky Victorian building, built in Jacobean Gothic style. It rose up with its dark stone façade, gloomy as a castle in Transylvania, its uppermost storeys shrouded in mist and overlooking a beautiful sweep of grounds through which the River Axe wound its way from where it had emerged in Wookey Hole caves a mile up the road. This was Glencot School, on the edge of the Mendips and which was to be my first taste of imprisonment. An imprisonment and regime that, though harsh, was not without its value – for it taught me how to stand on my own feet amongst other boys who were not far removed from savagery at times, and it taught me how to evade the authorities, which would stand me in good stead when I went out into the real world. We were incarcerated for whole terms in this dark, oak-panelled building and its grounds; entombed in classrooms as we wrestled with mathematics, were crammed with dates and we conjugated Latin verbs, whilst through the window the river, the woods and the fields beckoned and my attention constantly strayed, dreaming of adventure.

We were sixty-odd boys, watched over by the headmaster, 'Ned', as we called him, by his ferocious wife and a handful of masters and mistresses. Ned was a tall, dignified-looking and extremely erudite man, with a moustache and upright military manner who would impress the parents no end upon them meeting him when we arrived back at the beginning of term; we were in fine hands, as far as they were concerned. And it was true, as far as the teaching went – his iron discipline, his erudition and his manner of teaching stopped even *my* attention from wandering overmuch and I worked hard under his watchful eye, going from strength to strength, especially in Latin and French (the two subjects he took me for) to the point where I actually attained a flying pass into Marlborough. However, he had a weakness – the bottle. It would usually happen sometime into the term, with his sudden appearance in the dining hall at lunchtime. He'd be acting strangely and coming out with odd pronouncements, such as, 'There'll be no cricket today, boys – we'll have a feather hunt instead; the first one to find an ostrich feather will be let off prep'.

We fidgeted uneasily on our benches, not at all sure where this was going. After lunch we were sent out into the grounds to search, whilst he observed us from his upstairs study window. It would be a fruitless search, of course – there are no ostriches in this part of the world – but we all searched as if our lives depended on it, for we didn't know the consequences if we went back empty handed. Weirder still, and sinister, was when he roamed around the dormitories after lights out. As we lay petrified in our bunks, smelling the whisky which surrounded him like a ghostly vapour, he might start off with a joke or a riddle, such as, 'What is big and red and throbs between your legs?' and one by one he'd ask us, and one by one we'd answer, 'Don't know, Sir.'

'A big, red motorbike, of course,' and then, singling one of us out, 'Come with me, you've been misbehaving today – I'll have to deal with you,' and the poor wretch – Barkeley, as often as not – trembling in his pyjamas, would be led off down the corridor, absolutely at a loss as to what crime he'd committed. Silence throughout the whole school as we held our breath and listened and counted – one, two, three, four . . . sometimes the boy would cry out or start whimpering, and then we'd hear Ned's study door opening and his voice, 'Behave yourself in future.'

Ned's binges would usually come to a head on the third or fourth day when his wife – the ferocious 'Ma A.', as we called her – would take the situation in hand and lock him in his study, where he'd be hidden away like the monster of Glamys, or the Minotaur whose bellowing could be heard throughout the school, whilst the other masters tried to pretend nothing was happening. Finally, a vehicle would pull up around midnight in the dingy courtyard far below and we boys, peering out from the dormitory windows, would witness our illustrious headmaster – 'that fine, scholarly gentleman' – being carted out in a strait-jacket and on a stretcher, being loaded into an ambulance and driven away. That was Ned put away until the next time.

Although the place was run like a prison camp I enjoyed Glencot, except for my first couple of terms when I was bullied mercilessly by the captain of the dorm, a nasty piece of work who, when lights were out, would whisper, 'Lights,' and his horrid little henchman would leap up and turn on the light whilst my tormentor would come over to my bed, lower his pyjama bottoms and fart on my face. In the evenings, after prep, he'd come looking for me and take me out into the wood where he'd put me up against a tree and whack me with a thin cane. Those had been dark days through which I'd lived in perpetual fear of the nights. But that all ended when, during one of these thrashings, I broke down in tears of utter hopelessness and despair – which I think had been his aim – and he left me alone after that.

The school was set in the most glorious grounds, lush green lawns and playing fields, woods and overgrown paths and through which, as I said, the river meandered where we swam amongst the green, waving river weed and paddled little coracles. My great chum during these prep school days was a rascal of the first order called Barkeley-Smith. He was an adept at everything which went against the schoolboy code – he spat, swore, fibbed, and downright lied like nobody I had ever met. He broke every single rule there was or ever

could be and was called up by Ned almost daily for a caning or for
something more sinister, for Barkeley was his 'favourite'. I liked his
utter disregard for the rules and was impressed by his total lack of
any kind of morality. He'd been brought up in Chile and was a great
nephew, so he told me, of Lord Baden-Powell, though he seemed to
be in possession of all the qualities that are condemned outright in
Scouting for Boys. He was a master of survival and could be devious,
as he'd learnt he had to be to fend off his own abusive father and
I, who was sometimes shocked at his blatant iconoclasm, began to
see the necessity of breaking moral codes at times and that lies, for
example, were not evil in themselves; only black lies are, that harm
others, and I never heard him tell one of those; white lies are harm-
less and they can save a lot of unnecessary trouble, a thing I was to
find out later in life. I relished his company – he was full of mischief
and daring and, like me, was possessed of an irrepressible sense of
adventure. He taught me the first words of Spanish I would later
speak, after a fashion. As far as I could gather from the snippets he
told me and from reading between the lines, he'd had an unhappy
childhood and as a result there was something very vulnerable about
him which made him easy prey for predators like Ned. After all,
who could he run to, who could he tell? Certainly not his father, nor
even his mother who, he told me, was often confined in a hospital
and he didn't see her very often.

But, as I said, he did possess the greatest quality of all: the spirit
of adventure. We'd go far-afield together, slipping over the wall and
vanishing into the glorious Somerset countryside, steering clear of
the villages and farms because our uniforms, the corduroy shorts,
grey shirts and navy-blue pullovers, were as distinctive as the arrows
all over a prisoner's tunic and would betray our origins and a phone
call to the school would be no laughing matter. We'd make for the
hills, the Mendips, with their fabulous gorges and moss-covered ravines, its pot-holes, quarries and abandoned Roman lead mines, a
place of many marvels indeed where we'd lose track of time and have
to steal back into the school hoping we hadn't been missed, for if we
had we'd be in for a whacking.

And sometimes we'd climb down the fire escapes at night and take
the boats out on the river. Or we'd venture down the tunnels – ah,

the tunnels, how well I remember them and what an obsession they became. I was heavily influenced by the 'Famous Five' – I had all their books, all their tales of tunnels and secret passages which would be entered through sliding wooden panels and behind which such adventures, and sometimes treasures, lay. The tunnels beneath Glencot were accessed through the cellar and, to get into that, one had to unbolt the great wooden door in full sight of anyone who might be passing and, if that was a master or a prefect, you were in trouble. But once you'd slipped in there the tunnels were yours. It was a veritable labyrinth. One entered through the hidden entrance behind the fireplace, a great inglenook, with a mantlepiece of thick marble. It struck me strange that there should be a fireplace in a cellar and made me wonder what went on down there. Were there some kind of magical practices which, via the tunnels, connected up with the Wookey Hole caves, famous for their witches? Myself, my old friend Barkeley and my younger brother Tony when he came to the school, and sometimes a couple of other trusty friends, sworn to secrecy, would go on expeditions down there as often as we could, each with a torch and were careful not to lose sight of each other. They seemed to go round and round about seven times, we reckoned, until we came to a wall which blocked off the passage and, though it was difficult to calculate down there, for it was impossible to retain any sense of direction, we had the feeling that whatever was behind the wall would lead in the direction of Wookey Hole.

I revelled in the fact that the discipline was so harsh and that there were so many rules, because of the thrill of breaking them and the certainty of punishment if you got caught. The Spartans would punish a man not for the crime itself but for the stupidity of getting caught. That, I thought, was a very admirable principle as it kept you on your toes and developed cunning – and that, along with daring, were qualities which were to stand me in good stead when I was on the road and constantly in danger of falling foul of the law.

There was precious little free time, apart from the weekends, but even then we had lessons on Saturday mornings until lunchtime, and on Sunday mornings we'd have to go to church in Wookey Hole and straight after that we'd have to write our weekly letter home, which would then be censored by Ma A. before being posted, just in case we mentioned anything we shouldn't mention about the school and its headmaster. So in the end it boiled down to just the afternoons in which we'd be allowed out to do what we wished, until prep in the evenings. On weekday afternoons there was always games, which I hated. Cricket was not so bad, it was summer time and you could laze about in the grass when your side was batting and when fielding I'd try to get the position of 'long stop' which was so far out from the pitch that the ball rarely came that way and so one hardly had to do anything. Actually, if old Mr. Williams ('Willum Billum,' we called him), Latin master of the lower school, was umpiring we could get away with doing nothing at all—apart from the bowler, the batter and one or two others left on the pitch to catch the ball if necessary—because old Willum Billum saw nothing but the bat and the ball, so intent was he on the game and being short-sighted to boot. So we, the rest of us would be climbing trees and jumping in the river—far more fun. As for football, I just hated it; standing around on freezing afternoons or chasing like an imbecile after a ball and trying to kick it into a goal all seemed a thoroughly ridiculous waste of time. I'd rather have been playing tiddly winks.

Because of my long legs and my ability to run fast, though not because of my skill at the game, I was put into the first eleven, much to my horror, when I was old enough; this was like a death sentence as there would be no more free Saturday afternoons as we were obliged to play matches against other schools. It was one such match in which we were playing away against another school, I forget which one, and were near to winning the inter-prep school tournament and walking away with the cup. The match was nearing the end, just two minutes to go and neither side had scored a goal and it looked as if it was going to end in a draw, but then I scored a goal—and we lost the match. I'd kicked the ball into our own goal. I didn't have to play in the first eleven after that.

Despite these escapades I worked hard, for Ned, despite all his faults, was a brilliant teacher and I attained a flying pass into Marlborough. Although I was immensely proud to be at this great school and enjoyed the freedom of being able to stroll downtown and take off on long bike rides in the surrounding countryside, I felt like a fish out of water. It was more than just a change of schools, it was the transition from the idealistic, carefree world of boyhood to that awkward, disturbing realm of adolescence; I was reluctant to leave the enchanted world of boyhood I'd left behind at Glencot. The other boys all seemed so mature and serious and seemed to know already exactly what they wanted to do in life; they'd strut about 'Court', the main square, carrying books and brollies as though they were already the stockbrokers, lawyers, politicians, judges or God knows what establishment figures who would be calling the shots one day.

When I'd first arrived there my ambition had been to join the army and to charge recklessly, fearlessly, at the enemy, sabre glinting in the sun, as I'd seen in those old pictures of the cavalry on the North-West Frontier – that was the life for me, full of adventure, daring, honour and glory as I rode victorious beneath the castle walls, ladies leaning from the towers, showering me with kisses. I requested that I be drafted immediately into the 'Corp', as the CCF was known as, instead of having to wait until my second year, as was the custom, thereby wasting no time in precipitating my military training. My request was refused and I had to wait. I'd watch the parades around Court with envy – those lucky fellows with rifles over their shoulders marching to those stirring tunes such as 'Land of Hope and Glory' and 'The Old Bath Road', the latter being the school song, which reverberated on the ivy-clad walls; yes, it sent a shiver up my spine, it stirred my blood.

In my second year I joined up and was in my element marching with a rifle over my shoulder, firing rifles and machine guns on the firing range, with field days on Salisbury Plain, holiday camp on Dartmoor where we'd take part in manoeuvres against a real army regiment, the Green Jackets, who treated us as snotty public school boys and would give us a good kicking if they caught us in an attack – their one chance of showing us who's boss, I suppose, should any of us one day become their commanding officers. I thoroughly enjoyed all this but my world was suddenly turned upside down when I underwent a sudden, rather painful, change of heart in which all my illusions about glory and all that were shattered: Did I really want to kill? I asked myself; could I hate a man I'd never met so much that I'd want to kill him? And in the cause of what – love of country, glory, honour? Kill a man the other side of the world who wasn't even remotely a threat to me or my country? No, the more I thought about it, the more I realised the glories of battle were nothing more elevated than sordid squabbles over oil, gold or territory, usually at the expense of poorer countries. In fact, the cause, in most cases, was nothing more noble than the Economy and defending British interests overseas. I'd been reading Remarque's *All Quiet on the Western Front,* the very antithesis of the glowing stories from the North-West Frontier; here was the reality of war, the utter futility, the stench, the body parts splattered on the walls of trenches; and by this time I'd started writing poetry.

My great friend at Marlborough was Nick Muirhead. He was a giant of a man, even taller than I was, standing some six foot four with an upright, commanding bearing and a brilliant sense of humour that complemented the profound seriousness within him and the extremely sensitive nature of his soul. We would take off on long rides on our bicycles, heading for the downs, Savernake Forest, Avebury or Salisbury Plain where, flinging our bikes down at the side of the road, we'd lie in the long grass and talk about our dreams. He used to sing an old song from the First World War, 'Take me back to dear old Blighty,' and as he sang a strange chill ran through me, as though he didn't really belong to this world and that one day he'd get a Blighty wound and wouldn't return. He had wanted to be a soldier too and after Sandhurst went on to become a second-lieutenant in the Black Watch; but the reality of it all was too harsh for him – there was nothing glorious about Northern Ireland, to which he was deployed three times, and each time on his homecoming he was more jumpy, more nervous, more manic and deeply depressed. He would appear, if he'd heard that I was back in England, at my parents' house in Wiltshire, 'This is the one place in the world I can be myself,' he had said once as we walked over the fields under an autumnal sky, rooks cawing in the trees that surround the old henge and the smell of woodsmoke in the valley. 'The one place I don't have to pretend to be someone I'm not. Ulster is hell . . . '

I witnessed the beginnings of his crack-up but not the end, when everything had been further intensified with the complications of a girl in London who would not give her love to him, until finally there was a shot across the fields, from which there was no return. On the eve of his funeral, as a guest of his distraught parents, in a lonely farmhouse in Sussex, I heard footsteps running up the gravel drive below my window, the latch of the kitchen door lifting, and then silence. My friend had come home, but he'd left the world forever.

There was little point in my staying on at Marlborough – that was apparent to everybody. I'd failed all my exams, except English and French 'O' level, and instead of going up into the sixth form I was kept back to wallow in the 'removes', from which I was unlikely to emerge – ever. It was an ongoing struggle to keep myself out of detention and away from the housemaster's cane, of which one incident I remember well: It was just after prep when a prefect sought me out to tell me to report to the house-master.

'Come in,' called Mr. Isaacson as I knocked nervously on the door, not knowing exactly what I was wanted for but with the certainty it would not be good, for it was never for anything good I was called up by 'Bum Eye' as we called him, as he had an eye which swivelled in its socket in all directions and you never quite knew if he was looking at you or somewhere else. He also had a weird habit of prefacing many of his sentences with 'Wo'.

So as I entered he greeted me with, 'Wo, Ashford-Brown,' and he looked me over with disdain – he really, really didn't like me.

'We've just had a prefects' meeting, they tell me you've been in the punishment book more than everybody else in the house put together – I'm going to cane you. Bend over the chair.'

And then, for some reason, he asked me how many strokes he was going to give me. 'Six, I hope, sir.'

In for a penny, in for a pound, I may as well have the full whack, and it's hero's stuff to get six of the best.

'Wo, I'm sorry to disappoint you, I'm going to give you four.'

They were vicious, those four he gave me, they stung like mad, and I was quite glad it had only been four in the end.

Finally, as I recounted to Lamb, I precipitated my own dismissal with the cutting of the bell rope – the bell which would clang imperiously from morning till night sending us hither and thither with its iron-tongued commands. I'd stopped the system. I'd also engineered the end to my school career; now I'd go out into life – the *real* school.

Chapter 11
Vrpolje

Thanks to Lamb I can afford to take a train over the Yugoslav border. I board a train bound for Ljubljana. I shall get out after the frontier and strike into the interior.

What on earth's going on in these corridors – all these agitated youths rushing about with bundles under their arms? Right next to where I'm standing one of them's trying to remove a panel in the side of the compartment. Probably he wants to hide his package in there. The panel won't slide out, however hard he wrenches it – *'piska matrina,'* (mother's cunt) he curses. Turning towards me, sweating, he says, 'Please, can carry this you by frontier?' and he produces a pair of jeans and a denim jacket from the bundle he's carrying.

'Er . . . yes.'

'Thank you,' and he makes off swiftly down the corridor. I get it, American clothing, worth its weight in gold in communist countries. Better check the pockets for anything less innocent, just in case. We're off. And now a youth, not much more than a boy, leaps from the platform onto the running-board beneath the door of the carriage, gripping the railings, he's trying to climb in but another geezer has rushed at him from inside the wagon, kicked him in the face and he's fallen backwards from the now fast-moving train and smashed his skull on the platform.

We've pulled into the frontier station and dozens of brutal-looking guards, red stars on the peaks of their caps, have boarded the train, and all of a sudden I'm confronted by the red bloated face of one of them barking, 'Passport!'–whilst the others are pulling the carriages apart, unscrewing panels and lifting floorboards. Not a stone's left unturned.

Once over the border I alight from the train and make my way down to Rijeka. Coming upon a market I wander around, picking up fruit from the ground. I see some Gypsies selling carpets and, not being able to resist having a word with them, go up and say to the woman in front of the stall, *'Jarla maw pen,'* at which her hands go up in the air and she exclaims, *'I Rom!'* They crowd round me, a table is produced, a chair, food's put before me, and wine. Money–in the form of wads of notes–is stuffed into my pocket. I feel like an impostor as I sit here eating and drinking. All I did was to utter these three words and–hey presto–all this has materialised before me. Well, I'm not going to come clean and announce that I'm really a *gadjo*–that would be silly. After all, I'm a very good friend of the Gypsies and Tatta would be happy to see me right now, recipient of the lavish hospitality of his distant kin–and proud that I've had them believe I'm one of them–*'Bravo, mishto,'* he'd say.

I've turned inland. Every now and then I come upon a village, in the middle of nowhere, reached by the stony roads I'm tramping, and I'm greeted by curious looks. Men lift funny, narrow-brimmed hats (a little like my old pork-pie hat) as I pass; I wish I was able to do the same but, being hatless, I can only touch my hand to my brow in a salute.

'Ja sam Engleski,' I'm able to reply to them, in the few words of Croatian I've picked up. *'Dobro došli, Englez*–come and have a glass of slivovitz.' This invariably happens and, fortified with that potent fire-water made of plums and seventy or eighty percent alcohol, I leave the villages swaying a little and singing.

Coming into the plains of Croatia endless fields of maize stretch to the horizon on every side. Here and there the steeple of a church, shaped like an onion, rises up out of the flat landscape, its dome glinting. Bells sound over the fields in the evenings and frogs croak in the ponds. Haystacks, freshly built, make soft and fragrant beds at night–there's nothing like the scent of hay.

Walking along a stony road one morning, having just arisen from a perfect night's sleep on one of these ricks, a horse and cart pulls up beside me and the old fellow at the reins motions me to jump up beside him. He offers me a cigarette and we set off at a lively trot, through the glorious countryside. The old fellow smiles beneath his flowing moustache as I exclaim over and over again, sweeping my arms over the landscape, *'Jako lijepa Hrvatska, jako lijepa!'* The morning is so fresh, the fields still shrouded in the light mist of dew which is evaporating in the sun, and up ahead a golden dome rises above the red roofs of a village, like a shepherd surrounded by his flock. *'Vrpolje,'* he tells me, and we shortly arrive in the village where he lets me down in the central square. I sit on the terrace of the busy café and order a coffee whilst soaking up the sun. There are a few shops, a cinema and a kind of corn exchange, a huge barn, where horses and carts, tractors and trailers are loading and unloading. There are few cars and then only the small, cheap ones, like Yugos, Zastavas and Trabants, ubiquitous in Soviet countries. The roads leading into the square are unpaved, stony and dusty. I like it here, it feels like somewhere untouched by the modern world, and the more I get to know Vrpolje the more I feel I'm in a timeless place, in a place you might find in a fairy-tale. The coffee arrives in one of those small brass Turkish pots with a long handle, and is poured into my cup by a pretty waitress – it's black as tar and very strong and leaves a thick sediment at the bottom of the cup – just the job. *'Hvala lijepa,'* thank you, I say to her and she, with a graceful little curtsy, smiles and says, *'Molim,'* – my pleasure.

Two fellows come over to my table and start talking to me. They're about my age and one of them, who introduces himself as Baja, speaks very passable English, he's learnt it from listening to the Beatles he tells me. His friend is called Mato and it isn't long before we're all three of us walking through the village, Baja insisting on carrying my luggage, to his parents' house at number five, Radicéva utca, a little white house with a veranda shaded with a thick grape-vine, bursting with fruit, snaking around the trellising.

'You'll be our guest, for as long as you like', he says, putting my rucksack down in a little room which looks over the fields, 'You

must be hungry, my mother and sister will make us some breakfast when they come back from the shop.'

Vrpolje's the most enchanting village. It's just a main street, lined on either side with the small one-storey houses typical of the Balkans and through which an unpaved dirt road runs, with the occasional track running off to little clusters of houses bordering the maize fields and a large pond out the back where pigs wallow at one end and we swim at the other; a church, a few shops, the café-cum-restaurant, which is right in the centre, and a cinema.

Baja, big-hearted and wise, is studying mathematics in Zagreb. He has to shut himself in his room to study a couple of hours every morning but the rest of the day he gives over entirely to my wellbeing. He's the most attentive host and delights in taking me round the village, into the homes of his friends. After two or three days staying at his parents house and having this quite unprecedented hospitality lavished upon me I naturally begin to feel that I should take my leave of Vrpolje as I don't want to outstay my welcome. But Baja won't hear of it.

'It is a so great pleasure to have you here. You must at least stay for the festival at Dragotino.'

'What's that?' I ask, intrigued.

'On the fifteenth of August there's a big religious festival – at a place called Dragotino, a church on a hill, about twenty kilometres from here. Everyone goes from all the villages, plenty of wine and beer, plenty of girls – you'll like it, you'll see.'

That is still over a month away and, after Baja reassuring me that everyone will be very happy that stay on, I gladly do so. The people here are so friendly, welcoming and seemingly unspoilt by the modern world.

I just need to walk down the street to be invited for slivovitz, that fire-water distilled from plums, or for cakes and coffee, or *lubenica* (water melons) which they keep cool down the wells and draw up in the pail, straight onto the table.

On Saturday nights a film's shown at the cinema where all the young gather in front of the doors, talking and smoking and flirting. Baja, like the fine host that he is, makes sure that I get to know the girls of the village, introducing me to them one by one, two by giggling two.

'This is Ruzica, fall into those eyes of hers and you'll drown,' and Ruzica laughs, looks down at the ground, then at me, her dilated pupils like wells – yes, I could drown in those wells.

'And this is Vera, she'll break your heart if I'm not mistaken,' Vera smiles, curtsies, she's wearing a blue summer dress, the cheeky evening breeze lifting the hem and exposing her thigh, corn-coloured hair falling to her shoulders, cornflower eyes whose lashes are black with mascara. We gaze at one another. I feel myself toppling.

'Come on,' says Baja, 'before you fall into each other. Meet Lilija here, like as to a lily of the lake.'

I'm impressed by Baja's poetic description of the girl, who matches it, blushing coyly before us, 'this little lily turns pink,' he adds, and we all laugh.

'Here's Jasminka coming now – you haven't met her yet – she's my girl, sweet seventeen, you know what I mean.'

Some evenings we spend around the table on the terrace of the café in the village centre. Here the lads of the village hang out and I get to know all of Baja's friends. One of them, especially, I like, Ivan, a big simple chap always looking for fun and whose gigantic laugh amuses Baja, he being as loud and jovial as Baja is quiet and contemplative. Every summer an old gaffer arrives in Vrpolje with a cart-load of watermelons. He stays with them until they're all sold; at night lying down on the ground and sleeping beside them. Ivan tip-toes up, one evening, and steals one off the pile as we watch on from the café over the road, our breath held lest the vendor awaken. Ivan comes back triumphant, the melon stuck up his jumper as though he was heavily pregnant. We all retire to his house and eat great slices of the fruit and drink warm milk straight from the cow he keeps in the yard.

Baja's father's the stationmaster at the busy main-line junction of Vrpolje. I accompany Baja to the station when his father needs him to run an errand or something. On the way back we invariably call in at a house which lies on our route.

'You haven't met Zora yet,' says Baja, the first time we call, 'she's pretty and she makes the most fabulous cakes.'

She lives with her grandfather who plies us with Slivovitz whilst she, a lovely dark-haired girl, with a simple grace and wide-open smile, delighted to see us, brings cakes steaming hot from the oven.

'Please come whenever you want,' she says to me, 'I'll always have cakes for you . . . ' There's something wistful in her voice.

'She's lonely,' says Baja, on our way back to the village, 'she does all the work in the house and has to look after her grandfather – she doesn't come to the village very often. She likes you,' he says turning to me, 'but I think you fall for the dangerous ones, like Vera . . . '

Vera's house is near the bridge at the far end of the village where the river runs. Willow trees grow all along it, and plum trees heavy with fruit, now that it's August. Having been summoned, I arrive in the mornings and pay my respects to her – for in every way she evokes that response from a man, being as she is close to a goddess – as she languishes on her divan on the shaded veranda, smoking her long cigarettes and drinking Turkish coffee. She has me sit on a chair facing her, not too close, not too far and, as though it were a ritual, engages me in conversation just at the edges – not too close, not too far – of intimacy. Strange conversations we have and I feel at ease and I feel on edge and she knows that I'm longing for her in every fibre of my being and she knows that she can play with me – half seriously, half for fun – which amounts to roughly the same thing. Baja would say that I'm a clodhopper in such matters but the thing is, she does have a boyfriend with whom, apparently, she's soon to get married. You see, the whole thing is rather strange and more so when she suddenly announces that she can meet me in Rijeka, for she knows that I'll be leaving for the coast in a while, 'I will come alone', she says, 'and we can be together under the stars. Don't tell a word to anyone, this will be our secret.'

Almost insane with joy I walk home. Baja keeps looking up at me as he plays his guitar, but he doesn't say anything. I know he thinks she'll break my heart or at least, burst the bubble of my dreams. And now, sure enough, it's Saturday evening and as usual we're all gathered outside the cinema. I look around, she's not here and my heart sinks because the doors of the cinema have opened and we're about to file in, so I won't see her now. The film's pretty boring, it's a Western and so predictable – the cowboys win, all the Indians have been murdered . . . To my surprise she's outside the cinema when we come out, leaning against a lamp-post smoking a cigarette. She comes over to me and says, 'I can't meet you in Rijeka, I'm sorry,' and that's all she says to me and she drops her eyes and walks away.

It's taking some getting over and she's never given me any explanation. She doesn't summon me to her house anymore, sometimes I pass her in the street but she hardly acknowledges me. I know she's going to get married soon and I suppose that has something to do with it – and I suppose I ought to understand that.

The day arrives for the long-awaited pilgrimage to Dragotino. Everyone's been talking excitedly about it – I can see that it's indeed a big event.

'Don't worry,' Baja had said to me, 'you won't find yourself having to take part in the religious ceremony – the older people do that in the church. We, the boys and girls, are all outside on the tombs in the moonlight. Oh, and there'll be a beer tent,' he adds smiling, 'so you'll be happy.'

We're going to walk there and so, in the afternoon, we set off, taking paths which twist and turn through the fields of maize. There are five of us: Baja, Jasminka, Mato, Ivan and I. We pass other groups on the way, some walking, some in carts. Thousands of people for miles around are converging on Dragotino.

'Why is the festival so important?' I ask my host.

'It's the assumption of the holy virgin Mary into heaven,' not that he gives any credence to that, 'that's for the old folk, we'll have fun on the tombstones, all the girls will be there; and don't worry, no virgin Marys.'

We pass lonely cottages on the edges of the fields and the woods, the inhabitants of which bring refreshment to us – lemonade, slivovitz, cakes.

The sun goes down and a brilliant red lights up the sky in the west. The stars come out and the moon, swollen like Mary with child, rises up in the heavens and, as we approach the hill we hear the swell of an accordion. The hill's lit up with lights. Tents and stalls sell drink and food. The church perched on the top blazes with candle light. We circumvent the procession and come to the tombs on the other side where hundreds of young people are gathered, lying on blankets spread out, just as Baja had said, beneath the moon.

We find a contingent from Vrpolje amongst whom are Ruzica and Lilija (two to set my pulse racing for a start) and another girl, whom I haven't met before – her name's Vesne. She's from Bosnia. Raven-haired and flashing eyed, a Gypsy if ever I saw one. Baja doesn't know her so he can't introduce us – but he whispers to me, 'Watch out for this one.'

Baja's amused by my reaction to all the girls I'm meeting. He can see how bashful I am. 'You're so slow,' he says to me, shaking his wise head, 'they all like you, they're just waiting for you to say something. Vera would have sorted you out . . .'

Hymns rise up from the church. The immense flat landscape spread out below and all around us, is dotted here and there by the lights of distant villages shimmering like the stars above us. I feel like drinking some *pivo* (beer) and so I make my way down to the tents and the music. It's like a wedding feast down here. Whole pigs are being roasted on spits and there are great barrels of beer from which frothing pints are poured by the busy servers trying to keep up with their thirsty customers crowded around the makeshift bars. Lanterns are swinging from poles and intoxicated peasants, in their funny hats, are swaying in one another's arms to Slavonic dances played on rustic-looking bagpipes and accordions – it could be straight out of a scene from Bruegel.

Having swiftly despatched my glass of beer down my gullet, strong stuff which goes down beautifully after the long trek through the fields, I'm heading back to the bar for another when Vesne comes rushing up to me from the crowd, 'Come with me, darling,' she says, pulling me by the hand and out into the darkness.

'I love you,' she breathes, pulling my mouth down to hers and kissing me with such passion I begin to swoon. And then, breaking suddenly away from me, she rushes off into the night, suddenly vanishing in the same way she'd appeared.

'Maybe she's a heartbreaker, just wanting to hook you and drop you,' says Baja, shaking his wise head, when I recount to him the strange encounter. 'Maybe she just wanted to take with her to Bos-

nia an Englishman's kiss. You never know what goes on in the heads
of these lynxes.'

And then, looking at me with a bemused smile, he quietly sings,
'You must remember this, a kiss is but a kiss . . . '

But a kiss is everything to me.

We return from Dragotino in the back of a cart, dog-tired as we
bump along the stony tracks in the glaring dawn. We spend the day
recovering and, the following one, I bid farewell to Vrpolje and all
my friends promising I'll be back, and take the road south, the kiss
of a hot-blooded Bosnian on my lips, and all the sorrow of a love
which never blossomed, by the river where plum trees grow and willows weep.

Chapter 12

Zé

As though some mad music has touched me I'm taken away to the Cretan shore. Pan has come down from the crags and all the flocks are going wild, sown as they are with a mad longing. I copulate with Venus in the depths of my soul. 'You must love,' she says, 'and I offer myself to you in order that you understand.' The flocks have lain down and the sea is a deadly calm. The air has stopped moving and I fight for breath. 'You must love,' she says, 'and I will show you how, for you must not go without love and I will come upon you with all the intensity, all the immensity of it,' and the sea, aroused from its torpor, crashes demented on the shore and the flocks go wild. And it's as though the night itself has conjured her up–or is it she that's conjured up the night? The door handle turns and the turner of the turning materialises in the room. Time stops and a dog in a distant hamlet bays at the moon. 'I could go mad for you,' I think to myself and I feel what Sappho felt when she wrote:

> My tongue is useless;
> a subtle fire
> runs through my body . . .

'Meet Lala, just returned from the south, sleeping under the stars and in Gypsy tents,' says Inês, introducing us.

'*Olà,*' she says, '*enchantée.*' (And I truly will be enchanted.) We fill our glasses and drink. The women break into Portuguese and I listen, as though to music, to this lovely, liquid, language. The word *Lisboa* is forever on their tongues – *Lisboa, Lisboa!* I'll get there some day, with this woman I cannot take my eyes off. Corn-coloured, her hair flows down her neck to her shoulders brushing the collar of the jade silk dress she wears so loosely on her body and beneath which her breasts swell and in which I will bury my head, lose myself . . . forever.

Oh, but now she's getting up and leaving us. Dammit! She has to rush, she explains: her husband (my heart sinks at the mention of one) will be looking at his watch, wondering where the hell she is. It was not often they went out to dinner these days and now she was already going to be late.

'You liked her, didn't you?' Ashley and Inês tease me when she's gone – so they'd noticed.

'Yes, oh yes,' I say, a bit bashful.

'Actually, I think she liked you too, *mon vieux,*' Inês winks at me.

'You think so?'

"I know so.'

'She's married?'

'Yes, but what's that got to do with it?' Inês winks mischievously, 'She's not that married anymore. Anyway she's coming for supper the day after tomorrow; if you're interested in her, be here.' Phew! She seems serious, she evidently reckons I stand a chance – I'll be here alright.

But with the clear light of the morning, logic and reason return and I tell myself it's just another fanciful dream, brought on by the champagne. She's out of reach and even if she was attracted to me it could never happen that she'd get involved with me. I mean, look at me: ragged, penniless, an unkempt head full of dreams and poetry, utterly lacking any practical sense, in the worldly sense of getting on, making money; she looks like she has expensive taste, would demand a bit of luxury, a bit of pampering; no sleeping under bridges for her. But all the same – supper tomorrow night . . .

I wander around Paris in a haze. Sitting in the Jardins du Luxembourg I stare at the fountain, with its jet of water spurting into the metallic August sky and falling back lazily into the pond. Wooden yachts float on the water blown this way and that by the listless winds which spring up from all around, like mischievous little spirits weaving their spell. Trying to read I can only think of those eyes, blue as the sky, that hair like corn in August, those nails, blood-red, and that hungry, devouring look in her eyes, and I think further, of other things . . . and the book lies neglected in my lap, the errant breezes flicking its pages over – as though to say: no time for reading, get ready for love.

I wander along the quays of the Seine, as far as the Eiffel tower in the west and the Quai de Bercy in the east, oblivious to the barges drifting by in the sunset and Notre Dame, like a mallet against the western sky turns blood-red.

Turning off at Châtelet and down the rue St. Denis I wend my way amongst the women beckoning, *'Tu viens, cheri?'*

I'm testing myself by tempting myself, but why? I don't need tying to the mast, these sirens pale into insignificance all of a sudden, *'Non, merci,'* I say, and stride along the Boulevard des Bonnes Nouvelles with great resolve and then turn into the rue du Faubourg Montmartre and climb to the Sacré Coeur from which I look out over Paris, all glittering, the moon above blood-red. I've got to have her.

She's already there when I get to the flat and she looks up with a smile, a very discreet smile, barely perceptible, as I come through the door. Quite a company's turned up for supper, amongst whom are Franco, an Italian painter, who carries a gun and a bottle of whisky in his pockets who, on occasion, lets loose a volley of bullets into the Paris night skies and Leo, a Chinaman who's studying business at the university and living in such dire poverty he fights with the neighbourhood cats over the fish bones thrown out at the market – or so they say. He's brought a bottle of rice wine along. Here's João with the great bushy beard, who escaped military service and the futile war in Angola. There's Medeleine, journalist for one of the left-wing papers in Paris. Lars, a Danish guitarist of some renown. Harald, a young German photographer with whom I'd gone wandering down town and had run into trouble with the girls on the rue Blondel where he'd started taking snaps of them lining the street, half undressed. Furiously they rushed at us screaming and, surrounding us like Valkyries, ripped the film out of Harald's camera. And then a young man had appeared, small, menacing-looking, in a dapper white suit, dark glasses and black leather boots up to his knees, a truncheon in his hand.

'*On se fait pas ça ici*,' he warned, escorting us to the end of the street, 'one doesn't do that around here, now fuck off and don't come back!'

There are all kinds of spoils on the table: olives, caviar, a great wheel of brie and succulent grapes from the south. Franco produces a little concertina and bursts, full-throated, into Neapolitan song.

Amidst all this merriment I've moved over to the window in the hope that Zé might join me – an exchange of glances has left no doubt that something's happening between us – and suddenly she's at my side.

'So you've been in Italy this summer – ah, Italy, I love it so much,' she says, 'and I'm sure you liked it too, didn't you?'

'Oh yes, the rolling hills, the landscapes which look like tapestries woven into the rich earth, the vineyards, the olive groves, the little solitary farmhouses dotted around the countryside, the immense starry nights . . . ' I'm starting to wax lyrical and I can see that she's loving it, 'and the cities, what cities did you visit?' she asks, 'did you go to Venice?'

'Oh yes, I spent many days and nights there, floating barefoot along its winding streets and warm flagstones, leaning from bridges and dreaming . . . '

'Dreaming of what?' she asks, looking over her glass at me.

'Of love, perhaps . . . '

'And did you find it, did you look for it?'

'Yes, of course, but . . . '

She turns her glass between her fingers so that the rim's brushing her lip, 'Have you found it now?' she looks at me intently and all of a sudden lifts her hand and strokes my face with her fingers. The reply didn't call for words, I put my mouth to hers.

Now I walk tall and proud and full of joy through Paris and along the Seine, Zé at my side, and Paris, which until now had seemed like a world of beautiful, unattainable women, is transformed into a fairy-tale of romance and I, until so recently an untutored youth in such matters, am instructed in the arts of love by a woman divinely versed in them. She comes to me in the afternoons, to my little room the other side of the courtyard. With bated breath I wait for the sound of her footsteps on the stairs. I've opened the door before she's had a chance to knock and, falling into my arms I undress her, my feverish fingers fumbling with the buttons of her dress and the clasps of her bra – *'Doucement,'* she says, *'On n'est pas pressés . . .'* But I am always in a hurry. If you had known her you'd understand why.

She tells me about herself, little bits, the surface details of her life, but any deeper than that I cannot penetrate, she does not let me. She gives me her body, isn't that enough – isn't the rest best left a mystery?

'I was your age when I first came to Paris,' she says, her head laid on her elbow, as we lie in bed, the afternoon winding down into evening, 'I came looking for all the things I'd dreamed of since I was a girl, watching those French movies so full of romance and glamour and culture. Portugal was a dead end when it came to culture – we were living in the middle ages under Salazar! I could have lived a comfortable, respectable life there – my family wasn't poor, far from it – but what's a life, however much money you have, if you have to live in a backwater? and besides, Lisbon's like a little village, everyone gossips about everyone else. My affairs are my affairs and that's how I like to keep them.'

She rolls over and stares at the ceiling, 'I came to Paris, I got married, I had a child – all too soon. I was left little time for the pursuit of the culture for which I'd come and, as for romance, well it seems to me that dies pretty quickly in a marriage, one gets attached but the spark dies. Don't ever go and get married.'

She looks piercingly at me as though to elicit a response; I drop my eyes – there's nothing I'd like better than to marry her.

Yes she's mine! I walk proud and tall through the streets and down by the Seine. No longer do the sight and the scents of the Parisian goddesses pierce me with pain, for the most exquisite of them all has given herself to me, is mine, and only she will have the power to pierce me with pain from now on. Huge banners of joy are billowing about my being. She's my Helen of Troy and she's launched a thousand delirious dreams in me.

> I walk
> your hand in mine
> spin you on your heels
> kiss your crimson lips
> in the city of the Eiffel Tower and Seine

She's skilful at arranging things and as often as she can she'll spend the evenings with me downtown, in the Latin Quarter, where we'll seek out a quiet little restaurant, and as our ankles touch beneath the table and our eyes stare into each other's over the candle, over the flowers, she'll fill her mouth with wine and release it in little spurts into mine, so that:

> My heart aches, and a drowsy numbness pains
> My sense, as though of hemlock I had drunk
> Or emptied some dull opiate to the drains . . .

And madly, passionately, besotted, we walk back under the stars, hand in hand along the Seine in which the lights of Paris splash and dance, her peals of laughter rising up to the bells of Notre Dame as I turn her on her toes, kiss her crimson lips. Sometimes I walk her all the way to the *banlieue,* the suburbs, where she lives, falling fifty paces behind her as we near her *quartier* – in case her husband's driving about. Sometimes, just sometimes, she comes back with me and stays the night.

Browsing the shelves of Shakespeare and Company, that intriguing bookshop down by the Seine which Henry Miller called 'a wonderland of books', I came across a real gem of a book called *The Gypsies* (in the original French, *Les Tziganes*) by Jean-Paul Clébert which I now have in my pocket. It explains so much about their origins in India and subsequent wanderings through Asia and in

Europe. Things which I was always so immensely curious about and was never sure how much the Gypsies themselves knew, as though it was lost in the mists of time. Time for them is abstract for they live in the eternal present and in the company of their dead, their ancestors, who are very much alive to them and who give them a sense of continuity which stretches forwards and backwards, infinitely, in both directions. And this is what I always felt when I was with them, that it's non-linear, organic, and recurrent as the seasons. 'Historical' time, with its dates and years and centuries, watches, clocks and calendars, and marked out with battles and wars and shifting alliances, means nothing to them; except that they get caught up in these events, which they ascribe to the madness, the schizophrenia, of the gadje.

No, time for the Romanies seems almost mythological and their only real sense of it is their racial memory. I could never work out whether Tatta was aware of their origins in the north of India and that the language he spoke was derived from Sanskrit, still retaining the grammatical structure and a large part of the vocabulary, the rest of it consisting of words incorporated into it from countries they've spent time in on their peregrinations – there's Persian, Turkish, Greek, Slav, Hungarian, Romanian, German; in fact by analysing the language one can trace the countries they've traversed as though it were a linguistic map. But of course, to them it's their language, *Romani* or, more specifically, *Manouche*, which they've always spoken, and as for home, well that is wherever they happen to be, wherever they've set up camp, whether it be by the side of the road or a river, in the wide open expanses or deep in the forest. I was hesitant about asking Tatta too much about things like this for I was afraid of sounding like I was prying and trying to uncover too much of their secrets, of sounding like a spy or something; that old crone in the encampment at Pau could never get it out of her head that I was in fact one. The closest I'd get to determining where they came from would be to be given a vague answer, such as: *'partout'*, everywhere. But now, with this book in my pocket, some of the questions I was burning to ask are being answered, some of the mystery is being revealed. Briefly, here are some things I'm learning about them:

They originate from the Punjab and Kashmir in Northern India in the region of the *River Sindh* from which they began their wandering westward over a thousand years ago, possibly because of the Muslim invasions which were happening at the time. It seems they spent a long time in Persia, Iraq and Turkey, before entering the Balkans and Greece in the fourteenth century and Western Europe in the fifteenth. Although all of the same blood originally, they are divided into three main groups: The *Manouches*, who are to be found mainly in France, the *Kalderash* of Hungary, Romania and Russia, and the *Gitanos* of Spain and the south of France, where they're called *Gitans,* in fact the French refer to all Gypsies as *Gitans* and are terrified of them and deeply prejudiced against them.

I've been reading a lot lately as I have plenty of time on my hands and spend the days wandering the streets, sitting in the gardens and cafés where I can read and write for as long as I like over a coffee, or sitting on the quays of the Seine with a big bottle of *Jenlain,* a mighty potent beer of seven and a half per cent alcohol, and a volume of poetry, Apollinaire:

> *Ni temps passé*
> *ni les amours reviennent*
> *sous le pont Mirabeau coule la Seine . . .*

Or Blaise Cendrars, Rimbaud, Verlaine or François Villon, whom I always think of when I walk along the rue St. Jacques where he attended the university and where he got into a dispute with a monk and the monk stabbed him, or wandering through *Les Halles* where Villon would hang out, picking pockets as he rubbed up against the crowd. Oh, and then there's Gérard de Nerval, who really intrigues me and who wrote:

> *La femme est la Chimère de l'homme*
> *ou son démon, comme vous voudrez . . .*

in *Les Chimères,* that little volume of strange, melancholic, and mythical poems, charged with a kind of wistful nostalgia for the golden Mediterranean lands which work a spell on my mind. The day before his death he wrote to his aunt who he'd regularly visit, 'Don't expect me this evening, for the night will be black and white,' and the next morning he was found hanged in the rue de la Vieille-Lanterne.

Yes, I'm doing a lot of reading, working my way through some of the classics of French literature, largely neglected by me until now, like Sartre, de Beauvoir, Camus, Rabelais, Victor Hugo, Balzac, Alain-Fournier and his haunting one and only novel *Le Grand Meaulnes,* Anaïs Nin, her diaries and correspondence with Henry Miller – ah, Henry Miller, whose books did so much to loosen me up that first time I was in Paris and still very wet behind the ears, still terrified of the fair sex and prudishly moralistic towards matters of sex, I thought it shameful, but inside I was seething with unfullfilled desires and thoughts which would plague my mind and which I was powerless to dispel. Miller's writing helped me out of all that with his unashamed accounts of erotic romps in Paris. Inês, who had all of his works in Portuguese, which of course I couldn't read, gave me the first book, *Tropic of Cancer,* in English. I reckon she must have thought it was just what I needed.

In the mornings, working in a gallery in St. Germain, Zé is able to indulge her passion for art. It's the Renaissance artists for whom she has a particular penchant and I have my first taste of Michelangelo, Caravaggio, da Vinci, Botticelli, Fra Angelico, and co., as she leads me round the Louvre and all the other galleries in Paris. When I confess to her that in all my time in Italy, I'd not been near a gallery – except the church in St. Marco in Venice, from which I'd been ejected by a priest for not wearing shoes – she has a fit. 'But galleries cost money, Zé, and I preferred to spend the precious little I had on wine.'

'Philistine,' she reprimands me, but behind her mock horror at hearing this I can detect a note of amusement in her voice.

I'm tasting the good life now. But to meet the expense of these evenings with Zé, I have to apply myself to my trade with extra vehemence, the old flower business. Early evening, darkness falling, I slip trough the hole in the fence of the Parc Montsouri and fill a cardboard box with flowers, make them into bouquets and flog them around the cafés and restaurants of the Latin Quarter.

'Do you see yourself always living like that?'

'Living like what, Zé?' she's sprung the question on me out of the blue, and the tone of her voice dismays me.

'Oh you know, living from day to day, selling flowers, getting drunk, never knowing if tomorrow you'll have any money."

'Well, I don't know – I mean, what's wrong with it?'

'You have a brain and you're wasting it. You should be thinking about going to university – it's not too late, you know.'

'University, but Zé, life is my university,' I look at her reproachfully, 'I've learnt more in the years I've been on the road than I could in a lifetime at university.'

'Alright when you're young, but you're nearly twenty-three now. How do you ever expect a woman to put up with it?' So that's it. She's like the rest of them – money and all that's what counts in the end.

The balmy days and nights of summer are over; autumn has descended on Paris with her mists and the climate of our liaison seems to be changing with the season. Zé has become so critical of the way I'm conducting my life, 'You're going nowhere,' she says, with such scorn a kind of impotent rage wells up within me. I am bloody going somewhere, she just doesn't understand me, doesn't understand that I'd do anything for her, anything.

'Like what?' she goads.

'Well, like I'd go to work in a bank, or . . . '

'You'd sell your soul, you'd sell your soul for a woman – what sort of man would you be? You'd be a slave, that's what.'

'Yes, I know Zé, I wouldn't really ever do that – I just wanted to give you an example of how far I'd go to . . . '

'And do you think I'd love you the more for that? I would despise you.'

'Well, I'd go to the ends of the earth for you . . . I'd die for you.'

'Die for me? what's the use of that?' and then her face, a moment ago the picture of scorn, softens, clouds over, and there's a note of tender anxiety in her voice as she says, her eyes averted, 'Don't love

me so much. one day I'll fly away . . . ' I can feel the blood draining
from me as I stare up at the ceiling.

She mentioned once a former lover, quite a recent one in fact,
with whom she'd had an affair in new York, 'A poet, like you,' she'd
said, and I'd felt the first pang of jealousy. I don't want to hear of
anyone else who's known her. Supposing . . . supposing I'm not the
only one seeing her now.

I mean where is she when she's not here and she's not at home
either? Thoughts such as this have started plaguing me and, one
afternoon in late November, feeling a distance between us as we lie
together in the growing darkness, as though she's a million miles
from mc as she stares blankly up at the ceiling, I venture the question, 'Am I the only one, Zé?'

Her eyes swivel into mine in panic and she pulls my face down
and buries it in her neck, saying, 'Of course, you are – don't be silly,'
and then, suddenly angry, 'How could I have time for anyone else
with my life so busy with you, with my husband, my daughter?
How could I have time even if I wanted to?'

I really don't know what it is that's getting into me. Why am I
letting my imagination sow these fears? I just can't believe that there
aren't a whole host of other men wanting her – and perhaps getting
her.

'There's no one else,' she repeats emphatically; but I can't be sure,
can't be absolutely certain. If I could only be certain about us what
then couldn't I do, couldn't I build? Edifices of towering joy to celebrate our incomparable love that will never die.

But these nagging doubts and suspicions I can't hide, and they're
beginning to poison our relationship, perhaps even to drive her to
the very place I dread, another man's arms. Oh that we could be on
a desert island together, alone, not another soul in sight, ever, locked
in one another's embrace, forever and ever, amen. Such prayers I
mutter under my breath and begin to feel the prison I'm construct-
ing for us in my mind: one that will enclose us forever and ever, and
within which I'll be safe from that most excruciating of all emotions – jealousy. I'd go to the ends of the world for her: risk prison,
torture, death itself, to be the undisputed winner of the hand of her
who has become the sole meaning of my existence. Then one eve-

ning, towards Christmas, she announces that she's going to Lisbon. She'll be gone a month, a whole goddamn month.

Darkness has fallen. She said she'd be here at six, to say a brief farewell, 'And I mean *brief,*' she'd emphasised, 'don't try to detain me, I have a lot of packing to do before the morning.'

I'm pacing these cramped quarters, one eye on the clock, it's a quarter to seven. In the courtyard an icy wind's crashing about like a devil – lifting dustbin lids and cardboard boxes, banging doors and rattling window panes; all these sounds are ennervating and meaningless until I hear one distinct one which makes my heart stop – high-heeled shoes on the staircase. In one stride I'm at the door through which she blows.

'I can't stay,' she says, wriggling out of my embrace and making for a chair at the table where she sits, casting her eye over some papers scattered about on the table-top.

'You've been writing?'

'Yes.'

'That's good,' she looks up at me, 'about what?'

'About you.'

'You mustn't, you really mustn't. One day I'll disappear. Lead your life for yourself, don't live for me. There are too many complications in my life – I'll only make you unhappy . . .'

'No you won't, Zé, you make me so happy, so very happy,' she searches my eyes, worriedly, tenderly, for a moment. She ruffles my hair, I'm on my knees. She knows that she's already the source of so much unhappiness in me. I lay my head on her breast which is soft and warm and comforting. I want her forever and ever – I'll go mad if she disappears. I raise my mouth to hers and for a moment we kiss, before she pulls away, saying, 'I haven't time, I told you . . .'

She hasn't time? Why has she never time? Self-pity, rage, indignation are welling up, choking me – she'll be gone a fucking month and she hasn't time for a last embrace.

'Don't you love me?' I burst out.

'It's not that, it's just that I don't have time. Can't you understand that, can't you see anything but from your own point of view? You demand this, you demand that, demand that I come running to you every time you call; and because I can't you think it's because I don't want to.'

'I'm sorry, Zé, sit down, have a glass of wine, don't go.'

'No, I must go now – I didn't come here for this kind of scenario. You have no right to make me feel guilty for going to Lisbon. My mother wants to see me, she's old – you think you're the only one I have to care about?'

'Here, drink.'

'Just a sip. Ah, why do you make me so nervous?'

'Because I love you and I don't want you to go away.'

We fall silent, stare into the glasses of wine before us.

'I have to go – it's only for a month or so. You'd think it was for ever the way you're going on.'

'A month *is* forever, even an hour is, when one's in love.'

'Yes, it's quite an abnormal state to be in,' she says, getting up, adjusting her skirt and buttoning her jacket up to her throat.

'*Adeus,*' she leans over, kisses me fleetingly on the forehead, 'see you when I return. Try to be reasonable.'

And as suddenly as she'd come she's gone.

Her glass stands half finished on the table, lipstick on the rim. I lift it to my lips and drink – refill it and drink – and drink and drink and drink . . . and now aglow, enfevered, bold, a plan starts hatching in my head. Let's see . . . sixty odd francs in my pockets; that's some cigarettes and a meal somewhere along the line. Now, as much warm clothing as I can find into my rucksack, drain the last of the bottle and dash to the station – the Gare d'Austerlitz from which a train leaves every night, around midnight, for Lisbon.

Chapter 13

The Lisbon Express

. . . train rushing through dark night
– iron wheels – turning and smoke – turmoil . . .

Here we are, and here she is waiting, 'The Lisbon Express'.
Platform 3 23h.45. Orleans – Limoges – Bordeaux –
Hendaye – San Sebastian – Valladolid – Salamanca –
Guarda – Lisbonne.

This is it, my transport awaits me!

Slipping past the guard on the barrier was easy, he was distracted
by a lost-looking fellow wanting to know where he could buy a
ticket. I've climbed aboard and am leaning from the window. The
platform's crowded with Portuguese immigrant workers returning to
Lisbon for Christmas. Good, all this confusion should make things
easier for me. I fish a small bottle of cognac from my pocket, take a
swig – I'm ready for anything.

A whistle's blowing and the train with a jolt, with a clank, is in
motion and I, resigning myself to my fate, am stowing away without
credentials, except one: my burning love which no one will subdue
and which will get me to my destination, Zé's side, at any cost.

Stowing away on a train means keeping a constant watch. You
cannot afford to lapse in your vigil – a moment off-guard can cost
you everything. You must be ready to move, to become invisible.
There's no rest – though you must feign serenity – and sleep, except
in the very middle of the night – is out of the question. It means

being forever in the corridors, eyes darting from one end of the carriage to the other for the dreaded sight of the guard's uniform. It means to feel apart, alone, hunted. You find yourself with prayers upon your lips—there is a god at such times, there has to be. One thing I know for sure: Venus will be smiling upon this amorous plight of mine. Thirty-six hours I'll be in this state of anxiety. I'll have earned my ticket if I get there. Let's see, thirty-six hours with overtime and danger pay—hmm, I'll have earned the price of the ticket several times over, let anyone tell me I don't work for a living.

I've made a thorough inspection of the carriages—there's not a nook or cranny where I might hide. Even the spaces under the seats are blocked off. If only there was somewhere I could put myself and leave myself, that I could hole up in. I could hold out for thirty-six hours, could creep out in the dead of night for a piss. But these wagons are completely stowaway proof. Damn the makers of them! Damn the petty, mean makers of them!

Hiding in the lavatory is one way, I've done that before, but on shorter runs—and I've often got away with it—having learnt the trick of making it look unoccupied—but as often as not one gets caught, run to ground like a fox. No, on a long run like this my chances would be slim—I'll have to find another way—and quickly. We've been hurtling into the midwinter's night already a good half-hour—the ticket inspector must surely be getting busy by now. What am I going to do? A nip of brandy'll fire my brain—Mmm—brrrr—yes—Now think quick, where are you going to hide . . . how about the roof? Crikey, the roof. Open the window—bitter wind, ice cold metal—how can I climb up? But it's crazy. Yes, but I've got to hide. Hey, these railings and steps outside the door—Eureka! It should be simple enough: upon the approach of the guard I'll open the door and step out into the night, grabbing the rails as I do so, of course. Pull the door closed behind me and crouch down on the steps, my head below the level of the window. I'll hang there for as long as it takes the official to pass. Ha, the petty, mean, makers of these carriages didn't think when they were fixing these steps that one day a man, mad with love, would be crouching on them.

We're already some way south, the hour advanced and the merriment in the train all but subsided when I espy the guard working his way along the carriages, looking into the compartments and punching tickets. I open the door, catch hold of the railings, feel my way down onto the lowest step and close the door behind me. I'm oblivious at first to the icy wind cutting at me along the side of the train but it's not long before my hands, gripping on for dear life become painfully aware of the numbing cold and it'll only be a matter of minutes before they seize up. The ground's streaking beneath me like a rushing river that will dash me to death should I fall. I tuck my head into my chest and pray, not to God, but to the almighty guard, that he should not dawdle, or pause at this window to smoke a cigarette and stare out into the night. Pray guard, hurry! My hands arc numb with cold and I cannot hang here forever . . .

I raise my head cautiously to the level of the window and peek in – I've done it! I've done it! The guard's uniformed figure is disappearing through the dividing door into the next carriage. I fumble at the handle and clamber back inside – I've done it, my plan's worked. I jump up and down, stamp my feet and clap my hands to get the blood flowing and take the final shot of brandy. The train's cascading through the black, midwinter's night, clattering on the lines and shuddering, like me, in its whole being. I stand at the window and light a cigarette, gaze at the reflection of this strange beast in the glass – through it a glowing city looms up on the horizon and is snatched away again by the night.

The sky in the east is paling, the dawn light's extinguishing the stars one by one. I'm awoken by my own shivering, lying doubled up and uncovered on the compartment seat on which I'd finally lain down exhausted.

'Bonjour, monsieur.'

It's an old woman who's spoken, sitting opposite me, outlined against the brightening sky through the window. A little girl lies with her head in her lap.

'Ah, bonjour, madame.'

'I hope you've slept well,' she says kindly.

'Yes, very well, thank-you, madame.' It's true, though I can't have slept more than two or three hours I feel marvellously refreshed. Fishing in a bag lying at her feet she produces a thermos,

'So now would you like some coffee to wake you up?'

'Ah yes, madame.'

I sit up and she hands me a cup of sweet, milky coffee – piping hot. How good it is.

'Are you going far?' she asks.

'To Lisbon, madame.'

'So you are going to my country.'

'You're Portuguese?'

'Yes, I'm Portuguese from Porto, in the north. Now I've made my life in Paris. My husband, you see, went there for work – we went there many years ago; and when he died,' she crosses herself, 'I stayed there because we had a house and life is easy with a pension and you know in Portugal things have always been difficult – now there's been a revolution and things are changing, getting a little better but still, life is hard, people poor. But my son lives in Lisbon and my grand-daughter, Kiki,' she strokes the child's head, 'she is a Lisbonense.' The little girl's gazing at me with wide eyes.

'Will it be your first visit to Lisbon, monsieur?'

'Yes, yes, the first time.'

'Ah, the first time is always the most unforgettable – and it is such an enchanting city – coffee?'

'Oh yes, thank-you, madame,' She refills my cup. *'Muito obrigado, senhora,'* I add a little coyly.

'Ah, you speak Portuguese!' she exclaims with surprise.

'Oh just a little, so *um pocadinho, senhora . . .* '

'Que maravilhosa,' delighted, she clasps her hands together over her breasts. I remember so well Zé using that expression and making that very same gesture with her hands – it's like an expression of rapture. 'Have you studied our language, monsieur?'

'Ah no – no, I only speak a little – I learnt it from friends.'

'You have Portuguese friends?'

'Yes, madame.'

'In Paris?'

'Yes.'

'And will they be in Lisbon now?'

'Yes, for Christmas . . . '

'And you will stay with them, of course,'

'Er . . . yes, yes, I will.'

'You will love Lisbon, Monsieur – and especially now when it will be full of lights and music – everyone is so happy at Christmas time and you are young . . . I lived there once as a young woman – oh yes, I too was young once: not always was I the old lady you are looking at now. I was beautiful too. Maybe, young man,' a glint's come into her eye, 'maybe you will meet someone in Lisbon and you will never want to leave.'

The coffee's warmed me through and through as has the conversation with this congenial old lady – her presence is imparting to me a sense of safety, of protection. But I can't tarry here too long and lull myself into a false sense of security. People are beginning to stir, are moving to and fro in the corridors: there could well be an early morning inspection. I'd better get back on watch.

'You are going, monsieur?' she looks surprised at my sudden departure. 'Ah, but yes, of course,' she looks through the carriage window, 'You must have sensed it – we're arriving at the frontier . . . ' The frontier! A spasm of fear shoots through me – now I'm going to have to be on my toes.

Gathering into my demeanour and my voice all the calm which I feel a million miles from I begin to take my leave, expressing warm thanks for the coffee and wishing them both a *Boa viaje,* an agreeable journey.

'Au revoir, monsieur, adeus. And . . . ' she winks at me, 'good luck.'

Agonisingly slowly, we pull into the frontier station, Irun. I lean my head from the window into the crisp air and bright sunlight. A loudspeaker announces that all passengers are to alight from the train and pass through customs for a baggage inspection. There'll be a break in the journey for ninety minutes.

The platform's a scene of bustle and confusion: luggage is being unloaded from the carriages, children are rushing about, uncontainable in their excitement, their mothers shouting at them. Men are rolling around drinking from flagons and singing: singing of the land to which we're getting ever closer. I'm glad of this confusion: it'll give me a better chance of slipping through undetected. I join the general drift towards the *douane*, glad to be amongst these ecstatic immigrants.

Let's be relaxed about this. What have I to fear anyway? My bag contains nothing it shouldn't, my passport's in order, it's only the 'ticket touts' I have to worry about and chances are there won't be any here – so dinna ye fret, me lad. Just take the moment for the moment and keep yer wits about ye!

Look, I'm sailing through, it's a cinch. They're not interested in me, it's the Portuguese they're seizing on – like vultures they're ripping open packages, turning trunks and boxes upside down and inside out. Me, with my British passport and nordic appearance, they're simply waving through. It hardly seems fair, but I'm not going to start protesting.

To make absolutely sure the train isn't leaving soon (after all, having got this far I'm not going to get left behind.) I approach a railway official, 'You have time, monsieur, to have breakfast,' he assures me good humouredly.

I head into town and step into a little restaurant where I order a large bowl of soup, bread and a Spanish omelette stuffed with potato and onion. This'll set me up for a while. Already I sense Spain in here, smell it in the air with the joints of smoked ham hanging from the beams and the musty smell of wine soaked into the floorboards – I'd better have a jug of wine from one of these solid wooden kegs to celebrate the journey thus far and to fortify me for the next leg of it – och aye, a wee drop of wine will not go amiss. But dinna ye get blotto and miss the train.

Why do I keep breaking into Scottish today? Must be my ancestry coming through. Perhaps those kilted fellows swimming about in my blood are getting animated by this adventure and are finding their tongues through mine. And I'll bet they're glad of the liquor.

And now, before I drink too much of it and lose my wits I'm going to pay and head back to the station. Hmmm, I've just enough left for a packet of fags and a coffee in the canteen.

I feel good standing at the counter stirring my coffee and drawing on a cigarette – I've earned these moments, this heaven-sent lull in the drama, oh yes, I wink at myself in the mirror – I've earned this.

Twenty-four more hours of vigilance and anxiety lie ahead of me. People are clambering back on board–I'd better do the same. And now I'm leaning from a window basking my upturned face in the deliciously warm sun. There's a final check with clanking hammers of the wheels which have been changed. Doors are slamming, a shrill whistle blowing–we're off! And I'm on my toes again, all nerves. Thank god I have some cigarettes: a precious, light-blue, packet of Gauloises.

Ne pas se pencher au-dehors
Nicht hinauslehnen
E pericoloso sporgersi
Do not lean out

Four languages warn of the danger of sticking one's head from the window. Do such a foolish thing as that, me? and whilst the train's in motion? No, of course I wouldn't. Boy, am I glad of this sky-blue packet of Gauloises as I loiter, all nerves, in the corridor, one eye on the landscape flashing by through the window, the other darting from one end of the carriage to the other.

Late afternoon brings the first control. With a spasm of fear I see the guard come through at the end of the corridor. I'm in the middle of it, standing at the window, engaged in conversation with a young Portuguese fellow who has a little English and wants to practise it. He looks startled when I break away but I have no time to give him an explanation–anyway, what explanation would I give? As luck would have it once again the outer compartment at the end of the carriage is free of people. I open the door, clasp the railings and crouch down on the steps below the level of the window. It's less biting cold than the night before and I feel quite at ease, this time, hanging from the railings. The sun, a great ball of red, is plunging towards the horizon and will soon be swallowed by the blue sierras which line the skyline to the west. I take in the breathtaking beauty through my eyes narrowed to slits in the on-rushing wind.

'There, where the sun is falling now, my love is–Nothing stops the sun; nothing, No one stops me!'

All of a sudden, a station's looming up towards us – Fuck! – what now? – we're not slowing up and, at a gallop, and with a wail of the locomotive's siren, we charge between the crowded platforms. All heads turn and gaze, open-mouthed, at a monkey clinging to a pole and whisked through their midsts.

I'm on my way
I've always been on my way –

Blaise Cendrars. He too would have clung on here, jubilantly, with his only arm, his '*main amie*', the eternal cigarette stub blazing and sparking like a fire between his lips . . . I peek a look in through the window; the guard must have passed by now – indeed he's nowhere to be seen; his tour of inspection has passed me by. I'm making it.

The sun's edge is touching the line of the sierras and looks as though it will roll along it like a ball – but its course is set, like mine, and it plunges like a comet into the earth. Night falls. We're approaching the border, climbing steadily up, up, up – up a mountainside, up towards the stars. There's uproar and a great bout of singing as we pull into the frontier station. The customs men climb onto the train, check passports and we move into Portugal. Portugal! The land of my love! I stick my head out into the night and shout, tears welling up in a great ecstatic sob from the depths of my being, 'My love, my love, I'm coming!'

The stars flash and dance in the heavens.

But oh – so confident that I've made it I become lapse in my vigil. Oh let it be a lesson to me forever more: not to rest before the goal is reached. The ticket man's upon me – my heart sinks into my boots.

'No ticket? – then your passport.' He takes it away from me and tells me to go with him upon arriving in Lisbon in the morning. Glumly I nod my head, all the elation, of just moments before, gone – all my endeavours for nothing. Damn! Damn! Fuck! Damn!

Well at least I can lie down and get some sleep now, no need to look out for the guard any more. I can behave as though I've got a ticket from now on. I laugh grimly, unconvincingly; no point in forcing myself to be humorous at this point – the game's up and there's nothing at all funny about that. I'd rather swear blue murder and kick the door.

I lie in the darkness thinking. I'll go along with him in the morning but keep my wits about me – see if I can wriggle out of this predicament, with or without the passport – oh yes, I'll escape . . . Please Life, *please* you guardians of my life – let me escape.

Anyone who has approached Lisbon from the Alentejo at dawn has looked up to see a city, touched by the pink of the sun, loom up out of the mist which falls away from her like veils, like a woman emerging from a steamy bath – and this is what I see as my eyes open on Portugal for the first time. We are gliding, unhurriedly, dreamily over flat expanses of swamp through a blue-pink mist. It's my birthday, the solstice. According to legend the sun, at its nadir, is imprisoned in the underworld. Pray to God I don't suffer the same fate. I feel marvellously refreshed; I've slept the sleep of the just, and now I'm alive again. All the details of my predicament come flooding back – alright, I'm in a fix, but I've got this far, and twenty-three years along the road of life. I know, somehow, that the gods are smiling on me (above all Venus) and so what threat can a few piffling frowns from officialdom present? None – just you wait and see.

Propping my head up on my rucksack I look over the mud-flats. Zé, still sleeping, is quite unsuspecting of my stealthy approach. Will I be with her by nightfall? Will I *really* be with her? It'll be a miracle . . . oh yes, it'll be a miracle.

I'm among a bustling crowd, a crowd into which I could disappear and walk out, free, onto the streets. Should I, should I? Should I make a break for it, forget about the bloody passport? But no sooner have I stepped down onto the platform than my captor's hand is on my shoulder and I follow him meekly to the railway company offices.

After a consultation with the station master the guard turns to me: I must pay the fare from the frontier to Lisbon – they don't seem to know, or don't seem to care that I've come all the way from Paris, all they want is five dollars – that seems fair enough, and I'd pay it, had I the money – it would be a small price for freedom, an almost negligible sum; of course, I'd pay it if I could. But I can't.

And I don't think they believe me when I tell them I have no money.

'*Dinheiros,*' they insist, 'money.

'*Nao tenho dinheiros,*' I say, turning my pockets inside out. 'No money.'

They look at each other and then back at me,

'Travellers cheques.'

'I don't have travellers cheques.'

A policeman's spotted through the window, shuffling lazily about in the station, smoking, looking bored. He's called into the office. Oh, oh here we go – things are gonna get tricky. He waddles over, a round body on short legs and glares at me, 'Money!'

'No money!'

He looks perplexed and then says in as many words as he can muster in English, 'Pay ticket, you must, to frontier from here.'

I explain, as I've already explained, that I have no money.

'Then in prison you must are going,' and he crosses his wrists, one over the other, as if in handcuffs.

'Okay.'

'No okay! Pay ticket you!'

'I – no – can – pay – because – no – have – money.' I pronounce every word clearly and precisely so that it'll sink in, and register in his head once and for all, that I have no money.

'Prison you are must then going.'

'Okay, prison then I must am going.'

I'm having fun with this novel way of speaking English.

'No prison – pay must you.'

This is getting tedious. How many times must I remind him I have no money?

Well, finally he gets the message, and I'm told to sit down and wait. It seems like an eternity – there's no light from the sun in here and it seems like night, though high up, through the skylight of the station, I can see the bright winter sunshine and blue sky. Zé can't be more than a few miles away but, sitting in this twilit captivity, it could be a million. My captors are standing between me and the door – what chance would I have if I bolted? I look at the gun on the copper's hip: I suppose he might use that if he got it into his head. What are they cooking up for me, I who am so near and yet so far, they could scupper all my plans. Why don't they just let me go?

In the end they make it ridiculously easy for me. The *chef de gare* says, 'British Embassy. You go. Money give. Here come. Money give.'

'Okay,' I say, unable to believe my ears, but trying to conceal my delight, 'Money here bring, yes, yes, *sim senhor.*'

'You are coming here, today!'

'*Sim senhor!*' I assure him, 'I will need passport . . . '

Is he going to give me my passport?

Here it is, in my hand, clutched so tight that it will never be taken from me again, and here I am walking, trembling, out of the office, towards the station entrance, into the bright sunlight . . . Is it a mistake? Will a voice call me back, a hand clap over my shoulder? I'm ready to run, ready to run very fast . . .

Chapter 14

Lisbon

I find myself hurrying towards an Arabian archway and up steps which wind amongst colourful ramshackle houses, up and up and up, not stopping until I'm out of breath. My heart is dancing in my flight like a bird set free. Yes, I'm flying! I smile at everyone I pass, at every stone and step and house and tree. Out of breath I stop in a garden bright with bougainvillea and look out from a terrace over red rooftops to the great River Tagus sparkling in the sunshine. Ships of all sizes lie at anchor on the water and a magnificent suspension bridge spans it in loops.

I start to descend in the direction I feel must lead to the heart of the city, winding my way down stone steps that are as twisting and narrow as a goat's path and are flanked by gaily-painted, two-storyed houses, with washing all the colours of the rainbow hanging from their balconies; under arches, through tiny squares with fountains and palm trees. Children greet me; *'Olá, Olá!'* I laugh and disappear down other alleys, down countless flights of steps. On reaching the bottom I come into an enormous square alive with people and trams. Filled with the thrill of being I sit down in a shaft of light on the steps of a doorway and, propped with my elbow on my rucksack, I close my eyes and drift away . . .

There's a tap on my shoulder and I come to with a start. An old woman, dressed from head to toe in black, is handing me something, *'Boa sorte,'* ('Good luck') she whispers and disappears into the crowd. Thrilled, I examine the round, chunky, brass coins lying in my palm. I wonder how much they're worth; will they be enough for a cup of coffee?

One way to find out and so leaping up I look for a café and enter the first one I come to; the whole air's filled with the aroma of fresh coffee. I feverishly examine the price list displayed above the bar—have I enough? Why, I have more than enough! Bless that old lady's soul. Cigarettes, have I enough for a packet of cigarettes, just to make my happiness complete? I have. Buying a packet of the strongest and cheapest cigarettes I sit down at a marble topped table where I'm brought a steaming glass of milky coffee. Everything's working out—you see, I told you the gods were on my side. Perhaps the old woman was Venus in disguise, and the coins she handed me were forged in her lame husband's workshop—yes, they were still warm, come to think of it. Well, well, well, what a birthday present. I joke and laugh with myself. I want to do cartwheels over the table tops and hug every single person in the café and on the street. Everything's turning out better than I could possibly have hoped or planned. A canary is singing in a cage above me, its wistful agony is the one note of sadness in this otherwise joyful morning. An old fellow is wandering around the café with a handful of brightly coloured tickets. He's calling out, *'Amanha! Amanha!'* Tomorrow! Tomorrow! People call him over to their tables and buy strips of tickets. Who knows what tomorrow will bring. I feel I've already bought my strip and am winning at every turn of the wheel.

I take Zé's address from my pocket and examine it once more. Let's see, *Restelo*. Now that might be quite far out of town. The couple at the next table have been looking at me sympathetically from time to time; I have the feeling they might speak some English and be able to help me with directions.

'Ah longe, longe,' says the woman. 'It is very far, you must take the bus.'

I don't want to tell her that I have no money for a bus and so I let her write down the numbers I must watch for. And then, she pulls from her handbag a little map of Lisbon, 'It's here, you see, very far out.' I quickly take in as much as I can with my eyes and know now roughly the direction in which I must walk.

Out on the street I suddenly feel quite weak with hunger. It's nearing the lunch hour and smells of cooking are teasing my nostrils and tantalising my belly as I stroll along the narrow cobbled street called the *Rua da Sapateiros* which has little restaurants on either side of it. Right, this one, and, with a deep breath, I plunge through a door to find myself in the dark, warm, steamy interior with the clatter of plates being laid on the tables by the waiters preparing for the lunchtime rush, and a man I take to be the boss standing at the counter doing some sums. He regards me with some interest as I walk through the door, not the usual sort of customer. I walk straight up to him and explain my hunger, my penniless state and my willingness to wash the plates if he could just provide me with a little food.

He looks at me with perfect understanding as though to say: There's no shame in being penniless and it's human to be hungry, and then says,

'Sit down – I have no plates for you to wash but I'll send you over a meal,' and he signals over to a waiter to lay a table for me. I can hardly believe my luck as three great platters are set before me and a carafe of wine, a veritable feast, fit for a king. Oh my god, I'm overwhelmed by this kindness and I thank them all from the bottom of my heart as I set out fortified, and divinely drunk, to look for Zé's house. One day, if this little tavern still graces this street I shall pause a moment before its door, like I did then, take a deep breath and plunge in, 'I am he who you helped all those years ago – I have never forgotten your kindness. Your meal sustained me the whole day long and the wine made my spirit soar as I walked along the river to find the lady of my dreams – you understand that the morning you helped me was no ordinary morning . . .'

I start walking westwards along the river. The sun is swooping down behind the looping bridge and turning the sky into a blaze of colours. At an enormous statue of Christopher Columbus, which I noted on the map, I turn right, away from the river, and find myself on the road to *Restelo*. At dusk, I'm knocking with feverish anticipation on Zé's mother's door. When Zé opens the door she nearly faints, '*Mais comment . . . ?*' she breathes.

And now she's taking me through Lisbon in a taxi, her body pressed up close to me in the dark, her hand – the hand I would go to the end of the world to win – in mine. I write our names and draw a heart in the mist our two breaths have made on the window. And tonight in a little hotel where no one knows us she gives me the best birthday present a man could ever wish for . . .

As *um amigo ingles* (an English friend) I'm given a room and stay as a guest at Zé's mother's house for the length of my sojourn in Lisbon. It's a kind of attic room with a marvellous view over roof-tops to the estuary. On lucky nights, if Zé's home early from her visits, she tip-toes up the stairs and spends an hour or so with me. I can't complain that she's otherwise out – after all, she's made this rare trip to Lisbon to see old friends, to visit relations. I can't expect her to neglect her social rounds just because I've turned up on her doorstep. No, I accept that, I'm lucky, after all, but all the same, it seems sad that, rather than my being here being a joyful, romantic re-union, I feel that I'm a little in the way.

I spend most days alone, wandering around the city and along beside the Tagus watching the ships from every corner of the world inch their way beneath the looping bridge, and the ferry boats bobbing over the waves towards *Cacilhas* on the other shore. And when a mist comes down, quite suddenly over the water, the estuary booms with ships' sirens.

> In Lisbon harbour by the docks
> where massive vessels lie at berth along the quays
> you can loll against a column and steam across
> the Tagus with your eyes –
> you can hop on a ship and sail to China
> or over the wide Atlantic to the great Americas in your mind
>
> And in Lisbon harbour when the sun has sunk
> the colour of blood into the swell
> you can drink with sailors from every far-flung corner, who
> with their eyes on the girls and over a beer
> will tell of their lives at sea, the tedium

of weeks at a stretch beyond the horizons
without any women . . . the talk will drift
to prostitutes, punch-ups, prisons
on every longed-for shore, in every port from Reykjavic to
Rio –
to storm, to madness, murder
and the loneliness of the sea, too deep to tell

And in the depths of drink they'll weep
the debris of their dreams adrift
upon the tides, which rise and fall and are their lives.

I sometimes find myself in all the bewildering din and confusion of the market at the *Cais do Sodre,* a huge temple of barter and commerce which rings with the cries of the marketeers, their voices rising up to the rafters miles above. Vegetables are strewn all over the ground, turkeys are hanging from hooks along the walls. I keep my eyes skimmed for discarded fruit – oranges from the Algarve, bananas from Africa. What I can scavenge down here is all I eat from morning to evening, except for a cake around tea time at the *Brasileira*, which I come by through trickery. The *Brasileira* at *Chiado* is the most famous of all cafés in Lisbon, with its quaint, old-fashioned, elegance, its marble tables, its wooden-panelled walls, lined with mirrors. A place where the dandy as well as the Bohemian meets – intellectuals, artists, conspirators. I'm definitely of the latter category for every afternoon I conspire to obtain a cup of tea and a cake for nothing. It's surprisingly easy, in fact, as the old waiter's very absent-minded and I can outwit him quite easily by ordering what I want at the counter then taking it to a table so that he assumes that I've paid. I look forward to that cake all day long.

Glad of the distractions the streets afford me, I amble through them trying to fill my days. Just as the lady on the train said, Lisbon's full of lights and music and happy Christmas crowds thronging the squares and shops and cafés. Business booms for all, from the shopkeeper to the accordionist on the corner. Even for the beggars it booms – ha, the beggars – there are some wily ones indeed. Look at this one sitting on the *Rua do Carmo* shaking so violently one would diagnose his condition as the final stages of Parkinson's disease; that is if one didn't cotton on to the fact that he's an out-and-out phoney and the whole thing is an act. See how quickly the tin on the pavement in front of him is filling up with coins. And now watch him, thinking no one's looking, stop his shaking and fish a packet of expensive cigarettes from his pocket and with gold lighter and steady hand light the fag between his lips.

But the one that really takes the biscuit I happened upon yesterday when strolling along the *Rua Augusta*. From some distance away I heard a most sinister groaning and choking and gurgling. Gripped with curiosity I made in the direction of it and all of a sudden its author sprang into view. Sprawled out in front of a busy bank was the most ghastly apparition: a grey-faced old man writhing, twitching and emitting these flesh creeping cries as though he was in the throes of death. At first I was taken in by it like everyone else seemed to be; but then I began to notice the tell-tale signs of an act. Firstly, why'd he laid a newspaper out carefully underneath him? So as not to dirty his clothes of course. Secondly, why did he keep glancing slyly around and only start his caterwauling when he saw people approaching? So as not to exhaust himself unnecessarily, you may be sure. He was doing pretty well, getting lots of money along with horrified looks – he was getting rich in fact, the tin beside his head simply piling up with coins and bank notes. Everything was going like clockwork until a Good Samaritan arrived, knelt down beside him and, very concerned, was saying, 'Come with me to the hospital.'

The arrival of this altruist was the very last thing the old impostor needed right now – he was going to spoil everything. He carried on with his act trying to ignore his benefactor. But the 'Good Samaritan' was insistent, 'Hospital, You must come with me to the hospital.'

A crowd was gathering round, someone was despatched to a nearby café for a glass of water and finally the 'dying' man was obliged to acknowledge the presence of this meddlesome man by saying furiously to him, 'I'm alright.'

'No, you are sick, come to the hospital . . .'

'I'm alright,' hissed the beggar glaring at the fellow who was making such a damned nuisance of himself. 'You see, nothing whatsoever is wrong with me,' he said, raising himself up.

The Samaritan saw that indeed the grey-faced fellow was looking better and finally took his leave. When the last of the crowd had dispersed I, watching from a little way away, saw the old man lay himself down on the newspaper and resume his lucrative business.

'Do you sometimes smoke?'

This time it's a heavily accented German voice which has startled me out of my reverie. Sitting in the morning sun on the steps of the National Theatre I'd been drifting off with thoughts of Zé. Now I'm looking into the face of a tough, brutal-looking young fellow with cropped hair. I nod.

'Ja? so komm, I haf something . . . '

We wind our way up through the cobbled alleys of *Alfama* to the ramparts of the castle of St. George and flop down on a bench which commands a view over the Tagus and out to the wide Atlantic from which a fog is rolling in covering the ships on the estuary one by one. Sirens bellow over the water like distressed cattle, like my soul.

Marco is my companion's name – he hails form Hamburg. Renting a car in Germany – 'a Mercedes, of course, alvays,' he says with a grin – he'll drive it to Spain where he'll sell it at a good price and no questions asked. And so he's able to have 'long vacations in ze sun wizout having to vork like a slave.'

We smoke. The mist rises up from the river, stealing in over the city and enshrouding the red roof-tops in floating veils. The din from below has become muffled, blanketed, and all about us is now quite silent.

'It's different here,' says Marco, 'when I'm in Germany, I'm only feeling anger – anger at ze vay people live – zey don't live. It's different here, I am different . . . something makes me soft . . . there is a voman, I sink you understand . . . ' his voice trails off dreamily and there is a radiance about his face, a gentleness seeping through the callous exterior.

'Yes, I do.'

'Strange ze power of zem,' he says, staring out across the banks of fog to the deep blue wintry sky line.

I don't think Zé really knows what to make of me being here – on her home ground, as it were. She feels as awkward as I do on the occasional visits we make together to friends or relatives. After all, she's supposed to be a married woman and her husband's forever being enquired after.

'He's well,' she says, 'but busy. He'll come next time, he promises.'

Most of those she knows are the well-to-do whose houses and apartments are adorned with fine paintings and carpets which I hardly dare walk upon in my clodhoppers. Zé introduces me as a poet which always animates our hosts,

'Portugal is a land which loves its poets,' they tell me. It's true, I've come across more statues of poets in my meandering through Lisbon than in any city I've ever known. My favourite is that of Antonio Ribeiro, a sixteenth century satirical poet, which stands in the square outside the *Brasileira* and is less of a statue than a real live person. *'Chiado'*, he was known as, and after whom the whole district of Chiado was named. He's leaning towards you so far that the stool he's sitting on is tilting, almost to the point that he's going to fall off it; he's telling you a story, his hand in a sweeping gesture before him and a smile so wide it splits his face in two – there's invariably a pigeon perched upon the bonnet he dons on his bonce, which of course has been permanently dyed white by their droppings over the years.

They name streets and squares after their poets and put them on bank notes so that paying for a coffee in the *Brasileira* (that is, when I *do* pay*)* with a current note of a hundred escudos which bears the head of Fernando Pessoa, I smile to myself when I think that the poet's very spirit, or one of his many personas – for the name, Pessoa, means 'persons' and his poems are written from different parts of himself in kaleidoscopic fashion – might be sitting at one of the tables; for the *Brasileira* was his main haunt, and what better place for his different personalities to speak than this many-mirrored café. He might well have written this poem in here:

Não sei quantas almas tenho.
Cada momento mudei.
Continuamente me estranho.
Nunca me vi nem achei.

Which I roughly translate:

I don't know how many souls I have.
Every moment I've changed.
I'm ever a stranger to myself.
I've never seen nor found myself.

To be truthful, I feel quite lost in Lisbon. Most of my time is spent alone and, when I *am* with Zé, I'm never feeling she's altogether pleased that I'm here. It's a world which she prefers to keep private – and there are lots of things in her world she'd rather keep that way. She's aware of how I feel and so she's not altogether surprised when I announce to her, not a week since my arrival, my intention to depart in the morning.

'How will you go? Surely not the way you came?'

'I'll hitch,' there's not the same incentive to risk stowing away again. I feel more like just walking out into the snows of the sierras and dying. Quietly, bloodlessly.

It'll be more than a bit grim heading back to the wintry north. But thank God Ashley and Inês will be there at the end of the journey to bolster my sunken spirits. And at least I'll have an adventure to recount to them, I'll have a tale that I'll have brought back from my travels, that, if nothing else will have made it all worthwhile. They must wonder where I've been all this time. I slipped out of Paris without telling a soul. They must have worried when they found my quarters empty, a couple of 'starry-necked alembics' drained to the dregs on the table and all the signs of a hurried, probably drunken, departure. And they're not blind to the fact that things are becoming a little strained between Zé and I.

Zé's given me some money to travel with but, in my pride, I've slipped it into an envelope with the note I've left her, 'I love you, etcetera,' and I'm leaving Lisbon as penniless as I arrived. I'll survive. Nothing really matters anyway. It's my heart which needs attention: my belly will look after itself.

Chapter 15

Wintry Journey

Frozen drops fall
from my cheeks;
have I, then, not noticed
that I have been weeping?

Franz Schubert, *Winterreise*

I'm on the road which leads towards Coimbra and the north. I pick up a series of short lifts and finally a lorry stops which is going right into Spain. The driver's small and dark, with one of those faces one comes upon frequently in Portugal, thin and worn with hard work. Between us we manage to communicate, with Portuguese, with Spanish, with our hands and sometimes with just a look or a smile. He shares his food with me and plies me with cigarettes – how thankful I am.

We wind along mountain roads lined by fir trees sagging with snow. It's getting colder and colder, mist is on our breath and I shiver inside my greatcoat. As night comes down the sky's brilliant with stars, clear and cold as crystals. The lorry's straining its engine as we crawl up the steep gradients, a full cargo of timber's being hauled along behind us.

It must be two in the morning when we cross the border, and are waved through without ado by the guards, too busy playing cards to bother about the odd timber truck like ours, lumbering along at this hour.

'*España,*' says my companion.

'*España,*' I echo him, we smile in the darkness, and the glow of our cigarettes lights up our faces as we pull on them. A strange closeness has grown between us, as though the road we've travelled together has knit our souls for a flash of eternity. He explains that we'll be continuing for about fifty kilometres more along the road I need before he turns off to some remote corner of Galicia. I thank him from the bottom of my heart as I clamber down from the cab. It's three in the morning as I watch the rear lights of the trailer disappear into the darkness and then lie down, just where I am, at the side of the road, to snatch a little sleep, if I can.

The morning finds me curled up in a ball, frozen stiff. My head's inside my sleeping bag and when I peak out it's to see that I'm on a plateau, rugged and vast, stretching as far as the eye can see; like a patchwork of light and shadow thrown by the rising sun – it's brilliant, with the metallic sheen of an El Greco painting. Spread before my eyes, it uplifts me and makes me feel marvellous – all my troubles melt away in the face of it. I wish I was a painter like Ashley: I'd seize brush and canvas and paint it all. I'd immerse myself in this landscape so deeply that I'd cease to exist, I'd become this earth, this rock, bombarded by the sun, the moon and the stars and ravaged by the wind, for as long as the Earth remained and I'd need for nothing more than just to be. And my face, turned eternally towards the stars, would wear that serenity which to me, in my impassioned plight, is so far from me. I spring shivering from my sleeping bag, pack my things, sling them over my shoulder and set off with swift gait into a biting east wind towards the climbing sun.

I happen upon a discarded hunk of bread by the side of the road, it's hard as rock and being worked upon by a team of ants which I blow off, every man jack of them and, as I suck it, it becomes as soft as wool in my mouth. Breakfast.

I stick my thumb out when a vehicle approaches and my tongue out when it passes. It doesn't matter that they don't stop – I'm having the time of my life strolling along this road.

> As I was strolling along the road
> I sang to a flower and talked to a toad

I kicked a tin can and gnawed at a loaf
I spat out dough which stuck to a tree . . .

All my troubles seem so far away – oh yes, oh yes, I laugh for the
first time for a long time; I really laugh! I roar with the sheer exu-
berance of being and skip along lightly, singing that Beatles song,
'Yesterday, all my troubles seemed so far away . . . ' and I change it
to, 'Now today my one big trouble's miles away . . . ' and, with every
step I take she gets further and further away.

How good it is to be alive, anyway, and sound in every limb – I
should be damned grateful for it. And this morning I am, grateful
for every flower, for every blade of grass; grateful for the sky and the
air and the sunlight on my face, just grateful to be alive. Why do I
always have to cloud everything over with my taciturn thoughts and
storms of the heart? Being on the road makes me so simple. I'm alive
and that's the main thing. Hello sheep, Hello goats, Hello flowers,
sky, rivers, fields, clouds, sun, stones. Hello everything in creation!
Hello *me!*

Those words of Blaise Cendrars clang like bells through my mind:

All life is only a poem, a movement. I am only a word, a lo-
gos, a depth, in the wildest, most mystical, most living sense . . .

Night's fallen. I've reached Valladolid. Hitching is proving very
difficult and so I'm going to seek out the railway station and jump
on a train. Oh that I could get to rue Bézout in time for the New
Year's party – fat chance of that, I know.

Here's the station. Now let's see, a train'll be coming through in
about seventy-five minutes, bound for San Sebastien – that's the one
I want. 'Mercury, guide, god of travellers, thieves . . . ' I begin an
incantation to the gods beneath my breath.

I'm hungry, mortally hungry; I'm going to have to beg or steal.
Here's a canteen. I'm sizing up the possibilities of stealing something from the counter, but all the food's behind glass and a vigilant-
looking woman at the till's eyeing me suspiciously and I'm retreat-
ing onto the platform. So I'll make for the streets. Drawing a deep
breath, I approach a neatly-dressed fellow with spectacles whom I

think looks benevolent but when I request of him a few pesetas for something to eat, he barks at me, 'You're hungry? Go and work.'

I shy away from him like a whipped dog.

'Go and work,' he says.

Work! Work and be as smug and heartless as him – I should have knocked him down and robbed him.

Hunger and this humiliating rebuke have whipped me up into an animal ferocity. My nerves are tingling, on edge: it's going to be a lean, cold night if I don't act. Why's everyone staring at me now, staring at me with suspicion, accusation? What have I done? It's what I'm about to do, that's what they're watching for . . . I take a deep breath, plunge through the doors of a restaurant, sit down at a table. I order soup and bread and wine – I eat like a wolf, drink – order more, eat, drink – and now . . . NOW! – RUN! – into the street, down an alley, RUN! keep running, don't stop, as far as you can, as far as the grim, neon-lit suburbs . . . You're safe now, safe from the city from which your fear hears only the sirens of police cars howling like jackals.

A biting wind's got up from the north, bringing with it an icy rain. I'm heading straight into it and though my thick coat and boots are warm they're not waterproof. My gloveless hands, as they grip the straps of my rucksack, are numb and blue with cold.

> With something akin to poetry
> this madness in me
> I trudge head bent like Chikusai
> into the biting wind.
>
> Basho

Drenched, I arrive in a small town through which a railway runs. There's a station here. I can dry off a bit and carry out yesterday's train hopping plan. All I want is to get to Paris as fast as I can.

What a cosy little waiting room. The timetable tells me I have a wait of four hours for the next train bound for San Sebastien. Oh well, I'll be out of the cold – I can dry out and thaw out over the little radiator. There's no one else in the waiting room or anywhere in the station: it's quite desolate. The wind whistles through the cracks in the door and the window, shaking and rattling them. I look out over the grey landscape, darkness falling. Propped up over the radiator, letting the warmth soak deliciously into me, I pull a book from my pocket and begin to read. *A Day in the Life of Ivan Denisovitch* by Solzhenitzin. Now here's being described real misery and despair – mine's not even worth mentioning in comparison to theirs. Nevertheless I envy those hapless chaps the meagre ration of porridge they're doled out daily – porridge. Oh what would I not do for a bowl of porridge. I need to take a leak and venture out onto the platform in search of a pissoir – a sign's swinging in the wind: *Caballeros* In the dimly lit interior as I stand at the trough pissing, what do I espy? Why, money!

Someone has thrown some coins into the urinal, I fish them out. They're slimy and smelly, needless to say (certainly not hot off Vulcan's forge) but they're money and not to be sniffed at. I have thirty odd pesetas in my hand, no mean sum when a pack of Celtas cigarettes sets you back but six pesetas. I scrub the green slime off them under the tap and set off in the direction of the town in search of some 'goodies': a packet of cigarettes, a giant-sized loaf, some wine.

The ticket office is open when I arrive back (oh dear, I haven't left enough for a ticket – oh well, I'll just have to board without one.) A handful of people are on the platform; the train's due to arrive in ten minutes or so. I stand on the platform smoking. It's stopped raining and stars have appeared in the sky. The gloom I felt before has lifted, like the clouds, and I feel light and happy; just a little apprehensive about the next step of the journey, 'Mercury, guide, god of travellers ...' I intone under my breath. Now a train can be heard approaching from down the line and, suddenly rearing into view and with a blaring blast of its siren, is pulling into the station and jerking to a halt. We're climbing on board. The station master is rushing out of his office, pulling on his hat. Some mail bags are being loaded onto the rear of the train, and then, with a wave of a flag and the shrill blast of a whistle, we're off.

We've gone barely fifty kilometres when, quite without warning, the guard is upon me demanding my ticket. I tell him I'm not in possession of one and that my chances of my ever being are slim as

I lack the necessary funds. He hurries on up the carriage telling me to wait there – he'll be back. There's a particularly mean-looking old man nearby who has witnessed this and no doubt relishes the situation I find myself in. He's staring at me insolently, a leer on his lips. He's going to make sure that I stay put until the guard comes back. But fortune again is on my side and right on cue for, in the middle of nowhere, the train slows down and comes to a halt. Without wasting a moment I open the door and with a big grin at the old man, whose mouth has dropped open in disbelief, say, 'Adios,' vehemently and jump out of the carriage, scrabbling down the embankment to find myself in a muddy, ploughed field through which I run as fast as the sucking earth will let me. I stop to watch the train, a long line of lights in the darkness, move off into the night. Walking, hitching, getting short lifts from time to time, managing to sustain myself with scraps of food I find here and there, the odd cigarette from a driver, I manage to keep body and soul together and my spirits from sinking into my boots. I manage a song sometimes, a chuckle. I pick up a lift which takes me up into the Pyrenees.

New Year's Eve finds me huddled up in an alcove outside the station at Bordeaux, snow falling, no party. And in the morning I jump aboard an express train going up to Paris, dodge the guard all the way and, by nightfall, am walking into number sixteen, rue Bézout.

'Where've you been? I'd baked a cake for your birthday,' says Ashley, 'but when I went to look for you, you weren't there – we've been very worried . . . ' he looks at me a little sternly, as an older brother might, 'you might have told us . . . '

'I'm sorry, I should have, I know; but I was in a mad hurry when I left . . . '

A bottle of wine and a glass are put before me,

'Tell us all about it.'

And so I tell them everything I've been telling you. And some other things as well.

Chapter 16

Castle on sand

Who now enjoys you, thinks you gold,
Dreams you will love him, – Still, still hold
No hand but his, nor know
Winds change.

Horace

To be here again, rue Bézout, my harbour in from the storm, the stormy ocean which rages relentlessly outside, to drop anchor awhile in this homely port with the sole two people in the whole wide world who understand my present plight. Zé will be away for another two weeks; it'll give me time to reflect, to collect myself. I'm far from confident about our romance – I feel we've had our heyday and that now it's becoming a downhill slide. 'One day I'll fly away . . . ' and it's becoming increasingly obvious to me that she means it. It dawned on me some while back that she doesn't have the same dreams ('illusions', she'd call them), as I do about our future. I know that I bungle many moments by vexing about a future which seems to be increasingly uncertain – moments when we've been blissfully in the present, lying together in each other's arms, walking hand in hand along the Seine, the spectre of doubt has intervened: is she going to be mine forever and ever? Or will she fly away? Where to? *Who* to?

Panic stricken, I've seized her: Do you love me? I've choked – only to be met with her silence, and the silence says it all and all the harmony that had existed between us shattered. O God in heaven, I'm clumsy in these matters.

I'm glad to be back in Paris after all, and relieved that she's far away, if truth be known. In fact, I dread her return.

But return she does.

'Did you feel that I neglected you in Lisbon?' she asks me.

'Yes, a little . . . '

'I'm sorry, Lala,' she says, tenderly, as we lie in bed; she's stroking my face and searching my eyes.

'I'm very proud that you came all that way and in such a dangerous fashion to be with me . . . very proud . . . no one ever did anything like that to be with me before.'

She's looking at me intently; she wants to say something, I can feel it, something she doesn't want to say. But at last,

'You mustn't . . . you mustn't love me so much. You know what I've always said, from the beginning . . . that I'll fly away one day . . .'

'Yes, I know Zé,' I hate to hear those words.

'It frightens me the way you love me! You . . . you don't seem to be happy like you used to be . . . I'm afraid for you.'

'I'm happy when I'm with you – being with you makes me happy . . .'

She stares at me, unable to hide her look of alarm.

The blood of my lost love is pounding in my heart. I touch and smell her now, her wrists pressed against the pillow. My shadowed face lifts from hers towards the moon. It's evening and the flower sellers line the boulevard to sell to me, the one who is damned. They're coming at me in waves of blood roses, their eyes accusing – of what? of what? I've given her everything. Not yet you haven't, not yet . . . the evening is darkening and closing in on me.

On the pavement with a bottle. In the evening sauntering. I raise you to my lips – I drink, I fall. Love is a smelter of hearts; dreams are ships on the rocks. Love is a furnace and I'll have another drink.

Ah, thousand-thought troubled. This night is nothing but pain. You're somewhere here in the city, in your silk dress, your eyes painted like blue moons, being dined, 'entertained' . . . I can feel only heartbreak and pain in every fibre.

The summer, the summer of seventy-seven hot, humid, a horrible sticky heat which undermines my nerves . . .

> In your hand I saw the note
> you quickly read and saw you smile
> and now you're telling me you'll be back late . . .

The police got me last night. I was making bouquets and selling them on the Boulevard St. Michel when they came up and told me to stop it or they'd run me in. 'Run me in then you fascists!' I'd had a fair bit to drink and being confronted by the C.R.S. infuriated me; they triggered off the fury that was already seething in me, because of Zé of course – nothing can upset me like she can – she'd said to me in the afternoon during a brief visit to my room,

'Don't be jealous if you see me in Paris with another man to-night – he's an old friend who's invited me out to dinner, just a friend – don't be jealous,' she added again emphatically. It was the very way she emphasised it that aroused my suspicion. How could I know there was nothing between them? It's nearly a month now that she's not come out to dinner with me – she's always too busy – like last night, 'too busy' with this bloody 'old friend' of hers . . He'd better not be that geezer that was all over her at the party the other night.

Anyway, I vented my fury on the cops who were standing be-fore me. Well, they weren't having any of that so they shunted me off down into the warren of alleys in St. Michel up one of which a whole bus load of C.R.S. lurked. They formed a ring around me about thirty of them, and under the orders of a thin-lipped, bespec-tacled superior, *'Tappe-le,'* he barked, a big thug rushed at me in the centre of the circle and began to pummel me with his fists. I had so much drink inside me that I didn't really feel anything, just blind fury. No doubt the treatment being meted out to me would have continued indefinitely until I was mashed to mincemeat but sud-denly the cop stopped, at a command from the superior, as a young couple turned down the street and headed towards us.

The cops pretended nothing was going on, but the couple knew very well it was, 'Viens avec nous,' they said to me and, one on either side of me, holding me, they took me away from the ugly scene and into a café, where they bought me a coffee.

'We knew they would stop hitting you when they saw us coming – it's illegal what they were doing and they don't want witnesses.'

I recounted to them what had happened and confessed to them that I had provoked the situation.

'They don't need much provoking,' they said.

. . . strutting in my room, the radio gets on my nerves with this French opera – I flick the switch and silence it. My thoughts I cannot flick the switch on them they are gadflies and they goad me to distraction. I wish yesterday hadn't happened, I wish it could be wiped off the face of the calendar. I was drunk and when I told her she was always larking about in Paris but never bothering about coming to see me, boy, did she get mad! she came back with: 'if you think I'm just larking about, if you think I have nothing more important to do than come and see you all the time if you think that . . . ' Well then she ground me to powder right there on the pavement in front of her so that I was left raving and trying to convince her that I didn't mean it like that, which of course I had but even if I hadn't nothing I could do or say could reprieve me now, nothing could persuade her to look upon me favourably – just remember trying to hold her and her pushing me away, then hurrying to the metro, and I distraught sitting on a bench and feeding the pigeons with the remains of the loaf I'd had for lunch with that fateful bottle of *Jenlain*. Think I called in at a bar in Montparnasse on my way back, and after that putting a franc in a telephone underneath the Bouquet d'Alésia, and thank god she didn't answer! then nothing after that. Now, let me think . . . The history of Paris from the time of the year one . . . What's that got to do with it? I'm here now am I not – it's irrelevant the history of Paris, I know but I'm just trying to distract my mind that's all, it was a voice that popped the history of Paris into my skull, I don't know anything about the history of Paris except that I suppose that because there's a river here they built a town on it and a few bridges over it and populated it with frogs all croaking *oui oui* or *oc oc* or however they pronounced it then. And they all lived comfortably ever after until in the fifteenth century Villon came along and insulted them all—and jolly good for him! And then in 1453 the Gypsies entered Paris—no, that was the year that the Turks toppled the towers of Byzantium . . . then the fall of the Bastille in 1789, that must have been fun, get drunk and join the mob, that would have been something to take my mind off things, to get this rage out of me! But no, the only date of relevance to me is 1976 when she first walked through the door and I beheld her, radiant as the moon, as a dog shouted from a distant hamlet and time stopped—and I wish it had stopped forever right there, but it didn't, it kept moving mercilessly on! Monsieur, monsieur I've had a disgusting vision . . . Oh, do you want to go to confession do you want to tell us of this disgusting vision that has risen up before thine inner eye? No, not this year, non non definitely not! it's just that it rose up like a genie out of that bottle of rouge. . . O unbearable one fluttering at the corner of my mind, faceless tormentor, bloodless ghoul, horrible and merciless and cruel . . . and and . . . O kindly one have a drink on me, gorge yourself on my blood . . . O kindly one just let me have her and know she is mine forever and know that I occupy all her thoughts just as she does mine and I can forget my troubles and live again. . .

Ah, the Paris night! Everyone rushing around electrified in the flood of light, swimming in the sea of a city steeped in passion. *Liaisons dangereuses*! *Crimes passionnels*! Romantic Paris! *Ah oui, tres romantique, mon ami*! It was once—I tell you I've had my share of romance here—oh yes, my friend, you can be sure of that—but now I need to have another drink to bring a touch of that old-time magic back, to put some of that fire back into my veins . . .

Ho, in my hey-day (not so long ago) I walked head high, along these boulevards with my Helen who launched a thousand white sailed dreams in me—Oh listen, buddy! She was radiant as the moon—all the tides of my blood swelled towards her . . . And now, down here by the fountain, this sweltering summer, I go through such strange moods—she's always on my mind you see—always—I can't think of a moment when she's not. What's your story? Something similar? Oh well you understand what I'm talking about then.

Yes, thank you – a cigarette's just what I'm in need of. You say you knifed someone for taking your girl? Blimey, that's somewhat extreme, mate.

Amidst the sea of faces I see only hers. On the pavement full of feet, I see only her red shoes. Is that not her head and shoulders in the sixty-eight bus heading for Châtelet? I must chase it, over the bridge, over the flow of the Seine, over the hill and far away.

Night has cloaked me in black. A black so thick the stars cannot peep; only the moon, a murky red, looms like a lantern in the dark. I want to submerge myself in sleep and suspend thought. Look at me, Christ! My head hangs on the ground and my feet drag along behind me – can I blame her for turning away from me? No, but it's precisely because of her that I'm sinking. God, can't you see that? Precisely, because she torments me with doubt – because she'll never tell me one way or the other about things – about whether she loves me, whether we have a future together, so how can I be resolute? I mean, listen, to keep her I'd do anything, anything – even go to work in a bank or some such institution, I want her that much. She just has to say, 'Yes, I too love you and want to be with you forever, just find a way of supporting us,' and I'd be lined up with a necktie on (might as well be a noose if I think about it) applying for a job in a bank – not that I'd ever get one.

But she never gives me any cause for hope. And so I'm sunk to this: lifting a bottle to my lips at the fountain of St. Michel, in the company of others, some of whom perhaps had trodden a similar path.

It comes like a bombshell when she announces she's going away on holiday. She's had an invitation from somebody, she won't say whom or where she's going, only that she'll be away for a couple of months.

'But . . . but . . . you can't!'

'What do you mean, I can't?' she says angrily, 'am I tied to you?'

No, she's not; but I'm tied to her, in iron bonds. What a miserable, pathetic slave I've become.

It's a hot sultry afternoon. I'm sitting on the edge of the bed, my head in my hands. Some pigeons coo in the yard and on the street a motorbike roars by. How much more pain can I take? She's washing herself at the basin, pulling on her skirt, her blouse, her shoes. Watching her from the corner of my eye I feel I no longer have any right to her body, no more claim on her heart—it's suddenly gone stone cold.

> . . . you have all about you a distracted air
> you're making your face up but not for me
> in a moment I'll spring up and kick down the door.

I let her go.

'*Adeus* . . . ' she says as she lets herself, without a smile, through the door. Numb, as though all the blood and warmth have been drained out of my heart and out of my soul, I can't even cry, the well of my tears is dry. Sitting here, listening to the sounds in the room: the ticking of a clock, the creaking of the floorboards contracting in the heat, a fly hurling itself at the four corners of the room, I have no thoughts: they've stopped, as has my heart.

The room's grown dark. Dark as the grave. In the mirror, I'm white as a ghoul.

No hurried packing of things and rushing to pursue her this time—no, I wouldn't know where to follow her . . . or . . . or . . . perhaps I would, but I don't want to think about it.

'Better have a drink and make some plans for yourself,' I say to my reflection. I take a bottle of wine from the cupboard and pour myself a drink.

Ha, that's better, the precious liquid's putting the blood, the fire, back into my veins.

I'll get the hell out of here!

Chapter 17

Barcelona

The Ramblas, main artery of the city, with its stalls selling flowers, selling birds in cages, its lottery sellers: blind men tapping their sticks, calling out numbers with the promise of wealth '*mañana*' – the Ramblas with its flowing crowd, its beseeching beggars, its hawkers selling matches and shoe laces and soap; its entertainers, musicians, acrobats, fire eaters; its thieves mingling with the crowd (one bolts out and dives down an alley – shouting, confusion, police arrive – too late, far too late.) And, running along the entire length of this teeming thoroughfare, cafés with marble tables spill out onto the pavements, with their tourists and their dandies and their prostitutes. There's nowhere in the world like the Ramblas and, if you linger a while, leaning against the railings of the metro station you'll see the world pass along it, and a blind man with a stick tapping the pavement and calling out '*Waddi, waddi!*'

I've never been able to work out what it means.

Just arrived, I'm flat broke. I lack the means for a jug of wine. I'm going to have to change this state of affairs. I find a park which has a few flowers and I set to work making bouquets. I'll have no problem persuading the young couples out for an evening stroll to buy my product. But I'm mistaken – not the slightest interest is shown and, very pissed off, I fling the flowers which have drooped and wilted into the gutter; there's nothing for it but to go begging. This works and now I have enough for some wine.

I run into a fellow called Klaus who, like me, is sauntering along the Ramblas with a bottle in his hand. He's a young German from Düsseldorf who speaks good English. He's leaving for Ibiza this evening at ten o'clock. As the time's only about six we decide to have supper together. We find a very cheap restaurant where we eat well and get quite drunk. I walk with him down to the harbour where he boards the ship just in time and, as I wave goodbye, I think to myself I'll never see him again. I'm wrong. Ten days later I'm sitting on the steps outside the post office when suddenly I hear 'Hi Lala,' and looking up see Klaus smiling all over his face.

We retire to the little restaurant and get very drunk on the potent wine from the great barrels. And Klaus gets very, very drunk. He falls off his chair, crawls around in the sawdust on the floor, crashes into tables, puts his arm round the waiter and tries to waltz around the cramped little tavern before dashing for the door and out onto the street where he pukes up all over a motorbike parked outside. I rush out and pick him up from where he's fallen into his own wine-coloured vomit and manage to drag him to a pension. I take him up the steep, narrow steps (which is not easy) to the reception at the top where an old woman is seated at a table. I advance with Klaus to the table, clutching him by the arm, desperately trying to stop him from keeling over, and tell the alarmed-looking woman my friend urgently needs a room for the night as he's very tired. At this Klaus collapses onto the floor and I jerk him up to his feet re-iterating that he really is very tired and needs a good night's sleep. Her face is the picture of disbelief and disapproval – 'Pasaporte,' she snaps – and I search my drunken friend for his particulars and start to write them down on a form she's shoved to me across the desk. Klaus, meanwhile, who's been hanging his head in silence suddenly springs for the door and rushes down the stairs. 'Uno momento,' I cry to the woman and leap down the stairs after him. He's puking up again in the courtyard. I drag him back upstairs and explain to the woman, whose face has fallen even further, that he really is extremely tired and he must have a bed immediately. He's led upstairs by a boy and I go off to find myself a place for the night.

I venture into the warren of alleys that lead off *Las Ramblas.* This is the world of Jean Genet, this his sinister underworld of Barcelona.

I can just see cruel-hearted Stilitano, the Serbian deserter from the Foreign Legion, with his one-gloved arm leaning at the bar of one of these dim *bodegas* from which the fumes of alcohol and cigarette smoke belch forth as though they were the fumes from the infernal regions. Low-looking characters, drunks, transvestites and drugged-looking fiends slouch at the counter. Jean, sad-looking, sits at a table, a vial of some concoction or other before him and a heart breaking for the savage attentions of Stilitano.

However hard you look you can't see the stars from down here, even though it's always night, nothing can reach down into these depths. The only stars are from the juke boxes which are flashing or the glint of a knife or of a needle – you watch your Ps and Qs in the labyrinth of Barcelona.

I'm tipping back murky white wine at one or two pesetas the vial. An extremely incongruous looking fellow wanders in from the street. I'm surprised that he's got this far without having been robbed; with his lankiness, his long blonde hair, his beard and spectacles he looks like a student from some northern realm.

Coming straight up to me, a look of relief on his face at seeing another foreigner, he asks me if I know of somewhere to sleep, somewhere that's safe – he's been sleeping in the park and has already had his money taken. He's penniless now.

I'll be sleeping on the beach – there are thieves there, too, and rats . . .'

'Can you show me where the beach is?' he asks.

'Well, yes – but I won't be going there until late.'

'Then I will stay here with you,'

'Ok – if you want.'

His name's Bert, he hails from Enschedé in the east of Holland. Having finished his studies – computer technology (Christ, whatever next?) he's now qualified as a fully fledged computer operator (a programmer is apparently what they're called) and I'm doomed to spend the rest of the evening with him.

'Would you like a drink?' I realise by the way he's just standing there rather awkwardly that he probably hasn't two brass pesetas to rub together.

'Oh, thank you,' he brightens up; we clink glasses and drink.

'Do you . . . er . . . not get stolen from?' he asks me.

'I have been stolen from many times in the past, but I'm a little more wily now.'

'What is "wily"?'

'Clued up. '

'Glued up?' he looks astonished.

'No, no,' I laugh, 'not glued up, clued up, clever, wise.'

'Ah.'

'I'm still not very clever, but I'm cleverer than I used to be.'

We laugh. 'Have another drink . . . ' I'm beginning to enjoy his company – his constant look of surprise endears him to me. Glad of the wine, he's relaxing, beginning to look less lost than when he stepped over the threshold, less bewildered.

'Where did you put the money whilst you slept?' I ask him.

'Under my head, my pillow . . . '

'Your head can slip to one side of a pillow; whilst you sleep your body leads a life of its own – a thief will just watch and wait.'

I recount an incident that had happened to me once in Rimini; I had no money at the time so I didn't have to hide anything but my passport which I'd put in a plastic bag and buried in the sand underneath me. Suddenly in the dead of night, I was awoken by a movement beneath my pillow, '*Oi, che fai?*' I shouted at a fellow bending over me, his hand rifling about under my pillow.

'Ah, *niente, niente.*'

'Listen, if your are looking for money I don't have any, okay.'

'*Bene,*' he said backing away into the shadows. I fell asleep only to be awoken again by the hand worming its way about beneath my pillow, tugging at something.

'Oi!' I shouted springing up and facing him in the darkness, 'I told you I have no money – *non capisci?*'

'Well, what's this?' he had the face to ask me.

'What's what?'

'This . . . '

Now he was pulling out the thing which he'd been trying to get at, in order to show me.

'Oh that,' I laughed, 'that's my belt.'

It was a leather belt buckle that must have felt like a wallet to him.

'Ah, *una cintura . . .* ' he seemed almost a little embarrassed.

'You see, I told you I have no *soldi*. I'm a poor man.'

'*Scusi . . .* ' he said, his tone apologetic now, 'I won't bother you again, *amico*, and I'll tell my friend, who's also robbing on the beach tonight, to leave you in peace.'

'Thank-you,' I said, '*grazie,*' and then we both laughed, laughed hard and, shaking hands, bade each other goodnight.

'*Buona notte, amico, buona notte . . .* '

'That's a funny story,' says Bert, looking astonished; 'I didn't even see the thief running away in the park last night.'

'Was it a lot of money?' I ask him.

'Phew,' I gasp upon him telling me. 'Then, why on earth were you sleeping in the park and not in a pension?'

'To save money.'

'We'd better have another drink,' I turn to the barman. '*Dos vasos de vino, por favor . . .* and now, Bert,' I announce draining my glass in one tip, 'I'm broke.'

'Broke?' he looks at me alarmed.

'No,' I laugh, 'it doesn't mean I'm broken, not of one piece – it's an expression, it means "to have no money." '

'Ah, so you have no money, too?'

'Either, you mean,' I correct him pedantically, 'yes, momentarily, but I will make some more.'

'You are money-making here?'

'Yes, I'm money making on the streets – begging.'

'BEGGING?' Bert blurts out, flabbergasted.

'Yes.'

I stoop down, pick up my rucksack and sling it over my shoulder. 'And so I have to go . . . '

'Could . . . could I come with you?' Bert's all eagerness, 'watch you, see how you do it?'

'If you like . . . '

And so we head towards the *Ramblas* and I tell him how this particular form of money-making is done.

'And it turns out?'

'You mean does it work? Yes, watch.'

A likely-looking fellow's heading towards us, brightly dressed, a man of about sixty, bald headed, jovial looking. I take the plunge, *'Por favor, señor . . . Tiene un poco de moneda para comer, tengo hambre?'*

He looks at me, smiling amiably and, reaching into his pocket, hands me a hundred peseta note.

'Muchas gracias,' a hundred pesetas is a fair bit of money. I glimpse the look of astonishment on my new friend's face.

'You're together?' the man asks me, pointing at Bert who's a step or two away.

'Yes, we're friends.'

'Come along then, both of you, I'll take you to a restaurant.'

'You see, it works,' I say gleefully to Bert as we stumble out of the restaurant full of food and wine, having bidden farewell with warm thanks to our benefactor. Bert's more than just impressed, he's dumbfounded. I'm glad that he's witnessed begging at its best.

'I'm going to try it tomorrow,' he announces as we head towards the rat-and-thief-infested beach to sleep.

Now the beach of Barcelona must be one of the filthiest in the world. As you swim in its putrid water you're likely to collide with lumps of excrement, used rubber johnnies, blobs of oil, plastic bags which wrap themselves around your limbs like octopi. Nevertheless, upon arising in the morning, Bert and I religiously take a bath in the quagmire, to freshen ourselves after the previous night's heavy drinking in town. Besides, it's the only way we can have an all-over wash. On the way to the *Ramblas* each morning we pass a wrought-iron fountain with a handle which one pumps whilst the other washes face and teeth and hair. And so, by the time we arrive at the Ramblas and sit ourselves at a café in the Plaza Real for a coffee, we're fresh as daisies.

Bert's taken to panhandling with an ease and expertise which amazes me. We do a morning 'swoop' on the Ramblas, assemble the requisite amount for lunch and retire to a tavern, which lies in the thick of the labyrinth. The establishment's called *Los Galegos* and is run by an old chap, Pepé and his son José. The doors open at noon and Bert and I take our places at a table. Calling first for a jug of wine which José siphons off from one of the massive wooden barrels that line the walls. It's the kind of place to which I naturally gravitate, dim and dark, one's eyes needing time to adjust before they can make out the décor of this dive: the little bar at which old Pepé (*Tio Pepé*, we call him) sits and scrutinises you as you step over the threshold and into this oasis of refreshment with its enormous barrels round the walls, the sawdust on the floor, the wooden tables and chairs with their paper table-cloths upon which José tots up your bill, the grimy yellow ceiling, stained from years of tobacco smoke and a million cigarettes from which a pitiful, benighted canary sings from a cage. All this and then the smell of cooking, of fried fish and garlic, of pig's balls, *bolas de cerdo*, yes, pig's balls, *jamòn*, and the smell of wine (and urine if you're at a table near the gents) pervading all.

Let's have a look at the menu which is chalked up on the wall:

Caldo 5 pta
Carne assado 25 pta
Bolas de cerdo 40 pta
Bacalhau 55 pta
Bifstek 25 pta
Pollo (chacachacachac) 35 pta
Huevos fritos (2) 10 pta
Tortilla español 20 pta
" " frances 15 pta
Ensalada mista 15 pta
Patatas 10 pta
Legumbres 15 pta
Postres 10 pta
Pan y coverta 5 pta

I'll have *caldo*, which is a thin soup, the water poured off the vegetables, with some potato and cabbage adrift in it – it's good and hot; and then I'll have a *tortilla español* – a Spanish omelette, filled with potato and onion – and with that I'll have a salad and chips and with this amount of victuals in my belly I shall be guaranteed impervious to starvation today.

Bert's having more or less the same as me except that he's having the *pollo chaca chacachac* as he calls it – the 'chaca chaca chac' meaning cut into pieces as he makes a cutting motion with his hands – instead of the omelette. I guess he hopes to put a bit of flesh on that scrawny frame of his. We call for more wine and set to drinking and feasting. Other customers come in and the place is soon packed.

'I like this life,' says Bert, as we chink glasses, 'I didn't know it existed.'

I smile at the way he puts it, 'Everything exists,' I tell him, 'except nothing – nothing does not exist, as Parmenides pointed out.'

'Who?'

'He was a Greek philosopher who made a journey to the underworld in a chariot and met Persephone, queen of Hades, who instructed him in the secrets of the world and told him what I just said.'

'Oh, it sounds interesting. It makes me think . . . ' he pauses, contemplating the wine in his glass before him, 'it makes me think that life should be fuller than the one I'm headed for, the one I've been told is the correct and proper way to live: to go to an office every day . . . that's what all my studies are leading to. I'll have a good job, will make good money . . . but how boring it will be,' he looks up at me, 'don't you agree?'

How could I not?

There's a commotion at the door: a drunkard who'd come in and started falling over the tables is being ejected by José, who shouts, '*Fora*,' and shoves him onto the street.

'I don't know what I'll do when I go back to Holland – I am already committed to a company, making programs . . . programs . . . ' he says distractedly, lifting his glass of wine and taking a swig, 'my feeling is not to like to spend my life with a company making programs, my heart's not there,' he exclaims excitedly, 'my heart's not there.'

One morning when on our way from the beach to Los Galegos a vehicle loaded up with pumpkins passed us, with a loudspeaker mounted on the roof of the cab it was crying out, '*Calabazas! Calabazas!*' Gypsies, no doubt, hawking their wares around the houses.

'Pumpkins,' I exclaimed to Bert, 'I had a brief affair with a pumpkin.'

'An affair, what is that?'

'A love affair.'

'A love affair, you mean you . . . ?'

'Yes,' I called back as we battled through the traffic, 'I'll tell you about it when we get to the restaurant.'

Once there, I waited until the wine was brought and we'd charged our glasses, before embarking on the story, 'It was about this time of year, early autumn, I was walking along a coastal path somewhere south of Rome. The sun was going down into the sea and a great round full moon, the colour, and indeed the shape, of a pumpkin, was rising on the other side of the sky – you know how the sun and moon are as though on a see-saw at that time of the month: one goes down as the other comes up. Anyway, as I came over the crest of a hill I found myself walking alongside a field of pumpkins, big ones, deep orange, ripe, erotic. '

'Erotic?' Bert glanced at me his mouth open and with an expression almost of alarm, as though he might be in the presence of some kind of sexual deviant or, at best, someone who suffered from delusions.

'They looked voluptuous and as seductive as women lying in that field, in the soft blue air and under a full moon,' I went on, 'it was all very romantic.'

'Romantic?' exclaimed Bert in disbelief, 'pumpkins romantic?'

'They can be, they can be whatever you want them to be, with a little imagination of course; and I really wanted one of them to turn into a woman – I was young and so shy and unsure of myself when it came to real women – but I had a vivid imagination to make up for it, I mean, look at that Greek sculptor, Pygmalion, who fell in love with an ivory statue of a woman he'd carved and who, with the help of Venus, made to come alive,'

I don't think Bert knew what I was on about here but I went on, 'The one I singled out seemed to be the biggest and most voluptuous in the whole field as though she was the queen. Looking from side to side, just to make sure there was no one about, I made my way stealthily towards her and, kneeling down beside her I took out my trusty pen-knife and cut a hole in her. She was soft and warm inside.'

'Phew,' Bert's jaw had dropped to the table. 'That's a funny story,' he said.

Having had our fill of food and wine we roll laughingly down the Ramblas – it's about four o'clock and, having spent all the money, we start another stint of begging so as to provide for the evening in the *cervezerias* along the Ramblas, where we drink jugs of beer and eat *tapas* at the zinc bars.

Every night we pass this young Mexican fellow (a Mercurial look-ing fellow if ever I saw one) who installs himself on the pavement with a big sign before him, illuminated with candles and minia-ture icons of Jesus and the Virgin Mary so that it looks more like a church ceremony than a begging operation.

'I'm a Mexican,' it announces, 'all my money has been stolen and I want to return to my country. Can you please help me by giv-ing me what you can afford. God be with you and Mary the Holy Mother of Jesus.'

Well, he's just raking it in – he could go to Mexico and back fifty times with the amount he's making in an evening. But it's all going up his arm, we see him later in the lavatory of a bar shooting it up.

'Let's try it the Mexican's way,' says Bert.

'Christ, you're not embarrassed to sit on the street like that, like a hungry dog?' I don't like the idea at all, but here's Bert, the computer programmer, keen as mustard.

'No, I want to try it,' he says, and, finding a piece of cardboard we write in Spanish the message to the passers-by. We keep it simple:

Tengo hambre –
Necessito dineros para comer.
Muchas gracias.

I'm hungry –
I need money to eat.
Many thanks.

And so Bert takes the plunge and, although we've just staggered bloated with victuals and wine out of the tavern, he looks as he sits there on the pavement, like a victim of drought and famine and I, who have positioned myself a few yards away as a look-out for police patrols, watch amazed at the number of people who bend down and give the Dutchman money. He manages a wink at me through the crowd: it's working. I'm dreading my turn at this game but, now that Bert's started it, I know that I'll have to do my stint. And so, after some thirty minutes or so, I relieve him at his post and, hideously uncomfortable, sit there, holding my belly as though I'm suffering severe malnutrition. Looks of all kinds are cast in my direction: some hostile, some sympathetic. From time to time someone stoops down to ask me what's happened. This question makes me feel more pitiable than ever – as though I'm completely pathetic and helpless. But I just have to put up with this self-imposed humiliation, have to pretend it's not me sitting here – not the 'me' I take myself to be anyway.

And now, with this excruciating part of the day done, our pockets full of ill-gained loot, we race for a bar and tip gallons of cool beer down our parched gullets.

Bert and I have become inseparable and I'm more than glad to have his company; the fun and revelry we have together stops me brooding over Zé–Zé who seems a million miles away. Strange how carefree and happy I feel whenever she's far away and out of mind.

One evening we're drinking in a *cervezeria*, just off the Ramblas, when suddenly there's a stampede of people rushing down the street outside. The barman runs to the door and starts pulling down the iron shutters. A demonstration. We want to get out – demonstrations are a riot, especially when you've got some drink in you. The crowd had bolted down this street from the Ramblas, where the battle's raging, and now it's filtering cautiously back there. Bert and

I mingle in with the drift. We get out onto the Ramblas to be faced by a thick cordon of riot police.

'What's it all about?' I ask a student in the crowd.

A young Basque has been tortured to death in a prison cell, he tells us – that doesn't sound right so we join in the chorus and start shouting at the police,

'*Fascistas! Cabrons!* Death to Franco!' They open fire on us, *Pam! Pam! Pam!* with rubber bullets. Confusion, uproar, screaming. We run for the alley, in blind panic – someone's been stuck by a bullet and is being dragged along by his friends; he's doubled up, groaning. The shooting dies down: again we make our way up to the Ramblas shouting, 'Fascist bastards! Kill Franco! Long live the Basques!'

Again a volley of fire. A bullet whistles two inches from my face and clatters into the boarding of a shop window behind me. That scares me, I tell you. They may be rubber, these bullets, but if one strikes you on the bonce it's going to leave you with a deranged brain for the rest of your life; the better part of valour's to retreat now.

'Let's get out of here,' I shout to Bert above the din.

One late afternoon, just staggered from the Galego's tavern to take up our pitch for the evening's 'money-making', a young woman comes along . She's bending down talking to Bert who's sitting on the pavement doing the first stint. I can see Bert getting rather exasperated. I move closer to see if I can get a snatch of the conversation. Bert, whose face looks quite desperate, points to me and I hear the woman exclaim, 'But he can come too.' Bert motions to me to come over, 'This kind woman has invited us to a restaurant to eat . . . '

'To EAT!' I exclaim, dismayed – all we had in mind was to drink.

'She insists . . . '

'Yes, I take you for meal – you're hungry – you must eat properly.'

Reluctantly we follow her to a taxi rank, the restaurant she has in mind will take a taxi ride to get to. Bert quickly fills me in, 'I couldn't get rid of her,' a tone of apology in his voice. 'the begging was going very well.'

'Yes, it's a Friday evening.'

'When first she said 'come to a restaurant,' I said, 'I can't – I have to make money.'

'Make money for what?' she asked.

'For food . . . ' I said.

'So I will take you to a restaurant and you'll eat.'

'She had me there, what could I say? I couldn't say I wasn't hungry really, I was just pretending.'

'No, I suppose you couldn't.'

'So then, pointing at you, I said, "But I'm with my friend and . . . and . . . "'

'"But he can come too," she said.'

And now here we are, off by taxi to stuff more food down our gullets. I guess we were in the wrong place at the wrong time! Oh well . . .

The taxi takes us all over town: god knows where we alight at last, neither of us know the Barcelona that exists more than a stone's throw from the Ramblas. We walk into an elegant restaurant, where the waiters, dressed in smart red jackets and bow ties, snap to attention before us, causing the Dutchman and I to feel, with our unkempt appearance and ragged attire, like fish out of water, out of our river, the Ramblas. Dish after dish comes. Thank God there's plenty of beer with which to wash it down – we'd never manage it otherwise. And then, with our bellies bloated and heads reeling, the young lady, Rosa, puts us in a taxi which takes us back to the Ramblas.

We've agreed to meet her at noon tomorrow – she'll take us out to lunch.

And it happens regularly that we're taken off by taxi to some chic restaurant and lunched or dined. She has an antique business which is thriving; money's no object. It's after one of these luncheons and we've all three of us arrived by taxi back at the Ramblas, staggering under the weight of the food we've eaten and swaying as a result of the wine, that I, walking a little ahead of the other two, turn around to see them arm in arm, dove-like, the Dutchman cooing in her ear. Here we go, a little romance is in the air.

And sure enough it is; they become lovers and, if I may at this point jump ahead in time as I may not have the occasion to mention it later, they'll get married. And so, Bert, begging for beer money, has obtained a wife.

The season's on the change. It's mid-September. The leaves are turning brown and are beginning to fall from the trees which line the Ramblas. Autumn's coming; I can feel it in my blood, and in my mood. The old anxiety is welling up to the surface once more, Paris looming up in my thoughts again . . .

Bert has to return to Holland: his contract's due to commence and, now that he's considering marriage, he's going to have to be 'realistic' he says, a little embarrassed, to me. He has become more preoccupied and less carefree – just like I have now that the spectre of a return to Paris has begun to haunt me. Rosa and I have gone along with Bert to the bus station. It's a blustery day, the first real taste of autumn, as though it's timed, to tell us holidays are over, 'back to business' – I shudder to think of the 'business' before me. Rosa is in tears as the bus drives off with Bert's bearded, bespectacled head leaning from the window, and his skinny white hand waving in the air.

The next day, anxiety clutching at my heart, I set out for Paris.

Chapter 18

The Fountain of St. Michel

Stepping off the train I'm seized by dark forebodings which increase as I descend the station steps and feel the full impact of Paris and all that it portends. My impending fate is written into every stone, every tree, every leaf that I scatter with my feet. Wrapped in a black cloud I head for rue Bézout. If only I didn't have to be again who I was. If only I didn't have to have the same longings, the same feelings. I may as well be wishing not to have to live any longer, it adds up to about the same thing. I think of a line of Whitman, 'For these are the days which have to happen to you . . . '

Maybe one day I'll know why they had to happen. Maybe . . . if there's some kind of a divine plan to my life . . . if everything's for a purpose in the end . . . maybe it all fits – But I can't see the fucking point in anything now.

At number sixteen, rue Bézout, I'm faced with a little note upon the door, 'In Lisbon until the end of October.'

I freeze at the sight of it. Now what? No grub, no wine, no welcome. Nothing. *Rien, absolument rien de tout!* Just nothing! Nothing but the streets to go out into, with empty pockets. Zé, too, will still be away . . .

I head back down to the Latin Quarter, hands in pockets, eyes on the ground. What am I going to do now? Stay in Paris? Head back south? Retreat to England? I haven't the heart for anything – all that seems to have gone. A dark dread is gnawing away at me and working its way to the surface. A kind of beast with terrible teeth and tusks is tearing at the rock beneath the pavement on which I walk . . .

Drifting into the company gathered around the fountain I'm passed a bottle and drink. Hmm, that takes the edge off my misery – the wind loses its bite as I begin to glow inside. Darkness has fallen. I'll be needing some more of this liquor: the outlook's too bleak without it. I'll have to do a bit of beggary.

And so with, *'T'as pas cent balles, s'il te plaît?'* I'm approaching the passers-by; it's working – I'm getting enough to drink myself into a stupor before wandering off to look for a place to sleep. Not under the bridges, though the river's but a stone's throw from the fountain, for the quays of the Seine are exposed to all kinds of prowlers in the shadows: thieves, perverts, police . . .

Slipping into a doorway on the rue Bonaparte I find a cubbyhole under the stairs and curl up and sleep drunkenly. At dawn I'm awoken by a concierge screaming she's going to call the police. Shouting back at her, 'One day, madame, you'll know what it's like to be tired as death and have nowhere to lay your head – because your conscience won't let you rest, you bitch, you mean-hearted, stinking bitch!'

I become so furious that I nearly strike her.

At the counter of a café in the rue St. André des Arts drinking a coffee, I'm shaking with rage. What's becoming of me that this hag can have me screaming at her like a madman?

I'm losing sight of myself, I realise as I stare at the unshaven, uncertain, anxious, apparition in the mirror behind the bar – I'm losing sight of myself . . .

I become a regular drinker around the fountain – certainly not 'the fountain of life', nor is it 'the elixir of eternal youth' that we drink: it's more like 'the concoction of eternal damnation' – it being the surest way to madness, via delirium. It comes in bottles with stars around the neck sporting such names as: Gevéor, Préfontaine, La Petite Villageoise . . .

We're a mixed bag, an assorted lot, odds and sods, dregs, straggling about the fountain in every fit and state of drunkenness, like the flotsam and jetsam swirling in a stagnant eddy in the river of humanity that flows along the Boulevard St. Michel. We're at once a threat, a nuisance, an uncomfortable reminder to the passer-by who, sitting pretty though he might be at present, might not always be.

Not a man amongst us could be said to have chosen this existence (remember my aim as I set out on the glorious road was 'to find Romance and Adventure') Not a man amongst us had ever in his past said to himself, 'One day, if all works out, I shall flounder about the fountain of St. Michel in a permanently drunken stupor.' The wheels of fate have put every man jack of us here. Every one has a story; I've heard hundreds of them, each one on its ten thousandth telling, embellished out of all proportion, though at the kernel of it lies the stark truth like a clenched fist, and despair where once there had been a dream.

Guy, who fancies himself as some kind of gangster, is about the lowliest type you can find around here; his gangsterism extends little further than the environs of the fountain: he'll swipe your wine, your cigarettes and anything he can lay his hand on should he get inside your pocket. I don't like him and he knows it – nor does any-one else for that matter – but I've heard a strange story about him, though it's one he never tells himself. During the disturbances of May '68 he had been a student, had had ideals and he wasn't afraid to follow them through. But then, snatched from the midst of a crowd by the police, he grassed on his accomplices and by the time he was released had undergone a profound personality change. No longer the anarchist locked in deadly combat with capitalism he's now a self-styled gangster out to get as much capital for himself as he possibly can – from whom it doesn't matter, rich or poor, it's the same to him. He's known as '*Guy le Gangster*'. I've rarely come upon such a sneaky character and that scar puts me in mind of . . . well, you remember that geezer in the alley in Montmartre? Yeah, him.

By contrast there's this sensitive-looking soul, with a straggly beard and cracked spectacles, who tends to be alone but is often caught up in absurd disputes and sometimes reduced to tears by Guy who torments him without mercy. Moved to pity I've stepped in once or twice to defend '*le prof*', as he's known as, usually to grab

back the spectacles which Guy's snatched off him and is balancing on the end of his nose or threatening to crunch underfoot.

'Without those I'm lost, really and truly lost,' says the poor old fellow tearfully, 'I'm lost anyway,' he adds.

It's not a happy tale he relates to anyone who's prepared to listen, the details of which haunt him, 'The moment I came through the door and found them in each others' arms in our bed.'

He had been a professor at one of the universities, I forget which one, somewhere in the south, perhaps Montpéllier, 'Professor of Greek and Latin—I knew Homer backwards, could recite Virgil standing on my head. I was headed straight for the top of my profession, it was everything to me. I had a young wife, beautiful, everything a man can desire. I took her for granted. One of my students—uncannily like this bastard Guy, as though he's returned to haunt me—took advantage of my neglect of my wife. I had returned home from a lecture early that day, a headache.'

Here's Marie—everyone's after Marie, trying to get her drunk and get into her knickers under the bridges. But Marie doesn't drink and she's trying to stop all of us from becoming alcoholics. It's her mission here at the fountain. It was because of drink she got raped so many times by all those men who gave her money to keep her mouth shut—if she'd been in her right mind they'd never have got near her.

'You were a drunken whore, that's what you were,' Guy shouts at her, taking the greatest delight in reminding her of what she's trying so hard to forget, 'and you don't need to drink anymore because you're demented enough without it.'

Left to herself she sits for hours humming to herself and going through the motions of sewing. 'I'm making warm clothes for my man—he's away at the war,' she tells me when I ask her what she's doing, 'and you—why are *you* always drinking?' she looks at me with huge, bright eyes.

There was work going on in the building opposite and the café was full of dust and noise. I'd ordered *un express* which I'd downed in one gulp. That was hours ago when I first sat down at this marble-topped table and had taken up my pen and tried to write in my hard-backed note book, my *'cahier des ecoliers'* and nothing much had come but I kept moving my hand and things did start coming but now I'll put my pen down for my hand is beginning to ache, it's been moving for a long time, 'that's because you're not used to sitting down and writing,' I tell myself. It's true.

I shall order another coffee, I have enough money and perhaps I can get into my second wind though god help me if I can't, I'll have bought a coffee for nothing and must sit here for another two hours in this café filled with dust and noise to get my money's worth.

I get on quite well with the waiter, he doesn't look at me in the way some of them do–perhaps he thinks I'm a serious writer, even a well-known one, in spite of or perhaps because of my attire. (I must get the heel on my shoe fixed, I sound like a cart horse trudging about) *'LE MOT JUSTE,'* I cry.

'Non monsieur, c'est un café noir'.

How was he able to read my thoughts or did I really cry out? He has been to Italy, he tells me. There the waiters cry out *'UNA CAPOOCHA,'* at the top of their lungs if you order a cappuccino. I know about that and I chuckle. Italians are okay but they're a nation of cake eaters and don't really know how to drink, they like flashy clothes and there's not much depth to them. I'm over-dressed for this sudden spring-like weather and I'm sweating under my jacket and I must be just on the brink of stinking. I must go to the fountain of St. Michel and wash my armpits.

He's a most congenial fellow this waiter–his name's Maurice and we've struck up quite a friendship. 'I spent some time in Rome', he goes on to tell me,'but give me Paris any day–down there there are too many *bêtes noires*,' and I wonder what he means by that.

'C'est a dire . . . ?' I enquire of him.

'Oh, you know, just too many of them,' and I wonder if he'd been chased by bulls or some such thing issuing from the Colisseum, but he doesn't enlighten me further on the matter.

'Down there they called me Mauritzio,' was his conclusive observation about Italy before he excused himself to serve another customer.

Now this other customer is quite bizarre. Pretending that I'm writing I observe him out of the corner of my eye. Maurice has stridden off towards the kitchen, a strange expression on his face. I hear the banging of pots and the swing door creaking on its hinges. Out on the street a fire engine streaks by, its siren roaring. The customer has not moved but all around is sudden commotion and din. To my surprise he's still there when Maurice returns to his table. To everyone's surprise really. There really are too many *bêtes noires*.

I've run into a fellow countryman called John, a youngish man like myself who's found himself in Paris and penniless. A student at St. Martin's College of Art in London he had decided to quit the academic approach to painting and take up the romantic one: to sleep under the bridges and live on the street. Naturally enough he's drifted along to the fountain. We get chatting over a bottle of Préfontaine. He too is living by begging and between us we raise the price of *un litre* more and more swiftly as our mendacity becomes increasingly accomplished. We start moving further afield over Paris, having a drink on a doorstep on the rue de Rennes from which we watch the dresses of unsuspecting women fly up around their haunches as they pass over the grids on the pavements that blow out hot air from the metro below – we see some pretty sights – or down by the river, our legs dangling over the quay, watching the laden barges glide up and down and under the bridges whilst we talk of life, of women, of dreams and that kind of thing, and sometimes we go as far as Montmartre or the Champs Elysées, mingling with the crowds and ready to seize whatever opportunity might bring our way.

Outside the church of St. Germain des Prés, the bottle drained, we go in search of alms. Taking a stroll around inside the church we come upon the collection box – 'Pour les Pauvres' written upon it – who poorer than us? – it's a hefty wooden affair, square and four feet high: this must contain a pretty penny within.

It's heavy, it rattles with coins as we tilt it on one side, and it's all going to be ours. We've got it almost to the door when suddenly the hush of the church is shattered by a voice screaming, *J'appelle*

la police,' and a verger is rushing at us from out of the shadows. We drop the box of loot and run.

I've told John about Zé, of course, who every day I've phoned only to hear, from her empty apartment, the ringing tone sound like a distress signal at sea. And each time, hanging up, I feel a mingled sense of relief and despair. But then, one afternoon, suddenly, her voice,

'*Allo . . .* '

'Ah, Zé . . . you're back . . . '

'Last night, late,' no trace of emotion in her voice. 'I'm very tired . . . where are you, in Paris?'

'Yes, can I see you?'

'No,' then, hesitating a moment, she says, a note of irritation in her voice, 'alright, you can come up here, but I haven't much time so come straight away.'

She hardly looks at me as she opens the door, just a cursory glance, and turns her cheek to me as I move to kiss her on the lips.

'*Ça va?*' she asks, knowing full-well by the anxious, bedraggled, look on me that I'm not alright at all.

'Sit down,' she commands me, pointing to a chair, she perching on one on the opposite side of the room. God, how distant she is, how unpleased to see me.

'Been in Paris all this time, or have you been away?'

'Been away, in Spain.'

'In Spain . . . ' she says, absent-mindedly and looking down at her watch, 'where I've been it's only eight o'clock in the morning now – I haven't changed my watch yet.'

She didn't need to volunteer that bit of information, I could have guessed that. Anger and blind, impotent despair well up in me whilst she is so coldly sitting there winding the hands round the face of her watch – the little silver watch which would tick at her wrist as, once upon a time, we made love.

She looks up, 'It must finish between us,' she says abruptly.

A spasm in my stomach, a gulf of white despair opens, I'm on my knees, my head in her lap: 'NO!'

Her hands lie motionless beside my sobbing head. I hear the ticking of the watch, it lulls me; I have become numb, inert. And then, out of the silence, her voice, distant, matter-of-fact, 'Do you want to make love?'

She's white and cold and inert as a corpse. She stares up at me with blank dead eyes—she is not here, she has done what she had always said she would do one day, she has flown away.

The moment I'm spent she comes back to life, gets straight out of bed and starts to dress.

'Hurry up,' she says to me who am lying on the bed feeling as though the last of my life-blood, my spirit, were drained from me, 'I've got to meet someone in Paris at six.'

She has put on a tight black skirt and is painting her eyes and lips, but it's not for me.

'Don't call me,' she says, as we ride the metro into town, 'I'm going to be in Brittany for a couple of weeks.'

'So can I see you when you get back?' I ask, clutching at a straw.

'I don't think so. You're always doing nothing, but I'm busy these days.'

Who knows how long ago I stepped from the train which took her down the line to who knows where. Who knows how long I've been rooted to the platform at St. Michel. Who knows how many doors have opened and closed, how many people have gushed from them, how many sirens have sounded, how many trains have come and gone. I look up—it must be lunch time over there.

Chapter 19

A Jaunt in the Countryside

Down by the Seine we're raising another hard-won bottle to our lips, 'Ever made this stuff, John?'

'I've thought about it.'

'What d'you mean "thought about it?" '

'I've thought about crushing grapes beneath my feet and drinking the juice which squirted out between my toes.'

'Well, shall we go and do it?'

'Sure, where?'

'Down South.'

The hitchhiking is hard; it's taken us nearly three days to get to Lyon. Luckily the weather's been on our side, sunny and warm, and we've been able to get some good nights sleep along the way. At Lyon we pick up a lift that takes us straight to where we want to go and soon vines, laden with grapes, stretch as far as the eye can see. It's easy to find work, I'd told John, you just have to turn up at a château, ask the boss for a job and, bingo, you're hired. But every vineyard we come to has a full work force. We're penniless and hungry and, having drawn a blank at several châteaux, we realise we'll have to be a bit more practical about seeing to our bodily needs, about getting some grub inside us. So, at the next vineyard, upon being told there's no work, we state boldly our plight.

'*Vous avez faim? Attendez,*' and the kindly woman, disappearing for a couple of minutes, returns with bread, cheese and wine, for which we thank her profusely and stroll off down the road guzzling greedily and pulling on the bottle of cool Beaujolais.

This is the life, we laugh, as we stroll along. There seems little point in going to work now – we'll get along fine without it. We wave at groups of pickers as we pass them and filch food and wine from the hampers and flasks at the end of the lines. And if we happen to be passing at sunset when work is finishing, we can sometimes get ourselves invited into the château for dinner. The picking crews in this region are students – we haven't come across any Gypsies or Spaniards – so John and I pass ourselves off as 'wandering scholars', standing wobbling and swaying up on the rickety tables and reciting fragments of Keats or Dylan Thomas, Shakespeare or Blake (thank God there are no fluent English speakers about, so we get away with the mistakes in our renditions) causing much hilarity amongst the students who reply with juicy morsels of the French contingent of poets: Villon, Rimbaud ('*O saisons, O châteaux!*') Baudelaire, Apollinaire ('*Ni temps passé. Ni les amours reviennent. Sous le Pont Mirabeau coule la Seine* . . . ') Of course, no one seriously believes our story of being 'wandering scholars' – they see us for what we are: a couple of wandering winos. But on such evenings we're all scholars – wine flows and the poets of England and France find their voices on our slurring tongues.

'Under the new made clouds and happy as the heart was long, in the sun born over and over, I ran my heedless ways . . . ' Dylan Thomas booms through the dining halls of this fair wine country.

But there are some lean times too, such as arriving broke in Belleville this cold and blustery afternoon. The streets of the town are empty, desolate – not a centime to be squeezed from them. Let's get out of here, it's utterly depressing. We've managed to beg a bit of bread, so we have something to chew on as now we head for the road which once again is opening out before us. On the outskirts of town we pass a supermarket. Think of all the food in there – just think.

'Look, I'm going in there with the bottle.'

The empty wine bottle I'm carrying in my rucksack will be a perfect pretext for entering that glittering palace of grub, 'I'll cash it in, see what I can pick up on the way to the cash desk. Don't scoff the rest of the bread whilst I'm in there; I might be able to get something tasty to go with it.'

'That would be good,' says John, his face lighting up, 'good luck . . . and be careful. I'll be ready to run.'

Shelf upon shelf of food stretches to the horizon. 'Food, glorious food,' I sing to myself in an attempt to be jolly and put myself at ease. My stomach is in a knot – *courage, mon vieux, en avant!* – I go forward on my mission, by way of a meandering path.

Right, in the refrigerated section, a couple of Camemberts, and a couple of Camemberts into the poacher's pocket. Chocolate next, two bars of that, *dans la poche.* Now the biscuit section, mmm . . . Petit Beurre, I certainly can find a space for a packet of those.

Coming up to the cash desk now – assume to your utmost ability an air of naïve innocence . . . Look guileless, gormless . . . and remember: dinna ye fret.

A woman, as large as a house and built like a brick shit house is before me at the pay-out, with ten thousand francs worth of food which she doesn't need. My fear's mounting; I'm gripping the bottle in my two hands to stop them shaking. At last she's signing an enormous cheque, and it's my turn.

'*Voilà, trente centimes,* monsieur,' says the girl, not looking at me.

And now a woman with a cold smile's stepped up in front of me, '*Un instant, monsieur, s'il vous plaît.*'

I follow her as meekly as a lamb into a room in which a repulsive little man sits, pallid and sluglike, under a bright neon light. His whole demeanour is that of one whose mind concerns itself with little else than the price of 'commodities'. He looks like a 'commodity' himself, sitting there mealy-mouthed, importantly, like a thirty centime package of lard.

'Empty your pockets,' he snaps.

I pile up my spoils on the desktop whereupon he goes ape shit. And the sight of me standing before him grinning – for I've been reduced to a helpless grin – makes him so furious, so beside himself with rage, that he starts slamming his flabby fist on the desk top. He picks up the phone.

The police are here before you can say 'Jack Robinson'. I'm snapped into handcuffs and led out to a waiting van. We drive off at breakneck speed, lights flashing.

At the *gendarmerie*, having been divested of belt and shoe laces (should I get it into my head to hang myself) I'm locked in a cell and left. The hours pass. I look through the bars into an empty room, empty but for a table and a near-full bottle of *rouge* standing on it. Oh that there were no bars between us. If only I had that holy drop of liquor in here, this unprecedented interlude would not be so irksome by any means.

It's for a top up from this bottle that an elderly cop eventually steals into the room. I watch as he pours himself a glass, drain it then, smacking his lips, pours another. He's going to have a good binge, this old bugger. He's lifting this second glass to his lips when I interrupt him, 'Monsieur . . . '

With a start, spilling some wine down his tunic, he sees me peering out from behind the bars.

'*Ah oui . . . toi,*' he stammers, '*un moment . . .* ' and he turns towards the door and scurries out along the corridor. A minute or two later and he's back unlocking my cage and returning my belt and laces. I point to the bottle, 'Could I . . . just a little? . . . '

He looks at me a moment and then, with a conspiratorial wink and grin, he pours out a glass, to the brim, and hands it to me. I down it in one tip and a marvellous warmth floods my body.

'Lead on, monsieur,' I say cheerily to my old jailer and we climb two flights of stairs where we come to a large wooden door at which he humbly knocks.

'*Entrez,*' a voice calls from inside.

What a splendid room. Wooden panels, bookshelves, and books, learned-looking tomes, a quick glance at the titles: Montaigne, Rabelais, Cervantes, not at all the sort of place you'd expect to come upon in a police station. But then the man who sits at the desk before us is not at all the kind of man you'd expect to find in a police station – he's a gentleman.

'*L'Anglais, monsieur,*' my old jailer says and dismisses himself.

The *chef* cordially invites me to sit down in a plush leather chair across the desk from him and offers me a cigarette.

'I understand,' he begins gently, 'that they've found you shoplifting in a supermarket.'

'Yes.'

'May I ask you your reasons for this?'

I tell him, frankly, that the principal motive for my conduct had been to appease my hunger – he smiles – and I go on to say that I'm looking for work in the vineyards, have found nothing, have no money.

'No money at all? Really no money at all?'

'No, none at all – I'm *fauché*,' he smiles at my use of the antiquated slang and fishing out his wallet from his pocket hands me a coin, '*Tenez* – go and buy yourself something to eat.'

'*Merci beaucoup, Monsieur*,' a five franc piece nestles in the palm of my hand, '*Merci beaucoup*.'

'It's nothing – you can go, you are free,' he stands up and shakes my hand, 'Good luck in your search,' and then adds, 'he who seeks finds.'

'Thank God, I was beginning to think you'd be in there all night,' John rushes up to me as I step out of the gendarmerie. I show him the five francs. 'Wow, we're rich, but I ate the last of the bread, it was so cold and tedious waiting around, and I thought . . . '

'Never mind – we'll get some more – we have the means.'

We dive into the first shop we come to and find we 'have the means' for a baguette, a Camembert, a bottle of Préfontaine, two packs of P4's. We're set up for the evening and we set off on the road laughing and singing.

Bless that inspector's soul.

Chapter 20

Paris in the Fall

I am the shadowed – the bereaved – the unconsoled,
The Aquitainian prince of the stricken tower:
My one star's dead, and my constellated lute
Bears the Black Sun of Melancholia.
Gérard de Nerval, El Desdichado

Zé will be back in Paris upon our return. At the Gare de Lyon I make for a phone and ring her number. I'm trembling like a leaf. The phone's blaring like a ship's siren in her flat but no one's there. With relief I hang up. I dread speaking to her – only pain awaits me as far as she's concerned. I won't try phoning again this evening, I'll wait until the morning. John and I drink a last beer together at the station canteen and then part company: he to stay with some friends up in the north *banlieue* and I to go rue Bézout along with my cares.

I've been up all night. At rue Bézout they had gone to bed and I carried on with the bottle until the first crack of light appeared above the rooftops and the budgerigar on the neighbour's balcony over the court-yard started to cackle. I pull on my boots and run along the rue St. Jacques to the Seine, to watch the dark November sun arise from the bowels of the city. Too early to ring her I wander along to the Eiffel Tower and back again to the bridge of St. Michel. The city's coming to life, the down and outs are squabbling around the fountain, Georges will have gone to work and Zé – well, provided she was home last night – will be getting up. It's time now, and I'm sick with fear.

'Allo . . . '

'Zé . . . '

'It's over between us. It's *over. Comprends? C'est fini.*'

Click.

I walk up to the bar, order a coffee, have a joke with the *garçon* about the weather, which is drizzling: how fine it is and one really ought to be by the sea-side on a morning like this. I stand serenely a while, looking out onto the street at the roaring traffic, staring out from a blackness as precise as a night with neither moon nor stars; exactly as black as the coffee I'm drinking. How peaceful everything is, not a sound reaches me here – but listen, a bird's singing.

I pay the waiter, tip him, he says something, I see his mouth move, I say the same thing back, God knows what it is, *'Au revoir, bonne journée,'* or something like that, something banal and devoid of meaning. Really, I have ears for nothing but this bird's song – so pure and mellow, so sad – like a blackbird piping over summer lawns, evening falling, shadows creeping – like a blackbird chanting, 'It's over . . . it's over . . . it's over . . . '

I'll saunter back to rue Bézout and tell them the news. What a day to go to the seaside, just you and I. We'll go for a swim before lunch and then sit in a fine restaurant overlooking the sea, eating magnificent food and drinking champagne, then a long, sweet siesta in the drowsy afternoon.

'Hello everybody,' they have such worried faces as I tell them the news and pour myself a drink, 'this will cheer us all up. Have a glass, let's have a holiday.'

The world has stopped turning, and it's poised so delicately.

When no one's looking I'll slip out with the revolver, that handsome-looking hand piece that hangs on the wall, an ornament now, but once the instrument of a fatal duel in which some uncle of Inês was involved. If it had a bullet I'd put it through my heart – I swear I would. Big words, you laugh, but I swear I would. I shall take it anyway – it'll give me a feeling of power in my crushed, defenceless state and I shall take some of those pills from the cupboard. I shall be armed against the world and all my sorrows.

I've slipped past their vigilance and am out on the streets where great sky-scrapers of hope are toppling, tumbling piles of rubble – pah, dreams are dust.

Watch me stop the traffic – you see, it stops. They think I'm going to blow their heads off, shatter their windscreens – no need for me to wait for the lights, I can cross the road whenever I want – I just need to let them know it's a gun – and click! – I'm pointing at them, and they stop! *'ARRETEZ . . . !'* BUT WHY CAN'T I MAKE MY THOUGHTS STOP!

> The bloody Paris moon is crimson, bleeding
> she has all but killed me.
> I hate you now as I walk lone and bitter
> full of lost kisses along the quay –
> wearing out my strength with wandering
> my eyes with crying
> (it's still down here by the water, I wish I could linger)
> I used to love your peals of laughter
> they'd rise up the towers of Notre Dame
> I'd turn you on your heels spinning
> kiss your crimson lips

Things are crashing all around me . . . my fists are sailing through sheet glass, smashing . . . tinkle tinkle, little star, how I wonder what you are . . . splinters, blood . . . the river, a bridge . . . I kissed you beneath it . . . peals of laughter . . . rose up to the towers of Notre Dame . . . I turned you on your heels . . . spinning . . . kissed your crimson lips . . .

O sing, bellow, rage . . . Moon on the water let me flow in streams into you from this parapet . . . my blood, my tears, my seed . . . let me fall before you and drown in your countenance . . .

'Hey, pal.'

'Huh? Oh, it's you, you made me jump.'

'That's the last thing I want yer to do, mate. Who're yer after with that gun? Not 'avin' girl trouble are yer? You're a mess. 'Ave yer seen yerself?'

'No . . . '

'Well take a pull on this.'

He has given me something strange to smoke and then melted into the shadows over the bridge. Now I see myself. In the water my face is shredded into ribbons in the wake of a passing barge.

Chapter 21

Dark Night

Unless you have chaos inside you, you cannot give birth to a dancing star.

Nietzsche

It's a winter's night, cold, dark. The fog through the window is thick, dripping. Dripping like the ticking of the clock. Quite numb I feel, glum rhymes with none – I feel glum. Mad rhymes with sad, I feel mad. I am glum and full of pills which make me numb – make silly word rhymes, chimes, crimes. In the pool of light the lamp throws, pool in which I drown, dream . . . downstream . . . I am a poet and now I finally know it. I can say anything and everything rhymes – why, look at my name it rhymes with gaga . . . but where is she now? Is she by the Seine in her silk dress, her hair done up in tresses on her head, studded with diamonds like a crown, under the same moon I can see through the window? Does she ever think of me, will she have heard of what has become of me, taken back to England like an invalid, a broken wretch, fallen pitifully on the field of Amour? How bad I am! I want her to suffer with what she hears about me, to feel remorse, I say that I love her yet I want her to suffer. That doesn't make sense – but it does rhyme. No, if I hated her it would be different, it would make sense. But this love between man and woman is a strange kind of love. It doesn't make sense. I want her to suffer, to feel remorse, so that she'll be punished and crying her eyes out and tearing her hair out as I would be if I wasn't so numb. These pills . . . but why should I want to punish her if I love her for god's sake? Because she hurt me – how? – by leaving me. But didn't I drive her to that by my insane suspicions and jealousy? Yes, but I swore my life to her, everything I would have given her. And did I? I would've done if she'd only stayed. How could she stay with someone so obsessed he couldn't even see her anymore? But she'd never tell me one way or another . . . about what? About everything – whether she loved me or not. But why does it have to be spelt out for you, why was it so important that she say it – did you want her to sign a statement declaring it, 'I, the undersigned, love you'? She didn't verbalise her feelings like you do, everything didn't have to rhyme, you couldn't understand that. You couldn't listen to the things she didn't say and when you did you got them all the wrong way round and twisted them. She was as mad about you as you about her, in the beginning, until you started frightening her with your obsessive fears. You drove her away and now you want her to be punished with remorse – pah, I spit on you.

Yes yes, you're right, I'm wrong, I'm very wrong – and speaking from a part of me black with pain. I'm not in my right mind you see, not in my right mind at all – was I ever, I ask myself. You, you can tell me that – you seem to know me better than I know myself. Who are you? When everything was going right, for instance, in the beginning when we were happy together, was I more myself than I am now? Was it just the flip side of this – neither side myself at all – perhaps you're more myself than I am. After all, you seem to know me better than I do anyway – watching me in that knowing way as I blunder about my worldly pursuits. What would you do in my position, tell me, please?

'I'd throw away those pills and come back to myself.'

> When at dead of one very troubled night
> gazing into the embers of the fire
> I sought to parley with my soul
> when all of a sudden I saw her flit
> amongst the shadows of the coal –
> she wore a scarlet robe
> and had a glint of mischief in one eye

and of deep concern in the one she fixed on me.
'I know it's hard,' she said,
'but all that happens has to happen
to make you grow it's why you're here!'

I'm emerging from this bleak period now. I had consented to some psychiatric help with the delicate prompting of my father. He immediately made an appointment to see a young psychiatrist in the local town, Devizes, who, quite frankly, was useless. He was someone with virtually no experience of life, who didn't know what on earth to do with me apart from putting me on pills with the hope that I'd be numbed to the point where I'd no longer think nor feel. I saw him twice and that was enough. My father then made an appointment for me to see a doctor in Harley Street; he was an archetypal Freudian, full of importance in his plush consulting room, whose 'therapy' consisted of little more than asking me a list of questions, all of a sexual nature and with no sense of the spiritual, no sense of the soul. A Jungian was what I needed.

I finally had a session with R.D. Laing, thanks to my father who arranged an appointment with him at his family home at Chalk Farm, and, although at first I thought he was going to be as useless as the others, he somehow managed to sow in me the seeds of my recovery. He did this with what I later realised was great skill, the skill of a true physician of the soul so woefully lacking in the others I'd seen – he listened. He could hear what I was saying and, without dismissing it as merely a young man's heartbreak over a broken love affair, went on to reawaken the original spirit in me which had withered away in despair, and he started to ask me about my travels and my aspirations to poetry and, by so doing, made my present crisis dwindle in its overriding dominance of all my thoughts which went round and round in a kind of labyrinth with no exit. He provided that exit and opened the way again for me so that on returning to Wiltshire I threw the pills in the fire and said to myself: I can do it without these. And from that moment on I took the bull by the horns and began to confront myself and root out the misery which was eating away at me, and slowly but surely I started coming back to myself until I was finally able to command the shadows to be gone.

And now, on this eve of another departure, I pace the room, to which once more I must bid *adieu*—for something stirs in the depths of me that the long dark winter has nurtured and now, with the sudden onset of spring, has germinated. An urge which I will obey and I must away into the still untrodden future. Through the window—flung open onto the night, the great black uterus of night forever about to give birth—the stars beckon and the moon, sailing out in majesty from behind the linden tree at the gate, commands me to do her bidding, whatever that may be. And everything becomes alive, a breeze like a lover's breath steals in behind the curtains which billow out like sails. Something shimmers on the wall, shadow-like, and flits away, as though it were my life. A dog shouts out from a distant hamlet, perhaps at some poor traveller passing sleepless in the night, or maybe at nothing but the moon. A moth flutters around the lamp in a fury at the light which taunts it like a sun—and otherwise, but for the measured, unhesitating ticking of the clock, all is hushed, suspended, about to begin. And there's something already about me which is not here.

It's midnight—I've been counting the strokes from the belltower at the Grange—the night is passing.

I'm going to step over to the gramophone, put a record on the deck, *Songs of the Auvergne* will perfectly match my mood, with its wistful longing conjuring up all that has been submerged in me for so long now. I'm going to start packing—if you want to hang around whilst I do so, that's fine with me. I'm an old hand at last-minute packing—I should be a dab hand but I always forget something, so please do remind me of anything I may have forgotten—even if it's nothing. Pour yourself another drink. There are, when it boils down to it, no more than a handful of things one absolutely needs, so I shall start with them—this reminds me of going back to school at the beginning of term and the dreaded packing of the trunk, 'Have you got everything?' my father would ask as we drove out of the drive, 'Try to remember now so we don't have to turn back when we're halfway there—you're just like your mother, always something you've forgotten, so try to remember what it is now,' he'd say, with his usual dry humour.

Yes, I'd have a trunk full of old worn-out clothes when we set out for Marlborough, with patches and frayed collars, stouts with leather soles and iron studs which went 'clip clop' like an old cart horse as I strolled around Court, all passed down from my cousin who was a good generation my senior and then to my brother and finally to me, and this was increasingly becoming a sore point for the Master, 'Your son,' he wrote to my parents, 'is walking around dressed like a scarecrow, please invest in some new clothes for him.'

I was very proud of my scarecrow clothes – they were magnificent tweeds of the fifties, baggy yet elegant, warm as toast in winter and far superior to the run of the mill black trousers being worn now, and my jackets all had patches at the elbows and the stiff detachable collars were stained with ink. Ah, and in my trunk, secretly, I had my pipe which I would smoke in the long grass above the playing fields – what a delicious joy that was, especially so because if I was caught I'd be in for a whacking, and so I'd have to be very careful not to let the puffs of smoke, billowing up from where I was hiding, give me away.

There are no stiff detachable collars going into my rucksack to-night – just a few tee-shirts, a neckerchief to tie around my neck should it get nippy, a change of underwear, a few socks, toothbrush, soap, my trusty old Opinel pen-knife Dzingo gave me, a couple of books – the *Tao Te Ching*, Henry Miller's *Quiet Days in Clichy*, a volume of Tang Dynasty poems (ah, that makes three), an exercise book with a hard cover so that I can write more easily on my knee should there be no table, a couple of biros and a pencil – trousers I'll have on, as, ditto, boots and jacket and that's about it; weight is of the essence, as little as possible of it for maximum mobility and not slogging around with an over-sized, bulging backpack like an American student on a gap year 'doing Europe', with everything from boots and trainers, to water bottles and the kitchen sink hanging off the back of it. Now, let's sling it over my shoulder and see how it feels – yes, perfect. I wonder where I shall be unpacking it tomorrow night . . .

And now, silently, as in prayer, I take my leave of everything about me – my desk, my dark mahogany desk, with the books and pens, the brushes and paints lying in the pool of amber light the lamp throws. My eyes linger a moment on each object which comes to life, springing from its shadow, from its past. Here's a bottle of ink with its black liquid, like the blood I spill over the page in the hope that some rhyme, some reason, may arise. Here's a box of matches standing squarely before the mirror – *PANDORA,* boldly written in red across its faded yellow surface and which had lain once on a table in the waiting room of the Gare du Nord when she, upon whom all my hopes were pinned, came to meet me but she would not meet my eye – and I knew the end was near and not even hope remained. And here's a little carved head someone brought me on a tramp from southern seas. I caress it – a beloved face springs to mind. And here, rising up amidst these scattered things, a miniature Eiffel Tower, wrought from cheap alloy, bought for two francs on the steps of the Sacré Coeur, I can still see her handing it to me, her nails painted red, red as the blood she'd draw from me, and the sun sinking behind her into Paris.

Dawn's first light brings the clarion call of the cockerel in the yard, the first screeched command to arise and gird my loins. My things are packed and on my back, my boots are laced and my collar turned up against the icy March wind, I must be off – Farewell! farewell to the old house and my family who are still sleeping. I have much yet to gather for my soul . . .

Chapter 22

On the Road Again

This morning, a warm sunny morning in June, so unlike that bleak November evening all that time ago, I lean over the bridge and watch the sparkling ripples in the wake of a barge inching its way upstream beneath the bridge, and the houses all along the quays gaily reflected in the Seine. I've been back quite some time, and am at peace with myself and with Paris now. The bells of Notre Dame are announcing that it's noon, and I must hurry on towards La Madeleine where Tim will be arriving soon. And now, sitting on the terrace of a café, sipping a *café crème*, smoking a Gauloise and soaking up the sun I have a little time on my hands before the bus from London pulls in, and so I'll tell you a bit about Tim before he appears. Well, as you'll soon see, he's got a rather dark complexion, that I suppose is the predominantly Celtic strain in him, he's not very tall nor is he short, somewhere in between and quite stocky, muscular. He's of a taciturn cast of mind having seen the drawn-out deaths of both his parents while still barely a youth and this must to some extent account for the balding head and deep furrowed brow at such an early age. He grew up in Uganda, where his father was a surgeon and his childhood was spent in the bush with the animals and nature—he was in his element there. But, during the political turmoil of the sixties and seventies, the family had to move to England where the dismal pettiness of urban life in Reigate thoroughly depressed him and drove his father to drink and an untimely death, followed shortly by his mother who died of a broken heart. I met him little more than a year or so ago but we immediately became the deepest of friends, as though we were long lost brothers now re-finding each other after uncountable time and happenings.

He had just returned from one of his many journeys across the Atlantic, working as a deckhand on yachts and tramp steamers. He was an adventurer, having set off to Gibraltar at seventeen to look for work as a deck-hand on a yacht or ship, crossing France and Spain on foot with a heart full of grief at his recently deceased mother. By the time I met him he was already full of tales of storms at sea and one off the coast of the Sahara where they'd been wrecked and nearly died of thirst, 'All that sparkling water stretching to the horizon, but we couldn't remove the salt from it.'

Here we go, here's the bus – that's his balding bean framed in the window. Now look how he's coming along, just like a tortoise with all that stuff on his back and his head swivelling from side to side to see if I'm about – ha ha! now he has espied me and his feet have broken into an involuntary skip, a jig – and I daresay he has a hell of a thirst upon him after the journey, we'll therefore be heading immediately for the nearest watering hole . . .

And now, six very drunken days and nights later, we've managed to extricate ourselves more or less intact from Paris, we're on a train on our way to Spain and down to Gibraltar where we plan on finding work for awhile to fund a little holiday in Morocco. Our resources are practically dried up – I've just spent the tail end of an inheritance on the good life in Paris in which I'd been shacking up with Nicolette, a gallery owner, who had a *chambre de bonne* on the rue Bonaparte – the very street in which I'd slept curled up in a stairwell and had been so rudely awoken by the *concièrge*, perhaps it was this very tenement, number five, the stairwell certainly looks familiar.

It was a lovely flat right at the top of the building, reached by narrow creaking stairs and black iron bannisters. It was full of exotic plants and light from the sky-lights which looked out over the grey roof-tops of the city. We'd spend hours on end floating in a round jacuzzi, drinking champagne and listening to Mozart, Jacques

Brel and the Sex Pistols under a skylight which opened to the sky far above the grey rooftops of the city. She showed me a Paris I'd never seen before: jazz clubs, the most *chic* of the restaurants in the *quartier* and La Rhumerie where she'd gone to pick up many men over the years – she was quite open about things like that and once, when I'd got jealous about a trifle, she'd chided me, 'Come on, sex is like music, just because you like Bach doesn't mean you can't like Mozart too.'

She was also a poet and I had met her on the eve of the *Quatorze Juillet*, dancing through the night to a band of the *pompiers* at Châtelet and, as dawn began to light up the skies of Paris, she'd invited me back.

Knowing that Tim would enjoy the story, I tell him about about how one morning leaving the flat with Nicolette as I usually did when she was off to her gallery and, having kissed her goodbye at the metro, I found myself wandering along to Châtelet and down the rue Blondel, a smaller version of Pigalle and less well-known to the tourist. On both sides of the street the girls would be on display, lined up along the walls and outside the bars, in an advanced state of undress with little more than scanty panties and bras, others with long shiny black leather boots, straps and whips; though at this time of the morning the street was mainly devoid of these strange creatures, having fled to their lairs at the first light of dawn. This particular morning I was surprised to come upon the doors of a strip theatre already open and a sign on the cash-desk window read: Entrée 5 F. Wow, a bargain. Putting down my five francs I entered the auditorium. For a moment or two I fumbled around in the darkness and then lights flickered on, music started grinding out and an unsmiling waitress showed me to a table. A sleepy and very bored-looking girl came out from behind the stage curtains and started mechanically gyrating her lithe body whilst undoing the clasp of her bra and unleashing her small breasts and cupping them in her hands, which she then slid down to her knickers and started to peel them off, tantalisingly slowly. So hypnotized was I by this erotic display that I didn't notice the waitress standing at my table until she put down the drinks list in front of me saying, with a cold voice, 'You desire, *monsieur?*'

There was only one thing I desired, and that was the girl on the stage who was about to reveal everything . . . damn this waitress to interrupt just now. With one look at the list and its horrendous prices, I said, rather irritably to her, 'No thank you, I just want to watch the show,' at which, she snatched the list off the table, the music abruptly stopped, the lights on the stage went off and the girl, with a look of relief, pulled up her knickers and slinked off the stage.

'You can get your money back at the cash desk, *monsieur,*' the waitress said, a contemptuous tone to her voice, and showed me to the door. As I walked down towards the Latin Quarter I chuckled at the fact that I had, in fact, had a free show – however brief it had turned out to be.

That was a good time but an awful lot of money had trickled through my fingers and so, arriving in Gibraltar we both need to find work. I get a job as a barman in a rooftop bar overlooking the sea and the coast of Spain. It's a fairly pleasant and easy job, being up there in the sun and the fresh sea air, except when it comes to working out the change I must give the customer on buying a drink, arithmetic being not my *forte*. Everything goes well for a few days, it's pretty quiet on the day shift and so I don't have to do much more than serve the odd customer who comes up – one of them being Tim, who hasn't found a job yet, and to whom I slip a few bob from the till to keep him going until I knock off in the early evening. One lunch-time an elderly waiter from the restaurant below wanders in sits on a stool at the bar, orders a drink and then starts to chat to me confidentially, 'You should be thinking of getting a job as a waiter, you could make a lot more money,' and with a conspiratorial wink, goes on, 'for instance, if I take on five tables I'll only declare four when it comes to the count up at the end and can pocket the money from the fifth, they'll never notice that, it's a drop in the ocean to them.'

He sees that I look interested and far from any conscience at doing such a thing. 'Good luck to you,' he calls back to me as he walks through the door.

This evening I've been paid my wages and find myself back out on the street.

Fortunately Tim lands a job, the very next day, as barman in a pub called the 'Captain's Cabin', which we'd called into whilst spending my wages, and which every sailor that puts into the Rock knows. It's run by a splendid old alcoholic gentleman from England called Ron, who sleeps in the larder as he drinks all the profits of the pub and is permanently in a state of inebriation and insolvency. He always has a cigar sticking out of his mouth so that whenever he speaks all you see is a black nicotined hole half covered by his drooping moustache and thus we call him the 'Black Hole of Gibraltar'. Whenever he's out Tim plies me with beers and himself with rum. Walking into the saloon one evening, to find it empty and no sign of Tim, rather perplexed I'm about to go out of the door when I hear the sound of snoring or groaning or something in between, coming from behind the bar, and there he is, lying flat out in state on the floor, I bring him round with a squirt of a soda siphon.

We've been sleeping on the beach a little way from the town that Ron has always warned us about, 'It's full of currents in that particular spot,' he cautions, 'get dragged down by one of them and you won't emerge for four miles, round the other side of the rock.'

The pubs have closed and my great eternal comrade and I are heading for the beach; we're caught up in a drunken argument and cursing each other, I can't remember what it was that started it, but probably just for the sake of it as we often do, and which we both secretly enjoy, berating one another with thunderous cries, and telling one another to go to hell, etcetera, but nothing below the belt that can't be patched up in the morning, and the whole thing is actually quite cathartic. Arriving at the beach I stagger towards the murky deeps which seem luminous and inviting, saying, 'I'm going for a swim.'

'Don't be a cunt,' growls Tim.

'I'll do what the fuck I like,' and, plunging into the waves, start swimming out through the water which is warm and comforting and all-enveloping as the womb, when all of a sudden I feel a pulling as though the water had arms and is tugging me downwards and rapidly away from the shore. Panicking, I try to struggle against it, but I am as nothing against this terrible elemental force, I am its

puny prey caught in its sucking tentacles which are clutching at me and pulling me further and further down. Swallowing water, I know that I'm going to drown and that any attempt to escape is futile. I resign myself to my fate, and all of a sudden become very calm, looking up at the black rock towering above, I think, 'This is it, and that's the last thing I'll see – the towering black cliff jutting into a sea of stars,' and, almost elated at my imminent death, all the pictures of myself well up before me, all the things I've thrown myself about over in a rage of self-pity and self-destruction seem trivial in the face of this.

I've talked about putting an end to my life for so long now here it is being done for me. My thoughts come more as overwhelming feelings, rather than words – I am done with words, they have no more meaning for me; there's just this overwhelming feeling of remorse of how I've wasted so much that I've been given and why didn't I make more of it. There are souls queueing up in heaven for a chance to live – even the angels envy man, they say, for this opportunity given to him, to face the trials of life and to overcome himself. And now blackness, oblivion, resignation, acceptance, peace . . . this is my final farewell to the world and to this perplexed being I've struggled to understand . . . unsure whether it *has* been myself, and that it has not been some blind, maddened actor all along . . . a veil is being torn away, I'm returning to who I really am, who underneath it all I was all along. I'm at peace now, no more desires to torment me. No more sorrows and sadness and rage. No more longing. No more struggle – I'm going home now. And then as suddenly as I'd been seized by them, the water's arms are carrying me up to the surface and, in a great curve like a luminous ring, back to the shore, as though in the arms of an angel – my guardian angel. On all fours I crawl up the beach, clutching at the sand squelching between my fingers, salty brine spluttering from my nostrils, whilst waves of gratitude overwhelm me as, face down in the sand I whisper to the earth a jumble of words through my tears and, staggering to my legs, which are trembling like the legs of a new-born infant, I rush over to where Tim is, curled up in his sleeping bag – 'Tim, I'm alive!'

Now Tim, ever the realist, upon seeing me rush into the sea had thought, 'Well that's the end of him, nothing I can do – may as well get some sleep,' whilst dreading the morrow and the unenviable business of informing the police and my parents. 'Well sod him,' I can imagine him mumbling before slipping into oblivion himself.

He's overjoyed to see me, unutterable relief lighting up his face as we hug one another, 'You cunt,' he admonishes, laughing.

Yes Tim, with an ingrained pessimistic outlook on life and a dark, dry humour. Upon announcing to him once that when I died I wanted just three words written on my tombstone, he enquired as to what they were to be – 'I have *lived*,' I replied, lived life to the *hilt*. He was silent a moment and then, lifting his head from his wine, said, 'I'll be laid alongside you, and on my tombstone I'll have engaved in granite three words.'

'And what will they be?' I enquired.

'I have died.'

We had got here to Gibraltar via Morocco, as the border between Spain and Gibraltar is closed and we spent a few idle days in Tangiers in the company of a smashing Australian nurse called Suzanne, whom Tim had managed to seduce on the ferry from Malaga to Tangiers, much to my envy. We lazed about on the beach, smoking large reefers which we rolled from *keef* purchased from one of the old men in the teashops or from 'double zero' as it was known, dynamite hashish from Kitama, we acquired in the back premises of a shoe shop whilst drinking mint tea and puffing till we were blue in the face and then all the colours of the rainbow, on a hubbly bubbly hookah pipe, the sound of whose gurgling began to sound as though it were inside our very heads. Or was it inside the caterpillar's head who was sitting atop it? And we'd spent the evenings wandering around the tea shops and the soup kitchens in the Medina, starry eyed, prey to all manner of imaginings and jumping with alarm at the shadows which flitted before us in the labyrinthine streets and holding onto each other whilst laughing till the tears rolled down our faces.

We've been in Gibraltar a month or more now, Suzanne long gone, and are sick to the teeth with the place. It seems to be all the worst elements of England moved to a rock in the Mediterranean. Apart from the bourgeois respectability of it, the over-the-top Englishness and patriotism – union jacks flapping in the breeze wherever you look and even the police dressed like British bobbies – apart from that side of it, there are the squaddies and the sailors who are en masse in the pubs in town every evening, and not a woman in sight except for those plying their trade. And so, really, apart from the fact that we can get drunk for nothing at the Captain's Cabin, there's nothing to keep us in Gibraltar any longer than the time necessary to save enough of those red pound notes to get us the boat to Malaga, once again via Morocco.

We do a moonlight flit, neither of us telling our bosses (my boss being the carpenter with whom I got a job as general dogsbody after my dismissal from the rooftop bar) that we were off and wouldn't be along for work in the morning. We buy our tickets and gleefully sail away from the Rock which had almost come to seem like a prison. We'll stop over a few days in Tangiers and then, having crossed to Spain, we'll take the road for Portugal; meanwhile we'll have a little holiday in Morocco. But it's turning out to be rather a long holiday, not the three or four days we'd planned. What happened was this: on the fourth day having tasted enough of the life in Tangiers and eager to be on the road to Portugal, we'd gone down to the harbour to board the boat for Malaga. As we went through the customs we were subjected to a thorough search of both our baggage and our persons and then asked how much money we had – our fortunes had dwindled somewhat, down to having just enough for a bottle of something on board, and, not being able to show any more than that, we were not allowed to get on the ship.

'But look we have tickets,' we protested as they held us at the barrier and we watched helplessly as the ship's ramps were taken up, the ropes unhitched from the capstans on the quay and the ship steamed off towards the horizon. The customs men just grinned at our indignant fury.

As we were walking dejectedly back along the quay we saw another ferry onto which people and vehicles were boarding and, upon enquiring as to where it was destined, were told that it would be leaving in an hour for Malaga. Aha, we were being given a second chance. Approaching the barrier, our fingers crossed, we showed our tickets and, without any fuss were waved straight through: and here we were walking up the gangway and stepping on board. Once out of sight of anyone who might be suspicious and recall us, we did a little jig on deck, a jig of unbridled glee. Now to get a bottle of something and celebrate the next leg of the journey. We had to wait until the ship put out to sea before we could buy the desired bottle of gin displayed in the ship shop's window. Once we got it we sat out on deck in deckchairs at the stern of the ship and saluted the sun which was going down over the wine-dark sea in a blaze of colours and watched the flying fish as they leapt in the white wake of the ship. We were having a whale of a time laughing, reciting fragments from Dylan Thomas, Li Po, Villon and that ilk of poets which goes smoothly, harmoniously, at home with a bottle of liquor, when along came two pretty German girls, drawn by the merriment and unbridled glee we were exuding. They drank from the bottle we proffered them and sat down with us. Tim and I didn't have to revert to a chat-up mode; the girls were enjoying us just as much as we were them, as they too began to light up with the booze. They started singing lilting German songs which had a haunting beauty and we listened in rapture, falling silent, and in love, with the mädchens to whom we were slowly moving closer. They were students from Bremen travelling around Europe and going wherever the wind took them. Tim and I became the wind for them that evening, and when we suggested they come with us to Portugal, they jumped at the plan saying, 'Oh ja, wunderbar,' and already we saw who was leaning to whom. We passed the black Rock of Gibraltar, pinpointed with lights beneath the stars, and lifted the bottle in salute. We wondered how the Captain's Cabin was faring now that Ron had lost his able-bodied barman. We asked the girls if they had set foot on the Rock.

'One night was enough there,' they almost spat, 'it was full of soldiers trying to get our knickers off, ach, not very romantic!'

We were all holding hands in a circle now and the girls were try-ing to teach us the words of the songs they were singing – not very successfully – and we all collapsed laughing. Our heads coming to-gether in the centre of the circle we formed.

'In a month's time you will be singing just like us, for every day and every night we will sing for you.'

Tim and I relished the prospect of that, in fact the future looked pretty damned rosy. We told them about the trouble we'd had with the customs, and although we boarded this ship without any trouble we were still a little concerned about the customs in Malaga – they may not let us through if we can't show the money. But the girls told us not to worry, we were together now and they had travellers' checks.

We began to make plans for the trip to Portugal. We'd put up in a pension in Malaga that night and set off in the morning. I told them all about my time in Lisbon and what an enchanting city it was – '*Wunderbar,*' said the girls – *Wunderbar*, indeed, for tonight and for many nights to come we'd be making love to them along the starry way.

The orange glow of a city had appeared on the horizon – we were getting closer and closer to it and soon the lights of Malaga looked like an intense cluster of stars reflected on the water. We slugged down the last drops of gin and prepared to disembark as the ship slid soundlessly into the harbour. Our hearts were beating fast – we just had to get clear of customs and the way would be open for the most eagerly anticipated stretch of time which lay before us. The customs officials had installed themselves at the top of the gangplank in the entrance to the ship. As the four of us approached, the girls' pass-ports were stamped and they were waved through but we two, my great eternal comrade and I, were not.

'*No passa,*' snapped the official,

'What? *Por que?*' we exclaimed, outraged.

'*Por que no tiene dineros!*'

'They are with us,' the girls pleaded, waving their checks at the guards, 'we have money, we are together.'

'*Non,*' and the officials pushed us back on board and our sweet-hearts-to-be in the other direction. The girls waved to us frantically and blew kisses from the quay as Tim and I, sick as dogs and furious with impotent rage, leant over the railings of the deck. The ship was putting to sea again immediately and, as the lights of Malaga receded and our dreams evaporated, we thought of jumping overboard, and would have done, had we not known that we'd have been scooped up by the authorities as soon as we hit the water. With deflated spirits and already hung over heads we laid ourselves out on the deck, over which the empty gin bottle rolled from port to starboard with every lurch of the vessel the entire length of the night.

Waking from a drunken slumber and heaving to in Tangiers, as dawn cracked above our throbbing heads, was a most depressing thing. The dream evaporated, we were hungover and broke; we hadn't even the means for a coffee to revive us. We mumbled to one another glumly as we set foot on Moroccan soil once more. As we sat on a capstan watching the ships come and go and wondering what the hell we were going to do now, and cursing the fact that we were unlikely to ever see the lovely German girls again, I told Tim the story of Verūshka.

It was a chance meeting, or so it would seem, but I suspect an unseen destiny had a hand in it. We'd both taken a wrong turn when boarding the ship and found ourselves at a dead end and, laughing, we hurried back to the main gangplank by which the last of the passengers were boarding. It was the ship making the night crossing from Harwich to the Hook of Holland – I was going to Enschedé to see my old friend Bert. Verushka was her name and was very pretty, in fact quite beautiful, with the distinctive Slavic features and corn-coloured flaxen hair I love so well, in fact she reminded me of Vera in Vrpolje and the coincidence of her name almost made me think I'd met again she who I had been so mad about, she who had bewitched me and in the end had eluded my grasp. I invited her to come to the bar and have a drink, once the ship put to sea. Over a few pints we got to know each other's stories. She was Russian but had grown up in Australia. She was a concert pianist, her long, sensitive-looking, fingers attested to that, reminding me of a concert I'd once attended where a beautiful woman, also Russian, played, her nimble fingers moving crablike, from side to side of the keyboard and at the same time like a spider dancing over the keys as though they were spinning a web whilst casting a spell which I was well and truly caught up in. And now I felt that Verushka, sitting closer and closer to me, was casting a spell over me. She told me she was on her way to Berlin where she'd been living with a bloke, but they'd broken up and she was going to pick up the rest of her things from the flat. 'I'll be free then,' she said.

As we stood out on deck with a bottle of wine I told her all about Greece and that it was there I was headed after a brief stay in Holland. 'I would love to go there she breathed, I have always wanted to go there some day.'

'Listen, if you're serious about that, I'll forget about Holland and go straight down to Greece, would you like to come with me?'

'Yes, yes I would,' and she looked up at me, her green eyes gazing into mine and her fingers weaving into mine. Her face lifted towards me, and then the meeting of our mouths in a long, hungry, kiss.

'Come on the train with me to Berlin, I won't be long there,' she said, it leaves from the harbour soon after the ship docks.

'I will.' and I held her tight in my arms as we looked out over the grey frothing sea, the stars bright and twinkling appearing between the flitting clouds, and below the waves slapping against the ship's sides. As her hands stroked my face I felt as though all the music they knew so well and which were lying in potential within them – Chopin, Schubert, Brahms – flowing from them and into me, I felt them weave a spell. I wanted her red varnished fingernails clawing at my flesh . . .

'Let's get up there into the lifeboat and make love,' I said, pointing to one of the boats suspended above the deck. She clambered up the little ladder in front of me and, just as she got into the boat, the ship rolled violently and she reached and puked up over the side. By the time I'd heaved myself up to her side she'd turned a ghastly pale and was groaning. I managed to get her into my sleeping bag – room for one only, alas – and, the rest of the night I spent trying to keep her warm, pressing myself up to her body and stroking her divine corn coloured flaxen hair. Sometime after dawn the flat coast of Holland came into sight. Verushka had woken up, stretching out her hand to me.

'We're about to land,' I said, the announcement had blared out over the intercom and people were already swarming to the exit. By the time we'd packed up and climbed down from the lifeboat most people had gone and the ship was nearly empty.

'I'm just popping in here,' said Verushka as we passed the 'ladies' on the way out.

'Okay,' I said, 'I'll wait for you here.'

I assumed – ah, assume nothing, for nothing is certain in this life – that, being a woman, she'd be in there for ages, powdering her nose and all that, so I thought I'd have time to have a pee and splash some water on my face to freshen up a bit. It took me two or three minutes and when I came out I waited outside the ladies. It seemed like we were the last people on the boat and I began to get anxious that I might hear the gangplank being lifted up and us not being able to get off. I waited and waited but she didn't come and didn't come – and then it struck me she must have come and gone. I rushed out of the ship and down to the platform of the railway that ran along next to the harbour. I was just in time to see the train for Berlin moving out of the station, the one we were to catch together. I kicked myself. She must have popped into the ladies for literally just a second and when she'd emerged and not found me waiting, must have thought, 'The bastard, he said he'd wait for me,' and hurried to catch her train.

No, never assume anything – and because I did I never saw her again.

Chapter 23

Marooned in Morocco

Now, I'd had the wisdom to leave untouched a hundred pounds in my bank in England. Luckily I hadn't been tempted to grab for it whilst in Paris when I was coming to the end of the inheritance I'd been drinking my way through. And so we trudged around the modern quarter of Tangiers looking for the British Embassy. We managed to make a phone call and arrange for the funds to be sent to a bank in Tangier and we were also given a cup of tea and a doughnut. We stated our plight to the obliging fellow at the embassy who expressed no surprise at our being turned back; the Spanish authorities would allow nobody coming from Morocco to set foot in Spain, who was not in possession of a ticket that would take him over the frontier into France.

And so now we'll just have to hang out in Tangiers until the money arrives. Until then there'll be nothing for it but to beg – and this is going to be a challenge, with half the street lined with beggars there's going to be a lot of competition. The tourists on the boulevard in the modern part of the city would be the most likely bet, we decide, and so, without wasting any time, we steel ourselves for the humiliation of it all and plunge in. Walking along the boulevard together we take it in turns to approach our prey. Some are sympathetic and help us with a few *dirhams* – others give us crushing looks as though we're the lowest of the low and ought to be thoroughly ashamed of ourselves. It's tough going, especially when we've had a smoke and are feeling a little hyper-sensitive, paranoid and tongue-tied and, yes, ashamed.

I've been going along to the bank every day but there's never any joy – 'No, it's not here . . . come back tomorrow,' they say, but it's never there on the morrow either. Then where the hell is it? We find out from someone else who has had money sent to him in Morocco that the banks here, although they have the money cabled to them immediately and have been in possession of it since then, and will hold it for anything up to a month, so that they can scrape a nice bit of interest off it, whilst you are reduced to penury and beggary. And when it is ascertained from other sources that it's unlikely we'll see the bullion before the month is out, we decide, rather than hanging around the city any longer, to set out on a jaunt around the countryside and live off cactus fruit and whatever charity we might stumble upon in the villages. At least we'll be out under the open sky again and not huddled up in the smoking chamber of the tea-shop which has become our refuge. As things happen we thrive in the sticks, what with the plentiful supply of cactus fruit which grow around the villages like walls and which we've been shown how to skin and eat without getting our fingers and lips and tongues covered in the hair-like spikes which surrounded them. They're quite delicious, sweet as jam once you get inside them, and they certainly keep us going when there's nothing else to sustain us. Upon seeing us engaged in this feverish activity we are hailed and called into these isolated villages by the inhabitants who provide us with tea and pipes, doughnuts and dates or, if we're lucky, with a full blown spread of couscous, goat's cheese, olives and all kinds of spicy de-lights. Tonight, after such a blow-out, where we've been the centre of great curiosity for the villagers who'd gathered around us in the lamplit granary in which we've been eating, we're told we can sleep here on the heaps of corn and, as they leave, one by one bidding us good night, the key turns in an ancient latch and we are locked in for the night – just in case we're robbers, I suppose, who might steal out at dead of night to burgle and plunder, bugger and rape.

Today, not having had a drop of water all day, we come to a settlement that is surrounded by a stone wall, not a high wall, but a wall all the same, which strikes us as unusual. Upon entering the village we are surrounded by some thirty or forty youths and boys who, in Spanish not French, are demanding money from us. We have no money, we tell them, and we'd just like some water. There's a well in the middle of the motley collection of stone huts to which we point, saying, '*Agua, agua . . .* '

'*Dineros! Dineros!*' they demand, and they start picking up stones and threatening us. We back away, and then run, as a hail of stones and rocks are loosed at us, along with a volley of abuse. We run as fast and far as we can from that place with its sinister, brooding air.

It had happened to me once before, being stoned and cursed like that, in France, by Gypsies. I begin to recount to Tim what had happened that time:

It was up in the Cognac region. Trudging along the dank, autumnal roads looking for employment in one of the vineyards, I was hungry, my pockets were empty and my mood was sombre; I felt just like the landscape around me that afternoon: a fog lay over it like a blanket, not a breeze stirred, not a bird chirruping in the trees – there was nothing but the sound of my feet to break the uncanny silence, as they shuffled along heavily through dead leaves. Sunk in some revery, I was snapped out of it by a vehicle screeching to a halt beside me, narrowly missing knocking me into the ditch. A head stuck from the window saying, '*Tu cherches travaille?*'

'*Oui,*' I replied

'*Allez montes,*' the back door was flung open and I, foolishly, got in.

'*Anglais? Allemand?*' asked the one in the passenger seat turning to me with what was meant to be a smile but was closer to a leer.

'*Anglais,*' I said,

'English, you speaking English yah, yah? – money? have money?'

'No money . . . ' I was looking for work I reminded him, I was not a tourist.

'Give us money we find you work.'

'Imun kek lovi,' I said sharply. He looked at me in surprise – how did I know *Romanēs*? I told him I had friends in Pau.

'Manouches?'

'Ova.'

He wanted to know where they were now – were they around here? No they were in Pau I told him.

'So then we are your friends now, huh Englishman?'

He turned to the driver who'd been watching me in the mirror all this time. They jabbered very fast in Romani and I couldn't follow them – it unnerved me the way they kept looking back at me. I wanted to get out of the car, to get away from them. I could hear Tatta's grave warning, 'Be careful . . . be careful.'

We turned off the road and into a wood in the thick of which three caravans were drawn up in a circle around a fire, from which a thin column of smoke rose. 'A real Gypsy encampment,' I thought, this time with some alarm. Two women were at the fire peeling vegetables and stirring a cauldron and a youth was sprawled out beside it. They looked up as we pulled to a halt with a screech of brakes.

'The *gadjo* wants work,' my two captors announced as we approached them. 'You stay here with us, you find work with us,' they said, turning to me. They were all staring at me – not a sound broke the silence. Above us a grey sky scowled – what was happening, why did I feel that I couldn't leave?

They were *Manouches* alright – but it seemed as though they had a rotten strain in them. And it wasn't only in relation to myself but amongst themselves there seemed to be nothing but strife: constant cussing and quarrelling, kicking their poor mangey-looking, cowering dogs if they came too near the fire so that they slunk back under the caravans. Some chickens lay helpless with their legs trussed up waiting for the knife to slit their throats and then to be thrown in the cauldron that was suspended above the hissing fire. How different from my friends at Pau. Perhaps these ones were outcasts living in banishment from the main tribe; but then it may simply have been as Tatta once told me, 'There are good and bad amongst us . . . just like amongst the *gadji*'.

We stayed five days in that wood where I felt as if I'd been be-witched, as in some fairytale. There were around sixteen of them in all, grown-ups and children. I had one friend amongst them, a beautiful raven-haired, dark eyed, girl of fifteen called Zunda who would stay up with me around the fire as late as she dared, teaching me Romani, quietly, under her breath – for the others didn't like me speaking it. I loved those nocturnal lessons when everyone but she and I had gone to bed, the stars overhead, the whisper of the wind in the tree-tops – the wood seemed benign then – the embers of the fire glowing between us. One night, squatting before me, she suddenly lifted her skirt, like a veil, exposing her nakedness beneath to my fevered gaze and she said, '*minche*,' then jumped up hurried to her *kampina*, slipped inside and closed the door. I thought of tapping at her window, running away with her into the night . . .

Tiginni chaï amunsa
ano zenelo vesh . . .

Little girl follow me
into the green wood
we'll pick wild strawberries
and hide them in your blouse
I have an old violin with three strings on it . . .

But how uneasy I felt in that green wood during the day times. I felt that I was being watched, a plan being hatched, feverish whis-pering . . . I felt like the chickens, trussed up, ready for the pot. I must stay around the camp, not run away, that was the main thing – work? We'll find you work, with us. On the fifth day the two that had captured me that afternoon returned jubilantly to the camp, arriving with the hooting of the horn and the screeching of brakes as usual. They had found work. The caravans were hitched up and off we went. After some five or six kilometres we turned into the tree-lined avenue of a château where we set up camp on the edge of the vineyard and the next morning began picking. There were some peasants also employed there, as well as a handful of Arabs. My presence amongst the Gypsies was explained by the fact that I was a cousin – an English Gypsy.

I was sleeping out in the dewy nights next to the fire and getting a poor deal with the food which arrived from the château, much of my portion being divided up amongst the young children and old women who weren't working. And so I was hungry a lot of the time. And then one evening after work the boss of the château came storming over to us demanding to know who'd been knocking the drying sheaves of tobacco off the beams in the barns. All fingers started pointing at me – 'It was him,' they screeched.

I knew damn well who it was: two of the boys had brought back sheaves of the stuff the day before and were rolling enormous cigars with them which they were lighting at the fire, coughing and spluttering.

'*C'était pas moi,*' I protested – the boss was looking at me curiously – obviously wondering who exactly I was.

'*Si, c'était lui,*' a woman screeched.

'*Non . . . c'est pas vrai, c'était les garçons là,*' I said pointing at the two boys, and then all pandemonium broke out.

'Quick, follow me,' the boss could see where this was going and that he must extricate me from the now howling pack and he led me into a barn, barricading the great wooden door against which volleys of stones began to clatter like cannon fire. I stood just behind the door, trembling, terrified that they burst in and knock the living daylights out of me. Shouting and screaming, they hurled all manner of curses at me as I heard engines revving up and watched through a crack in the door the furious fist-shaking departure of the Gypsies.

'You're lucky,' said the boss, letting me out, 'they would have made off with all the money you'll make here – they told me when you arrived that you were all together and I'd have paid your wages to them – and they'd have vanished, leaving you without a centime.'

'Blimey,' muses Tim as I finish recounting the tale, 'sounds a bit hair-raising – though I'd have been tempted to go through the whole ordeal just for that glimpse up that girl's skirt at the fireside that night.'

Nearly three weeks have elapsed since we sent for the money and we dare to think that it just might be there by now, so we head back towards Tangiers. A Mercedes stops and gives us a lift for a few miles. The driver and his companion are in the front seat engaged in conversation between themselves. Tim and I, sitting in the back with our rucksacks on our laps, hardly say a word, apart from 'salaam alaykum' ('hello') and 'shokran' ('thank you'). They seem quite oblivious to our presence but, as we're getting out of the car the driver leans over to us saying, 'Tenez, prenez ça,' and he pushes a ten pound note into our hands, a fortune in Morocco.

The car speeds off in a cloud of dust and Tim and I dance with boundless glee in the middle of the road waving the bank note above our heads as though it were a spotted handkerchief in a Morris dance. With quickened strides we make our way to the city talking feverishly of all the things we can eat when we get there.

By the time we go along to the bank this morning every single penny of the ten pound note has been spent – we had a blow-out in the evening and now, drawing a blank at the bank once again, we're sickened at the thought of having to go panhandling once more. But first we head for the beach to swim, to bask in the sun, to smoke a joint. Reclining with our heads on our rucksacks, I'm just taking the first pull on a joint when it's snatched out of my mouth by a Moroccan who's stolen up behind us and who snaps, 'What's this?' breaking the reefer open, 'hashish! I am police – what are you doing with hashish?' Well, Tim and I are fairly shaking with fear at this sudden violent interruption. Visions of Moroccan police cells loom up before us.

'It's only a little,' we meekly stammer.

'A little, a little what?' he barks, he can see we're shitting ourselves; 'A little keef,' we quaver.

'Passports,' he commands, 'give me your passports,' and with trembling hands we surrender our passports to him, to this horrible looking specimen with the thin lips, the dark reflecting sunglasses and the pock-marked face.

'British! – okay give me three hundred pounds, then no more problem for you!'

'Three hundred pounds?' we gasp, 'We don't have money, we are waiting for money . . .'

'One hundred, then.'

'We don't have anything . . . '

'Then we'll have to go to the police station – that ring,' he blurts out, pointing at the gold ring on Tim's finger, his father's wedding ring I think it was, the only item of value we have between us, 'give me that ring,' he demands.

Tim is just taking it off to hand it over when suddenly I know that this man's not a cop, he's a trickster, a thief, who preys on gullible fools like us, who are stoned and not quite ourselves, and makes a living at it.

'Don't give it to him, Tim,' I breathe urgently, just in time.

'What do you mean?' snaps the villain, slapping me across the face with the passports.

'Right pal, let's go to the police station,' I hiss at him, getting up, 'come on, let's go,' Tim twigs immediately and the thief begins to get anxious. Now that we've seen through his ruse we've recovered our composure and courage and, with determined strides, start towards the town. He begins to lag behind us, and now, before he tries to sidle away, we turn on him and yell in his face, 'Now give us back our passports.' Now he looks as full of panic as we did just a few moments ago and, pushing them them into our hands, hurries away. We watch as he's joined by an accomplice who'd been hovering around and they disappear quickly down the beach. Two days later, the money still not having come, we sell that ring in the *medina* for the price of two teas and a loaf of bread.

When, finally, the loot does arrive we head straight for a travel agent and, after buying two tickets which will take us all the way to Perpignan in France, what, lo and behold, do we have left over? Enough for another two teas and a loaf of bread. It infuriates us that the tickets have swallowed up all the money – we aren't even going to have enough for a bottle on board. But there's no time for regrets; we've got our passage out of here and we hurry to the harbour to board the first ship leaving for Spain.

The journey through Spain as far as Barcelona is a blur. We must have raised some money in Malaga for we had been drunk the whole way to Madrid, became increasingly so in the station in Madrid whilst waiting for a connection and we were finally finished off somewhere on the line to Barcelona when we fell into the company of some Spanish soldiers who had a supply of black hash from Kitama and had invited us to help them smoke it. As dawn cracked somewhere above our heads, I came round. Where Tim was I didn't know; in a daze I got up and went off in search of him. His torso was half in and half out of the filthy khazi, his balding pate laid out in state beneath the pan.

I told Tim all about the Ramblas and how Bert and I had pan-handled along it, and sat with the cardboard notice in the middle of the passing human tide, some two or three years ago. 'We'll be sitting up having lunch in *Los Galegos* by noon, you'll see.' I say to him as we alight from the train.

And who should we run into as we step over the threshold, peeling spuds on a stool by the wine vats, his shaggy head bent over his work and his dog sprawled out in the sawdust at his feet? Why, no lesser person than Jürgen, under whom I'd studied the art of *la manche*, in Marseille.

'*Ach, mein freund,*' he exclaimed, looking up, 'it is you!'

'Yes, it is me, so you remember me?'

'*Ja,* how could I forget, you are still in ze same clothes. I have ze good life here,' he went on, 'I am having all ze *wein* required by myself and all ze food which I am in ze process of helping to cook. You see, I am helping in ze restaurant and I am experiencing not one single point of worry for ze daily existence,' he knocks back a vial in one tip, 'I am sleeping on ze floor here and Wolf he is munching many bones, all ze days and all ze nights'.

'So you don't need to go begging anymore?' I ask him.

'*Ach nein, mein freund,* it is not necessary.'

I told him that I'd made some progress since Marseille and explained about the cardboard trick which my old friend Bert had cooked up in this very restaurant. '*Ja,* ze cardboard,' he says, shaking his head disapprovingly, 'ze cardboard is not real begging, it is not being honest with ze people and zere is not ze human element of ze speech, of ze sob story . . .'

Tim and I sit down and order lunch, not letting on to Jürgen that we'd employed the cardboard method to raise the funds for it.

'It is good to see you again, my friend, I was feeling in Marseille we would one day be meeting again. You see ze vorld is small and ze people of our nature we are always finding ourselves in ze same kinds of places,' he motions his arms around the dim, grubby interior of Los Galegos, the same kind of . . . of . . . '

'Dives?' I suggest to him the word he might be looking for.

'*Ja*, dives,' he likes this word and chuckles into his beard, 'dives, my friend, that is a very descriptive vord – it implies that one is diving by the headfirst into ze . . . ze . . . '

'Depths?' I prompt,

'*Ja*, into ze depths,' and dipping his purple nose into his wine, and then tossing his head back, empties this vial in similar fashion to the last. Tim and I follow suit.

'Maybe ten years since ve are seeing each uzzer on ze *Cannebière?*'

'Let me think, that was around 1972 so it must have been seven or eight years.'

'Many sings are happening in zose years, *mein freund* . . . '

'Yes, many sings . . . '

Before leaving town we pop along to the blood bank where we each sell a litre of blood – blood which must be somewhere in the region of forty to fifty percent alcohol – and make a fair bit of pocket money for the journey up to France. I've told Tim that we can find work in the vineyards, as the *vendange* will be underway and then, apart from the fact that we'll have to work our fingers to the bone, all our financial problems will cease to exist and we'll have food and wine galore.

Things don't turn out quite as simply as that. Around Perpignan the picking's been underway for too long for the vineyards to be taking on fresh hands and so, drawing a blank at every château we enquire at, we race for Bordeaux. Here we run into the hospitality of some students who are playing guitars and singing in a pavement café in the winding, cobbled back streets of the old quarter, which seem to exude from the very stonework of the houses the dank, musty odour of centuries-old wine. We are plied with wine and both of us fall head over heels with a dark-eyed girl who's singing – her mellifluous voice rising up through the narrow opening between the roof-tops to the sky, with all its October stars flashing.

The following day we board a train which will be passing through
the wine growing areas. We are ticketless of course. It won't be difficult I assure Tim, who is travelling in this manner for the first time
and is a little edgy as the train moves out of the station. I tell him
about the trick of hiding in the lavatory but not sliding the latch
into the occupied position. He thinks that this is a jolly good way
of fooling the guard. But when the guard does arrive he comes at
such lightning speed through the carriage that he's almost upon me
when I look up and see him; he has spotted me and in a matter of
moments will be asking to see my ticket. It's no good my trying to
hide, but to Tim, who's round the corner and out of sight, I say in a
fierce whisper, 'Quick, hide!' and he bolts into the thunderbox.

'*Billet, s'il vous plaît.*'

'Er . . . I don't have a ticket, monsieur –'

'Huh?' he looks at me, has he heard me right?

'You see, monsieur, I have no money and I'm looking for
work – for work in the vineyards and I have to get there quickly so
that I can help to produce the finest wine in the world – French wine
from Bordeaux.' I'm beginning to wax poetical and when I exclaim,
raising my arms in a dramatic gesture, that I'm going to work for the
glory of France I know that I'm stirring his Gallic pride and that I'm
winning him over; he suddenly smiles and then, laughingly, '*Alors,*
this time, just this time, *pour la gloire de la patrie,* you can travel
for nothing . . . ' and, by now thoroughly in the spirit of the whole
thing and with a big, benevolent smile on his face, he's just turning
away to continue his tour of inspection of the carriages, when – oh
no! – I hear the lavatory door opening right beside us and there's
Tim! The guard swivels round, '*Billet.*'

'He's my friend, *mon copain,*' I say urgently and then, adopting
again a heroic tone, 'he too is going to toil *pour la gloire de la France,*'
and the guard, now fully in cahoots with us, with a wave of his hand,
goes off chuckling into the next carriage.

As soon as we see slope upon slope covered with vines, through
the window, we get off the train. We find ourselves right in the
middle of where we want to be – it's a good thing to be in the middle
of where one wants to be. The little town is alive with tractors, with

trailers laden with grapes rushing to the cooperatives to unload and then racing back to the vineyards.

We set off immediately to find work but end up wandering for days about the countryside, once again drawing a blank at every château we come to. The workforces are complete and need no extra hands. We do, however, get food and drink wherever we go and it turns out to be a fine amble through the autumnal landscape, with its ever-changing skies and its dank earth saturated with the first heavy dews which bring out the exquisite smells of the earth and of the turning year. Tractors with trailers piled high with red grapes on the way from the terraces pass us on the narrow roads, and in the evenings the pickers going from the fields to the châteaux in carts, exhausted but singing and hailing us as they pass, darkness falling and the smell of woodsmoke in the valleys.

Passing through a village, we come to a cavern lit by a dim bulb, in which we can see large barrels of new wine and a young man syphoning off some of the lovely liquid into bottles. He looks up and sees us staring in, *'C'est bon le vin nouveau,'* he hails us, *'vous voulez gouter?'* It's a silly question: of course we'd like to taste it. He invites us in and ladles out the frothing liquid into glasses; it's delicious, refreshing and invigorating – there's a tingling on our tongues and a shiver of warmth runs through our bodies. He watches, happy at our rhapsody as we savour the sparkling stream and, filling two large bottles, hands them to us, *'Pour la route,'* he says, winking, and we, thanking him profusely, set off merrily along the moonlit road. We haven't gone far when we come upon a hay-rick, standing in the middle of a walled field. The whole scene, with its patchwork of silver moonlight and jet-black shadows, holds the enchantment of a mythological landscape, this four-square field with its crumbling walls in the middle of which rises this round rick like a tower, a magic tower of poetry. We run over to it and throw ourselves into the hay, leaping and somersaulting and springing as high as we can towards the stars, as though on a trampoline, arms outstretched to embrace the vast expanse of the heavens and finally collapsing spreadeagled in the soft sweet smelling hay, our bodies wracked and rattling with uncontainable laughter and we break out with garbled utterances which are nonsensical to the normal ear.

Chapter 24
Halkida

I have been staring into the water below me for so long I've fallen into a revery and, when I come to with a start, it's to see that the sun has plunged into the sea and the first stars have appeared over the distant mountains of Evia. A gaily-coloured fishing boat chugs up the current below me, inching its way beneath the bridge. I wave to the weather-beaten, moustachioed fellow at the tiller and he waves back. Way down the strait, in the distance, against the backdrop of the dark, foreboding cliffs of Evia, little boats, catching the last of the evening sun, are throwing out their nets and bobbing about on the deep-blue, turning-black sea. I linger thus for some time, watching the last play of light on the water and then, pulling myself out of my revery, I shoulder my belongings and proceed along the bridge and onto a long promenade, already teeming with the population out for the customary evening stroll, the *volta*. No time to lose. It's time to cast out my own nets and catch the flashing coins in my hat. Walking the length of the promenade once or twice to get the feel of it and finding just the right place, where it gently curves and the crowd is thick, I pull my whistle from my pocket, the dolls from their bag and, laying them out before me, start piping. The surging crowd is only too pleased to come upon some novel entertainment on their evening perambulation and the hat in front of me starts filling up rapidly. People are smiling, amused by my little family of dolls. It's a Friday evening, one of the first nights of spring and, as the fresh wind off the sea bathes my face, I take great lungfuls of it and exhale it as ecstatic notes fly from my whistle into the warm spring night.

It doesn't take long before I'm able to say, 'I have enough,' the hat is full and heavy with drachmas, plenty for a meal and a good draught of wine. I thank the people passing by and head off down a side-street. It has been a long, long day and a long, long march on an empty stomach with precious little water and now my pockets are jingling with coins and I'm going to find refreshment.

I happen upon a splendid place which is entered by a great green door, the other side of which is a huge interior like a barn, with rafters and barrels reaching up to the high ceiling and with a still-ness, a hush which is almost holy, as in a cathedral. Three or four bare light bulbs hang down on long leads which barely illumine the dim interior and throw shadows around the ancient, peeling, musty walls. This is the place! I install myself at a red-chequered table un-der one of the lamps. With such grace the landlord had put the jug of wine before me, with a little bow and '*Oriste, Kyrie* . . . ' before retiring into the shadows to prepare my supper. I contemplate a few moments the cloudy looking wine before me which he's siphoned from one of the huge vats which stretch along the walls and gleefully tip the musty, potent, nectar down my gullet. Ah Greece! I drink to your spirit, I drink your pure light, your sweet air scented with pine and the sea. I drink.

You might well be wondering how I suddenly pull a whistle out of my pocket and with it conjure up this wine, and my supper which is on the way – I've never spoken of any musical ability before. Well, it must have been about a year ago in Athens, when during a chance encounter with Sean, a fellow from Killarney on the west coast of Ireland, and a fine musician, over several beers in a bar in Plaka I'd ruefully expressed my regret at never having learnt a musical instru-ment and must have spoken at such length and so wistfully about the passion that music stirred in me and how marvellous it must be to be able to express one's emotions through music that Sean, reach-ing into a bag he had with him, produced a penny whistle – a tin whistle they call it in Ireland – which he handed to me, saying, 'It's never too late to learn. Here, take this as a gift, practice a little every day and, before you know it, you'll be playing like the Pied Piper.'

The full import of what learning to play this little instrument would mean dawned on me. Not only would I be able to express my feelings with it, playing quietly to myself by the side of the road or by the sea in the blue of the evening but, once I was proficient at it, I'd be able to make a living playing to the passers-by on the street. And so, with gusto, I set myself to learning it as fast as I could. At first, as can be expected, not knowing one end of the scale from another or, hardly indeed, one end of the whistle from the other, a veritable cacophony shattered the atmosphere around me – lizards took to their heels and birds bolted into the sky, their fingers stuffed into their ears – what kind of song-bird was this? But little by little, to my amazement and delight, the notes began to tinkle into tunes and I'd leap into the air and do a jig. Okay, bravo, you say, but what about the dolls, what the hell are *they?* Let me explain:

One evening, in one of the many pubs around Plaka in Athens, I was drinking a beer at the bar when I espied the head of a doll, a beautiful blonde-haired damsel with flaxen hair and blue eyes, who was lying discarded on a shelf in a dingy corner. It was possibly the effect of the alcohol, for I was already on my fourth or fifth pint, but it seemed to me she was staring at me imploringly – could it be that she was in distress? Was I seeing things or did she really wink at me just then . . . ?

'The doll there in the corner, whose is it?' I asked the woman behind the bar.

'*I kukla? . . . then'xero'* – the doll? I don't know' – she shrugs.

'May I have her?'

'*Nai, veveos . . .* '(*Nai* means yes in Greek, and I thought Greek was supposed to be such a logical language) – and so I rescued her from the place she'd been abandoned. I didn't know exactly what I was going to do with her but somehow, in an uncanny fashion, she'd compelled me to take her with me. Well, I realised that with eyes like that she could make money.

I called her Monica. The name came to me just like that – I don't know why. We would work together on the street. I found an old broom handle, on the bottom end of which I fixed a tin can so that it would act as a stand, and on the other end Monica's head. So now she had a body, be it ever so thin, and she could stand beside me. Putting a bowl in front of us and a plaque, written in Greek and English, explaining our predicament: that we were newly-weds on our honey moon but awfully hungry as we'd spent all our money on the moon and honey and could the passerby be so kind as to throw a coin or two this way. It worked. The Athenians were tickled pink by it and, lo and behold, the bowl began to fill up – clink clunk clink – with coins of the realm of all sizes.

Later I found another doll, a very funny looking one with a big shaggy head, like a mop. In his mouth I stuck a cigar and in his hand which protruded from his body and his potbelly, I glued a miniature ouzo bottle. He was our son who we christened Romulus. And then, rummaging around in a skip, I found a little toy dog, Skillo. So now we were a complete family and, carrying them in a canvas army bag, I've been travelling the length and breadth of the country.

Sadly, Monica had lost her blue blinking eyes and had now only the dark sockets where once they were. I made a trip out to the island of Paros, which was about as close to paradise as one can envisage, with its long golden beaches, emerald water, dazzling light and the cooling winds blowing in from the sea. I slept out on one of the further beaches which was almost deserted and I ran naked along the sandy beach at night, dipping in and out of the sea. The sky was always thick with stars and, as I lay in my sleeping bag looking up at them I seemed to slip into many dimensions which revealed themselves to me in the immensity in which they swam. There was a lively little town where in the evenings I'd hit the bars which were bursting with life. I ran into an English fellow, Jack, at the Saloon d'Or, a lively place on the harbour front, full of young foreign tourists and blasting out loud western music, alright for a couple of beers but not my cup of tea – he was of the same mind as me so we palled up and set off to look for a bouzouki joint or suchlike as we both wanted to hear something Greek, which was proving to be rather fruitless in this town, which catered almost exclusively to the tourist trade, to my disgust, but then we heard the sound of bouzoukis coming from the other side of the harbour and we made a beeline for it. It was a bit dark inside, full of cigarette smoke, and there was a throng of young Athenian men drunk and loud, ones to be avoided for sure, and just one girl sitting at a table alone. I told Jack to find a place to sit while I went up to the bar to get the drinks. Out of the corner of my eye I saw him making a beeline for the girl and sitting down beside her and the next thing he was being set upon by the blokes and shoved and punched out of the door. I rushed into the fray and belted one of the aggressors, at which the whole fury of the savages was focused on me and there was little I could do to defend myself against this mob and then a policeman appeared, at which the others stopped, but he himself punched me in the face, took my doll, Monica, and smashed her on the street, her blue eyes popping out of their sockets and now for evermore she would be blind.

'You leave the island in the morning,' the cop barked at me. What became of Jack I don't know, but I was left scrabbling around for my things: the shattered face of Monica, a photograph of Agatha and the eyes which I could not find.

Now perhaps is the time to tell you something of Agatha, for it was with her that I first came here; it was as though I was led by a goddess to this enchanted land. That was nearly two years ago. I'd met her quite by chance in London when she was visiting her sister. I myself was just visiting London for a couple of days where a friend was going to put me up. Ringing at his door in the early evening there was no reply and I was about to leave and retire to a pub when the heads of two extremely pretty girls appeared in the window upstairs and said I could wait upstairs in their flat. Well, who was I to turn such an offer down and her sister, Ilse, came down and let me in and led me up to her flat – and there was Agatha. She was a brunette with electric blue eyes contrasting so vividly with her dark waving hair. She stood before me silently for a moment as though struck by a premonition of all that was going to be and then stretched her hand out to me which was warm and her smooth skin was soft as silk and slightly trembling. We drank a lot of wine that evening, turned on the gramophone and danced, the three of us, Agatha, Ilse and me. I came to live with her in Regensburg on the beautiful Danube, along which we'd walk, hand-in-hand, heart-to-heart, through those delicious spring nights . . . and sitting in monastery gardens, the hills and fields yellow with rape and blue with lucerne and the corn turning golden on summer evenings, a jug of beer in one hand and my sweet love in the other.

She was a teacher and when her holidays came in August we set off for Greece, by way of Venice, where we spent one of the sweetest nights of love in a hotel overlooking the lagoon, listening to the bells ringing out from the churches and the songs of the gondoliers drifting up through the wide open wooden casement. From Venice we hitch-hiked down through Yugoslavia where we slept in the hayfields listening to the croaking of frogs, the clicking of crickets and fighting off mosquitos. We crossed the border into Greece on foot one night and woke the next morning in a field of watermelons with a herd of goats, their bells tinkling all around us. 'This is exactly how I imagined it,' she said, looking up at me from the pillow, 'seeing your face smiling down at me from a deep blue sky.' We drank watermelon juice for breakfast and walked through the morning. You wore a green silk dress with a pattern of flowers, so that you seemed to be part of the landscape we were walking through. You were divine that morning, agatha, and as I ravished you in a meadow I felt we were re-enacting the timeless tale of Persephone.

And now she comes to see me whenever she can. It's always a joy but at the same time it's a dilemma, you see I'd like to be absolutely faithful to her but with such long stretches between seeing each other it's difficult – it's not in my nature to not be attracted to other women, and here in Greece they are so pretty and so approachable, so temptation is great and I sometimes feel that I'm in chains. Last summer we took a boat out to Serifos, Medusa's island, where the strange shape of the frozen rocks bears witness to the men she turned to stone, an appropriate backdrop to what was to unfold. We went down to the sea-front one evening and were drinking beer in a little taverna right on the shore. From somewhere around the bay the sound of bouzoukis drifted to us at which my ears pricked up and I got to my feet and said, 'Let's go there.'

Agatha was reluctant, for she knew how I could be when music and wine got into my blood, she knew that I could become possessed, crazy, irrational. 'Come on, let's go,' And I grabbed her by the hand. It was about a mile away and when we got there we found a makeshift stage, a dance floor and a small bar with a barrel of retsina and another of ouzo. It was swarming with boys from the villages round about – and a few girls, who were dancing on the stage, the boys looking up at them with suppressed desire. I started pouring both ouzo and retsina down my throat, Agatha looking on with mounting apprehension, and then, wasting no time I leapt onto the stage. The girls were interested in this foreign man and started dancing up close to me – this didn't go down well with the boys and the tension in the air was palpable. 'Let's go back,' Agatha implored when I got down to top myself up with more ouzo and was about to leap back on the stage when she started pulling at my sleeve, 'let's go back, come home,' she implored. Angrily I pulled the keys from my pocket and threw them at her, 'You go back.' and she went off crying in the direction of the hotel. I was up dancing with the girls again and then I dimly remember fists and oaths, '*Malaka*! . . . *puste*!' As dawn was cracking I came round under a tree in a pool of blood. Everyone had gone home and the stage was empty. 'Oh my god,' I groaned, 'oh Agatha,' I sobbed, and the rippling waves of the sea were mocking me. I crawled and staggered back to the hotel where Agatha was sitting up waiting. 'I'm sorry, my love, I'm sorry . . . ' I sobbed, as I took her in my arms, begging for her forgiveness. She dabbed the blood from my face, tears streaming down her face, and down mine through streaks of congealed blood. I deserved to be turned to stone, I deserved the savage fury of Medusa unleashed to act on Agatha's behalf and turn me to stone.

And now here comes supper – he carries a steaming bowl of bean soup before him, '*Oriste Kyrie*,' – he fetches bread and oil and a magnificent salad of tomatoes and olives and cucumber and goats cheese and any number of herbs, '*Kali Orexi*,' he smiles – bon appetit.

I glance at him from time to time as I tuck into the feast he's provided me with. He's taken a seat near the door and is looking serenely out into the night. There's something about him that makes me want to hug him and say, 'I love you,' for he has an air of infinite kindness and nobility about him. His name's Andrea, I gather, for

one of the customers at the far end of the taverna has been calling out for another jug of wine, '*Andrea, Andrea, feri mas allo krasi,
parakalo.*'

I've since learnt that he was a partisan during the occupation
and perhaps that goes some way to explaining why, the moment
I stepped over the threshold, I would be safe here, as in a sanctuary, from whoever was trying to get me – something which will be
proved to be true. I come here every evening, sitting in an alcove
quietly reading, or writing when the wine takes hold of me, by the
light of one of the dim bulbs which hangs down from the ceiling
miles above. Sometimes I get into conversation with the old men at
the other tables, or with Andrea himself, who pulls a chair up to my
table and tells me about the town. And he talks about the time of
the Colonels and the screams that could be heard from the police
cells some nights, 'No true Greek could do that to another Greek,'
he says, 'that's something the Turks brought. Be careful of the police
here, some of them are still from that time.'

Well, it's been ten days or so since I arrived here, falling into an
easy rhythm of busking on the promenade in the evenings and retiring to Andrea's to wet my whistle and stoke the furnace. I've just sat
down and am slaking my thirst with the first jug of Andrea's wine,
when in come three youths who sit down at the table next to mine.
They're talking quietly amongst themselves and frequently glance
over in my direction. After a while one of them rises and comes over
to me. He's small, very small, swarthy and has a tangle of hair on his
disproportionately large head.

'*Tu parles français?*' he asks me, shyly. When I reply in the af-
firmative his face lights up . He doesn't speak English and so I shall
translate everything he says from the French.

'My name's Gary,' he says, stretching out his hand to me; I tell
him mine but for some unknown reason he'll always call me 'Papa',
or simply 'Pa' for short.'

'I'm Belgian, half Italian,' he stands before me, swaying a little,
and then suddenly exclaims, 'I knew we'd meet. We had to.' And
seeing my surprise at his emphatic, emotional pronouncement, he
explains, 'I saw you on the promenade, I heard you play – I was with
my friends here; I said to them I have to meet that man – it must

have been the music, it went straight to my heart and I knew that if we could meet we'd understand each other, we'd be friends.'

'Take a seat, call your friends over,' and I motion him to sit down.

'This is Vangelli, this Achillea,' Gary tells me as his two friends take their seats at the table. We shake hands and greet one another, '*Yeia sou . . . yeia sou*. Let's drink.'

We chink glasses, '*Aspro pato!*' (literally, 'white bottom', down in one go) says Achillea, and we do just that.

'I've been here a long time', says Gary, starting to tell his story, 'about two years . . .'

'Four,' interrupts Vangelli who seems to understand some French.

'*Quatre, alors* – I love Halkida, I have many friends here – and the girls, ah Papa, the girls here are so beautiful and I'm in love with them all.'

Vangelli casts his eye at him, 'Oops, I mean, just one,' Gary quickly corrects himself and picking up his glass and squinting through it he emits her name with something like a gasp, 'Evi, just Evi,' and he tips the murky contents down his throat.

'I used to chase all the girls here in Halkida, but now only Evi, only she I want to chase, chase around the woods . . . but Evi is so serious. Every evening she is at home, studying for her exams and my heart is longing for her but I cannot see her . . . but then,' and he turns to me with a broad grin, 'at least this way I can have a little drink in the evenings.'

'She doesn't like you drinking, then?' I laugh.

'Every time she catches me drunk she says she'll leave me. I have to go on my knees, implore her to forgive me, make all kinds of stupid promises that I won't drink again – no, never again – please, this time forgive me *agapi mou*, I had to have a drink, I was lonely without you, I was thinking of you and I thought maybe you didn't love me, not as much as I love you . . .'

I'm beginning to get a picture of this passionate little fellow, beginning to like him immensely. Andrea comes over with more wine. We charge our vessels. Gary goes on, 'I'd had enough of Belgium, a horrid, cold, dismal place always raining and the people just like the weather, ugh,' he spits, 'they don't know how to live – the only thing they know how to do well is make beer, and that, ah Papa, they know how to do like nobody else – ah, give me a jug of *Chimais* now, with its dark beautiful body so silky smooth, frothing over with its beautiful head . . . '

He's talking about it just as he'd been been talking about his girl a minute ago.

'I'd do anything for a glass of *Chimais* or *Trappiste* – anything. Ah, if you knew of some of the things I've done . . . but I could not tell you, I'm ashamed even to think about it now . . . but you see, when I was fifteen my step-father, *Espèce de salop, cannard!*' and he makes to spit again, 'he threw me out on the street with nothing, with absolutely nothing, *rien de tout,* and my mother imploring him to let me stay and him shouting at her to shut up, he didn't want to see her filthy son in the house ever again, ah Papa, if you knew what it was like to see your mother treated like that, I swore revenge, I learnt to survive, easy when you've nothing to lose but everything to gain, I tell you, Pa, you can kill then . . . '

He went on to tell me about Charleroi, the city he had the misfortune to be born in, 'It's a vile industrial town, perhaps the ugliest in all of Belgium, lots of the factories are closed now and half the people on the dole, they watch television, eat chips, drink beer and get fat and they don't care about anyone else, they won't help you if you're hungry, so sometimes I had to help myself, you understand, Pa? It's not like here, people are kind here, Greeks are kind, Papa.'

'Yes, I know that, Gary,' and how true it is: it was the first thing that had struck me the first time I stepped into Greece, how different they were from any other people of Europe. 'The Greeks don't let you starve,' he went on, 'and I have good friends,' he points at Vangelli, '*Coonelos*, rabbit, we call him because he has long ears, and Achillea, he's *trelo*, completely crazy, nuts, and his father's a general in the army here and very embarrassed about his son, sometimes kicks him out of the house when he comes home drunk.'

His two friends laugh and look fondly at Gary who's obviously enjoying himself and, as his monologue goes on, is beginning to slur his words and squint, 'Yes, two very good friends,' he concludes, clinking their glasses – then mine, 'we are going to be good friends too, I think . . . '

'I'll drink to that,' I say, raising my brimming glass and draining it with one tilt of the hand, '*Aspro pato,* as Achillea would say.'

Gary follows suit saying, '*Moi aussi*, Papa,' tipping it back in the same manner and hic! he has hiccups now and starting to squint so much he holds a hand over one eye, 'and one for Evi,' he says, filling his glass, 'to Evi!' and down his neck it goes, 'Evi . . . Evi . . . where are you now? Evi . . . ' his head has fallen into his hands and he's moaning, 'Evi . . . hic . . . where are you . . . hic . . . Evi . . . ?'

Wherever she is it's lucky for Gary she's not here – he'd have a lot of explaining to do, a lot of promises to make.

The three of us help him to his feet and bid Andrea goodnight.

'Goodnight, my boys – see you tomorrow.'

And we go down to the promenade, deserted now at this late hour, where Gary comes round in the bracing wind that's coming off the strait.

Gary and I become inseparable friends. It's his utter spontaneity that I find so unique, so refreshing. His moods, his feelings, move visibly across his face, so that I know if he's sad or happy at a glance – he sometimes makes me think of a dog in that dogs too act in a manner that perfectly reflects their feelings, nothing hidden or suppressed – like a performing dog, running around, its tail wagging and barking at the air when he's happy, but I come upon him from time to time when he's sad in the depths of a tavern, bottle before him, usually ouzo, head in hands, tears running down his face, stone silent. If he's not too far gone I can usually coax him out of his gloom. I sit down in front of him, charge our glasses and enquire as to the nature of his woes – needless to say, it's always to do with Evi.

'Ah Papa, how can she love me? How, how, HOW can she love a drunkard like me? You see, she doesn't like – hic! – me drinking, Pa . . . '

I brace myself for a tale of woe.

'Papa . . . Papa . . . it was – hic – like this: she told me yesterday she wouldn't be able to see me today, she was busy preparing for exams . . . of course, I was sad at first, but then,' and Gary's face lights up despite himself, 'that meant I didn't have to stay sober today, I could have a little drink. So I came looking for you – perhaps you too felt like a drink. Ah, you know, hic, the morning was so perfect for a little drink down at the promenade, all the girls passing . . . whoops! No, Evi, I only want you, *agapi mou, mono esi thelo*,' he breaks into Greek as if she was before him and he really was talking to her, and is metaphorically on his knees begging forgiveness – and then, looking up at me, 'I looked for you everywhere, Papa, I asked everyone – *pou ine o inglezos?* I listened for your flute, I couldn't find you, Pa . . . *Alors*, I went along and bought a little,' (he always calls a bottle little no matter what size it is) 'bottle of ouzo and went down to sit by the water alone . . . Hic! . . . I finished that one and was on my way through the town to get another one – ah Papa, why did I not look at the clock, why, why did I not look at the clock?'

'Evi was getting off the bus?'

'Oui Papa, Evi was getting off the bus . . . *MERDE!*'

Until I arrived in town Gary was staying anywhere he could – friends put him up. He shuffled around from one house to another, getting a bed, getting fed, but for the funds required for his spare time hobby, drinking, he had to do a spot of beggary now and then. It was for these little bottles of ouzo by the waterside (should he have a day off from meeting Evi) that he needed pocket money. When I come along and he hears that I sleep on the beach he decides that he too will live under the stars – why not? It's summer now, so he gets hold of a sleeping bag and we set up camp on a beach not far from the town.

There's no need for him to beg anymore; I play the promenade in the evenings, making ample for us both to eat and drink our fill. Gary takes it upon himself to do the chores, such as lighting the fire and making tea in the morning and running errands into town to get things we run out of (though I can never be sure when he'll come back, should he run into a friend or Evi or a little bottle of ouzo.) The pace of life we set ourselves suits us down to the ground; we're awoken early by the brighteyed sun whose rapid ascent into the sky drives us out of our sleeping bags. First thing is to dive into the sea to freshen up and shake off any vestiges of a hangover – marvellous to float about in the crystalline water, feeling alive and vigorous and looking up at the deep blue sky and then sipping bowls of tea on the warm pebbles by the fire before heading into town and a café on the seafront where, if on the counting of our resources we find enough remains after the previous night's excesses in the taverna, we order breakfast: yoghurt with honey ladled from a barrel, fried eggs, toast and coffee. Gary often slips away after this to see his old chums who he digs up here and there or to see his *Dulcinea*, whilst I love to amble along the promenade at this time of the morning, when the day is still fresh and the town just beginning to stir, stopping to chat with an old fellow, Stavros, who's always to be found near the bridge with the swift alternating currents, dangling a line over the railings.

'*Yeia sou philé,*' he always hails me as I approach, '*ti kaneis simera, kala?*' He knows my Greek is still very basic so he speaks slowly and with a lot of gestures – gestures being almost a language of their own in Greece – and he tells of the waters here and the mystery of the currents for which Halkida is famous; you see, they change direction every six hours and no one understands why, even Aristotle, who was intrigued by them and visited the town many times on account of that, even he was non-plussed and others had tried to plumb their depths but had invariably drowned, even when attached to a strong chain. The bridge spans the swift flowing waters and connects the mainland to the island of Euboea (Evia), that long, mountainous island of which Halkida is the first city and which had seen many struggles and sieges and bitter fighting with the Turks who had finally taken it and erected the now ruined castle on the hill, overlooking the strait and the town, nestled amidst tall, sombre cypress trees which surround it like sentinels, a reminder of its dark past. And he tells me of partisans and the struggle against the Germans and how the mountains of Evia were a haven for resistance groups, and of firing squads and executions in the town square.

The line twitches, he starts tugging and then – hup! – something silvery flashes in the sunlight and lands at our feet wriggling, squirming; it's a sword fish, 'there are lots of these just here,' says Stavros, 'I think they are the guardians of the mysterious waters.'

Halkida is indeed full of history and legend and pervaded by a strange atmosphere, almost sinister. That's why I've stayed here.

All along the promenade there's the clatter of tables and chairs being set up outside the cafés and people beginning to sit at them as soon as they're set up and ordering coffee, no one in a hurry and an early morning hush everywhere broken by the occasional cry of a lottery seller walking around the tables with his strips of tickets, announcing the draw, '*Simera! Simera!*' Today! Today! A soft mist is evaporating over the water, and the air smells of newly landed fish from the boats just in from the night's catch. I sit on a capstan, its iron already warm from the sun, and take everything in, store in my memory the impressions, the sensations of a morning of April which will never come again.

I go to the market, the belly of the town, to get the things for lunch – bread, cheese, usually feta but sometimes, if I have enough, *kaseri*, (a delicious hard, salty cheese something like parmesan), olives, the little black wrinkled ones, or the big, lush green ones, tomatoes, big and red and juicy, and the cheery fellow calling out, '*agoori, agoori,*' hands me a cucumber from his cart, I then go looking for my funny little friend and we set off for one of the further beaches near the lighthouse where we sit in the shadow of a rock and eat. The afternoon we spend swimming, lying on our backs looking at the sky, or at the girls who've come down to bathe, their lovely, lithe limbs and olive skins barely covered by their skimpy bikinis – ah, need I say more . . .

'Evi's father's a judge, Papa . . . '
'A judge Gary – Christ, you do pick 'em!'
'He doesn't like me, Pa . . . '
I start laughing and rolling about on the sand, 'I'm not surprised,' I exhort, helpless with mirth, 'You must be the very last person on earth a judge would want to see his daughter with.'
He doesn't know whether to be offended or amused by what I've just said – he looks hurt. 'Oh Gary, you know what I mean, people like that: judges, politicians, bureaucrats, cops, the whole load of scumbags of that ilk, don't like the likes of us – you should feel honoured to be disliked by them, because you are different, you are human . . . ' He's visibly cheered up by this, and goes on, 'He doesn't like me and he's always trying to make trouble for me here in Halkida; he talks to the police – you know, I was in prison here and tortured because of him, said I'd stolen something from a shop,

it was a lie, I've never stolen anything in Greece, people give you if you're hungry, not like in Belgium,' he spits, 'you can be lying in the ditch and no one will help you – here things are different, you know that, Papa.'

'Yes, I know that. Go on . . . '

'He'll try to get rid of me, make me leave Halkida, I know he will. He was asking Evi about me yesterday and whether she'd seen me.'

'And what did she say?'

'I don't know, Papa . . . ' he's throwing pebbles into the sea, 'why is life so hard, Pa?'

'I don't know, Gary – perhaps it's to test us.'

'Test us for what, for God's sake?' he chokes, a kind of rage welling up within him.

'I don't know . . . '

One evening, Gary being off with his beloved somewhere and I, finding Andrea's taverna closed, go into another restaurant for a jug of wine and a quiet read. I pull out my volume of Whitman which falls open on 'Song of the Open Road':

> Afoot and light-hearted I take to the open road,
> Healthy, free, the world before me,
> The long brown path before me leading wherever I choose . . .

Ha, this is the stuff! I tip back a vial or two and read on:

> I am a dance . . . Play up there!
> The fit is whirling me fast.

Ha, sublime! More wine! More wine! Ecstatic with Whitman's words and the wine I pull my plpe from my pocket and start blowing, whereupon a jug of wine is dispatched to my table from a company of diners the other side of the room. The restaurant's full and the atmosphere's getting merry, as a Greek taverna will at the appearance of a musical instrument, people are clapping their hands calling out '*Pexi, philé, pexi,*' 'Play, friend, play!' – this applause fires me up to fever pitch and I play with wild abandon with Whitman's words in my head:

> You road I enter upon and look around, I believe you are not
>   all that is here,
> I believe that much unseen is also here . . .

And jugs of retsina are dispatched to my table from every corner of the taverna. It's too much for the owner, however, a scowling fellow, who comes over to me and snaps, 'STOP.'

'NO,' I bark back and carry on, at which he gathers up the jugs of wine on my table and takes them off to the counter at the far end. A silence descends, an apprehensive hush over the whole scene.

I get up, pick up my empty glass and make for the counter at which the boss is standing. Seizing one of the jugs I charge my glass and throw the contents of it in his face. He stands there a moment, wine dripping down his suit, fuming, speechless with rage. He grabs the telephone, 'I'll get the police here.'

'Get them,' I taunt, grabbing one of my jugs of retsina and taking it back to my table. I sit down and drink, lifting my glass in salute to the assembled company, my benefactors, around me. They're displaying a mixed reaction of mirth and anxiety. They applaud my action, my stance, my defiance in the face of the disagreeable owner but they're anxious about my fate – they know the police will be here in a minute.

And so they are. The boss, trembling with rage and set on vengeance for this humiliation in front of his customers, is furiously pointing me out to them and one of them is at my table saying, '*Ela mazi mou,*' – 'come with me.'

'No,' I look at him defiantly and, not knowing what to do, he retreats to the counter. A young fellow, a student, gets up from his table and is beside me, imploring me to see sense, the gravity of the situation, and escape with him before it's too late. The urgency in his tone brings me to my senses and together we rush out onto the street and down to the promenade.

'It was very funny what you did,' he says to me, 'the owner of that place is a nasty man, no one likes him; we only eat there because it's cheap and the food is good; but him, he's no good – doesn't like mu-

sic or any fun, as you saw – he's an ex-cop and he'd have made sure you had a really hard time if they had taken you.'

'Well, I owe you a great debt, dear friend, for sparing me all that,' and I clasp his hand as we say goodbye in the invigorating wind off the strait.

The evenings are given over to money making, feasting and drunkenness. Appearing on the promenade when the moment's ripe, when it's aflood with the crowd, I put my pipe to my lips. The hat begins to fill up – clink go the coins, clink, clunk, clink (music to my ears) and Gary, if not already around, materializes as though conjured up by the call of the pipe, its strains flying far and wide along the winds. And there he is before me, an eye in the hat and a tilt of the head which says, 'enough yet, Papa?' meaning is there enough to repair to the tavern or, or perhaps enough for a little bottle of ouzo to be going on with, 'Take what you need Gary, but don't be unintelligible by the time we get to the tavern.'

In a while he's before me again, swaying a bit and hiccuping, proffering a bottle, drained but for the last quarter which he has managed to save for me. I down it in one tilt and resume my playing, all afire. At a nod of my head he bends down and, taking from the hat what's needed for a jug of wine, melts into the shadows towards the taverna where I'll join him as soon as fortune allows.

Once the good people of Halkida have filled the hat I release the last note, like a bird, into the night, and take the winding back streets to Andrea's. I step over the threshold into the cool, dim, interior greeting Andrea and his good wife Eleni, '*Yassas, Kali 'spera,*' and my eyes, accustoming themselves to the darkness, make out that great tangled head of my little pygmy friend of the melancholic disposition bobbing over his vial. We set to feasting and drinking. Eleni brings us great bowls of piping hot soup, bread, olives, salad, feta, as Andrea fetches retsina from the huge vats around the walls.

Some nights the walls resound with the ecstatic twang of a bouzouki as an old fellow, as old as Greece itself, plucks the strings and sings, his voice rising up into the rafters high above our heads, just as they must have done in Homer's time. On one such night a sailor called Niko, whose ship's been lying out in the harbour for some weeks now, staggers from his table in the shadows of an alcove and, pushing some tables and chairs aside, takes to the floor to illustrate his life with a dance. We watch him jerk into movement beneath a dim light bulb which hangs down over him and lights him like his guiding star in the voyage of his life. This man, weather-beaten, scarred, lined like the lanes of the sea, cap pulled low over eyes which are looking beyond us, beyond this time, into distances, dances. It's the dance of a drunken man, an entranced man, but it's steady, deliberate, studied as he tells with his movements the whole, incomprehensible mystery of his existence.

We too are entranced, we stop within ourselves and follow him: here's a young man setting out on a journey, here's a ship, the sea – we feel distances, homesickness, the loneliness of the sea too deep to tell – we walk in faraway ports, taste wine, women – we are intoxicated, draw knives, thrust, a terrible madness comes upon us . . . As he's about to fall to the ground, and we with him, he gathers himself up and salutes the sky, the sun, the moon and the stars which have steered him. The bouzouki dies away on the air, he returns to his table. We remain silent, dumbfounded, all at sea in our emotions and, raising our glasses that glint like dark gold, we salute the man who, though slumped now like a dead man across the table, has *lived*.

So the days and nights go on through the summer with its raging heat and life would have gone on blissfully and carefree had the police not laid a trap for me – you see, I was in their sights too as I was very prominent with my whistle on the promenade in the evenings and now it had got about that I was walking out with a girl, daughter of the owner of a haberdashery on Avadon the main shopping street. I went into the supermarket I usually used for provisions for lunch; the cop must have been waiting for me as the moment I stepped over the threshold he was upon me flashing an ID card in my face – Gary had warned me there were a lot of plain-clothes cops about, that's how they catch you, 'Come with me,' he growls, grabs me and marches me to the police station where in the usual sort of grim, bare room I'm pushed down into a chair with a fat man sitting across a desk from me, a menacing leer on his face, 'you've been begging.'

'I've not been begging, I've been . . . '

'*Begging*,' he barks, 'now get out of Halkida – if you're here in the morning you'll go to prison.'

'I knew it Papa. I knew it – they'll get me next . . . '

We're sitting on the rock at the headland below the lighthouse, sharing a bottle of ouzo – a large one. 'Ah Papa, I'm scared, I know they'll be coming for me next; it's Evi's father, you can be sure, that's got the cops looking for us ah merde, merde, merde!'

His head is in his hands and he's pulling so hard at his hair I fear it's going to come out, 'Merde Papa, he wants to force Evi and I apart, you see, I told you what he's like – I cannot leave Evi, ah Evi, Evi . . . ' The waves lap at our feet comfortingly – the sea loves us. But what can even the sea do against a judge that has all the law of the land behind him?

Sure enough, Gary's caught the very next day, threatened and told to beat it out of town and not come back. We decide to hide out as long as we can on a beach a mile or so east of town. We have a little 'holiday' here, hopefully undetected, before going our separate ways. The beach bar which we are blessed with stays open late and it's here we spend our evenings drinking with the fishermen, with the pocket money our girls bring us, along with food packages they make up from their larders at home. Sometimes we pay a visit to Andrea's taverna, sneaking along the winding back streets when darkness has fallen. Once there we're safe – we're home. Andrea shakes his head when he hears what's happened, saying, 'it's not right . . . it's not right.'

Chapter 25
Into Anatolia

The first strange sight that meets my eyes as I come out of the station in Istanbul is a patrol of three soldiers in battle gear, their guns at the ready as they stalk, looking to left and right of them, in a column through the street. I spend the morning wandering through its labyrinthine streets which are full of unfamiliar sights and smells, of traders and porters, donkeys and beggars, mosques and wooden houses. Finally, towards noon, I sit down in a café near the market and drink tea from peculiar little glasses with undulating curves and scarcely bigger than thimbles – I say I drink it from glasses, plural, because I call for several doses of this refreshing aromatic tea.

By chance I come upon the famous 'Pudding Shop' which is in all the guidebooks and all travellers to Istanbul talk about, it being a meeting place for people passing through the city on the way to the East or returning from it. It's lunchtime and so I go in and have a meal. The food is excellent – such a colourful array meets the eye as one scans the display at the counter – but the place itself is disappointing; it has a western commercial atmosphere and I can hardly hear myself think for the grating, drawling of American voices all around me. I can't see any seasoned travellers about – a few with brightly coloured, cumbersome, backpacks – but that's not it. If these guys take themselves for travellers then I'm a Dutchman.

After lunch I go to the Süleymaniye *hammam*, one of the most famous Turkish baths and one of the oldest, famous for its dome and geometrically aligned chimneys and built in 1557 for Süleyman the Magnificent—whoever he was: no doubt some fat, pompous git with a turban and an extremely high opinion of himself. As I go in I'm given a towel, a bar of soap and a bowl with which to douse myself. This reminds me of one of the tales of Nasruddin (*Hodja*, as they call him here in Turkey, meaning 'Teacher') of whom I've spoken before and I'll speak in a minute. Going through the arched doorway I find myself in a great domed hall with eight marble columns surrounding a central massage stone on which some fat Turk is being drubbed and slapped about by a bald-headed, equally fat, masseur with sweat pouring off him onto his customer—it looks like some bizarre sacrificial ritual. Some twenty-odd pot-bellied men are lounging about in the shallow pools, Do I want a massage? I'm asked—no, I think I'll give that a miss. I sit by a trickling fountain dousing myself for an hour or so until I get bored—yes, I get bored, I want to be out on the streets again exploring this fascinating city. But before I go, I'll tell *Hodja's* tale:

Upon his arrival in a strange town, he decided to take a bath to get the dust of the road off him. He was as ragged as a beggar when he got to the entrance of the *hammam* and the door-keepers treated him with the contempt they'd show a beggar as they handed him soap and towel at arms length, and almost to the point where they were holding their noses. Upon his leaving the baths a couple of hours later, he gave both the doormen a solid gold coin. Returning to the baths two days later, the doormen were all over him, rubbing their hands obsequiously, giving him the best soap, sweetly scented towel and generally treating him like a *pasha*, a lord. *Hodja* took it all in his stride, reacting no differently from the other day, when they'd treated him like a pariah. Upon his leaving, a couple of hours later, he handed each door-keeper a brass penny, saying, 'That's for last time, the last time was for today.'

Out on the street the full effect of the bath comes upon me—I feel marvellously clean and invigorated. I wind down through the narrow, cobbled, streets to the Bosphorous and lean over the Galata bridge for awhile, watching the hurrying, scurrying street life of this teeming city. I notice that down below the bridge, actually underneath it and just above the level of the river, is a café where men are drinking tea. It would be nice to be down there drinking tea, watching the ships passing, and the sun going down and so I find the steps which lead down and am soon installed at a table before a thimble of tea. Several men are disappearing in clouds of smoke, with tubes, leading from a glass bowl at their feet, looking like the caterpillar in *Alice in Wonderland*. I wonder if it's hashish they are smoking – surely not, not openly? And then the waiter, noticing me staring at the pipe of the fellow nearby asks if I'd like one – yes, I say. And so the whole paraphernalia is brought along to my table; the glass bowl, the tubing, and, filled already with a dark brown tobacco, burning charcoal is put on top of it and I am left to suck away. The smoke comes bubbling through the water in the bowl and up the tube in a coolish stream to my mouth. At first I get a pleasant buzz but after a while I feel myself going green and have to lay down the tube, humbly admitting defeat.

There are some deliciously sleazy beer dens in Istanbul where in a dingy twilight one stands or sits on high stools at counters and is brought frothing beer in pint-sized glasses the shape of fezes. Lovely, sensual Turkish music issues out of speakers on the walls – a woman wailing like a siren to the accompaniment of a *saz* (a stringed instrument with a long neck), a clarinet, deep-toned and sensual sounding, various shrill, frenetic pipes and a drum. You down that first pint in one or two long draughts to cut the edge off your thirst and a signal to the waiter has another frothing jug coming out of the murky depths towards you.

I reside in a building site, a construction of five storeys high, commanding a magnificent view from its topmost floor over the river to the eastern, Asian half of the city. Although it's a rather perilous climb up those flights of steps in the dark, it's to the top I always head late at night and, rolling out my sleeping bag, sit for some time watching the lights of legendary Constantinople thrown into the Bosphorous and the ships passing along it silently, like shadows, and I look out over and beyond to the islands scattered about the strait and into the darkness beyond which is the great land mass of Turkey itself. I'm awoken at dawn by the cry from minarets, the call to prayer rising up over the rooftops. I love this mystical chant of the East, with its subtle tones and quavers and its phrases abruptly broken off. And as I look out over the tapering minarets of *Sultan Ahmet*, I watch the rising sun illuminating them one by one and I think of the opening lines of Omar Khayyam's *Rubaiyat*:

> Lo! The Hunter of the East has caught
> The sultan's turret in a noose of light–
> And from his sling he's loosed the stone
> Which puts the stars to flight.

One of my favourite places in Istanbul is a wide, flag-stoned piazza outside the university, scattered with café tables under a canopy of trees from which the first leaves are beginning to fall. It's alive with students sitting in groups in discussion or reading from learned-looking tomes. I sit here and read too, over endless thimblefuls of hot sweet *chai*. I'm reading *Jamaica Inn*, of all things, by Daphne Du Maurier, and looking up from it after being immersed in its pages I feel somewhat disorientated and it takes some moments to adjust as I drag myself back from the wilds of Bodmin Moor to this square in the Orient. I found this thoroughly good read in the stalls – not dissimilar to the stalls along the quays of the Seine in Paris – that line the streets around the university. It's a marvellous old Penguin edition with an orange cover and its price, two and six, in the bottom corner – it makes me feel at home. The only other books I have with me is the *Tao Te Ching*, which I always carry with me to guide and instruct me at the many crossroads I come to, both inner and outer, on my travels, a slim volume of reconstructed fragments of Sappho's poetry, and Dostoyevsky's *The Idiot* which I've finished and will try swapping for another book, as I'm famished for more reading matter.

I take a train to Izmit and from there start to tramp south. I don't have to stick my thumb out, for cars and lorries stop and pick me up. The people are all very friendly and curious and, like so many country people, absolutely unable to comprehend why I should want to be travelling around with nothing but a rucksack, and why I didn't want to stay in my country, making money and having a family. Had I told them I was restless and was looking for something more than money and a family they wouldn't have understood – what can there be more than money? So I say I'm still young and I want to see the world before making money and having a family. This makes them feel I'm a little less mad than they thought. But still, they insist, I could make some money first, and have a family, and *then* I could see the world with my family and stay in hotels and not have to sleep outside.

I'm passing through a village one afternoon, around lunchtime when I'm hailed by a family sitting on the veranda of a house eating and who invite me to come and join them. What a sumptuous array of food is before my eyes: *chorba* (soup), made of pumpkins and paprika, yogurt, *pilaf* (rice), goat's cheese, grapes, melon and, to wash it down with, this delicious curdled milk I tasted in Istanbul called *Iran*, drunk ice-cold and ladled from a bucket. They are extremely kind, a simple peasant family with a yard full of goats and hens, and some fields of cotton and peanuts around the house. The mother, aided by her two daughters, bustles around the table keeping our plates and glasses full – she has a voluminous skirt and a shawl tied up round her head and under her chin – she beams at me saying all the time something in Turkish to which I can only reply with *Çok güzel, Çok güzel,* – Very nice, Very nice, – One of the very few expressions I've picked up at this point. And although it's always to the food I point when I say these diplomatic words, it's really to her two daughters I'd point if custom didn't restrain me, for they are lovely to the point of ravishing. There's to be some kind of religious feast tomorrow, so I gather, from one of the sons who speaks reasonable English, would I like to stay for it? There'll be a dance in the village tonight and tomorrow eating and drinking. I'd be very happy to do so, I say.

Under protest my clothes are taken off me and carted off by the mother to be washed. I only washed them two days ago in a river near Izmit. Nevertheless, they are going to get the full treatment now and I'm dressed up in an awful American style sports outfit in which I feel like a monkey and, at the dance which takes place in a ring of lights at the far end of the village, I feel so awkward and ridiculous that, although I'm taken by some girls onto the floor to dance, I can do little more than wiggle my hips and blush and feel ridiculous. And there's not a drop of alcohol to make me feel more at ease.

At least I've awoken this morning without a hangover and I've slept like a king in the bed they made up for me on the veranda. I'm allowed back into my own clothes which have been washed and ironed. I see that it's going to be a good day, for two of the neighbouring fellows come around at breakfast time with a bottle of *raki*, a very potent fire-water, like that in Greece. There's a newspaper on the table – where on earth has a paper sprung from in this tiny village? – it has a photograph of a defiant-looking ram, with twirling horns, gracing the front page. I ask the significance of it and am told that everyone eats sheep on feast days like this and yesterday a man was trying to kill this ram to roast for the feast but the ram charged at him and killed him instead. I laugh but quickly stop – it would be rather inappropriate to laugh at such a thing. We drink a tot or two of *raki* and then set off in a clapped-out car to a wild fiesta by a river where men dressed in black are playing crazy pipes, I don't know what they're called, but they're like bagpipes without bags and sound like the buzzing and droning of hornets at the gates of hell – I love them and this time I dance, as though possessed, and drink and dive into the river fully clothed – my clothes get a third wash in four days.

The following day, somewhat the worse for wear, I set off heading south, touching the coast at Marmaris, an exotic harbour and paradise for the rich, yachting set – I could probably make a fortune busking here, I think, sauntering along with the multitude which throngs the promenade. But I am not quite down to my last bean and so don't have the goad of necessity to have me pulling out my pipe and playing. I'm a little apprehensive about plying my trade in Turkey – the stern face of the régime looks as though it wouldn't smile kindly on that sort of carry-on. It's later on, in Antalya on the southern Mediterranean coast that I'm to find myself, money spent, singing for my supper again. Nervous at first, I timidly let fly the first tremulous notes into the air and before long I have the most attentive audience surrounding me – Turks eagerly following my dancing fingers on the tin whistle and throwing money into the hat – all paper money for there are hardly any coins in Turkey and so, when I stuff my winnings into my pocket, I feel like a billionaire.

I've come along the coast from Antalya heading east and I've come to a beach where I fall into the company of some fishermen who share their food with me and take me out in their caïques to spread nets in the evening. The sun has just sunk below the horizon as we head back to the shore and, alongside the boat as we heave to at the jetty, a solitary head is bobbing about in the water.

'Hello,' says the head.

'Oh, hello. You sound English . . .'

'Dan, Dan Stoker from Brighton,' he extends his hand up to me and to my two companions in the boat, 'been out fishing?'

'I've just been out helping these fellows lay their nets – it's beautiful out there with the sun going down over the water. So you're English – goodness, we'll have to have a chat.'

'That's better, I can see you now,' says Dan, putting on a pair of wire-rimmed spectacles, 'Yes, I'm afraid I'm as English as can be. That was a quaint little caïque you were in, how did you fall in with them?'

'The fishermen? Oh, well I was wandering along the beach earlier on and they were sitting here mending their nets, they greeted me – invited me to sit down and have some lunch with them. When they asked me if I wanted to go out and lay nets I jumped at it.'

Dan's drying himself off, shivering in the fresh wind which has got up off the sea. The sun's sunk and the sky's turned crimson.

'I've got a bottle of wine in my rucksack,' says Dan.

'Ah great.'

'Yes, look – almost the same colour as the sky,' he says, holding the bottle up to the sunset. 'I don't suppose your companions will drink, huh?'

I call over to them. They shake their heads.

'They're wise, perhaps – this is veritable rot-gut,' grins Dan, 'but I've kind of acquired a taste for it.'

'So have I.'

'Well, cheers, down the hatch!'

He has been in Turkey about the same length of time as I have; he up from Syria and me up from Greece and so we've been travelling in different directions until our meeting here on this remote beach some miles east of Antalya on the southern coast.

'I'm travelling on a grant from Cambridge University,' he chuckles, 'studying the political and social infra-structures of the Middle Eastern countries. I'm studying politics at Cambridge, you see. Politics. I don't give a fuck for politics. But I'm studying them anyway. Have you tried this *raki* stuff yet?'

'I certainly have.' And I tell him about the revelries by the river and how I somehow survived and lived to tell the tale.

'I had a similar experience to you in one of these Turkish villages . . . that stuff can drive you absolutely mad. You don't look like a holiday maker,' he says looking at me with a wry smile, 'or perhaps you are a holiday maker – I mean someone that's permanently on holiday.'

'There you have it,' I laugh.

'And so what about money . . . I mean, is money not a problem for you?'

'Money's always a problem. I have to try and make it as I go along . . .'

I tell him about the various ways I've made money on the road, the bottles, the flowers, the 'sleeve' – but now I play the penny whistle.

'Ho man, that's great,' says Dan chuckling appreciatively. The wine's glowing in us – I relish evenings like this with some liquor and a witty companion. It could be fun to pal up with him for a while.

'Listen,' he says as though voicing my very thoughts. 'I've got money, a generous grant from Cambridge, more than I can ever spend in a cheap country like this, you could probably do with a break from all your enterprises, and have a real holiday, all expenses paid, how about travelling a bit together?'

'Ha, that sounds good.'

'Hey, great. Drink! Guess what?'

'What?'

'I've got another bottle of this stuff in my luggage!'

'What . . . what's that?'

'I said, are you still in the land of the living?' Dan's propped on his elbow, his specs skewiff on the end of his nose.

'Yes, I seem to be.'

'Your fishermen friends have been calling over to us – they're making tea. Want some?'

'Yes.'

It doesn't matter to Dan that he's retracing his footsteps as we head eastward along the coast.

'As a matter of fact I'm glad to be,' he says, 'I meant to take a look around Capadoccia on my way – but I didn't get up there. I guess I was in a hurry to get back to the west, I'd been in so many remote places and too long alone. But now, with your company, it'll be different. You've heard of Capadoccia, haven't you?'

'No.'

'Oh well, I think you'll find it's worth seeing.'

We dine in the restaurants along the way, Dan footing all the bills.

'Don't thank me, thank Cambridge,' he always says as we step out onto the street. 'Let's look for a beer house now for a beer or two to wash it down with.'

Arriving in Mersin, the last town on the coast before we turn inland to Capadoccia, we buy a couple of bottles of wine – *šarap*, as it's called in Turkish, which sounds like 'shut up' – wrapped in newspaper, as they always are in Turkey to disguise their frowned-upon but just-tolerated contents – and sit on a bench to have a quiet drink and a chat. It's not long before dozens of boys are surrounding us looking agog, incredulous, that we're drinking in a public square. Oh well, we're used to this by now and carry on conversing oblivious to all the pairs of eyes on us.

'How about a night-club before we leave the coast?'

'Hmm, sounds good, Dan.'

'Yeah, I've heard they're quite something in Turkey.'

We're sucking on a hookah, going green. We have whiskies in our hands. The lights are red and the girls before us are going through the throes of Oriental nights with that irresistible blend of the sensual and the mystical – the music's goading them on as they move amongst the tables, flaunting hip, thigh, breast . . .

'I hope the grant's going to stand up to this.'

'Relax,' says Dan.

We cross the Taurus Mountains. Capadoccia opens up before us every bit as strange and desolate as Dan had described it. Yes, he was right, it's like the moon: bone-white, strewn with pillars of chalk whittled into weird shapes by the wind.

'You can see how easy it was for the Christians to chisel out their grottoes here, can't you,' says Dan, 'this place is riddled with caves and tunnels. There are whole cities underground. Imagine the states of mind they must have got into hiding there, hardly seeing the light of day many of them, for years – and when they did peek out of their holes, to see this.'

We arrive in a little town right in the middle of this region and are sitting on a wall near the baths, drinking a bottle of wine when an unctuous looking fellow comes up, all agitated and rubbing his hands – would we like to go to his house with him? What for? We're quite happy where we are. To drink some wine, he says, cunningly seeing that it's the occupation which most interests us, 'Ah, yes,' we say and off we go, making sure that he buys some bottles on the way. He leads us into a building with a long corridor, several doors leading off it – sshh! – he puts his finger to his lips as we tip-toe to the door at the end; slipping a large key into the latch he lets us into a room. He motions us to be seated on cushions on the floor and we begin to drink. We've soon polished off the three bottles of wine and Dan and I get up to leave.

'Ah no, stay here,' he says, jumping up and motioning us back onto our cushions. 'Three bottles more I buy.'

He puts his finger to his lips as he slips through the door – we're not to make a noise and we're not to go – The latch is turned with a loud clack. He's locked us in.

A few minutes later he's back, feverish and sweaty, with the three bottles. Obviously not accustomed to the quantities he's tipping down his throat our host is losing control of himself: looking lecherously from one to the other of us his eyes are wandering over our bare legs, clad in shorts as we are. Suddenly he dives across at Dan making a grab for him between the legs at which Dan, with a reflex action strikes out, planting his fist square on the nose of our host who drops like a fly, blood pouring from his nostrils.

'Christ Dan, did you have to?'

'I couldn't help it, I just did it without thinking,' says Dan, white as a ghost.

We can't bring him round – he's well and truly out for the count. We slap him, shake him, rattle him – but he's gone. Blood's bubbling up and through it he's emitting ghastly groans.

Carting him over to the bed, we plonk him down, prop his head up with cushions and make a hasty retreat to a building site to sleep off our drunkenness.

'Allah Akbar . . . ' wails over the town from atop a minaret and we hear many slippered feet gliding over the pavement below heading for prayer – dawn is cracking above our splitting heads.

'I must go and see if that bloke's alright,' says Dan anxiously, sitting up.

'Okay, good idea, I'll meet you in the tea house on the corner.'

I'm sipping my second glass of tea when Dan returns, more worried-looking than ever. 'I knocked repeatedly on his door but there was no response from within.'

It's best to leave.

Evening and we're strolling through the countryside, raiding tomatoes from the fields – sweet, juicy ones, deliciously ripened by the sun. The scarecrows dotted about the place might fool the birds but not us. Some of them look pretty stylish and we're joking about them modelling the latest Paris fashion.

'Hey Dan, look at the marvellous trousers that one's wearing.'

'Ha, yes, real Turkish bags!'

'I'm going to get them off him.'

What perfect replacements for my shorts now that Autumn's coming and the evenings getting chilly. I creep up through the crops, bow deferentially to the scarecrow, mutter a little apology as I slide his trousers off and climb into them myself. They're pure wool, held together with a thousand and one stitches and patches and they fit like a glove. Oh, I can't leave you with nothing on, Sir, you'd better have my shorts.

Dan's a little envious, 'I wish I'd spotted them,' he says and then shaking his head, laughingly, 'Imagine me turning up at Cambridge to present my thesis on politics and social structure in the Middle East dressed in a Turkish scarecrow's cast-offs.'

We arrive in Kayseri. So this is the famous Caeserea which was forever popping up in those Latin texts at school; it certainly seems to be a remote citadel, an outpost, with its huge crumbling battlements. The main square looks like the right sort of place to do a little piping; a crowd gathers around and money falls thick and fast into the hat in front of me. It's a nice reception for a 'wandering minstrel' but I'm beginning to get anxious at the way the multitude is swelling around me; it's taking on the dimensions of a political demonstration. Suddenly I'm faced with two-plain-clothes policemen and 'taken down to the station.' Three cops in the entrance stand to attention and salute me – is that because of my fine attire? We come to a door at the end of a corridor and enter a room in which a fat pig of a man sits behind his desk. After a bored scrutiny of me, he shrugs his shoulders and growls to my captors who promptly lead me out of the office, past the three cops in the entranceway, who once more stand to attention and salute – perhaps I should do as Nasruddin at the bath house and give them three gold coins – and I'm released onto the street.

Dan's hanging around in the square, surrounded by boys.

'Ha, thank God,' he says, 'I had visions of Turkish jails.'

And now, reclining on the grassy bank outside a house in the suburbs of town, we're basking in the last rays of the sun and working at a bottle of *šarap*. Inside a ground floor window's a man with a pointed beard, reading the Koran, just like from the pages of the Arabian Nights. Overhead, three giggling girls are peering down at us from a balcony. Dan and I start to flirt with them, blowing them kisses which they catch and place on their hearts.

'Mmmm,' Dan and I look at one another, and this silly but delightful play goes on for some time and we become bolder and bolder with our gestures the more we drink. The girls giggle and nod as we make to pretend we're holding them in our arms, kissing them. I dare say we'd have become bolder and bolder, to the point of being obscene, if the venerable old chap, smiling and beatific-looking, wasn't inviting us to come and eat in his house.

He's effectively put a stop to our carrying on with his daughters while we sit up at the table with him discussing God, our tongues hanging out for more wine which isn't, unsurprisingly, forthcoming. The girls wait obediently on us bringing food and water from the kitchen and the most we can do is to give them the occasional sly wink when the old fellow has his head bent over his bowl.

'You can sleep here tonight,' says our host at the end of the meal. Oh really, we can sleep here? Yes, we can sleep here, and he leads us downstairs and out into the yard where there's a Volkswagen camper.

'In here,' he says and he locks us in, bidding us goodnight. No fool he.

Dan and I part company in Ankara. He has to make all haste back to England, to Cambridge. I miss him as I trudge through the suburbs and out onto the road leading north on which I stick my thumb out and manage to get to a small town near the Black Sea and, as evening's falling, I decide to rest the night before pushing on up to the coast in the morning. Having supped on a loaf of bread and some goats cheese I'm strolling around the town, digesting my meal, when I hear pattering feet behind me,

'Excuse-me, Sir,' a small man with a large forehead and spectacles has spoken, he's out of breath, panting.

'Yes?'

'Excuse-me, Sir, but are you spikking Engleesh?'

'Yes.'

'Ah, I'm happy, very feeling happy. My name's Mustapha,' he proffers his hand, 'I am Engleesh teacher, you understand – you coming dreenking tea with me?'

'Thank-you, yes, thank-you.'

He leads the way to a tea-house at the corner of the square.

'Sir,' he begins.

'Yes?'

'Weel you do me a favour?'

It depends what, I think to myself, looking at the fellow with some reservations.

'Oh, you will. I thank you very much . . . I am Eengleesh master with class of boys – all of them have not seen an Eengleeshman. You are Eengleeshman – thank-you. I am asking you to come in tomorrow on the morning to my class and you are spikking weeth my scholars.'

'Come to your school? Me?'

'You, Sir.'

'Well, I . . . '

'You will? Oh thank-you, sir, much pleasure this will be making me and my scholars.'

Mustapha's the picture of joy when I arrive at the school. He must have been watching for me from the window for he's out of the door and seizing me by the hand before I've even got to the top of the steps.

'Thank you, Sir, an Englishman is always to his words being true. I am so happy that you are coming in this morning – come!'

He leads me into the building along a corridor where we halt before a door,

'Here my scholars are waiting for you – you the first Englishman they ever will be seeing.' Thirty-odd impeccably polite boys, dressed in black from head to toe, rise from their desks as we enter.

'This is an Englishman,' my benefactor says, proudly presenting me and getting me to climb up onto the dais as though I were an exhibit and he a successful trophy hunter returned from Safari with a real Englishman.

'Now, sir, please you are asking them some questions – you are asking them, yes, for a kick off, their names . . . '

'Oh . . . right . . . what are your names, chaps?' And one by one these serious scholars introduce themselves: Mahommed, Mustapha, Ali . . .

'Please sit down now.' They all, as one block, sit. The master's rubbing his hands with unrestrained glee, 'You see, sir, they are all quite understanding you. Now please ask them questions from this book.'

He hands me a text book with illustrations. Here's a Mister Thompson with pinstripe suit, bowler hat, a copy of *The Times* under his arm hailing a taxi with a brolly – this is what they imagine an Englishman to be like: not this scruffy-looking fellow before them with flip flops on his feet and patched-up baggy breeches, who'd sooner be seen standing in a field keeping the birds away than hailing a cab in London.

'Where's Mister Thompson going to in a taxi?' Hands go up eagerly.

'Mister Thompson is going to office, Sir.'

'You're right, Mahommed, well done. Now what kind of work does Mister Thompson do?'

'Mister Thompson is businessing man, sir.'

'Yes, Ali, you're right, he's a cunning little business man.'

'I your pardon beg, Sir?'

'He's a businessman, Ali.'

At the end of the lesson Mustapha grasps my hand, thanking me profusely, 'I'm very gladdened for the education of my scholars that you have appeared to them as an Englishman. Now the headmaster is having the wish to talk with you, if you are time indeed having.'

'Oh yes, time indeed I have.'

He leads me upstairs and along a corridor to a door at the far end. He knocks; a voice calls from inside.

'Please go in,' says Mustapha, wringing my hand.

The head-master, a large, pompous-looking fellow, sits in a luxurious leather chair at a massive oak desk on either side of which are placed small flags: the crescent moon and star of Turkey and the stars and stripes of the United States.

With a perfect American drawl he says, 'Sit down, boy,' and waving me to a deep armchair picks up a phone and orders coffee.

'So, you're English – we don't get many Englishmen here in our small town. Mustapha told me with excitement about his meeting with you. My masters have little chance to practice their English; they make a lot of mistakes.'

I chuckle.

'Yeah, you've noticed it, boy. I have a proposition to make to you . . .'

'Yes?'

'Well, if you would . . .' There's a knock on the door and a maid brings in coffee, pours it out, hands us each a cup, and discreetly leaves the room.

"I get this brand straight from the states, I always drank it in the States."

Now he's off telling me about how great the States are, how exemplary the education system is there, how everything's right there – big, big, big – therefore good, etcetera – weird how childish important men can be.

'You been there, boy?'

'No.'

'I have a proposition to make to you,' he takes up from where he left off some minutes before, 'my masters speak very bad English, they need practice. I understand you are a traveller – you like travelling; but if you would like to stay here in this town for a while, converse with my masters so that their English has a chance to improve, I would be very happy. What do you say?'

'Well . . .'

'Have some more coffee – think about it.'

He pours me another cup and as I drink it I rapidly weigh up the pros and the cons. The pros obviously are that I'd be put up, have my bodily needs in the way of food and shelter provided, and I'd get to know this rather intriguing little town at the same time as picking up the language. But the cons really outweigh the pros: I think of evening after dreary evening sitting up in tedious conversation with the likes of Mustapha and his colleagues – being very polite and correct, conjugating verbs and discussing past participles. No, I have my heart set on the Black Sea coast and some carefree wandering in these last glorious days of autumn. And besides, he made no mention of remuneration.

The headmaster can hardly conceal his disappointment when I tell him my decision. 'It's a pity,' he says, 'it's a great pity. Oh well, you're a traveller, I guess, and the Black Sea is really beautiful. Now, at this time of the year, there are nuts,' and, as if to conclude our conversation, 'I wish you luck, boy.'

I get up, thank him for the coffee, express my regret at not accepting his offer and leave the room.

I'm walking out of the town when a huge black limousine pulls alongside me, a door flies open and voice calls from inside, 'Get in.'

I freeze with fear for a moment, thinking it's the police, but nevertheless I do as the voice commands. I find myself in the back seat of a luxuriantly upholstered Daimler and, grinning at my side, the headmaster, 'I'm taking you for lunch, boy.'

We're pulling up outside a fancy restaurant, the chauffeur opening the car door for us and waiters ushering us in seating us at a table. And here I am feasting like a king, in trousers that I bagged off a scarecrow in Capadoccia. It pays to be an Englishman at times.

Sinop's the first town I come to on the Black Sea. It's a port, ships lie along its quays and some kind of industry's going on. Darkness has fallen and I make straight for a tea house. I step into a cosy, green-walled place lit by a solitary bulb which hangs from the low ceiling and is shrouded in the fug of a hookah an old fellow in the corner's smoking. I'm brought tea and then a 'hubbly bubbly' is brought over to me, paid, the proprietor gives me to understand, by the chap in the corner emitting clouds.

'Teşekkür Ederim,' I call to him, he smiles and inclines his head in a little bow.

I begin to turn green as the walls of the tea house after a while and I have to lay the pipe down. Kemal Attatürk glares down at me from a photograph above the bar, 'Ha, the British can't take this Balkan blend!'

And at Zonguldak, the next town on my route, I'm drawn towards music and the sounds of festivity coming from the direction of a restaurant by the shore, from which people are spilling out in great gaiety onto the road running by and along which I'm walking. I'm hailed and invited to come in; it's a wedding feast and I'm sat at a long table and given food and lemonade there is a distinct absence of raki or wine. There is a spectacular performance of dances, one of which is so bizarre I'll never forget it. Several men dressed in what appear to be black sacks are shaking and quivering and leaping in the air to the sound of a Pontic lyra. I can only describe the dance as macabre, sinister – but for the audience it's one worthy of the utmost applause. It seems that it's a warrior dance though whether Pontic Greek or Turkish in origin I have not found out. The lyra is a hypnotic instrument of which I've already spoken much.

It's like Cornwall, this coastline; full of blackberries and bracken, apples, pears and hazlenuts. The waxing moon accompanies me on my night wanderings, knitting her silver beams into the sea and into my dreams as I journey.

I was born on the night after the full moon; the Gypsies say that to be born then is to find fortune in faraway lands. I want to find wholeness, to find the meaning of my life – that would be my fortune.

I'm on the road back to Istanbul but, before returning to Greece, I'm going to make a detour out to Troy and perhaps Gallipoli, which I see is nearby. On the map there's a town called Çanakkale which is right on the Dardanelles and is within easy reach of both these places; there should be a promenade there and I might be able to make a bit of money. Hitching has been going pretty well here along the Black Sea coast and I've picked up a lift all the way to Istanbul; once there, I'll go to the bus station and buy a ticket.

Çanakkale is a very pleasant little town with a kind of holiday air about it, with a promenade full of people strolling and taking the evening air. The people are very friendly and the hat before me fills up in no time, full of paper notes which I have to keep an eye on as every now and then a gusty breeze off the strait threatens to blow them away. After about an hour I count my winnings and find that I'm a fairly wealthy man – not only do I have enough for a good drink and supper but I can probably afford the price of a room in some modest hotel; the evenings are getting chilly and I don't fancy sleeping out down by the water. I go in search of a small hotel up the back streets and enquire the price of a room at the first one I come to – it is so incredibly cheap I book in for three nights. I've made up my mind that this is going to be a little holiday and this will give me time to explore the town and to take in the two sights I came here to see and in the evenings to return to a little luxury and a good night's sleep.

Unless one is an archaeologist there isn't much to see here in Troy, apart from crumbling walls, many overgrown with fig trees, and a great big wooden horse which you can climb up inside; no towers or battlements, along which I imagined Helen to wander, disconsolate, looking down on the Greek fleet and thinking of faraway Sparta, her longed-for home (though some say she never left there and it was only her phantom which passed along the high battlements of Troy, perhaps it's like that with all women of great beauty, they are only figments of our fevered imagination) nor is there any sign of the great gates through which the horse was dragged by the joyful citizens; in fact I'd find it all a little disappointing if it was only for the relics of a fabled city I'd come – but no, sitting on this wall looking out over the plain below to the sea is quite enough for me, I can imagine it all as once it was, and as it will always be, defiant against the ravages of time, and I can imagine Hector sitting here in the lengthening shadows of evening, the rustling of leaves of the fig tree, a lizard stood stock-still watching him, just like this one with the unblinking eye sizing me up as I write in my notebook what Hector might have felt all those years ago:

> Greeks, why do you persist
> why don't you go home to your wives
> who wait for you, tears in their eyes
> and your children who will become fatherless
> if you don't pack up and go–
> take Helen with you, she's brought nothing but sorrow
> to us who grieve here
> our women who lose their husbands
> our children their fathers
> our young men and girls
> who've never known the joy
> of walking barefoot along the shore
> where now the black hulks of your ships

like sinister harbingers of death
are pulled up on the beaches
and the tents of your marauding warriors
ring with the shouts of their drunken carousing
in the evenings which once were full of peace
which we've all but now forgotten . . .

This morning I've awoken with somewhat of a hangover, having returned to the hotel yesterday evening laden with cans of *Efes Pilsen*, which is really a very drinkable lager and which slipped down so easily, and joyfully, after the day at Troy. I also had a big bag of nuts, walnuts, almonds, cashews and others I don't know the name of, which are so plentiful in Anatolia, salted and delicious, which are so good to munch whilst refreshing oneself with beer. I sang, I did somersaults on the bed, I scribbled some things in my notebook, which are barely legible as I try to read them this morning. Outside, dark, ominous looking clouds have driven away the azure blue sky of yesterday, and today I'm going to cross the strait to Gallipoli.

It's a steep climb up the hill from the ferry, the clouds hang low and everything is dank and autumnal and when I reach the top I shudder at the sight which greets me: a vast garbage tip which seems to stretch out over the whole hilltop and halfway down the other side to the sea. Walking through it is like walking through a cemetery of rotting corpses and the stench is so great I'm close to vomiting. Two half-starved little puppies suddenly emerge from this hideous terrain of the dead and come running up to me, as though I'm the only other thing alive and that I can save them. Oh, how my heart goes out to them, I can hardly bear to think of the misery life has brought them. They tag along behind me and, as soon as we're away from this stinking place I sit down on a small tump overlooking the sea and open the bag in which I have a picnic. I break off some cheese for them and some bread which, with their tails wagging and little squeals of delight, they wolf down and look at me pleadingly for more – their need is greater than mine and I end up giving them most of the food I've brought with me – how could I not?

I look out over the slate-grey sea and imagine how it must have been, like a heaving cauldron full of dark menacing ships firing indiscriminately at the hillsides to dislodge the Turks entrenched all along the slopes, and down below landing crafts spilling doomed soldiers onto the beaches with the incessant cackle of machine guns mowing them down, and how Attatürk, perhaps sitting on this very same tump I'm now sitting on, watching the whole bloody show with a grim smile of satisfaction. Darkness has started falling and an icy wind's got up off the sea – shuddering, I get up and hurry away from this place, back through the cemetery of rotting corpses and back onto the track which leads downhill; the two little puppies are following along behind me and want me to take them home – but I cannot and, with tears in my eyes I know I must lose them, abandon them to their fate.

Chapter 26
Saloniki

I arrive in Thessaloniki in the middle of a huge march by the Communist Party, the KKE. The streets are full of red flags and the crowd protesting the presence of NATO and the Americans in Greece and demanding workers' rights – '*Psomi kai doulia kai elefteria*' – 'bread and work and freedom,' they chant – and police everywhere. I tag along just for the hell of it as the procession shouts its way through the streets to culminate in front of the United States embassy where a thick cordon of police in riot gear confront them. There's some stone throwing and the reciprocal charge with batons when everyone scatters. The Communist Party of Greece – the KKE – is very active in Thessaloniki. I'm enjoying the excitement of this march amidst these red flags billowing in the wind off the harbour, and the feverish chanting which is almost hypnotic, and with a bottle in my pocket I drink to get my blood boiling like those around me – I may as well be in the thick of it just for the hell of it. There's something of the thrill of the battlefield which brings my martial nature to the fore and dim ancestral memories, perhaps struggles against the *Sassenachs* (the Saxons, i.e., the English) and I may well have stayed till the bitter end that evening – and apparently the end *was* bitter – had not a fellow, watching with scorn from the pavement, said to me who was just in front of him, 'Stupid politics. Come on, I'll show you some better things in this town than this.'

And so I let myself be led out of the fray which I'd been really quite enjoying until his statement 'stupid politics' had suddenly brought me to my senses and I asked myself why I was getting ridiculously immersed in it, so much so that I'd probably have ended up throwing stones at the police just for the hell of it and then being bashed on the head with a truncheon, or felled by a rubber bullet.

His name's Yurgo, 'Call me George,' he says. We go into a bar in the back streets called *Selini,* one of the very few places young people gather in the evenings, mainly students, and would-be anarchists who are dressed in black. There's a heavy metal group playing on a little stage and a fair bit of head banging going on, the rhythm gets into me and, just as I'd thrown myself into the marching and shouting a while back, I now throw myself into a kind of frenzy on the dance floor.

She caught my attention the moment I entered, as she's extremely pretty, lynx-like, a type I find irresistible, but know that they're almost invariably tricky. But it's only as the joint's closing, sometime after midnight, that I actually get a chance to speak to her. Breaking away from the company she has hitherto been surrounded by, mainly young men, she comes straight up to me and asks if I could take her home.

We sit on the floor in her apartment and she pours us a drink. She then produces a pack of cards, telling me to make a wish as I shuffled them – I hardly need tell you what I wish – it's not that England should win the Tiddly Wink Tournament, or that I'd become a millionaire or that the morrow would be a fine sunny day or anything like that.

'Take three cards,' she says, 'and lay them face down on the carpet.'

I do as she commands. Then one by one she turns them over with her long slender fingers and then, looking at me solemnly, pronounces that my wish isn't going to come true. There's little point in staying any longer and so I put on my coat and bid her goodnight.

I plunge headfirst, wholeheartedly, into the life of the city which is so much more appealing to me than Athens. Not that visually it's any more beautiful, most of the old town having been destroyed in a fire, and it is now a mass of concrete and car-crazy streets; but there is the enormous harbour where you can breathe and escape from the teeming city and here the people are more courteous, more open and friendly and, whereas in Athens I had hardly met a soul who was not a foreigner like myself, here in Saloniki, people come up to me in the street and start talking, curious as to where I'm from or, seeing me walking barefoot and in a threadbare coat, concerned about my welfare—it seems like I'm virtually the only foreigner in town and they feel responsible for my well-being in some way.

George becomes my guide around the town, taking me to bouzouki joints where they play *rebetika*. These are underground, rebel songs that came to Greece, along with the bouzouki and hashish, when the Greeks were expelled from Anatolia by Atatürk in 1923 and thousands of refugees flooded into Greece, especially Thessaloniki and Athens. They sing of love, of injustice, of women and hashish:

> *Otan kapnisi o loulas*
> *esi den prepei na milas . . .*

> When you smoke the nargilhe
> You mustn't speak about it . . .

They're sometimes called the 'Greek blues,' defiant as they are against authority and the terrible injustices meted out to the refugees, many of whom were homeless and sleeping on the streets of the cities. They were outlawed for a long time and gatherings would be broken up by police raids and their participants, the *mangas* as they were called, beaten up and imprisoned.

It's nearing the end of November and the lagoon is blanketed with a thick mist through which ships are barely discernible, emerging into sight from time to time they look for all the world like monsters from the deep silently moving against a dismal grey background. I'm sitting on a bench down by the waterfront having some lunch and looking rather gloomily out on all this, when suddenly standing before me is Jean-Michel who I'd got to know in Athens back in the summer and who was a fabulous musician; he'd studied the guitar at the Lyon conservatoire and beside whom I was just an amateur, but whenever we met he'd insist on us playing together around the cafés, 'Just start playing your crazy pipe,' he'd say, 'and I'll pick up the rhythm.'

'*Condé!*' I exclaim, incredulous at the sight of him suddenly materializing before me, as though out of the mist, and I leap up to embrace him, 'what are you doing here?'

'Just hanging out like you, *Psilé*.'

Condé I call him, which means short chap in Greek, for he's about Gary's height – a funny looking fellow with a pointed beard, a beret and a permanently excitable manner, which I partly put down to drink. He in turn, calls me *Psilé*, which means 'tall chap'.

We recount to each other our adventures and our dubious fortunes as we gravitate with accelerated pace towards a wine tavern in the market. This is the beginning of a three week binge and high old time in that crazy, wonderful time of the year, the build up to Christmas, when the lights go on in the cities, the bars and restaurants are full and the streets bustling with people of exceeding good cheer – it's a marvellous time to be on the main drag and there's money to be made. And what luck to have Condé accompany me with his guitar and his high spirits. 'You lead,' he says to me, 'and I'll pick up your crazy rhythm . . . ' – which he does with impeccable skill, shifting and improvising chords at every unpredictable turn, swoop and soar of my whistle.

'*Ide, Psile, ide,*' he'd prompt and goad in Greek, '*Allez, grand ivrogne, allez,*' ('Go on, big drunkard, go on') And, with the hat full, we repair to a taverna and order plate upon plate of food and jug upon jug of wine. And then we'd start to play at the table – customers at the other tables start singing and drumming on the tabletops, wine flows and gushes down our gullets.

A young man at one of the tables takes a bouzouki out of its case and starts singing:

> *O dromos einai skotinos, oute fengari exei*
> *Einai tholos o ouranos, kai arxisei na vrexei*
> *Einai tholos o ouranos, kai arxisei na vrexei . . .*

> The road is dark and there is no moon
> The sky's overcast and it's begun to rain
> The sky's overcast and it's begun to rain . . .

He's Dimitri (Mitso) and he invites us to stay with him in his apartment near the Rotunda, right in the centre of town, where he lives with his girl friend, 'You can stay as long as you like,' they say, giving us a key to the flat.

Christmas is on its way and my heart's beginning to cry out for Agatha. But how am I going to get all the way up to Germany to be with her? To be with her is the one thing I long for now; I need her sweet love to calm the turbulence I feel within – I need the deep healing she would bring to my soul. I need her to forgive me . . .

The weather's turned bleak and cold and Thessaloniki's enveloped in a dank murky fog which comes like a thick, wet, blanket off the lagoon and I've heard reports of thick snow all the way up through Yugoslavia. Hitch-hiking is out of the question. It'll have to be a train for which I'll somehow have to raise the money and so I go to the station to enquire about prices – not cheap, and I doubt I'll ever make enough to get all the way to Munich, let alone Regensburg. Looking at the large map on the wall of the ticket office I ponder things awhile. If I can get up as far as the Austrian border that'll be the whole length of Yugoslavia traversed and the back of the journey broken, the rest of the journey I'll just have to be on my toes.

I make up a new sign which states that I'm trying to get back home for Christmas. I play like fury in the colonnades of Aristotelous and the generous-hearted people of Thessaloniki soon fill my hat.

A cold rain, turning to sleet, is falling as I buy the ticket first thing in the morning.

Chapter 27

Journey to Regensburg

It looks dark and bleak as I look from the window at the steppe-like landscape. Thank god I'm not out there, and I shiver at the thought. The telephone cables which trail along beside us are sagging with the weight of snow and the wind moans through them as it does through the cracks in the carriage corridors – and I thank god I'm not hanging on outside the carriage. I'm snug in a compartment which much of the time I have to myself so I can stretch out and wrap my sleeping bag around me. I've brought a plentiful supply of bread and cheese and some wine which has me merrily singing along with the rhythm of the wheels on the lines. I fit lines of verse to their clatter as they doggedly take me ever closer to Agatha.

Suddenly there's a screeching of brakes on the lines, we're arriving in Skopje where Gypsy urchins clamber into the carriages as soon as we come to a halt. A wild-eyed one with a head cropped like a bullet pulls back the door of my compartment, 'Money,' he demands, his hand struck out like a punch towards me. '*Imun kek lovi,*' I tell him in his tongue – he looks at me taken aback, 'Money,' he repeats, quietly this time, looking at me very carefully, not at all sure what to make of me.

'*Imun kek lovi, maw praal, deek,*' and I pull my pockets inside out to show him. Completely at a loss as to who I am and how I should speak to him in his own language, he stares at me, muttering, '*Kek lovi . . .*' and dashes on up the carriage.

The further north we go the heavier the snowfalls become. The miles pass monotonously with seldom a break in the white landscape through the window. Perhaps the onion-shaped steeple of a church, a line of grey steel pylons, like miniature Eiffel Towers striding across the flat landscape, a solitary factory chimney or a row of naked poplars along an icy riverbank will jut through the blanket of snow. From time to time a flight of geese or swans will slice through the heavy lead of the sky. Night falls and everything disappears; no stars appear, nor moon.

Lulled by the monotonous clatter of the wheels on the lines and sleepy with the aftermath of the bottle of wine which is now empty I must have dozed off for some considerable length of time for when I come to the train is slowing down and we are crossing a bridge from which I look down into a wide river with the lights of a city thrown into it. A lot of people are filling the corridor looking like they're about to alight. Opening the compartment door I ask someone where we are – Beograd, comes the reply.

Towards the frontier I start to get nervous. My 'legality' will be expiring there and for the rest of the journey I'll have to be on my toes. At the frontier both Yugoslav and Austrian customs officials get on and check passports and luggage and then, without too much delay, we're rolling into Austria–outside the lights of the carriages light up the snow which lies alongside the tracks.

A good thing about these compartments is that there's nothing to stop you sliding in under the seats, which I'm about to do immediately after we start off into Austria–determined not to be taken by surprise as I had been that time in Portugal when I'd not expected a control so soon after the frontier station–but then, just now dammit!–a young man comes in and sits down opposite me. This is a definite spoke in the works of my plan–what should I do? Should I just go ahead anyway, regardless of what he might think; or strike up a conversation with him, to test the water, as it were? I observe him out of the corner of my eye–he looks alright, a little bohemian in fact, probably a student.

I'll have to manoeuvre quickly and so I say, *'Guten abend.'*

'Ah, good evening,' he says in excellent English and smiles, 'Are you Irish? you look Irish.'

'A little bit,' I know he's going to be on my side so I waste no time and say, 'Look, I'm travelling without a ticket and so please excuse me, I'm going to hide under the seat.'

'Ha, yes,' he says, his eyes lighting up, 'I want to see this.'

And with a smile of gratitude towards him I carry my plan into action. Not a moment too soon for almost immediately the compartment door slides open and a pair of jack boots are two feet from my head in my dark lair.

'*Reisepass, bitte,*' I hear him demanding, and then a click of the heels and he's gone.

'Ha, ha—how splendid,' exclaims my new-found friend, 'what a magnificent adventure—you are a stowaway.'

'Yes, I am—and thank-you for being on my side, for playing the game.'

I look up at him grinning from under the seat.

'*Natürlich.* Of course I'm on your side,' and, reaching for his bag, he pulls out a bottle of schnapps, 'perhaps you'd like a little of this . . .'

'Oh yes,' and taking a couple of good swallows, I shiver as a delicious warmth steals through my whole being.

His name is Franz and is a student reading political history at Salzburg University.

'Not such a bad subject', he tells me, 'there are some interesting characters—'rogues' I think you would call them—like Guy Fawkes, a man I particularly admire. He nearly succeeded in blowing the whole of parliament to smithereens.'

I laugh at his use of the word 'smithereens', his English really is good and I'm embarrassed that my knowledge of German goes little beyond '*Prost,*' as we raise the bottle of schnapps in salutation to one another. 'There are quite a few governments that could do with a barrel of gunpowder under them,' he goes on, 'and every November the fifth I blow myself to smithereens with a bottle of schnapps.'

We get onto the subject of poetry. Lit up with the schnapps and flat on my back beneath the seat I've been waxing poetical about life and the adventure of travelling.

'You sound like a poet', he says, 'in fact the way you speak reminds me of the poems of Hermann Hesse. He was a true romantic, do you know him?'

'Oh yes,' I exclaim, delighted at the mention of him; one of the most precious books in my library in England is his *Wandering*, which has extracts from his diary, illustrated with pencil sketches, which he wrote on his journey on foot from Germany down through the Austrian alps to Italy, and which I'd given to my mother one spring day as I set off on my travels south – it seemed to encapsulate everything I felt about my own wandering.

'Yes,' says Franz, obviously pleased that I've read him, 'that is a beautiful book . . . many people dream of doing what he did, just leaving everything behind, including their old selves, and setting off into the unknown – though of course very few people actually do it. I think you have followed in his footsteps,' he laughs, handing me the bottle, 'and you should read his poems, you will like them – they are so sensitive and romantic. Oh, and another poet I think you would like is Rilke, do you know him?'

'No.'

'He too was very sensitive, and very spiritual, mystical, as though he was inspired by something beyond this world – in fact, *The Duino Elegies,* the work he is most well-known for, was inspired by an angel who appeared before him; the first line goes like this, "'Who, if I cried out, would hear me amongst the angelic orders . . . ?" He was Austrian, by the way – you should definitely read him.' I promise him I will – perhaps Agatha will have them and will be able to translate them for me as we lie in bed drinking wine.

The schnapps is working wonders – I'm glowing with it in my dark cubby hole under the seat – and I like Franz very much; he's warm and humorous with a glint in the eye. He'd be fun to go out on the town with, sink some beers, chase some girls. Perhaps I'll get to Salzburg some day and he'll take me on a tour of the beer houses. I can imagine old cobbled streets, bridges over whatever river it is that runs through it, snow-capped mountains all around, beautiful flaxen-haired women.

'Innsbruck,' says my friend, bringing me back to earth, 'this is where I have to get out.' My heart sinks.

'It's been a marvellous journey we've had together, look me up if ever you're in Austria again,' and he hands me a piece of paper on which he has scribbled his address, 'Good luck with the rest of the journey – keep the bottle,' and grasping my hand which I've extended to him from under the seat, he takes his leave.

The train pulls slowly out of Innsbruck and thankfully nobody else has come into the compartment and so I'm left alone with my thoughts and what remains in the bottle. My heart leaps at the thought of being with Agatha again – oh how my heart leaps! I see her blue eyes and dark hair, can almost feel her hair sweeping over my face as I lie here. I can feel her breath as she whispers in my ear, 'You have come, you have come.'

I can feel her joy. I take a swig of schnapps and tears well up in my eyes. Her love is very sweet, very precious – oh why am I so restless, why can't I be happy staying with her, what am I looking for that she can't give me? She gives me everything, dammit, why am I like I am? Why do I have to keep leaving her? Oh my love, I'll be with you soon . . .

I don't know whether the guard passes again or not during the rest of the journey – I'm oblivious to everything as my sobs blend with the rhythmic clatter of the wheels on the lines and the shudder and sway of the carriage.

We pull into Munich which is under a blanket of snow. It's going to be a cold night, the last train for Regensburg has left. I'm scanning the timetable for the times of the trains in the morning when a smartly dressed man of fifty or so approaches me saying, 'Have you missed your train?'

'Yes,'

'In the morning there are more trains – come, you need a place to sleep tonight, probably . . . ' I know perfectly well he's homosexual as I say, 'Yes,' and follow him out to his swish-looking Mercedes parked outside the station in the snow; but I need a place to sleep and I'll be able to handle any untoward situation. We drive to a club, where he buys me a disgusting cocktail which I nearly gag on. He's looking at me in that way I find so unpleasant, which women must find themselves subject to so much of the time. I ignore him and watch the cabaret going on in the centre of the room, which is certainly holding my attention as two girls in leather skirts and nothing else swivel round a pole.

'We go now,' he says abruptly, standing up and I reluctantly follow him to the door – I'd been enjoying the show – and once more we're driving through the winter night, the streets banked up on either side with shovelled snow. Not far from the centre we turn into a narrow street and then into a garage in the basement of a luxury apartment block, and take a lift up to the fourth or fifth floor where, behind a thick metal security door we step into a luxurious penthouse. He motions me to an armchair whilst he fishes some beers from the fridge. I look out of the window, it's snowing hard now, swirling silently and settling on the window ledge – thank god I'm not out there, imagine trying to crawl into some stairway or some nook or cranny in the station . . . brrrr . . . I shudder at the thought; it's warm in here and nice to look out over the rooftops thick with snow, in from the cold, beer at hand, to be alone, put some Mozart on the hi-fi equipment, to sit and drink and dream, without this tedious guy who's obviously going to try it on before long. And sure enough, no sooner have we sat down to drink than he's standing up saying, a feverish tone to his voice, 'We go to bed . . . '

Oh shit, why can't he just go to bed and leave me to enjoy the beer? I tell him I can sleep here, pointing to the floor which is covered with a thick carpet on which I'd be very comfortable.

'No, no, the bed is big – you sleep on the bed.'

'But here is good . . . I have a sleeping bag, I will sleep well here . . . ' but he's insistent and quite determined that I'm not going to sleep on the floor. And so reluctantly I get into the bed, keeping my clothes on, and then of course he follows.

'No! No! 'I say firmly, as he tries to cuddle up to me.

'Just to hold you,' he says pathetically,

'No,' I say getting as fast as I can to the extreme edge of the bed – 'No, nein, nein,' I shout as his hand tries to pull me back, 'I will sleep on the floor,' and am about to jump out of the bed. He's whining in a throttled voice now, 'I'll be good.'

Well, he doesn't bother me after that and for some time I hear the sound of him doing something under the blankets, terminating in a stifled cry. Then there's silence and I sleep the sleep of the just until the morning. He makes a good breakfast and is all kindness and a little sheepish-looking about his performance in the night. He looks as though he's probably some respectable businessman. He offers to drive me to the station which I'm glad of and on the way ask him if he could give me the price of the ticket to Regensburg.

'*Natürlich,*' he says.

I manage to call her from the station and, with feverish excitement, board the train. At high speed we flash through the brilliant white landscape, gleaming in the bright mid-winter sun. And now here she is, running along the platform and throwing her arms around me as I alight from the train. How beautiful she is in her green coat and silk head scarf, tying her flowing hair behind her neck like a Gypsy girl.

'You've come,' she cries in my ear, 'You've come back to me.'

The banks of the Danube are white and chunks of ice float under the bridges, the coloured lights of Regensburg, all lit up for Christmas, are sprinkled like stars in the water as we stand for a while in silence on the bridge.

'Do you know Rilke?' I ask her,

For a few moments she's quiet, as though she's remembering something, and then, squeezing my hand she says, so quietly it sounds like a prayer:

> Isn't the secret intent
> of this taciturn earth, when it forces lovers together,
> that inside their boundless emotion all things may shudder
>   with joy?

> (Translated by Stephen Mitchell.)

It's so good to be back with her again and we spend all that Christmas holiday in bed making love and drinking wine. Her body has never seemed softer, warmer, as we lay beneath the skylight through the dark cold days, snow falling outside. Sometimes we go out for walks along the Danube or to wander around the glittering streets of Regensburg with its magnificent cathedral and cobbled streets and beer houses bursting with life and merriment, warming ourselves by the wood stoves. And wandering over the bridges, feet crunching in the snow and invariably ending up at the Roter Herzfleck (the Red Heart Spot) under the stone arch, its warm Sienna-red and ochre walls lit up by the lantern above our heads, where we kiss and swear undying love. At times like this I think to marry her, we could be so happy, if only I was different . . . But I know in my heart, and it is such a horrible thing to know, that I will abandon her one day.

And now spring has come along and with it the old restlessness, the calling of the road, and I suddenly feel trapped – the sweetest of traps, the nets of Venus, and the hardest to disentangle oneself from. But when one evening in April the phone rings and it's Tim telling me to hit the trail up to Kiel on the Baltic, right up in the North, where he is on the good ship Sinbad, a tall-masted yacht, where they are chartering the boat to tourists for excursions round the bay, I jump at it and, leaving behind a tearful Agatha, depart the very next morning, sticking my thumb out on the autobahn and, incredibly, reach Kiel by nightfall.

As instructed by Tim, I signal that I'm here by flashing a torch from the harbour wall in the direction of a tall-masted yacht lying at anchor some three hundred yards out to sea which I reckon is theirs. I laugh uproariously as Tim comes over in a dinghy to pick me up.

I laugh until my sides split at his appearance, he looks just like Shakespeare in some of the portraits, with the balding bonce and what remains of his hair reaching to his shoulders, with the tufted goatee beard, the earring in his ear and his teeth flashing in the lights of the harbour, the very picture of a pirate. I need not tell you that we drink like pirates that night, and through it until dawn – Tim and I and Ian, the skipper.

The weather's glorious on the ensuing days. In the mornings we take on board a handful of day trippers, sometimes as many as fifteen of them, and then after freeing the ropes from the capstones and pushing the boat off we set off around the bay, mine and Tim's job done for the morning. While Ian, the skipper and proud owner of Sinbad is at the helm, holding the tourists enwrapped with tales of the sea, many of them, according to Tim, wild exaggerations and others entirely made up but they keep his audience enthralled – all part of the day's excursion. So while he's thus engaged and oblivious to everything else, Tim and I smuggle a crate of beer up to the foremast, a reasonable distance from the wheel and out of sight as we sit behind it, and entertain ourselves with bottles and bottles of strong Pilsner.

A week or so passes with these daily excursions around the bay and then one evening nine journalists and photographers come aboard, sober and terribly serious-looking. They have chartered the boat to take them to a tall ships race in Copenhagen – so that makes thirteen of us, including Brian the engineer. We, the crew, have been drinking gin and tonic all day long on board another yacht in the harbour so that by the time we put to sea the four of us are at least three sheets to the wind. The journalists are all extremely serious and rather alarmed to find the crew in such a state.

We head out into the open sea where a favourable wind fills the sails and we cut along nicely towards Denmark. After a while Ian, our illustrious skipper, announces that he's going below for a kip and leaves Tim at the wheel. Tim of course is an accomplished sailor and has no trouble keeping us on course. The sky is full of stars and the invigorating wind buffets our faces and keeps the sails filled to their magnificent capacity as the noble old vessel streaks through the waves, every sinew in its body taut and quivering like a thoroughbred stallion.

We have a bottle of schnapps which we lift high, toasting the stars and the gods of the sea. And the more we drink the merrier we become, laughing and joking and throwing all caution to the wind. After a while Tim has to take a leak.

'Take the wheel,' he says, and wanders over to the railings to piss over the side. Of course, leaving me at the helm is rather a rash thing to do. The compass is swinging from one side to another and it seems to me the thing to do is to steady it up and try to keep the needle in the centre. I swivel the wheel from side to side in an attempt to right it. All of a sudden there's a thunderous crack and wrenching sound, the boom swings violently overhead narrowly missing Tim and catapulting him into the black churning cauldron of the waves. The whole ship shudders, the sails are wrenched from their fastenings, there's screaming from the journalists below and Ian rushes up to the deck to take the wheel which is twisted and no longer responding. The sails are flapping wildly and collapsing all around. And then the journalists, white faced and panicking, clamber up from below, their pallid faces appearing at the hatch, screaming and yelling, '*Mein gott, was geht? Hilf uns!*'

Pathetic they are really and Ian shouts back at them, 'Shut up you lot or I'll throw you overboard!'

With the waves washing over the deck and the ship, rudderless now, lurching and drifting at the mercy of the wind which, until now, had been so benign and obliging in its swift conveyance over the waves, we stagger around the deck hauling the soaked, heavy sails in from the sea. With the adrenaline, and of course the schnapps, pumping through my blood I feel no fear, only a kind of wild exhilaration, as I battle with the seething elements. I feel god-like, invincible! Only the realisation that this was all my fault tempers a feeling of pure exultation.

Brian, the engineer, has tried to start the engine but it's flooded and besides, with the steering gone, it would be futile to get it running. With a walkie-talkie Ian manages to contact the harbour master in Kiel, some twenty odd miles behind us. They'll launch the lifeboat immediately. It will of course take some time to reach us and we must keep constant radio contact to help them find us. When it does finally appear on the horizon we send up Very lights to guide them in. And then poor old battered Sinbad is towed back all the way we'd come.

As I said, my conscience is uneasy about the whole misadventure but Ian, gentleman that he is, only blames himself and his own inebriated condition for the whole disastrous escapade. All the chartering money will have to be returned and Sinbad will have to stay for months at the repair shops in Kiel.

It's already May by the time I get back to Regensburg and Agatha can sense that the journey has changed me and that I am already far away. She knows it and she silently grieves.

'We can meet in Italy in June,' I say, knowing that she has holidays then, 'that's not far off.' It goes some way to consoling her, but I catch her crying sometimes and it breaks my heart. Nevertheless, I set off one early morning heading for Munich.

Chapter 28

Munich

I hitch to Munich through the early summer landscape, the beautiful rolling hills of Bavaria with their fields of yellow rape. Arriving in Munich I swallow a bottle of wine in Marienplatz and fall in with a load of musicians, jugglers and drifters and spend a marvellous night of drunken revelry in the streets and bars, such as I haven't done in a long while. This decides me on staying here a bit, a week or so perhaps, giving Munich a whirl – it's still an unknown city to me.

I've drunk all the money Agatha put in my pocket to help me on the way and so this morning I set up the dolls on the busiest shopping street which runs off Marienplatz, the Kaufingerstrasse. I've made a new plaque in German saying more or less what the other one said and, not without a little apprehension, I stand here on the pavement and wait to see what kind of a reaction it will cause in the Germans. Well, it certainly is very different from the Greeks, very different. This is a typical scenario:

'Zat is your family?' says the puzzled person before me.
'Yes,'
'*Ach so*,' followed by an inspection of me from head to toe, and then down at the dolls again, 'and zat is your vife?'
'Er . . . Yes, that is my wife.'
'Ach so. She has no body?'
'Yes, look, that's her body,' I say, pointing to the stick.

'*Ach so* . . . ' always this damned '*Ach so*,' as the logical brain tries to grasp the situation, 'she is very tin zen . . . '

'Yes, she is very thin – she is hungry, you see, very hungry.'

'Are you hungry too?' my interrogator asks in a way that seems to be trying to catch me out and admit that it's because it's really me that's hungry, so why don't I say so, instead of making up this stupid story with these dolls.

'Yes I am,' I say, feeling thoroughly ridiculous by this time.

And, like squeezing water out of a stone, at last a coin might fall in the bowl – not a healthy clunk but a *plink* – ten pfenigs, or twenty or, if I'm lucky, half a mark. No, the Germans are a little short on humour – but perhaps my show really isn't very funny – and they have to know exactly why and what for they are giving me alms. They obviously can't understand why I don't just be honest and tell them straight out that I'm hungry. I'm sorry, I'm being hard on the Germans and I feel a little bad about this as I remember the very first time I was in Germany when I was eighteen or nineteen and how on a couple of occasions when hitchhiking the driver would give me twenty or thirty marks as I got out of the car, telling me to enjoy my stay and how once, in a small, mediaeval town, with half-timbered houses and cobbled streets, just as you see in the old fairy tales, in a little inn, finding my supper had been paid for by the people on the next table who had already left when I came to pay the bill and then the pretty young waitress, the daughter of the owners, asking me where I was sleeping that night and upon my reply, 'Out in the fields', her turning to her mother, saying something and then turning back to me, 'You will be our guest, you will pay nothing,' and then being shown to a delightful room with low beams and a big soft bed and little wooden-framed windows looking out onto the square.

I awoke in the morning to the sound of a gentle tap on the door and the maid telling me breakfast awaited me downstairs in the dining room. They all gathered round me wishing me a '*Güte Reise*' as I slung my rucksack over my shoulder. Thanking them from the bottom of my heart I set out, rested and refreshed and with a memory I shall never forget as long as I live.

It's fun being on the street again and always manage to make the requisite amount with which to eat and go round the beer houses in the evenings. Ah, Bavarian beer, nowhere have I found such scrumptious ale as this. Thurn und Taxis, Postmeister Doppel Bock and other hoppy, sparkling golden ones, I pour down my gullet.

It's to the *Hofbräuhaus*, the most renowned of all Munich beer houses, I head most evenings. It's really an outlandish establishment, with its great hall-like, echoing interior and long tables, row upon row of them. Big buxom Bavarian women serve the tables, carrying as many as ten '*Masses*' at a time – a *Mass* is a glass stein about a foot high and which holds a litre – their biceps bulging and their tongues sharp and shrill – one minds one's p's and q's with these fräuleins. In the middle of the hall is a stage on which beefy fellows in lederhosen and trilbies play sentimental songs from the Bavarian woods along with rousing drinking and marching songs, on drums, trombones and accordions whilst, in their midst an enormous muscular frau, with blonde hair and blue eyes, blows with all her might into a trumpet which stirs the beer-swilling multitude to their feet and, from their enfevered souls, the most grotesque renditions of song rise up into the upper reaches of the hall – a far cry from the melodious songs of Greece. I have to confess that, after a couple of those jugs of beer, it doesn't really matter what or how you sing as long as you're singing.

Some memorable evenings I spend in here, sometimes alone sometimes in the company of other drifters like myself. This is the place that Lamb would haunt when he was mugging businessmen up alleyways. As long as one has the price of an initial *Mass*, the three or four marks or whatever it is, one can remain in here the whole evening and get completely pie-eyed by means of 'minesweeping'. 'Minesweeping', as I've said before, means going around the tables polishing off unfinished '*Masses*' of which there are plenty some half full, others hardly touched – but being very careful not to catch the attention of the fräuleins.

I'm living in the station – or rather around it, for I sleep in a building-site nearby so as not to be disturbed by the *polizei* that come along at night with batons and dogs; but I frequent it often

during the day: starting in the morning, with coffee in the canteen. It's good coffee and seems to be the cheapest in town, and the canteen is a lively place, being full of Turkish *Gastarbeiter*: the sound of their voices being more musical to my ear and easier on my hungover head at that tender hour than the rasping, guttural German. And besides, in a railway station, whose atmosphere is of constant coming and going, of transience, the very essence of which is change, movement, I feel at home. I can spend untold hours in them—wandering along the platforms, feeling the pulse of the vibrant locomotives about to spring into the unknown, going through timetables and letting the names of cities work upon my imagination and hearing their names roared thunderously from loudspeakers in the eaves high above: destinations, distances, dispersion—the hours ticking like hammers, like our lives, towards departure and the unknown future.

In whatever city I find myself I'll never resist the temptation to come in off the street and immerse myself awhile in the supercharged atmosphere of the main railway station—just as in Paris, at times of supreme anguish, I'd sit in a church whose peace and silence and the figures of Mary cradling her infant was like balm to my troubled soul and my thoughts would stop turning, churning, and I'd step back out onto the street calmed and strengthened. But stations fill me with something else—nervous, electric energy, which conjures up movement and visions of distant cities.

> From the walls the names of cities boom
> on electric tongues
> which conjure up distance, dispersion, as the hours
> ticking like hammers strike
> everything present into the future . . .

There's a soup kitchen in the *Hauptbahnhof* in Munich where one can eat absolutely free of charge, run by the railway company itself and called the *Bahnhofsmission*. In a dingy, rather sinister little room at the top of some stairs that lead up from the platform one is served a thin soup and a chunk of bread by an unsmiling woman behind a grubby counter. As you sit down to eat at one of the wooden tables a policeman from a little office next door—from which they watch through a peep-hole, everyone who comes and goes – comes in and inspects your papers. It's all so reminiscent of Nazi Germany and it gives me the creeps. After having one's broth one can stroll over to the other side of the station where there are offices of the Red Cross run by nuns who serve you tea and biscuits.

One afternoon, whilst thus partaking of tea, I fall into conversation with another tea partaker. His presence on the table next to mine had been making me a little nervous, what with his cropped head and frightened eyes which were darting all over the place. He fixed me with his stare a moment and then began to tell me his story in pretty good English but with a heavy German accent.

'I'm on the run. I escaped from the Foreign Legion in Marseille and I'm trying to get back to Berlin, once there I'll be safe, I'll be able to lose myself in the city, but I have to get through the checkpoint at the frontier, they are sure to have my name there and they'll send me back – you can't imagine what hell that would be, *mein Gott*, worse than death, *ja, viel schlimmer als der Tot*, much, much worse than death,' he's wringing his hands, his face contorted, 'if only I had time to grow my hair, but if I am staying around here I'll get picked up.'

Well, I can see how easy that would be, I just need to think of the surveillance at the soup kitchen. He'd got mixed up in a raid on a post office in Berlin – an armed raid with a bunch of amateurs – they got caught, of course, immediately, and given heavy prison sentences. And it was then that he heard about a scheme that if you served five years in the Foreign Legion, as a kind of option to prison, your sentence would be annulled, you'd be issued with a new passport and any past crimes would be wiped off the slate. 'That's why the Legion is full of thugs, really nasty characters some of them – it's hell, I tell you – from morning till night it's hell.' I look at him, he has quite a sensitive face really, certainly not the face of a criminal. I wonder how he'd got into this mess in the first place.

We retire to a beerhouse on the Kaufingerstrasse where I'm able to help him with the price of a beer or two which steadies him up a bit and some of the anxiety goes out of his face, to the point where he can crack the occasional smile as he recounts the whole stupid turn of events and his incredible naïvety, 'I guess there's a kind of roman-

tic appeal about the Foreign Legion, something heroic – ha! – heroic!
something exotic even . . . yes, I'd even pondered the idea of joining
up when I was young – you know the kind of crazy notions one has
as a youth,' he says, looking at me, his head cocked to one side, 'and
so, when I was sentenced to eight years – eight years. Stuck in a cell!
I requested the option of joining up instead. No problem – in no
time.

'I was in a uniform in the Sahara and having my head beaten
about by my companions, the other Legionnaires . . . initiation for
a new recruit wet behind the ears,' he looks pretty glum as he stares
into his beer, 'and then I was sent into my first engagement with the
enemy, we had no idea who they were but the Foreign Legion always
has to have an enemy. We were dropped by parachute over a village
in the middle of nowhere from which as we came down we were being shot at. As we landed on the scorching sand and were scrabbling
for cover the only person I'd become friends with, another German,
suddenly fell down at my side – he was dead. *Tot – mein Gott* – he
was dead! I went mad and started to run, run away from where the
shooting was coming, but one of the others came after me, caught
me and struck me in the face so hard I collapsed. I was lucky they
didn't leave me there but back at base camp I was beaten without
mercy and put on a ship to Marseille where they were going to put
me through a tribunal and the commandant shouted at me as I was
leaving, "*Vingt ans! Tu vas avoir vingt ans!*" *Ja, zwantzig Jahre* . . . you
see, if I'm caught now at the frontier . . . *ach!*

His head's in his hands, a look of utter despair on his countenance.

'Have another beer,' and I call over to the buxom fräulein.

'I got away as we were coming off the ship, something totally irrational happened which distracted my guards – it was a miracle – if
it was not a miracle then I cannot explain or understand anything
anymore . . . ', his face has lit up and for the first I detect a ray of
hope as in a man who is suddenly unburdened of the gravity of his
plight.

'So don't worry,' I reassure him, 'forces which you can't see are
obviously on your side.'

I see him off on the evening train, his hand stretching from the window of the carriage window, grasps mine, '*Danke mein Freund,*' and the train moves off towards his uncertain fate.

'Look, we're getting nowhere like this.'
'Yes we are'.
'No we're not'.
'Yes we are.'
'We aren't,'
'We are,'
'Aren't!'
'Are!'

I love that sort of argument because I always defeat my opponent, simply because I can go on and on, ad infinitum, until I wear him out. I don't tire of that kind of conversation, I don't find it the slightest bit tedious, in fact I relish it. It's like with arm wrestling, at which I've rarely been defeated, not because I'm bulging with biceps but simply because I go into an arm lock, truly locked, not budging, though my opponent be straining and puffing with all his might to push my arm over but never can, for I've concentrated all my force there while at the same time remaining very relaxed, I suppose it's to do with the gathering and directing of *chi,* as martial artists do in the orient, and I can stay that way until my opponent has exhausted himself and then I simply flip his arm over with ease.

Yesterday I strayed unwisely into this dingy bar in search of a beer and had instantly regretted it as my eyes adjusted to the darkness and made out the customers in there – a bunch of drunken seamen staring at me in a hostile, belligerent manner as I made my way to the bar, by which time it was too late to turn on my heels and beat a retreat out of there. Somewhat nervously I ordered a beer from the landlord who looked as villainous as the rest of them and I was beginning to fear for my safety.

'*Du, Ausländer, komm hier,*' commanded one of them and with a brutish gesture motioned me to sit at the table of him and his leering mates. They'd been sparring with feats of strength and this one had emerged the champion it seemed. 'Fight,' he barked and he

planted his beefy, tatooed arm assertively on the table and barked
into my face, 'Fight, *Ausländer.*'

Assuming an air of macho calm, which totally belied my nervous apprehension about the menacing atmosphere in that place,
I took up the challenge and immediately applied the lock at the
upright. It soon became evident that what he thought was going to
be a pushover with this puny *Ausländer* was going to be otherwise
as he pushed and strained, tried twisting my arm, and any other
ruse he could think of to get the better of me, all the time sweating
and cursing '*Scheise,*' and petitioning encouragement from his mates
who were all beginning to realise that their champion was on his
way to a humiliating defeat as I simply would not budge. Little by
little I sensed his huge straining muscles begin to slacken and then
I began my offensive, his arm by now offering no resistance to mine
and in no time his now limp arm lay on its back on the table with
mine on top of it. '*Ach, Scheise,*' he muttered in defeat and I was
treated to a lot of beers after that, and pats on the back from the
whole drunken crew and, despite my wobbling about a bit, I walked
out real tall from that dive – the muscle man, the cock o' the walk,
the indisputable champion.

Chapter 29

A Stroll in the Mountains

I t's time to leave Munich, summer's arriving in all her glory, and the road is calling. I'd have left this morning had not I run into an Irishman, Peter, yesterday evening who, over a beer, told me he was making money for nothing—for lazing around in a summer garden during the day and at night sleeping in a soft feather bed and, on top of that, being fed three square meals a day. Needless to say, I was nothing short of intrigued and pressed him as to how he'd stumbled upon such singular good fortune and, after a long Celtic preamble, he came to the point, 'There's a clinic in the suburbs in a very pleasant part of town, where the grass grows green and roses bloom, which tests medical drugs on human beings, the likes of us, who need to make a fast buck—me, myself, even as you look at me, am in fact in the very process of defining the qualities, both good and bad of a drug which, until now, has only been tested on gorillas and, though it may have taken me millions of years, or perhaps the equivalent number of beers, to evolve beyond the state of a gorilla am now, as a fully-fledged human being, getting over a hundred marks a day for my troubles, which are not really troubles at all, and am forsworn to fifteen days and nights of this enforced idleness, at the end of which I'll be getting a pretty penny, nearly two thousand marks which in this day and age stands at around five hundred pounds.'

He gave me the address to which I've presented myself this morning, and they've offered me a three day course on some heart drug, a beta blocker or something, which I eagerly accepted. I'm glad it'll be just three days because the road's calling very loudly and urgently to me now that summer's here – I'll make four hundred marks, half of which I'll send to Agatha to buy herself that dress she'd seen in a shop window, and with the rest I'll wander around Austria awhile before descending into Italy.

Just as my easy-going Irish friend Peter told me, it's an easy way of making money. I'm given a tablet in the morning, weighed a few times, have blood and heartbeat checked – and that's that. There are superb meals, a lovely garden to lounge around in, reading, and talking with the other inmates, who are mainly British; two of them are in for six weeks and are planning to go to India with the money they make. And now, at the end of this three days of enforced idleness, as Peter put it, I get paid, send the money off to Agatha to buy the dress she'd seen in the window of a shop and at which she'd expressed such delight, and head for the *Hauptbahnhof* where I'm going to jump a train to Kufstein, just over the Austrian border. Here, as I lean against a column on the platform, I watch the rushing to and fro, the hurrying to catch trains, the boarding, the alighting, the joyful meetings, the tearful farewells – people caught up in an urgency, a compulsion, a frenzy in this place between places. The headlines of a paper, behind which a man walks blindly to a departing train, are written in black, 'Wall Street Shudders.' I wonder what's afoot as the worry written into the fellow's face is black as the print. A man and a woman saying goodbye – look how forlorn she is in her grief, how her face is washed like marble with her tears while he is comforting, promising and gesturing but already far away, one eye darting restlessly into the distance, unable to perceive the pathos of the present in which he abandons her and from which she cannot take flight, for how can you flee from love when it consumes your whole being and binds you with iron chains?

> The station clock is waving its hands over its face
> in a frantic gesture compelled by time
> in two minds torn weeping we turn away . . .

There's a bookshop in the station which has a section of English books; there isn't much of interest, mainly the sort of trash one finds in airports and stations, and I'm just about to turn away in disgust from the shelves when my eye, as though guided by forces I can't detect, alight upon a title which shines out at me: *Buddhism*. I reach for it. What an extraordinary sounding woman I think as I read excitedly about the author: Alexandra David Neil, who had travelled on foot alone all through the Alps, when little more than a girl, and later through the Himalayas and had got into the forbidden city of Lhasa – the first Westerner ever to do so – disguised as a beggar. Now that's an adventuress. In this book she set down the fundamental precepts of Buddhism, the subject of which it's high time I should inform myself. The price I see with dismay is exorbitant; but I have to have it to take into the Austrian Alps with me and so I slip it into my coat pocket and walk out onto the platform. How excited I am to feel this strange volume which will eventually lead me to such vistas of the soul, pressing against my heart.

> *Kennst du die Perle, die Perle Tirols,*
> *das Städtchen Kufstein, das kennst du wohl;*
> *Umrahmt von Bergen, so friedlich und still . . .*

The air's exhilarating in Kufstein, pure mountain air which goes to my head and makes everything about me so vivid; colours spring from the depths of the shadows and sounds out of the silence are alive and speak to me and I listen, intensely present to the world. Leaning on the railings of a bridge which spans a fiercely rushing current below, I watch the sun go down and listen to a cuckoo's last call, coming from the woods which flank the river upstream; I hear some cattle lowing in the distance, a blackbird's heart-rending song mingling with the voice of the river below. Everything is purple and soon will turn silver with the light of the waxing moon. I get hold of a few bottles of beer and go down to the river bank to celebrate this May night, to raise my brimming bottle to the heavens, to the stars, and to rejoice that once again I'm wandering.

I couldn't be in a more receptive mood for my preliminary studies of Buddhism than I am in these weeks, wandering around the mountains and villages of Austria. Alexandra David Neil laid out the precepts of this doctrine in a clear, concise, manner but without ever a hint of academic dryness. Here is one of the finest of the rare breed of adventurers that has set out to find the truth of her life and the meaning of existence. My pursuit of romance and adventure is at heart no different from this, but whereas I have pitched myself into the world – for that is where my particular need of instruction lies – she went straight to the mountains, scaled the heights, where she knew that in the rarefied air, the awesome immensity of silence, and in the mouths of certain sages, lay the Great Secret which she sought. To have no desires except for the overwhelming one, to know oneself – that's where freedom lies. What single-mindedness, intensity of purpose she had. Me, I am driven by something relentless within, truth I suppose, the meaning of myself, but I am entangled and torn apart by all manner of terrestrial desires; my craving for alcohol and women keep me rooted to the Earth.

But during this sojourn in the mountains it is not difficult to transcend my nature and walk for a while on the dizzy heights by the side of this dauntless, striding woman. There can be no doubt that this dichotomy between the sensual and the spiritual side of my nature has been the cause, the root of my greatest trials and tensions. I have an enormous capacity for the lusts and pleasures of the flesh coupled with the equally ardent drive towards the total denial of them. This violent swinging from one extreme to the other, unable to steer a middle course between them, is what has brought me to my knees both in prayer and in despair, time after time. And how bittersweet life is: one moment the peaks of joy, exhilaration, ecstasy – the next, floods of tears, despair. We are as subject to our moods as to the violent storms which come raging in from the ocean, and we sway, absurdly helpless, on the swell like little boats with no rudders and no keels. When things happen to us, come rushing at us from the unfathomable depths of existence, there's no one reliable to be found to take the helm, all the selves we take to be ourselves are not who we really are and they run amok whilst the ship's sinking, each one assuming the role of captain, whilst the true captain's locked in the hold – and there's no use now looking up, crying for deliverance.

How many times did I find myself in this plight, did I find myself face upturned to the heavens that, in all my dreaming I thought must hear me? Not surprising that they turned a deaf ear for I would only turn my gaze upward when enstormed; whilst at other times, when about my worldly pursuits, I was none too concerned about the attentions of the heavens; in fact, I was altogether more comfortable if its gaze was directed elsewhere – paradise on earth was what I wanted, with this woman in my arms in this forbidden bed. So no wonder, as fortune's wheel turned from pleasure to pain, joy to sorrow, from ecstasy to despair, no wonder that I should find myself out in the night, as I so often did, bottle in hand, fist raised to the heavens, cursing, and the gods laughing at my supplications, my futile pleas.

I was a youth and sadly wanting

It was in a wayside tavern in the Tyrol
I sat drinking a draught of beer and smoking my pipe
whilst the waitress in an apron with lovely flaxen hair
moved from table to table with the grace of a sprite
and every now and then she glanced my way
seeming with a question in her look
but panic-stricken, tongue-tied, knotted-up inside I
    dropped my eyes–
for I was a youth and sadly wanting
in such things as these

And I wondered on my way home,
pausing on the bridge over the rushing river
torrid as the longings tormenting my soul,
how she'd take the little note I'd slipped
under the beer mat and whether
on the morrow I should go back
a little bolder and see–
or just be inept, leave it at that
sling my rucksack over my shoulder
and go on my way.

A steady downpour of rain is falling as I approach the Brenner Pass, the frontier of Italy. Crossing on foot I'm likely to be asked to

show the money I have on me – that would be precisely none – and
that's exactly what does happen, 'No money? Then you must go
back to Austria,' says the guard, pointing me back in the direction
I've come.

'But . . . but I have money waiting for me in a bank in Rome,' I
lie.

'You go back to Austria,' he repeats, and I know that only the
sight of banknotes or travellers cheques would change his mind. So
I have to turn back through the Austrian customs again and wander
about getting drenched in the pouring rain. I haven't even enough
for a coffee; my spirits are pretty low as I stand under the awning
of a building and debate as to what to do. I am determined to get
into Italy and the south: so somehow I will. I'll wait until dark and
then cross the border through the mountains, I think to myself, I'm
sure there won't be guards everywhere and that I'll be able to slip
through. Suddenly a boy in the petrol station the other side of the
road is hailing me through the rain. He's motioning me to come
over and take shelter in the office.

'Oh, danke,' I say gladly as I step in out of the rain.

'You like some coffee?'

'Oh yes, yes please,' this is a very unusual experience, being given
shelter and brought coffee in a busy service station like this. The
young boy is extremely kind and asks me from where I come and,
when I say England, his face lights up and he says, 'Oh, my brother
is speaking English,' and he points out of the window at a young
man who has been dealing with a customer and is now on his way
to the office. He comes in and introduces himself, shaking my hand.
He starts speaking English fluently, telling me he spent some time in
London and with a glance through the window laughingly asks me
whether the weather reminds me of my motherland – 'Not a little,'
I reply. He asks me where I'm going and when I tell him I'm trying to get into Italy but have been turned back for lack of money
he is most sympathetic, 'Everything always boils down to money,'
he says, 'Look at those big cars – some of them contain criminals, I
mean people who exploit others by cheating and lying and so have
big cars, lots of money and the guards are very happy to see them
and let them through – good stay in Italy, good stay in Austria, they

say – well this is the world isn't it: upside down – always will be. You're hungry maybe . . . '

'Yes . . . ' I say, and with that he leaps up and into a little kitchen where in next to no time he's prepared for me a cheese omelette and toast.

'Thank you, thank you,' I breathe, overwhelmed by this hospitality. As I eat I tell him of my plan to cross the border through the mountains, 'that would be very dangerous,' he says, 'listen, is the only reason for them not letting you into Italy the lack of money? I mean, you have a passport, I suppose?'

And on my nodding, he says, 'Then I can help you,' and with that he pulls a wad of banknotes from his pocket and puts them into my hand, 'now you should have no problem.'

I'm speechless with gratitude as I grasp him by the hand and take my leave. The guard is somewhat surprised, if not suspicious, at seeing all the money I present for his inspection – as he stamps my passport I can't discern whether it's a smile or a scowl that hovers at the corner of his mouth; whatever it is, we both know that money always does the trick and is the one sure thing to move an official's heart. I pick up a lorry moving south, the rain eases up and the sun breaks through the black storm clouds as we descend into Italy through the towering black Dolomites.

I had not been long in Italy when by a chance phone call to England I learnt that my younger brother Tony was to be wedded to Tacye, a girl from Ireland, towards the end of June and this was not to be missed of course. I was glad that it was still a few weeks away as I'd be able to meet Agatha as arranged but as far as my further plans which were to go down to the south of Italy and cross over to Greece they would have to be changed.

Agatha arrives with her brother and his sweetheart and we spend marvellous days and nights in the south Tyrol, clambering around the mountains, picnicking, lying in the long grass beneath azure skies of June, lovers entwined in one another's arms, flesh and spirit coming together in harmonious rapture. At night we go drinking and walking out under the stars, the scent of hay and honeysuckle blending with the song of indescribable yearning of the nightingale.

I drive north with them as far as Regensburg and her parting words are, 'Please wish your brother all happiness in his marriage. His wife will be happy too,' for a moment her voice chokes, I know what she's trying to say and I can only stroke her hair and look away into the distance, 'There's always this sadness in me since I know you,' she says, 'there is this sadness and I know it will accompany me until I die.'

Chapter 30

Marden

I take the road to the Channel, arriving in Marden in the nick of time, the very day before the wedding. So here we are, home with a capital 'H', for it's always been home to me and a refuge whenever I've been weary of the road and in need of recuperation. I've not yet spoken about the house in which I grew up and any story which purports to be an account of my life would be incomplete without it. Nor have I told you about my family who are all gathered here now, except for Kingsley, the oldest of my brothers, from whom a wedding gift for Tony has arrived from Cairo with Kingsley's unmistakable scrawl. Well I never, 'old Tone,' youngest of my brothers and with whom I grew up and went to school, is about to tie the knot. Here's my mother now, who has just extracted herself from the chicken house where she's been trying to catch a cockerel that has a chronic condition of bumble foot, and is rushing towards me her bare feet skimming unflinchingly over the gravel to give me a hug, 'Just in time,' she says, 'lovely to see you.'

Here is my father striding over, his hand outstretched, greeting me with a welcoming joke, 'You're arriving in such a grand manner and with such a reception one would think it was you that was getting married.'

And who is this coming round the corner of the barn, none other than Ashley – no need to introduce him. He has been busy on one of his eccentric projects, making scarecrows out of old bits of timber, rags, battered hats, nuts and bolts and other bits and pieces he finds

lying around. 'Ah, excellent,' he greets me, and glancing at my attire, 'you can pose as a model for me.'

We are standing in the yard now, drinking champagne when the very most characteristic sound to be heard at this homestead, along with the clucking of hens, the crowing of cocks and the cooing of pigeons, is suddenly all around us: the yelping and barking of hysterical hounds, the beagles, the mischievous little beagles that have arrived back from the hills with Wendy, my sister – Wendy who is like the huntress Diana with her pack of baying hounds; Wendy who spoils me rotten when I'm home. So here we are, the gathering of the clans, 'If only Kingsley was here,' my mother is saying, 'then we'd all be here.'

Here we are, in the yard of the rambling Old Vicarage, which stands in all its tumbledown elegance beneath the tower of the church of All Saints, Marden, a little village in the valley between the Marlborough Downs and Salisbury Plain. This is the house I grew up in from the age of six or seven when we moved from Market Lavington a village some five miles west, the one in which I was born – in a house on the High Street – on a midwinter's night in 1953. My parents had recently moved down from Scotland where my father was partner in a practice in Edinburgh. My mother wanted to return to Wiltshire where her roots were – just as my roots are, although I feel plenty of highland blood swishing about in my veins, giving me a somewhat fiery, martial temperament and the reddish hair. According to my father we are descended from Bloody Graham of Claverhouse, famous for his savagery in the struggles against the English. But in the union of my parents Scotland and England were harmoniously knit. I could not have hoped for better parents; I consider it one of the greatest assets of my life that fortune blessed me with the family I was born into. I don't know whether, as incarnating souls, we choose our parents, or whether they've chosen for us. The most satisfying explanation I've come across is the one in the Kabbalah where it says that when a soul is about to be incarnated it is brought down to a level just above the Earth by two angels, the guardian angels I suppose (and my god, do I not have a lot to thank them for) one on either side of it, who wait for the couple, who are to be its parents, to join in love and at the moment of conception bring it down and plant it in the woman's womb. They remain with it during the nine months of pregnancy and show its whole future life as though, like an acorn, the soul contained the whole tree which would be its life. It is shown every event, every situation it must resolve, every person it will meet, and every choice and decision it will have to make. After this intense Instruction and at the moment before birth the angels blow a flame out, and the soul forgets everything it has been shown, as it emerges into the world. But, deep inside it is all remembered. And then it goes through life with everything happening to it exactly as it was shown in the womb. What happens normally is, instead of fighting against its natural inclinations, it will invariably take the easy way around things, thereby lacking the essential strugglethat would lead to the growth it came here to accomplish. Unless, by chance, it hears a little voice through the din of its daily life and it remembers something: remembers who it is and why it came, and what it had to do. The angels remain with us throughout our lives, prompting us, guiding us, pulling us out of ditches, trying to stop us dreaming – to wake us up and make us see.

This theory not only sparked off a whole train of illuminations for me but it threw light onto the old dilemma as to whether everything is foreordained or whether one can change the course of one's life. And the answer to that, I suddenly realised, was yes and no. Usually no, in that one follows blindly the path already laid out, taking the easy option, and so changing nothing in one's fate – but one can, if one struggles with oneself against one's inclinations, one's desires, change the whole course of one's destiny and strike out into infinite possibilities, into uncharted waters. I can remember my mother asking me, quite out of the blue, when I was eleven or twelve years old, 'Don't you think that life is but a series of tests we must go through?' and it must have jolted something in my memory and I replied, 'Yes I do, Mum,' with perfect conviction that that was what it was all about.

Combined with a deep wisdom and compassion, for she loved her children and she loved animals, I have yet to meet anyone with a more spontaneous response to life than my mother. What chance did any of us have of being serious pupils at school when, from time to time when we were at kindergarten, she would burst into

our room on sunny mornings saying, 'Up! Up! We'll go for a picnic in the hills – it's far too nice to be sitting in stuffy classrooms,
you'll learn far more from nature,' and off we'd go with a hamper of
goodies to the White Horse or the Wansdyke, the Devil's Den, Old
Sarum or to the stones of Avebury or Stonehenge – what splendid
spontaneity and disdain for the things which, like sitting in stuffy
classrooms on bright sunny days, darken our childhood. What exu-
berance, what love of the wide-open spaces – the precious days of
our lives were instilled into us by our mother.

It was a happy, perhaps I could even say idyllic, childhood, in
which we were allowed to roam free, to set off on foot or on bikes
into the hills and woods, often with mine and Tony's great friend,
Errol Manners, with whom we'd get up to all kinds of antics and
set out on exciting, sometimes daring, adventures, floating on rafts
down the river, climbing church towers and walking along the high-
up ridge of the Old Vicarage from chimney to chimney with a sheer
drop on either side; Errol was the champion at that, he seemed to
have a better head for heights than either Tony or I, who found the
whole escapade quite terrifying but had to do it to prove to each
other, and to ourselves, we weren't scared. One slip on a loose slate
and that would be that.

Errol's mother, Mary, was our mother's best friend and they were
both fond of a drop or two of gin. I remember how, with a good
half bottle of the stuff in her, driving back in our mother's open top
Morris Minor, we young 'uns perched up above the seat in the back
she, on approaching a hump-backed bridge over the canal, would
say, 'Hold on tight,' and she'd accelerate and we'd fly in the air as we
took the bridge at full-speed, the car almost taking off, just as she
might have done on her horse when she was young, and giving us
the delightful feeling in the stomach one gets on a ride at the fair.
My mother of course was half-cut on gin but she'd never have put
her children in peril because in those days there was very little traffic
and besides she was a very good driver having, after finally giving up
nursing during the war, it not being exciting enough and always falling foul of her superiors and their over-strict regime, she drove staff
cars and lorries for the army on Salisbury Plain up behind the guns;
her hearing was always somewhat impaired after that. Whilst train-

ing for driving lorries she'd become very adept at reversing because she just went backwards until she hit something.

And behind our mother's wildness was our father a silent tower of strength, quietly amused, and often bemused, by his spouse's excesses whilst deftly averting the calamities brought so nearly by her extravagances. My father was a model to me of how a man of infinite discretion and noble duty should be. As a father he stood in the background, never meddling with our affairs never raising his voice or losing control, giving us the free choice, of which I've been speaking, to make all the mistakes in the book and then stepping in to help us when we were in the thick of things. As a doctor he was the most loved and respected in the villages for miles around. The centre of his practice was Market Lavington, and it stretched over the Plain as far as Shrewton and Tilshead, to which he could be called out at any time of the day or night, as he ran the practice single-handed and was on call twenty-four-seven.

He inspired confidence in his patients, gave birth to the hope in them, with his attentive, reassuring, bedside manner, which is the greatest art of the physician and is at least fifty per cent of the cure. Our house, Merry-go-Round, as my mother renamed it, was situated a few paces away from the pub, *The Green Dragon*, the very pub in which the poet Rupert Brooke stayed on numerous occasions, along with Virginia Woolf and other members of the Bloomsbury Circle, who used it as their refuge in the countryside. Rupert Brooke was my favourite poet when I was young and would sit by the fire smoking my pipe dreaming of Syra.

My father spent four years in Burma during the war, behind the Japanese lines, bringing the wounded back to the field hospitals, if there were any and, if not, having to amputate legs and limbs himself with high doses of morphine. He was twice mentioned in dispatches for his selfless service.

The story of his meeting my mother for the first time is rather amusing, and I would not be here, nor any of my siblings, had it not been for a flying kettle. Let me explain: before being posted overseas, my father was deputed to act as medical officer at an ATS convalescent depot at Cornwell Manor in Adlestrop. One day a VAD nurse turned up (VAD standing for Voluntary Aid Detachment and was, in my father's words, 'recruited from upper-class young ladies who didn't know one end of a bedpan from another, but who felt they must do something to help the war effort') – it was my mother, who'd been banished from St. Hugh's Head Injuries Hospital in Oxford for throwing a kettle at the Ward Sister, knocking her nearly senseless, and had been sent to Cornwell Manor as a punishment. She appeared before my father in a white nurse's uniform covered in red crosses and a hole in the heel of her stocking. It was love at first sight.

My mother grew up in the land-owning class, the so-called landed gentry, her father farming some fifteen hundred acres and owning all the houses except for two in the village of Berwick St. James on the other side of the plain, with all the men of the village employed, in one capacity or another, on the farm, in the gardens and the stables. The way my mother described it to me it sounded very similar to Plato's ideal republic, with each one having his station. There were the general labourers, the shepherd, the dairyman, the cartwright, the blacksmith, the gardeners, the grooms, with some of their wives and daughters working in the kitchen and as maids. So everyone knew their place and all was right with the world. She spent her childhood riding and hunting with the Wyle Valley Hunt, of which her father was joint-master. So really it never occurred to her that one should ever have to work for a living – that was for the 'lower orders', as she would put it.

Not so my father, whose father had been an engineer on the Clyde and had had to scrimp and save to put his son through the medical faculty at Glasgow University. For him money had to be hard-earned, it didn't just grow on trees, and it must have made him despair when it became increasingly obvious that I showed no inclination to do anything serious in life or take up any profession, especially when it was reinforced in me by my mother who'd said on occasions, 'A gentleman shouldn't have to think about money.'

So the instrument of fate, the flying kettle, had brought my parents together. I shall let what he later wrote in his memoirs, *Cold Hands*, continue the story,

I proposed to Pom and was accepted. However, I still had to get the approval of her parents. Therefore, it was arranged for me to visit her home – Berwick House – to get her father's agreement. Pom was there on leave and so also was her sister Joy with her current boyfriend, a captain in the Canadian Army. I expect Pom's father was much discountenanced by all these peculiar boyfriends – a Canadian and a Scot from Glasgow – chasing his daughters. And his third daughter was being pursued by a Belgian in the RAF!

Anyway, I had a very difficult time tracking down Pom's father. If I entered the drawing room he would sneak away out of the French windows and so on. In time, with my superior field-craft, I was able to corner him and ask for his daughter's hand in marriage.

He opened his inquisition by asking me if I hunted. On hearing my reply that I did not, he asked if I shot. Again I had to say 'no'. Next he asked me if I was a fisherman. Once more I had to say 'no'. Taken aback by all this he finally asked me what I did do. Actually I was a member of a golf club in Scotland but I did not mention this as I thought golf would be beneath his notice. With no answer from me he asked if I could support his daughter in the manner to which she was accustomed. I lied and said 'yes'. Whereupon he gave me permission to marry, but he was a very puzzled man.

And so, back to the present, here we all are, the spawn of the flying kettle, along with Tim and his brother Patrick and Greg, an old school pal of Tone's, raising glasses of sparkling champagne when we hear a vehicle making an infernal row with the revving of a clapped-out engine and chronic backfiring, as though it had been fed on beans. It must, it has to be headed for here and it must, it simply *must*, be Ian Macnab behind the wheel. He gets out of the car waving a bottle of whisky with an enormous grin on his face and wearing an old boiler suit with the back blown out. He's to be Tony's best man and whole tomes could be written about him, renowned around the Somerset pubs and about his disastrous attempts at being a businessman – businesses like mobile canteens and selling potatoes in their jackets, their dinner jackets: all of which initially take off at an unprecedented gallop only to fall with a thud at the first hurdle, the ensuing liquid celebrations of success, in which an entire fortune is disposed of. One little anecdote I'll recount, as I cannot resist it: his finances were in an appalling state of disrepair and so he was hauled up in front of his bank manager who said, 'Mr Macnab, your present enterprise is obviously not a success as I notice that you're now two thousand pounds in the red.'

'Yes, oh yes,' says Mr Macnab, 'but don't worry I've got something else up my sleeve.'

'So you will deal with this overdraft?'

'Oh yes, oh yes, not a chance I won't.'

A month or so later he's called up again, 'Mr Macnab, you assured me you were going to deal with this overdraft–I see that you have doubled it.'

'Well, er . . . oh yes, oh yes–but now I've got a new scheme.'

'I am tired of your schemes, Mr Macnab,' the bank manager shouted, banging his fist on the desk

'Alright, Alright,' said Macnab, 'don't get so worked up–after all, it's only money.'

Ian Macnab had been at Glencot where he became Tony's best friend. He had been expelled from another prep school for incorrigible misbehaviour and had landed up at Glencot which had a reputation for accommodating misfits, but little changed as far as that was concerned; he was always up to some prank which got him into nearly as much trouble as Barkeley-Smith. The best one, I think, was his putting hymn books inside the piano on a Sunday, just before Ma A came into play some hymns. Instead of 'All things bright and beautiful' there was a dull thud as she brought her hands down on the keys.

How good it is to be back again. I step indoors and smell all the familiar fragrances of the house, each one bringing back a feeling, a memory, conjuring up parts of my being sunk in me–how evocative the sense of smell is.

I go into the rooms one by one, the smell of wood polish here, of mothballs there, of geraniums in this one, drying linen here, wood smoke in the kitchen and coming up through the floorboards the musty smell of the cellar. I linger on the staircase and walk slowly along the corridors, letting the breeze from the open windows bathe my face with its fragrances of flowers and mown grass from the garden, hay from the fields beyond. And then, pausing a moment before the door, I burst into my room and swivel in an ecstatic circle in the centre of it—hello room! I close my eyes, breathe it all into me—I am home.

Old Vicarage
I can return to you any time in my mind
however far away I am
to any verdant corner of the garden my fancy takes me
To the orchard with its cool shade in summer
lying face down under the apple trees
and breathing the perfume of the grass
or through the arch in the hedge
and cross the croquet lawn barefoot in the dew

Or sitting in the old beamed kitchen in the inglenook
I can listen to the crackling and spitting of the fire
and the old dreams that once I dreamt of come to life in the
    flames
with the wind and rain lashing the window panes

I can stand again on the landing and listen to the sounds of
    the house
the creaking of wood of the floorboards the rustle of curtains
    in the breeze
pigeons cooing in the barn swallows nesting in the eaves
the striking of noon from the clock-tower at the Grange

Or at the casement of my old room where once I held her in
    my arms
I can drink in the air
sweet with the scent of the elder flower and the fresh-cut hay
and the soft summer rain falling on the lawn outside
and where once on such a night

I held her in my arms

Old Vicarage
nestled in the valley
between the downs and the Plain
through which a river runs
and from which in the distance in the dead of night
the clatter of the night train on the lines
which took her away

Perhaps we should all adjourn to the pub. A suggestion which meets with vociferous approval. And so in a gaggle we amble down to the New Inn, where we are welcomed warmly by the landlord and landlady, Henry and Bet, who start pouring pints from the wooden kegs – Wadworth's 6X, a full bodied brew from the local brewery in Devizes. Mr Macnab, or 'Nabby,' as he's known as here, is pulling a bundle of banknotes from his pocket – wouldn't his bank manager like to see this? – and insisting on paying for the round as he's just at this moment doing extremely well in his new business, selling potatoes in their jackets at the country fairs and festivals.

'I'm glad to see you've got some shoes on this time, Lala,' Henry says to me, 'Are they prison issue?'

'No Henry, they were presented to me by the country Ramblers Association.'

I have to be on my toes with Henry, he has a quick, dry humour and he's a dab hand at repartee. Yes, one has to watch one's Ps and Qs with Henry – he's an ex-soldier and he doesn't stand for any nonsense: no cussing, no swearing, no banjos, bugles or other musical instruments, no dancing, no dogs – and shoes must be worn at all times. A plaque in bold red lettering, placed above the bar, sums Henry's humour up in a few words:

Don't ask for credit
as a smack in the mouth
sometimes offends

Here are Malc and Ernie, pulling up on their tractors out-side–coming in for a lunch-time pint–I have to be on my toes with them too, especially Malc.

'Here, why aren't you out there helping us with the haymaking?' he's already started on at me, 'Always down there basking in the Mediterranean sun,' he looks at me, grinning, 'the 6X brought you back, eh?'

Malc and Ernie keep one of the farms in the village ticking over, Godfrey Stradling's farm. At this time of the year they're busy with the haymaking and later there'll be the harvest; during the winter months they're mainly to be found in the ditches of the western perimeters of Marden, on the Western Front–so that when I'm on my way to the hills I'll suddenly come across them, their heads just above ground level and the occasional–very occasional, I might add–shovel full of earth and mud being tossed into the air above them. Down with the shovels and out with the tobacco pouches when I come along, Malc deftly rolls a cigarette in the icy wind and Ernie puffs on his pipe. Yes, they are defending the village against the German advance, or is it the Russians this time?

'We reckon you've got a bit of stuff up there,' they wryly com-ment, nodding towards the hills, 'Always disappearing up there just as it's getting dark . . . what's her name?'

'Verushka,' I confide with a wink.

'Ha, so it is the Russians we're facing up there?'

'Da.'

'Does that mean "arrr"?'

'It does.'

'Then it sounds like we should be able to understand each other if we meet,' says Ernie, 'we'll be able to negotiate a peace treaty.'

'And if oi say "da" to Verushka, she'll say "arrr" to me?'

'Probably not, Malc.'

Whilst on the subject of pubs, there were others I'd frequent as well, for instance the Prince of Wales in the neighbouring village of Hilcot, with it's delightful landlord Lez, one of the old school of publicans whose father and his father's father had had pubs in Wiltshire. And he was the greatest connoisseur of 6X I have ever known. The best drop of this brew was to be found at the Prince of Wales. I'd wobble back from there after dark on my bicycle with no lights and no brakes and as I passed the crossroads at Puckshipton, where a man without a head is supposed to pass in a horse drawn carriage, on moonless nights with the black silhouette of the pines against the sky, my hair would stand on end and I'd sing hymns as loudly as I could to deter the headless man from crossing my path and inviting me to step into the carriage which, local legend had it, he was reputed to do.

Old Lez would often be at the fire as you walked in, stoking it up into a good blaze so that on a winter's night you'd be met by a blanket of warmth and his welcoming, 'You'd be in need of a drop of the good stuff.'

'Good stuff? Oi've drunk better bloody 'orse piss than this,' this coming from the old fellow with a shaggy beard and the purple nose, propped up on a stool at the bar – it is a roundabout way of saying it's a jolly good brew. This is 'Frosty', poacher by trade and the biggest imbiber of 6X for miles around. 'Frosty' is a funny name for sure – he came by it after being found in a field one morning, a stone's throw from the pub, frozen stiff as a board with frost. It had taken hours to thaw him out by the fire in the Prince of Wales and gallons of whisky to get the blood flowing in his veins and his purple nose once again.

'You won't find better in all Wiltshire,' Lez, to counter Frosty's derogatory remarks, reminds me as I contemplate the amber liquid he's set before me.

'I'm aware of that, Lez,' and, lifting it to my lips, I dispatch it in two long drafts down my throat, so that my Adam's apple does its customary dance.

'Now that's what Oi like to see,' he grins, 'a man with a healthy thirst – 'nother one?'

And just at that moment, through the door comes Brian Drewitt – well timed. 'Make that two pints, Lez.'

Now Brian was what was known as an 'oiler' at Marlborough; that is he worked in the kitchens and dolloped out our grub at mealtimes. He was a bit of a teddy boy in those days, with straight black, greased-back hair, a kiss curl and winklepickers – he is more like a teddy bear these days, I tease him, being rather rotund and wobbly as he walks.

'Oi remember that morning you cut the bell rope,' he never tires of telling me, 'there we were, all lined up in the kitchen to serve you your breakfast and no one turned up. You might have told us in advance, then we could've had a lie-in too.'

He and I would drive to barn dances in the summer, often finding ourselves walking home as he was too drunk to drive; under marvellous starry summer nights we'd amble back, wobbling and reeling and laughing. And that brings to mind another friend, Dave Taylor of Marden, whom I'd come across from time to time drinking at the New Inn or the Yeoman in Chirton, a village a mile or so away, and with whom I'd return with him mounted on the back of my rickety bicycle. We had to negotiate a steep hill as soon as we came out of the pub at some unearthly hour of the morning, with no brakes or lights, and then a long stretch of unlit road. Both of us being three sheets to the wind it was not all plain sailing and we usually ended up at least once rolling and laughing in the ditch, which was always full of stinging nettles in the summer.

He confessed to me the story of how, long before we became friends, he'd come out of the New Inn late one summer night and thought, 'Ha, Oi'll go and get some of them apples from the Ashford-Browns' orchard,' and once there, was merrily filling the plastic bag he'd no doubt asked Henry for before leaving the pub, when he heard the dogs barking and dashing through the garden in his direction. He took to his heels and, in the pitchy dark, didn't see the primitive pit we used as a swimming pool and, well, he got a right scolding from his mum when he turned up at home, not only dripping wet but plastered with mud from the newly ploughed field he'd had to negotiate, with the dogs in hot pursuit. Good old Dave.

And I remember how once, when we had a little shindig at the Old Vicarage one summer evening with a fire in the garden. Dave, who I'd invited to partake of a little liquid refreshment, turned up completely plastered. He'd already been refreshing himself down at the pub and, by the time he arrived was almost completely incoherent. He sat down by the fire for a few minutes and then suddenly got up up and wandered into the darkness. We thought he'd just gone to

relieve himself or something but, when he'd not returned after ten or fifteen minutes we wondered where he was. I called out, 'Dave, Dave, where are you?' at which we heard a faint, strangulated, cry, 'Oi'm over 'ere . . . ' coming from the direction of the orchard. On going over there I heard a groaning and there he was, stretched out on his back in the long grass. I helped him to his feet saying, 'Come on Dave I'll help you home.'

'No Lala, Oi'll be alright, oi know the way.'

'Well, I'll accompany you.' seeing that he might have some difficulty negotiating the road that led to his house some five hundred yards the other side of the river. It was pitch dark outside, it being well after midnight and the street lights were turned off, and he was wobbling all over the place. We got down to the pub and started to go over the bridge. He'd suddenly become agitated and said, 'Oi'll be alright now Lala, Oi can find my way back now . . . '

'Are you sure, Dave?'

'Yes, Oi'll be alright.'

So, knowing he was nearly home and realising he didn't want me to take him all the way there, I left him to his fate and headed back to the party. The next day the report came back, from two of the guests who'd been staying and taken an early morning walk through the village, of their coming upon a pair of boots sticking out of a ditch just beyond the bridge – the wearer of them was Dave who was upside-down and hadn't been able to extricate himself. His reluctance for me to take him home and his sudden agitation when we got to the bridge, I guessed was his mortal terror of coming home drunk at that late hour and having to face his mother, who no doubt would have given him a good scolding as so often had happened in the past.

His mother was a sweet and gentle soul who'd been a maid at the Old Vicarage in byegone days and 'lived in', her room being a little maid's room, at the top of the back stairs, that overlooked the church yard on the north side of the house. I once spent a whole winter in that room and it was really very gloomy, never getting a ray of sunlight and always cold, though there was an open fire in it which made it quite cosy in the evenings. I must say, it affected my mood and it was a very gloomy winter I spent there, what with the troubling shadows in my heart at that time. I don't know who owned the house when Dave's mum worked there but I think it was probably the old colonel who died in the bath, and who was rumoured to have buried a small armoury of munitions somewhere in the grounds. He also, I suspect, was responsible for the opium poppies which popped up in the summer all over the garden and the milky white juice it exuded when the bulb was cut, I unsuccessfully tried to dry out and smoke. He'd no doubt brought them back from India or the middle east.

Dave's father was a remarkable man who I once listened to at the pub reciting the whole of Gray's *Elegy in a Churchyard* off by heart.

Marden, little village in the Pewsey Vale, with its church, its pub, its river and bridges, it's tumbledown mill, its thatched roofs, its meandering road, its rookeries which fill the evening with their earthy, grating, chanting, the very voice of the trees. Marden with its pines and its poplars, its linden and its beech, willows, chestnut, oak, elms, its hawthorn hedgerows.

I roam about in the hills looking down on a little village nestled in its trees. I search the sky above me, the earth beneath me, the warm chalkland beneath my bare feet which spring on the sheep-trodden turf.

This was all so essential to my inner world, this returning from time to time to charge my batteries and to reconnect with the earth and the landscape which had nourished my soul through the time of my childhood. And sometimes I would come home and hibernate through the winter, sometimes sleeping through the short days and getting up around teatime to wander around the starlit villages, the moonlit hills and to burn a lonely lamp half the night as I stared through the window of my room. It was hard for my father at times, to see his son with seemingly no desire to lead a normal life and, apart from some hazy notion of being a poet, of writing a book someday, no direction in an irresponsible, reckless life. Oh, how he must have despaired. Sometimes we clashed and it was painful, but mostly he was sensitive and understanding, deep down, perhaps, seeing the value of my aimless existence and wanderings, and fondly calling me the Prodigal Son – by which perhaps he meant that I'd one day see sense and that I might even bring something of worth back with me that would atone for it all.

For my mother, too, it must have been hard, but in a different way, a mother's way; it was not that I was not achieving anything in life that troubled her but the unvoiced things that were going on inside me. Her mother's intuition told her I was grappling with things of which I could not speak.

> Mist on my breath and a ring round the moon
> the cries of the rooks
> are the voice of my heart

Chapter 31

On the Rock of Socrates

The approach of Christmas has the whole of Athens in a whirl; to set foot into the street is to step into a torrent – you're swept away in a human current intent on picking the shops clean of their wares. Emerging from the underground station in Omonia Square, and riding the human wave down Athinas Street, I let myself be washed into this eddy, this palace of ouzo, at the counter of which I'm now leaning. It would appear that I'm just having a warm up to give some fire before plunging into the crowds to drum up a drachma or two with my whistle and, to all intents and purposes, that's all that I'm doing. However, what neither you nor I suspect is that is that I'm unwittingly waiting for Gary to step over the threshold. In fact, right now and unbeknown to me, he's riding the wave down Athinas Street. I call this place a palace because of its size, its high ceiling and vast walls along which shelves stretch to the horizon glittering with bottles, into which walls huge vats are sunk, from which vats is siphoned the ouzo I tip down my gullet. It's rare that I leave this place in any manner other than swaying for the cheery chaps behind the counter delight in topping up my glass when my back is turned and the mean-looking boss at the till near the door is not looking. Needless to say, I turn my back to them quite often to give them a chance to perform this discreet service and to give them the pleasure of my feigned surprise when I turn back round; I have only to take care that I don't get hiccups if I'm going to play my whistle when I get back out onto the street (it's impossible to play with hiccups, as you can imagine) nor to get as relaxed as the purple nosed gentleman flat on his back on the flag-stoned floor near the exit; he was at the counter until a minute or two ago: he must have tried to make a break for the street but lost his legs at the threshold. It's just as well he has toppled this side of the door as he'd be trampled underfoot out there by the rushing crowd and perhaps even have been slung up as a carcass on a hook in the meat market. The cries of the butchers and the slamming of cleavers on wooden blocks are chopping up the very air around our ears. It's not too far-fetched to entertain the idea of staggering blindly out of here and ending up in a pot.

Ending in a pot this evening would not perhaps be the worst of all fates, it would at least be warm and it's cold outside. However, I'm well clad, what with the thick woolen breeches (not unlike that fine pair I nicked off the scarecrow in Turkey) which I picked up at the flea market and the great-coat and boots donated to me in Thessaloniki. That was a good time in Saloniki, meeting up with that drunken minstrel Jean-Michel and drinking the citadel dry – we'll run into him again later – meanwhile, no it can't be . . . it IS . . .

'I knew I'd find you here, if anywhere, Papa.'

Our paths are crossing once more and we're gonna drink and raise the rafters high with laughter:

> . . . for tonight two pals have met
> that time apart had torn
> and they've bottles and barrels
> to last them till the dawn . . .

The evening's crystal clear, the sky full of stars and at our feet all the lights of Athens are glittering like a lake of diamonds. We're up at the Acropolis, on the rock at the foot of the Parthenon, a not-little bottle of *ouzo* passing to and fro between us.

'Socrates used to hold discourse right here where we are now, Gary'.

'Who, Papa?'

'Socrates.'

'Ah yes, him . . . '

'So you have heard of him, Gary?'

'Course I have, Pa,' He pauses for a moment, stares, seemingly transfixed by the *ouzo* bottle and then, like an oracle, suddenly proclaims, 'I already know much, for I know that I know nothing'.

I look open-mouthed at my pigmy pal, startled at his erudition, 'Where did you get that, Gary?'

'Achillea, Pa. he wrote it all over his exam papers.'

Gary's been in Italy since I last saw him.

'My grandfather has a little vineyard there, I stayed with him, Pa.'

'Ah, that must have been nice – holidays in the countryside and no doubt all the wine you could drink.'

'It wasn't like a holiday, Pa.'

'What do you mean?'

'I had to drink all day and all night with my grandfather.'

'Ho, Gary, that can't have been a hardship for you.'

'Don't laugh, Pa, I nearly went mad – his wine was strong enough but that was only part of it, you see, he distilled his own grappa too.'

'Well, you must have been in your element, Gary.'

'Pa, I had to get away from there – in the middle of the night I ran away.'

This has me rolling around in stitches, 'you ran away because you couldn't face the drink – ho! ho! you're pulling my leg.'

'No, Pa, I had to escape – you see, my grandfather wouldn't take no for an answer, I had to keep up with him. I took a train to Venice, I thought I could make some money there because you told me you sold flowers there and the tourists would give money, you see, I wanted to get back to Greece, I wanted to be with Evi, but I got arrested, Pa, and sent back to Belgium.'

'Oh, what happened?'

'I was broke when I arrived in Venice and hungry – I could have murdered for a loaf of bread.'

'And a nice little bottle of something to go with it, eh?'

'Ha yes, I'd got my thirst back by then – well, Pa, I had to do some begging; first of all by going up to people and asking them but that didn't work well, I don't speak much Italian and I don't speak any English so I couldn't explain to the tourists what I wanted, they shied away from me as if I was some kind of despicable thing And then I remembered you telling me of that trick with the cardboard and so I wrote out a message in Italian and English–I had some one to help me with that–and sat down on one of the little bridges. It started to work, Papa, and I went every day sitting for three or four hours and making plenty of money. I even drank wine as I sat there and quite enjoyed my self. One day I noticed a geezer looking at me. Alright for a minute or two, but he'd been there ten or fifteen and enough is enough, 'Oi, you!' I called over to him, 'You've seen enough haven't you? And I waved him away with my hand; he stepped over to me and flashed a card–end of holidays in Venice.'

I chuckle, I love the way he tells his stories in that morose way so characteristic of him. I look at him, outlined against the Parthenon–the same dark, unkempt head, with its tangle of locks, like a kind of cross between Dionysus and Caliban, bobbing above the bottle–how happy I am that our paths have crossed again.

'What then, Gary?

'Belgium, Papa, I was sent back to Belgium–Charleroi–you know, the place you can't pronounce.'

We both laugh; he's not forgotten my connection with his home town. Years ago, hitching through Belgium on my way to Paris, I was walking along the *autoroute* when I came upon a full jar of peanut butter lying on the side of the road. I seized upon it and started to dive into its contents–It was absolutely delicious and I'd crammed my mouth full of it when, quite unexpectedly–for I hadn't got my thumb out–a car pulled up, a Daimler, with an extremely beautiful and refined-looking lady at the wheel, who rolled down the window and asked me where I was headed. Now, Charleroi is difficult enough for me to pronounce at any time (as it is for most Englishmen, who cannot roll 'R's) but, with a mouthful of peanut butter all glueing up my mouth and stuck around my teeth, it was absolutely impossible. I tried to be articulate but could only emit a mangled sound, something like this, 'Charrrlerrroi . . . Charrrrlerrroi . . .'

Horrified, she looked at my filthy gurgling mouth, which must have looked as if it was full of excrement, *Je vous en prie, monsieur,* she exclaimed, in undisguised horror, stepping on the accelerator and speeding off towards Charleroi. Ah, what cruel fate had put that jar of peanut butter in my path, and to what sweet fate might it have led had I not had its contents stuck around my teeth?

'So, back in Charleroi what did you do there?' I went on, intrigued by his adventures.

'Drank, Pa.'

'What, all the time?'

'Yes, back in my old haunt at the Château d'Eau.'

'L'Étoile Verte?'

'Yes I drank and thought of Evi. I had to get back here, it would be over if I didn't.'

'So?'

'So I had to get some money. I broke into my father's house and took everything I could find; that solved the problem – he deserved it, he's stinking rich and he never ever gave me a penny. He's not my real father, Pa, he's my stepfather; I never had a father,' I listen with my eyes closed – there's a biting sadness in his voice.

'I got out as fast as I could – life's sad in that grey, industrial, filthy place, Pa, and I got the train back here.'

'And Evi, you still seeing her?'

'From time to time when she comes to Athens, oh Papa, I try not to think about her – it's painful – you know how it is. I think we're drifting apart but I try not to think of it. Anyway,' he says brightening up and lifting the bottle to his lips and kissing it, 'A man can't have two loves they get jealous of one another.'

Dawn is cracking above our heads as we reel out of the meat market, the very place the nocturnal binge began. We've been drinking in the tripe restaurant; the dingiest, most fetid-smelling dive you can imagine, stinking of rotten carcasses and situated in the very bowels of that place of carnage, where they slop out tripes and retsina and they never ever close.

Since my arrival back in Athens, and it being winter, I've been living in a rundown hotel called the Byron – Gary also takes up residence here. A stone's throw from Omonia Square, it's more like a dosshouse than a hotel. We sleep in squalid dormitories with all kinds of other drunkards and down and outs, but it's a roof over our heads and we do have beds, flea ridden though they are. We pay a hundred and fifty drachmas a night, which is minimal but there are times when it takes a herculean task to raise even that amount, or rather, to have that amount left to us at the end of our night's drinking.

There's a Cockney called Colin residing at the Byron. He had spent some fifteen years in the army, had been discharged for irredeemable alcoholism, and had taken to roving around the southern parts of Europe where wine was cheap. Despite the fact that he has but one or two teeth left to him, a face shrivelled and ravaged by booze, bloodshot eyes and three fingers missing, he's a cheery fellow and is usually to be found at the bar of the Byron, cracking jokes, should you be looking for him. For a couple of hours in the morning he is out begging, or 'toutin'', as he calls it, with a little card written in Greek stating his plight, 'I am an ex-serviceman, unable to work due to illness. Please help me.'

One evening I return to the hotel to hear that he's been carted off in an ambulance. He'd been set upon by some fellow at the bar and kicked down the twenty odd stone stairs to the street. He returns two days later, his face cut and swollen and hobbling along on crutches once again.

'They took me to a lunatic asylum – I was just coming round when some bleedin' nutter threw a radio at my head and knocked me out for the count. I'm a right bleedin' sight now. But it will be good for toutin'.'

Christmas comes and goes. The metropolis, which was ablaze with lights and given over to feasting and revelry, returns to the sober, work-a-day routine. People have spent their dough and they don't feel like throwing much in the direction of the street musician until the first touch of spring puts the smiles back on their faces and the spring in their step. It's an uphill struggle to keep the two of us fed, watered, and stabled now. What's more, the weather has turned nasty, driving us all off the streets and down into the metro below. For the first time, Gary and I work together. We go up and down the line to Piraeus and back. Jumping from one rickety, rattling, carriage to the next, I put my whistle to my lips and Gary sways along the wagon with the hat. Every now and then we take a break, climbing onto the streets of Athens, Piraeus and at the stations in between and retire to a taverna for some refreshment.

We're in Maroussi, it's the fifth stop tonight and, three sheets to the wind, we're sinking another litre of *krasi* before a final run back up to Omonia – at least, that's the plan.

'I bet they're cops, Pa.'

'Who, Gary?'

'That lot over there,' and, with a hand over one eye, a sure sign that Gary's seeing double, he points over to a table with three men and their wives, 'They've been staring at us.'

'They're probably just curious Gary, or bored, perhaps, they're with their wives.'

'I don't like it, I know that way of looking – they're having black thoughts about us – it's the "evil eye" they're giving us, Pa.'

'The "evil eye"? Ha, Gary,' I laugh, 'relax, the wine's making you imagine things.'

'I don't like them staring at us, I've had enough of them, Pa,' he starts filling his glass with wine and staggering to his feet, starts heading for their table.

'No, Gary . . . Gary NO!'

But there's no stopping him and now he's bolting out of the door with three enraged men dripping with wine hot on his tail. They get him, throw him down onto the pavement and kick him viciously, the street ringing with their oaths, 'You mother fucking bastard, you shit arse, wanker, weasel, rat!'

I plunge into the fray to extract my imperilled pygmy pal and am promptly laid about myself with blows and kicks and a volley of furious abuse. Gary manages to get to his feet and slips away into the darkness leaving me alone to fend off the onslaught, and not doing very well.

'Stop! *Stamata!*' I shout.

'We'll give you "stop" you motherfucker,' and they carry on lambasting me. I've never been so happy to see a police car as I am to see this one now screeching to a halt on the curb. I have never been so thankful at being shoved into one and driven away.

And as for the cell in which I'm languishing now, how could I ask for more congenial company to share my confinement? A whole contingent of prostitutes. I'm not shy as I sit down amongst them: what fun if they all dived upon me and buried me beneath breasts and thighs. The little brunette next to me says she's cold, she shivers – no wonder, she has the flimsiest of negligées; it's the most natural thing in the world for me to unbutton my coat and invite her to snuggle up next to me whilst wiping the blood from my face. The others tease her that it's taken her all evening to find a man and it had better be love not business, for this one (meaning me) obviously hasn't a brass farthing. One of them gets up and starts screaming through the bars, 'You fucking wankers! You impotent perverts! Caging us because you want a fucking eyeful of pussy, a furtive little feel if you can – because you can't get it with your fucking wives!'

She's a formidable sight as she spits and screeches through a smudged, blood-red mouth, running mascara and with a hideous scar on her neck out of which a tattooed rose seems to sprout. A volley of abuse has brought the coppers who are unbolting the cage and, seeing me having a bit too much of a good time, snuggled up with the brunette and feeling her slight, shivering body next to mine, they're hauling me out, one of them shoving me along the corridor whilst the other goes into the cell with a vicious murderous look on his face. And then I'm suddenly out on the street, wishing I was back in that cell with the girls.

I find Gary back at the Byron, anxiously huddled over a beer at the bar, 'Oh Papa – forgive me . . . hic . . . for running away . . . but they were . . . hic . . . Papa, they were going to kill me.'

'But Gary if only you had stayed you'd have had a great time at the police station,' he looks at me puzzled and I recount to him my brief sojourn amidst the street sirens.

'You have all the luck Papa. I shouldn't have run away,' he stares morosely into his beer, a tear splashing into the frothing brew whilst an agonised utterance, full of self reproach, issues from him, 'Papa, Papa . . . I should . . . hic . . . have stayed to protect you.'

Chapter 32

Kalamata

Athens truly is miserable at this time of year. I tell Gary about Kalamata, a town of almost tropical climes at the far south of the Peloponnese where I'd once spent a month or so living on the beach.

'It was at this time of year Gary and it was so warm I could walk around with no more than a shirt on and sleep out under the stars.'

'We must go there, Papa.'

We take the funny little train, which seems like a toy, south the next morning crossing the Corinth canal and on into the Peloponnese, stopping in Tripolis for the night. Tripolis is cold, it's snowing and it's like a little town in the Himalayas. It's almost impossible to make money on the deserted streets, everyone being at home, and we look longingly through lighted windows and think how warm it must be in those little houses. We're hungry. I've made just enough for a glass or two of wine and no more. Passing a little *kafeneion* we can see men huddled over a stove wrapped in greatcoats it looks warm inside and we step over the threshold. Weather-beaten faces turn towards us.

'Yassas,' they greet us, and motion us to a table, the landlord bringing a jug of wine and they start asking us questions – where we are from, where we are going and where are we going to sleep on such a night. In response we tell him that we'll be sleeping outside at which he surmises that we have no money, '*Po po po,*' he exclaims and he goes back to the kitchen and returns with a plate of food, telling us that it and the wine are on the house.

We raise our glasses to the assembled company and toast Dionysus.

'Did I tell you that I've been to Dionysus's island, Gary?'

'No, Papa, it's true?'

'Yes, a couple of years ago, I went with Tim,' (Gary knows about Tim as I've spoken about him a lot), 'it was winter-time, just like now, and freezing cold . . . '

'Tell me about it, Pa.'

And so I told him the story.

We had decided to make our way out to an island and at random, by one of us closing his eyes and bringing his finger down on the map, the finger fell on Naxos, not knowing then that it was the very birthplace of Dionysus and that it was there that Theseus was to abandon Ariadne.

It was an island of extraordinary rugged beauty on which, had it not been so perishingly cold and had it been possible to make some money on the streets, which it wasn't as there was very little sign of life on them, we would have stayed. We decided to leave for Athens after just three or four days. Actually, as it happened, my stay was to be two days longer than Tim's, due not to design but by circumstance. With the little money which remained to us we had bought the tickets to Piraeus and were waiting in the harbour for the ship to arrive from the southernmost islands of the Cyclades. It was blowing a tempestuous storm; the sea, like a dark witches cauldron, was hurling itself in towering white-crested waves at the harbour walls, the rain lashing the windows of the waiting room, in which we'd sought refuge, along with the handful of other passengers waiting for the ship. We were wrapped warmly in our thick coats and were relishing the prospect of a stormy crossing.

'Got everything safe?' I enquired of Tim, meaning the tickets and the few hundred drachmas which remained to us which he had in his trusty keeping.

'Safe as houses,' he replied, tapping his breast pocket.

Lights began to grow out of the darkness on the horizon. It was our ship, coming closer and closer, until it came to a standstill outside the harbour walls, where it dropped anchor.

'*Ti eginé?*' I asked what was happening.

'The ship can't get into the harbour because of the condition of the sea,' I'm told, 'we are going to have to go out to it in a fishing boat.'

We started climbing aboard a caique which was pulled up along the quay and as soon as we were out beyond the walls we were being tossed about like a cork; but the boat held its course as we cut through the spray and alongside the great throbbing vessel, ablaze with lights, towering above us and which had let down a rope ladder by which, one by one, we were to clamber up onto the deck. Things were going fine, with helping hands pushing from below and pulling from above. Tim shinned up in true nautical fashion and I, who was next in line, was about to follow suit when someone pushed in front of me and, just as he'd got onto the ladder, an immense wave lifted our little boat high up in the air and away from the mother ship. However much the helmsman tried we simply could not get back alongside her and, after a good twenty minutes or so of futile attempts, he gave up. The ship weighed anchor, its siren echoing around the harbour walls, with Tim leaning over the railings shouting, 'Look for me in Piraeus – I'll hang around there,' and the ship lurched forward into the swell, its lights receding back into the darkness from which it had emerged. We, that remained in the boat, returned to the harbour – I without ticket or money.

There was a bar called Lalo's in which Tim and I had huddled from the cold much of the time we were there and in which, as virtually the only tourists on the island, we'd become known to the owners and the locals. So when I reappeared there I was greeted by surprised looks, 'We thought you'd taken the ship to Piraeus.'

'*Po po po,*' they said when I told them what had happened, and my stranded, penniless, state was met with sympathy all round. The sister of the owner, a lovely so-Greek type of young woman, thrust a whole wad of bank notes into my hand, saying, 'That will get you a room for the night,' and someone else had a meal sent over to me. As for wine, well, I was supplied with that for the rest of the evening – all hail Dionysus! They told me I should go to the harbour master in the morning and explain my predicament.

'But how will he believe that I had a ticket in the first place?'

'He will have to believe you,' came the reply, putting my mind at rest.

And so, the next morning I went along and told my story. At first the harbour master looked at me a little suspiciously and asked why it was that my friend had both the tickets.

'He just had,' I replied. He smiled, and issued me with a ticket for the ship which would sail the following evening.

When I arrived, late, in Piraeus, I didn't know where in hell to start looking for Tim; it proved as difficult as looking for the proverbial needle in a haystack – except I knew that, if Tim had the least sum of money on him, I wouldn't have to look further than the bars, where he'd be transmuting the coins into liquid gold. But there are a lot of bars in Piraeus, where to start? I reckoned he'd be somewhere in the area of the port from which he'd not have strayed too far. So I started, as methodically as I could, going along every street which led from the harbour, peering into every drinking establishment I passed. Walking along one of the narrow, dark, streets and beginning to abandon hope of ever finding Tim, I suddenly found myself being hailed by a black African from down the street in the direction from which I'd come. My first impulse was to hurry away from him but he was insistent and, sizing up the situation quickly, I saw that it didn't look threatening; he was trying to communicate something to me.

'Your friend,' he called out, 'in here your friend,' and he pointed to a sleazy-looking joint nearby, all flashing red lights and loud music.

'My friend?'

'Yes, your friend, he's looking for you.'

'Ah, he's in there?'

'Yes, come.'

And we walked into the infernal interior of this hellish dive to find Tim sitting up like Kurtz, from Conrad's *Heart of Darkness*, surrounded by Africans and with a foaming jug of beer before him.

Gary likes that story, saying, as we step out of the taverna into the freezing night, 'Papa, Tim is a big drunkard,' (*un grand ivrogne,* as he put it), 'and I think he perhaps is Dionysus.'

'Yes, you could well be right,' I laugh.

We spend the night in a construction site on the third floor sleeping on cement sacks and freezing cold concrete. In the morning getting up we shake ourselves like dogs and, with no money for coffee, we trudge down through the snow on the road to Kalamata. We had found a couple of stale loaves thrown out from a bakery which we're gnawing at as we trudge along; it's dry and hard as rock, not really the ideal thing to eat first thing in the morning, so we leave it for later. As luck would have it, we pass a field full of frozen cabbages and so, as nobody's around we pinch one, and then determined to make some soup with it – that'll warm us up. Up ahead of us we can see an old dilapidated-looking building, which turns out to be an abandoned cement factory – we'll be able to make a fire in there. And sure enough it's still partly covered and there's lots of dry timber littered around from the broken beams. In next to no time we have the pot bubbling away. We've added some salt and garlic which we had in our rucksacks and soon have a piping hot pot of cabbage broth with which we wash down the rock-hard loaves which melt in our mouths. And so, with our blood running warm, we hit the road again and, before long, pick up a lift going all the way to Kalamata. Soon, before our eyes, the landscape opens up and we can see the sea, deep blue, streaked with the red of the winter sunset and descend into the plain through the dark green olive groves which surround Kalamata.

It's warm, beautifully warm, and we stroll through the town which brings Italy to mind; the narrow twisting streets, the faded yellow walls reflecting the warm glow of the street lamps, the sound of our feet on the flag-stones and, looking up, stars between the rooftops. '*C'est beau ici,* Papa, *romantique,*' Gary's face is lit up and his voice wistful as he turns to me, 'I wish Evi was here with us.'

'You do, Gary, really?' I chuckle, 'but think, you've been talking of quenching your thirst ever since we arrived and she wouldn't let you do it.'

'You are right, Pa.'

We've been doing a round of the *kapheneions* with pipe and hat and now are looking for a congenial taverna to repair to, in order to squander our gains. We smell appetising whiffs of cooking coming from up the street and track them down to a ramshackle taverna with two pipe-like chimneys belching smoke from the tin roof. Staring in through the steamed-up windows, we see a cosy scene inside – a blazing wood stove with people pulled up on chairs around it, a woman cooking, and tables, stretching back into the dim interior, at which groups of people are eating and drinking. We walk in and take a table close to the stove. One of the most beautiful girls I've ever laid eyes on springs up and comes, smiling, over to us – what eyes she has, what wells of sparkling water, what hidden depths, her raven-black hair tumbling in waves to her shoulders. We look at each other straight in the eye, and time stops an instant before she breaks off saying, '*Ti thelete?*' ('What do you want?') 'I want you,' I'd like to say, but that would be a bit forward and instead say, 'wine.' She spins on her heel and has a word with the woman cooking who smiles over at us, and then she returns with a brimming jug of retsina.

'This is a gift from my mother and welcome to our *taverna*,' Gary and I rise to our feet, raise our glasses in salute and exclaim, 'we drink to your mother and you, er . . . '

'Olga.'

'To you, Olga.'

We take up residence on the beach and every evening we deliver ourselves to what we've come to call 'chez Olga' – the romantic tavern on Faro Street. We've become right regulars and Olga's mother addresses us as *paidia mou,*(my children), and provides us with soup and *patatas* every night, charging us only for the wine we drink, most of which is paid for anyway by customers at the other tables. And so an evening chez Olga costs virtually nothing – in fact we usually stumble out richer than when we entered for, with a nod of consent from Olga's mum, I pull my pipe from my pocket, let fly with some wailing air into the steamy interior whilst Gary wobbles around the tables with the hat–after which Olga asks whether we have enough for breakfast. If, on inspection of the proceeds, we find we are lacking the requisite amount she drops a coin or two in the hat saying, 'Now you have it.'

Whenever Olga has some moments to spare she pulls a chair up to our table, she has a sparkle in her eye and loves to hear about drunken escapades in Athens and Halkida. 'It's a good life you two lead,' she says, 'I'll have to come along with you sometime.'

'Oh yes,' I say, jumping at such a wild idea, at the thought of being out on the razzle with Olga–I wonder how she would be away from the watchful eye of her mother: she is very Greek, the dutiful daughter; but she's also Greek, the passionate woman which could magnificently, sublimely, disobey the rules.

'But it would be difficult,' she says with a sigh, 'Girl's life, you see.'

'She likes you, Papa,' Gary says to me.

'Do you think so Gary?'

'*Mais, oui papa.*'

'What makes you think so?'

'The way she looks at you.'

Gary is well-versed in the whims and wiles and ways of women–he is somewhat of an expert, in fact.

'So do you think there's a chance, Gary?'

'*Je n'sais pas, Pa*–you'll have to find out. But I think it will be not easy from a practical point of view.'

'What do you mean, Gary?' I want him to enlarge upon what he's said but he's getting to the point of incoherence, his head's beginning to droop towards the table. '*Je ne sais pas, Pa* . . .' and he's gone.

The following day, bloated with luncheon, we're stretched out on the beach. Gary's nodded off and I've pulled my notebook from my pocket and am doodling. I draw a picture of Gary and myself striding out along the winding road, exaggerating the difference in size between us so that he reaches hardly higher than my waist–I think it's rather funny, I'll show it to him when he wakes up. I start to practice my hand at writing Greek – 'Olga,' I write, '*s'agapo,*' I love you – '*isse poli orea,*' you are very beautiful, '*Thelo na kano erota me sena,*' I want to make love to you, etcetera etcetera, and I decorate the page with hearts. I slip the notebook back in my pocket and fall asleep.

This evening at the taverna I suddenly remember the drawing, 'Oh Gary, I forgot to show you this,' and I hand him the notebook open at the sketch. He's delighted at it.

'Papa it's us,' he exclaims and, turning the page, sees what I've written about Olga – 'you're really in love, eh pa?' he grins, putting the notebook down on the table. In a while we're joined by both Olga and her mum who pull chairs up to the table.

'What's the book?' asks Olga, pointing at the notebook.

'Look,' I say proudly, handing it to her open at the sketch of Gary and I on the road. 'Oh,' she exclaims with amusement, 'Just like you.'

'He *is* a little bigger than I am,' says Gary, charging our glasses, 'but he is exaggerating there.'

Olga, who's been flicking through the pages of the notebook, suddenly has her hand to her mouth and is giggling. We look at her puzzled, then Gary lets out a great bellow of laughter as he clicks as to what she's giggling at – and then the penny drops, 'No Olga, don't read,' I shoot out of my seat, red-faced, panic stricken, to grab the book containing my overt declarations of love – but it's too late – she's read it. Her mum, completely bewildered at all this is saying, 'What's going on? Why are they laughing?'

'They're mad,' I say, whilst thinking, 'I'll never be able to look Olga in the eyes again.'

'Yes you will, Pa,' says Gary, reading my thoughts, 'women like that sort of thing.'

Of course, our intake mounts as the evenings go by – the antiquated jukebox in the corner, which had not been working previously, suddenly sparks into life and we keep it turning with five drachma bits. Romantic songs scratch their way through their verses:

Kapou nichtoni
O ilios pagoni . . .

Drunk with ecstasy one evening I leap to my feet and dance between the tables – whereupon Olga rushes over and takes to the floor with me. We swirl round and round and leap in the air. Her eyes like black shining stars are in mine, her hands like conductors of unseen currents brush my body make me spring intoxicated with every fibre of my being towards her – we are flying in the air. Then the twangs of the bouzouki fade away, we collapse laughing, exhausted in our chairs under the disapproving gaze of her mum and to the appraisal of Gary who says, 'Magnifique, Papa.'

Olga goes back to clearing the tables, the taverna's closing up and Gary and I find ourselves hobbling back to the beach; 'I'm going to tell her what I think of her,' I say to Gary, 'the way she dances, her eyes . . . her lithe body . . . her . . . her everything – she was speaking to me . . . she wouldn't have danced like that and so up close if she didn't like me, would she, Gary?'

'No, papa, I told you she likes you and she knows you like her, women know these things – they're not stupid.'

'You don't think then she just thinks I'm a drunkard?'

'Well, of course she knows that, Papa, but women have an ambiguous attitude towards drunkards – they are either repelled or intrigued at what lies behind a man's drinking – it often dawns on them that they might be the cause: and that really intrigues them.'

It's a bright morning, the memory of last night's like a dream which won't fade. Gary makes a phone call to his Dulcinea; he comes away from the kiosk looking very glum. 'Papa I've got to go back to Athens, it's all over if I don't.'

'Evi's missing you?'

'I don't know if she's missing me, I just don't think she likes me being away so long – 'Are you drinking? she asked me – *agapimoo* I lied to her, she doesn't believe me: she knows I'm with you.'

'And that's proof enough that you're drinking?' I ask, amused.

'Yes, Papa.'

So Gary wants to leave immediately, he's filled with anxiety all of a sudden, an anxiety which I full well understand.

'Let's stay one more night – I just want to have a word with Olga to know one way or another.'

'Okay Papa.'

Tonight then is to be the final night, unless something's ongoing with Olga in which case I'll stay on. I am already roaring drunk by the time she comes along–big mistake. Gary and I've been here a good two hours and are launched upon our fourth jug of retsina. I bungle the whole thing by staggering over to the stove where Olga's sitting with her mother and, throwing all caution to the wind, sit down beside her and gasp, '*S'agapo*,' whereupon, alarmed, she leaps up goes over to Gary and out onto the street with him leaving me in the full glare of her mum's outraged stare.

Gary is looking somewhat sober – a worrying thing indeed – when he comes back in; he calls me over to sit back at our table.

'Papa, she likes you very much, but she says you mustn't dream. She's getting married in the summer.'

Tomorrow we'll leave for Athens.

Chapter 33
A long Sojourn in Athens

Summer's come; I've taken to sleeping rough in Athens – anywhere I happen to find myself, or have fallen, after the mighty turn of the taverns: under the rock of the Acropolis, on the hill of Lykavitos, in a doorway in Plaka. Gary's gone into an alcoholic decline from which I can't coax him out – it's to do with Evi, you see – but I do know where to find him: in an *ouzerie* on Solonos, a winding back street up above the Academy, and much frequented by students, and to which I render myself from time to time to share a bottle with him and listen to his woes. Evi has left him and so he's turned his full attention to the lethal liquid. We clink vials, toast Dionysus, and Gary recounts to me the final sequence of events,

'She could never understand, Papa, how I could love her and at the same time love ouzo. I told her that the two things were so different that they couldn't be compared.'

'Hah,' I laugh, 'I bet she was glad to hear that,' and I paraphrase Shakespeare's sonnet,

'Shall I compare thee to a bottle of ouzo?

'Thou art more lovely, and more distemperate . . . '

'Perhaps, Papa,' continues Gary, seriously, 'but what she couldn't . . . hic . . . understand was that I only drank ouzo because she wasn't with me, because I was sad. I expected her to understand that, and to forgive me this time for being drunk. you see, she'd come to Athens by surprise and found me . . . hic . . . drunk, Pa, but do you know what she said then?'

'I suppose I could start guessing but it might take all night, Gary.'

'She said, Pa, that I would drink when I was with her too, if I dared. She was right, Pa.'

And then the real cause of his misery comes out: 'Do you know, Papa?'

'No, Gary, what? tell me.'

'I think there is someone else – she is silent when I ask her – I don't like it when she is silent, Papa, it means she's not saying something.'

'I suppose it does.'

We knock back a vial and he goes on, 'We were walking through Omonia, Papa, I'd been drinking all morning and now the sun was beating on my head and she silent and saying she was going back to Halkida – but *agapimou* I say, you have only just come, and then I started to have all kinds of suspicions – Why was she going to Halki-da? Didn't she love me anymore? It was her silence, Pa, that drove me mad and when she went towards a kiosk saying she had to make a phone call I had visions. You know the little station at Halkida with all the eucalyptus trees and the sea and my Evi arriving there, and someone on the platform waiting, I grabbed her, Papa, "who are you phoning?" I shouted and she just looked at me scared and I threw a fit, Papa, I was jealous, you understand that – I was in a rage in the middle of Omonia and people had to pull me away from her and hold me back while she climbed into a taxi and got away, escaped from me, Papa . . . the last thing I saw was her white face in the taxi. Ah Papa . . . hic . . . '

He slumps over the table, sobbing.

There's nothing much I can do to aid Gary in his plight; he's bent upon a liquid form of self destruction and, when I manage to extricate him from the *ouzerie* for a little jaunt around town, he is either incoherent or doubles up in the middle of the street with pains in his liver. The best thing is to go along from time to time and have a little chat with him over a bottle at his *ouzerie*. It's heart-rending to see him like this.

I rarely go short of a bite to eat and make damn sure I'm in possession of the requisite drachmas for wine and beer by the evening. I'm sleeping out beneath the Acropolis, or wherever I happen to fall, and so there is no rent to pay. Plaka, the old picturesque area below the Acropolis, is always lively, being full of bars and young people and where you can drink and dance until the early hours. I spend the evenings there meeting people from all over, many coming from, or going to, the East, Athens being a kind of crossroads between East and West, where Orient and Occident meet, and that's a distinct feeling one gets in Greece, that there's more than a touch of the Orient about it, and yet it's where our western civilization all began.

One of the ways I make a living in Athens is by flogging stuff at the flea market in Monastiraki. Here everything can be sold, from German army tin hats, some of them complete with bullet holes, to dilapidated pieces of furniture, old army boots, ragged, patched up jackets and coats, goat bells, donkey harnesses, rusty door hinges . . . I find plenty of junk in the streets and dustbins in my long ambles around the city. A few days ago I found a splendid anatomical diagram of the human body and skeleton, in glorious colour and complete with cardboard pull-outs, typical of a product of the twenties, when it had probably been made, and which had been thrown out from a chemist in Kolonaki, the fashionable quarter of Athens. It really was a splendid relic of those times, with a great grinning skull and faded yellow bones, and I sold it for a hundred drachmas to an American from Milwaukee who absolutely raved about it, 'It'll be a sobering reminder that I'll be looking just like him one day,' he laughed.

I'm spending most of my time around Plaka, often in the company of Jean-Michel and some other, mainly French, musicians. We centre around a flat in Rangava Street where Julie, an American journalist, lives with a menagerie of cats, dogs and chickens. She holds open house for all of us other strays and drunken, wandering minstrels. We turn up laden with wine and vegetables from the market and cook huge suppers, veritable feasts which on warm evenings we eat on the roof with its delightful view over the tiles of Plaka and up at the columns of the Acropolis towering above us. There is a concertina player amongst us and a mandolin player, both from Brittany and there's a priceless fellow called Jean-Luc who plays nothing but takes the hat, or rather the coconut shell, around

for Jean-Michel, my old friend Condé, in the metro. I first set eyes
on Jean-Luc shortly after my arrival back from Santorini. It was in
the old Neon Kafeneion in Omonia Square. I was drinking a coffee
and reading at one of the marble tables when I heard this insidious
voice starting to work its way into my consciousness, in English
with a very strong French accent, coming from the table behind me.
The first words I could clearly discern were, 'I am very romantic.'

Overcome with curiosity as to who the author of this statement
was I peeked a look behind me to see a pallid face, long greasy hair
hanging in front of it and a few rotten teeth in a mouth that was sali-
vating at the corner and from which these words had been emitted,
addressed to a pretty, dark-haired, very innocent looking Greek girl.
This was my first glimpse of Jean-Luc, an incorrigibly romantic chap,
of whom I was to see much more over the next few months; heaven
only knows his story before he showed up in Athens—I imagine it
consisted of a somewhat seedy, depraved, existence in Paris, from
where he'd emerged. Jean-Michel had come upon him eking out a
living begging around Omonia Square, preying on young females
like the one in whose company he was now, at the Neon.

'I ask them if they believe in Jesus,' he tells me later, 'and when
they say yes, as most of them do, I tell them that he had said one
should give to the poor, "I am poor," I triumphantly announce to
them.'

Anyway, Jean-Michel, being a fellow with a big heart, had taken
pity on him and, although he wasn't the most presentable looking
specimen, had taken him on as his 'bottler', the one who takes the
hat round, and was splitting the winnings fifty-fifty so that Jean-
Luc began to make a fair wage as Jean-Michel was a truly remarkable musician who'd studied at the Conservatoire in Lyon and went
around the restaurants and cafés as well as up-and-down on the sub-
urban line. Jean-Luc's 'hat' was half a coconut shell which, according to Jean-Michel, he would rattle in the face of the customers in
a way which, understandably, some of them took exception to—so
much so that on one occasion a passenger on the metro pushed our
'romantic friend' away from him so hard that he crashed to the floor,
all the money spilling over the compartment. The most excruciating
part of the whole scene, according to Jean-Michel, was the spectacle

of Jean-Luc scrabbling about under the seats, whilst having a good peek up women's skirts, and in every nook and cranny, for every single drachma, which he counted audibly as he did so. And then, when they were getting out onto the platform to change carriages, Jean-Luc was slow about things and got his foot caught in the sliding doors as the train started to move out of the station. Jean-Michel couldn't do anything as he watched, from the next carriage up, Jean-Luc hopping along the platform signalling desperately for the train to stop. Luckily for Luke it did, just before they entered the tunnel.

I begin to like Jean-Luc, the aura of failure and depravity he carries about with him, as well as appealing to my sympathy, amuses me. Underneath it all he's a sensitive, probably over-sensitive, being with a lot of problems. His one great problem, his overriding obsession, is premature ejaculation. He corners anyone whom he thinks might have a sympathetic ear and pours out his misery and frustration which centres around this curse, the focal point of his existence, 'I cannot even get the tip inside before the whole thing is over,' he groans.

Julie is going out of Athens for a month and she leaves me in charge of her apartment in Plaka. During the three days of the full moon I am awoken early every morning by a knocking on the door; it's Jean-Luc, white as a spectre as he steps over the threshold and immediately begins to recount his nocturnal rampages. The first two evenings of the full moon he'd started off by going to a cinema—where they show those *filmes pornographique—ah la la, il n'y a pas des* 'holes barred', ' he tells me, which gets him heated up and excited and then, after a drop or two in the bar round the corner he'd gone around the brothels, spilling out his woes to the girls—or rather, the hags you see leaning in the doors of Athinas Street—and they tried to help him, but it was no good, he couldn't get it in further than the tip.

On the third morning he staggered in, more ghastly pale than ever, saying, *'Qu'est que je deviens? Qu'est que je deviens?'*—what is becoming of me? what am I becoming? The previous evening he'd well and truly gone on the rampage—starting off on the shopping streets around Omonia he'd gone up to passing females, slapping them on the bottom and running away. 'I was doing this for three hours, I never touched so many bottoms in my life . . . and then I ran off to the brothel and cried in a girl's arms . . . what am I becoming?'

'It sounds like you're becoming a werewolf, I'll have to call you *Jean-Loup* at the time of the full moon,' I retort laughing, unable to contain my mirth at his woeful tale.

It's turning out to be a long innings in Athens broken only by the occasional trip to one of the nearby islands, sometimes with Glenys, a Welsh Cypriot, with whom I've become a very close friend. She sometimes takes the hat around for me and even, on occasion, bursts into song; she has a very good voice but is quite shy about singing in the street and has to be coaxed. She's employed as a chamber-maid at the hostel I stay in when I have the money, for which she's paid a pittance but she always reaches into her pocket to give me a fistful of drachmas when she knows I'm skint – even though she also knows I'll spend most of it on wine and beer.

Although she doesn't drink very much herself, she often accompanies me when I'm doing the rounds of the watering holes in Athens and, because of her natural ebullience, her *joie de vivre,* and her very lively mind, she seems perfectly at ease in these places, sipping a glass of lemonade. We talk about artists, like Van Gogh and Chagall, who capture the magic, the dreams, the energy of life on their canvasses, and writers like Henry Miller, Anaïs Nin, Kazantzakis, John Fowles, Lawrence Durrell and Jung whose insights plunge into the depths of the mind. Being a Scorpio, Glenys is naturally interested in the things deep down inside us, in that other life we usually encounter only in dreams. Like myself, she wants to get to the bottom of things and find the meaning of her existence. I quote Socrates, 'The unexamined life is not worth living,' and she comes back with, 'The unlived life is not worth examining.'

Abundance and generosity are two words that readily spring to mind when I think of her, and a natural joy at the beautiful things of life – the sun, the sea, flowers, good food, feasting and good company. Of course, there is the darker side to her nature, the tendency to depression, when she recoils from life and goes inward and faces the intense emotions that lie there—her mother died in a car accident when she was young, leaving the inevitable scar such trauma inflicts—but it's through these things her soul has struggled and emerged into the light, strong, enduring, ready to face all that life brings, the sorrows, the joys, whilst embracing everything which is beautiful and good and, open to everyone she meets, she infects them with this hard-won zest for life.

At weekends I head out to sea-side towns like Raffina, on the east coast of Attica, which is easy to get to by bus, and is full of Greek tourists at the weekends and where I can pick up a small fortune with my whistle and feast and drink and breathe some lungfuls of pure sea air. Athens in the summer, being the bowl that it is amidst the surrounding hills, is a veritable sea of pollution. But better still, though further away, is Halkida to which I introduce the whole troupe of French minstrels, and, to my joy, Pat. Pat is Irish, though she grew up in Glasgow and has a charming Glaswegian accent. I first came across her when she was playing her guitar and singing on a street near the market. Her voice and her demeanour, not to mention her looks, arrested me. Unseen by her I stopped a while and listened to her, she was singing 'The Green Fields of Ireland,' in a voice filled with so much emotion it sent shivers through me. She was quite dark and small, Celtic-looking, I suppose one could say, and she had pluck as she stood there before the bustling crowd. I knew that I wanted to get to know her as I walked away somewhat intoxicated.

Well, I have got to know her and have started to fall into a not altogether unrequited love, with every possibility of blossoming beyond the odd, passionate kiss had she not a boyfriend in tow. We install ourselves in Andrea's taverna for a few days and nights of feasting, drinking and raising the rafters with unrestrained laughter and song. Pat's voice rises up to the ceiling high above us as her fingers slide over and pluck the strings of her guitar and her voice pulling on my heart strings, my tears flowing into my glass as I listen to her. Andrea is delighted to have such a company of fine musicians and is most attentive to the state of our wine jugs, passing frequently to replenish them, and with his kindly manner saying, '*Oraia mousiki, pedia mou . . .* ', 'We are all his children now.' We sleep out at the rocks under the lighthouse on the strait beneath the swirling, whirling stars.

I'm a bit shaky after another night's heavy drinking in Plaka and so I'm taking it easy this morning, trying to recover and drinking strong coffee in the sun outside Vasili's place, the *Taverna Kalamia*, just down from the Tower of the Winds. Old Vasili's a rum character: he looks more Turkish than Greek, like one of those illustrations from *A Thousand and One Nights*, a beefy-looking fellow with a bald cranium who one can imagine barring the entrance to a cave full of treasure, with bangles in his ears, a forbidding look and holding a scimitar. No one can fathom him, he's silent most of the time, hardly speaks, and when he does, it's a kind of mutter – but you pay attention because you'd better listen to what he's telling you. Although he looks as though he's far away, even standing with his eyes closed sometimes, he observes, he knows exactly what's happening – and he always remembers a face. It's always advisable to keep on the right side of him for he can suddenly, and without any apparent reason, erupt and eject you from his taverna, and there's no coming back.

Only Pete can get away with murder here. Pete can trash the place, he can turn the tables over, smash glasses, insult the customers, cause mayhem and Vasilli will just keep smiling his impenetrable smile – and will always let him back, no matter what he does. He loves Pete, in a way. Pete can do no wrong in his eyes, even when he's trashing his tavern and driving the customers away.

My first sight of Pete was up near the market when I rounded a corner to find out what all the noise was as I was idling along Athinas Street one hung-over morning in late November. In the centre of a crowd which had gathered around him was a tall, wild-looking bloke with shoulder-length straggly hair, a large drum on his back, a harmonica on a metal frame into which, between the lyrics he was shouting out, he'd blast and splutter whilst his huge, strong hands would manically pummel the strings of his guitar. He was doing good business, his guitar case pushed out in front of him was filled with notes and coins thrown into it by his astonished audience who, I daresay, had never seen such a whirlwind of furious energy on the streets of Athens before. Spotting me in the crowd he called out, 'Hey, yer couldn't get me a bottle of beer could yer?' and stooping down to pick up a handful of change handed it to me saying, 'and get one for yerself.'

Well, naturally enough – inevitably one could say – we became drinking buddies, which is to say, something like friends and, although I was a little wary of him at times, we started to hang out quite a bit together. He was from Coventry, had been born during the Blitz, 'I listened to bombs dropping as I lay in my cot, I think that put a stamp on my character in this life. Sometimes I explode, something to do with this stuff I suppose,' he grins as he twirls his glass in his hand.

'I used to have a parrot which perched on my shoulder when I played, people don't often see a one man band and with a parrot on my shoulder the show was complete, I made a fortune – everyone had heard of Pirate Pete and the Rock 'n' Roll Parrot.'

I asked him what had become of the parrot. 'I threw him off a cliff in his cage,' he said, 'he kept on screeching in my ear and I'd run out of drink so I couldn't bear it anymore.'

Just the other night I went bottling for him on the metro line down to Peiraeus. His drum was too big to get on and off with so he just had his guitar and harmonica, with which he can make quite enough noise. He was well pissed up, bursting into the wagons like an atom bomb playing his usual song 'Travelling Blues':

Well I'm a one man band
with a shaking hand
and an empty bottle of booze
travelling blues. . .

It went down well and in a mere forty minutes I'd bottled over a thousand drachmas. At Maroussion we retired for a drink and ordered Metaxa. We downed a few glasses in rapid *aspro pato* fashion and then, just as we were about to leave, Pete got wound up by a remark from some French fellow with a beard on a nearby table. A slanging match ensued and the waiter pushed Pete down into his chair. This really infuriated him and he leapt up again. And then the door to the street flew open and he was on the floor having his head kicked in by twenty to thirty boys from the street. I tried to extract him, crying to his assailers, 'Stop! he's drunk that's all! Come on Pete for fuck's sake let's get out of here, quick!'

But would he come? No. As soon as I disentangled him and they stopped the kicking he leapt back for more, shouting, 'Where's the frog?'

And now it seemed like the whole neighbourhood was on to him as he lay curled up on the floor being kicked to death. At last they decided he'd had enough and I managed to get him out on the street and very gradually steer him in the direction of the metro station. Blood was dripping from his mouth and pouring from his nose as he shook his fist and swore at the horde of hoodlums now thankfully behind us.

Getting to the metro he asked me to smear the blood over his face, saying it would be better for the show and bursting into a carriage of the next train which pulled in he threw himself into a frenzied performance, hurling himself around the carriage and lying flat on his back as his fingers hammered the strings of his guitar whilst bellowing out his furious songs.

> . . . travelling blues
> I got the travelling blues
> an' I ain't got no more time to pick or choose.

My peace is shattered at the sound of English voices and a lot of cursing and swearing. Two blokes in an appalling state of inebriation have sat down at a table and are calling out for wine. I try to keep myself as inconspicuous as I can and keep my eyes down and on a page in the book I was reading before they appeared, in order to avoid catching their attention; an exchange with these pissheads is just what I don't need at this fragile hour of the morning. One of them gets up and his opening words as he stumbles over to my table are, 'I'm gonna sit at your table – I'll try not to give you any problems,' at which he slumps down across from me and calls his friend over, whilst shouting at old Vasili to hurry up with the bloody wine, 'we're not gonna wait here all day for you to finish wiping the tables, you should've done that last night.'

Vasili's a master at containing himself, up to a certain point that is, but oh boy, pushed too far and he can explode, one more word from this insolent fellow could detonate him, one more word from this arrogant Englishman . . . I've seen him charge like an enraged bull and knock the likes of him off his perch and kick him out onto the street. But he carries on doing what he's doing and then he goes to get the wine.

When it arrives, slammed down on the table by a scowling Vasili, I know there's no way I can refuse their invitation to drink – I know that it would upset this fellow who was cussing and swearing in a curiously educated accent, 'that old landlord should be dragged out onto the street and shot,' he says, pouring me a glass of murky retsina, and then, 'life stinks,' he blurts out. I disagree with him on this, coming out with some platitude like 'it's what you make of it.'

'Like fuck, it is,' he snarls, and I decide to pursue this no further, feeling myself on thin ice and knowing how easily a man in this advanced state of inebriation can turn nasty over a seeming trifle. So I remain noncommittal to most of the things he spouts forth, nodding my head occasionally in agreement – although the wine, which he is copiously pouring, is having its effect on me and I'm becoming less intimidated by his aggressive manner and I have to restrain myself from having a bloody good argument, which is something I greatly enjoy; it can be a very pleasant way of exercising the mind and one's sparring skills, as long as the other doesn't flip and turn nasty.

The other fellow has a strong Irish accent and seems a little less pissed than his friend, whom he's continually trying to humour. He's a jovial type, cracking jokes and making light of things, and seems the perfect antidote to his companion. But the very drunken one is the one that interests me, he's far from being just a drunken sot, there's a lot more to him than that I feel. He starts ranting and raving about how he's going to cause damage to someone during the course of the day and break a few windows and things. I'm on the edge of my seat ready to dash at the first sign of this happening.

'Don't take any notice of Richard,' said the Irish one, 'he gets like that when he's upset. My name's Kevin,' he says cheerily, stretching his hand to me, 'what's yours?'

'Lala,' I say, 'rather a funny name, I know.'

'Funny as fuck,' blurts out Richard.

And then he follows up with, 'Please don't take any of my re-marks personally. I'm upset, that's all – saying goodbye to my wife always leaves me like this.'

'Aspro pato!' he says, raising his glass and downing it in one tip.

'We're not meant to be here, we've arrived from Crete by mis-take.'

'By mistake?' I look at him, a little surprised – I know one can ar-rive in places you'd not intended to, if you miss your stop on a train or take the wrong turning in a car or something, but to get on a ship in Crete and arrive in Piraeus, you surely can't do that by mistake.

'We were on board saying goodbye to my wife and her boyfriend,' he went on, 'when the ship started moving and we found ourselves on the way to Athens. We kicked up a stink when we realised what was happening and demanded the ship be turned around – went up to the bridge, but the captain couldn't be reasoned with – I think he was at the point of having us thrown overboard, we were a bit out of order you see,' he chuckled, 'In the end we accepted our fate, went down to the saloon and consoled ourselves with a bottle of *raki*. Hence, we're not exactly sober this morning, are we Kevin?'

'Not *exactly,*' he replied, in the accent of a Dublin man, 'in fact we're probably more drunk than sober.'

'Er, yes, that's a good way of putting it, we probably are,' Richard glances sideways with an amused smile at his companion and, turn-ing to me, 'he always puts things so succinctly.'

'Drunk, not by half,' his Irish friend added.

'Not by half,' mused Richard looking thoughtful for a moment, 'and would you say that was a good thing?'

'It depends on which side of half; if it was the further side I'd say it was.'

'Then, in conclusion, the state of drunkenness which has de-scended upon us must be something in the manner of a blessing. Is that what you're implying?'

'In a word or two: yes.'

It sounds like a Socratic dialogue to me and, laughing, I'm begin-ning to enjoy their company.

Richard's father had been an Albanian partisan during the German occupation; his mother was Russian. He himself had been born and brought up in Wales. He'd gone to Sherborne and had been thrown out, he doesn't say why, and after that he'd been on the road, one way or another, all his life, and speaks nine languages, one of them being Greek which he speaks fluently (it had been funny to hear him swear at Vasili in Greek.) He has striking features, one could almost say noble, and a glint in his eye.

Kevin's of a totally other background, a happy-go-lucky Irishman who, according to himself, had been a prominent member of the IRA. As the day progresses and the wine never stops flowing he bursts into Irish rebel songs, like 'Come out you Black 'n' Tans, come and fight me like a man,' singing with a beautiful, passionate voice, usually at the request of Richard who sits slumped in his chair smiling, his thoughts obviously soothed by these renditions. It reminds me of a king with his minstrel-cum-joker, with whom he travels around to cheer him up and keep him out of trouble.

'Would that be some kind of riddle you're putting to me there, Kevin, or would it be some kind of fact?' is one of the things he occasionally asks his jester. The fluency Richard has with languages Kevin has with accents, suddenly breaking into Cockney or Geordie, English toff, Scouser or Welsh, or a Frenchman speaking English, a German speaking Irish, a Chinaman speaking American, an American speaking Chinese . . . This cracks up both Richard and myself.

By the way Richard speaks I'm beginning to suspect he's a writer, or even a poet. This is confirmed when, asking if he might write something in my book, he writes this:

This day Katerina

The times we cried away all
our fears, we sat and thought
that Somalia was a long way
away. Sometimes I live to
listen for a breath, but my
breath leaves me in huge gusts.

How long do we continue sailing
in these rotting hulks as we
are passed by a time unknown
to us?

A shiver goes down my spine as I read it. He's published in England, he tells me, and I'm not at all surprised to hear that – the poem's pure genius.

'Do you know what I'm terrified of?' he asks me, 'That they're gonna kill my poetry by trying to explain it in the classroom. Let me leap in through the schoolroom window, pissed up as I am now – then they'll understand it.'

Chapter 34

Crete

I knew that I'd have to go to Crete some day, it seemed to have been calling me after hearing so many reports of travellers coming from there: of somewhere more intense, more scorching, more anarchic, more Greek than Greece itself, and now Richard's tales about it have served to reinforce my determination to go there as soon as possible. Thus, without further ado, as soon as Julie returned to Athens, I packed my things and came down to Piraeus where I boarded the night boat to Hania, on the deck of which I'm standing now as I look down onto the quay where the ropes are being unhitched from the capstans and the propellers are churning the oily water and, amidst the usual shouting and seeming confusion which Greeks are so good at creating whenever a ship is docking or putting to sea, the ship starts moving out into the Saronic Gulf. Soon the great mountain ranges of the Peloponnese are towering up to westward, the coastal villages twinkling with lights as we slide past them, as are the islands Aegina, Hydra and far out to starboard distant Spetsai and then the coastlines fall behind and away from us as we break out into the open sea. Steering due south with a bottle of ouzo and a warm, almost hot, wind from Africa bathing my face, visions of mermaids and all manner of strange creatures well up from the depths and flood my mind. Up above, suspended over Crete, a constellation, half-man, half-bull, seems to bellow for the earth and for the wine-red blood to course around its veins again. I listen to a tale told by the dolphins, that leap amongst the waves, that there

lies at the bottom of the sea a chest which contains all of Sappho's
lost poems—they are the words she whispered in the dark before
she wrote them down and they are guarded by mermaids. And if
you should take it into your head to search for them there are three
things you should arm yourself with before the descent into the sea:
a bag containing the winds of the six directions, and a seventh for
luck; a jar containing the condensed light of the stars, and a box
containing the voices of a thousand things. And don't forget to take
an umbrella.

I try always to have at hand a pen and a notebook when I wander
in the hills or along the seashore, for her lost voice can sometimes be
heard telling a poem in the song of a bird or the cresting and falling
of a wave, in a breeze as it whispers in the long dry grass of summer,
or in a storm which shakes the trees and moans like a soul, or in a
stone, which seems so mute but isn't; if you listen with your inner
ear you will hear them, they will forever be there; for did she not
herself write:

> Although they are
> only breath, words
> which I command
> are immortal . . .

I once had a dream which I couldn't see—it had come to me
enclosed in an envelope in the middle of the night, I knew it was
there but I couldn't open it. I needed a knife . . . no, a key. I went
in search of the postman who must have brought it and found him
saying prayers in a church.

'You'll have to go a locksmith,' he said, 'every letter of this kind
requires a different kind of key.'

'But why a key to open a letter?' I asked, perplexed.

'Because this is a dream,' came his response.

All of a sudden the locksmith, a funny little man with a pixie hat
and shining eyes, was standing before me and was handing me a key
which, upon turning it in the letter's tiny lock, I woke up and all
around me saw the objects in my room lit up like silver by the moon
as though they were the scintillating fragments of her poems which

now, worked upon by the beams of the moon, were being restored to their original wholeness.

We slip into Souda Bay just as the sun is rising and lighting up the magnificent mountain range which forms the back-bone of Crete. Here, according to legend, Zeus was born, hidden in a cave by his mother, Rhea, to save him from being gobbled up by Cronos, his father, and was fed on goat's milk and honey. Here also Paddy Leigh Fermor, one of my favourite writers, disguised as a shepherd, hid in the caves from which, with the brave men of the Cretan resistance, he would venture out and carry out operations against the occupying Germans.

A short bus ride takes us to Hania and, alighting at the bus station, I make my way by twisting streets to the harbour which more than meets my expectations. A great circular harbour of solid stone, built by the Venetians, curls around to a lighthouse at the entrance to the sea. It's full of fishing boats, big and small, with fishermen and their wives mending nets that are spread out along the quays. And all along it, from one end to the other, it's lined with *kafeneions* and tavernas with their colourful awnings, offering welcoming shade against the scorching sun, in which you can sit drinking coffee in the mornings, the sun sparkling in the green, translucent, water splashing almost at your feet, or in the afternoon, taking refuge from the fierce heat with bottles of ice cold beer, the condensation running down the sides of your glass; and in the evening with supper on a chequered table, and retsina from amber-coloured tin jugs, whilst the population passes before you on the evening *volta*, the proud, upright men with their high boots, flowing moustaches and black bandannas, their arms around their dark, pretty wives and their children running round them.

Following the curve of the harbour towards its western end are the ancient warehouses and workshops where fishing boats and trawlers are repaired. Along the quay nets are spread and fishermen and their wives sit mending them and here is to be found a large, cavernous taverna, so spacious it must at one time have been a repair shop too; bare-walled with creaking wooden tables and chairs and a bar at the end with barrels of raki and the deep red murky wine of the local hills called *mavro krasi*, black wine. Above door, on a wooden plaque is written *O Lyraki* ('The Little Lyre') and in the evenings the fishermen and workers in the repair shops gather here and sing *mantinades*, high-spirited songs and laments peculiar to Crete, accompanied by the whirling, intoxicating *lyra*, a three-stringed instrument played with a bow and held vertically on the player's lap; and by the *laoúto*, a kind of large lute with four double strings plucked with a plectrum and which has a deep resonant sound similar to an oud in Turkey; and a *baglamas* which is like a small bouzouki with a long neck, shrill, vibrant, high-pitched and usually played very fast with an insistent almost frenetic dancing rhythm.

As for the *mantinades* themselves, many of them are written down and remembered down through the generations, whilst others are entirely spontaneous, improvised on the spot, the musicians responding to one another as in the fado of Portugal, so that it becomes a delightful repartee, quick, unrelenting and highly skilful. Full of raw emotions, yearning, love's joys, love's sorrows, sometimes mischievous, sometimes bawdy, a typical stanza from a *mantinade* might go like this:

> O would I were the salt sea-wind
> And you upon the beach
> Would bare your breast and let me blow
> Until your heart I reach.

Or like this:

> When you go to Aghio Tapho
> And not get drunk there,
> It's like going to the Virgin
> Without saying a prayer!

I've been scribbling in my wine-stained notebook, trying to catch my emotions as I listen enraptured to the manic rhythm of the ever quicker and quicker repartee of the musicians, when I look up to see a company of tourists come through the door. Few tourists come here normally, as around this end of the harbour it's poorly lit and the quay's strewn with the nets, buoys and mooring ropes of the fishing boats, making it easy to stumble if you don't take care. They look a little awkward as they take their places at a large table next to mine. They're talking German amongst themselves. One of them's a very pretty girl with blonde flaxen hair who seems a little removed from the others who are talking loudly and seem quite oblivious to the music. She looks over at me rather wistfully, as though she needs rescuing and I motion to her to come over and sit at my table. As she comes over I notice how truly lovely she is, her slender body clothed in tee shirt and jeans and flip flops on her feet – simplicity at its most perfect.

'They're alright really,' she says sitting down, 'they just get a bit rowdy when they've drunk too much – I don't think they can really take this *raki* and the strong local wine. They're Swiss, like me, so they're always asking me to come along with them. My name's Heidi, by the way, and she proffers her slender sun-kissed hand to me, and you? You look Scottish or Irish – I bet your name begins with a Mac or something like that,' she smiles.

'Well, my middle name does, it's Mackenzie and my first name is Alastair – very Scottish but most people call me Lala.'

'Lala? but how did you get a name like that?'

'My sister gave it to me, when I was born – before they had time to christen me Alastair, so that is my real name reallly, it's closer to my soul.'

'I love it,' and she clasps her hands in front of her breast.

'Are you a writer?' she asks, glancing at my notebook on the table, 'a poet perhaps?' she looks at me with bright blue Alpine eyes and to my reply, 'well yes, sort of . . . ' asks if she may read something I've written or, better still, read her something. Yes, but I warn her these are really just a jumble of semi-coherent scribbles jotted down for the most part when in a state of advanced inebriation.

At which she laughs and says: 'That's how some of the best poetry was written – read me something, the more drunken the better.'

Happy to oblige her I pick up the book, flick through the pages and am about to read when a chair is slammed down between us by an odious fellow – one of a small group of ne'er-do-wells who are often in here trying to chat up any tourist girl who may wonder in.

Turning his back on me, he began aggressively imposing himself on Heidi.

'*Figé!*' I growl, 'piss off!'

He turns to me, hissing: '*Skáse malaka!*' and swivels back to Heidi who is edging away from him in disgust.

'*Figé apo tho!*' I shout, grabbing him by the arm, 'Get the fuck out of here!' at which he leaps up seething and pointing outside, hisses, '*Exo!*'

I'm out here on the quay before him, fists raised, ready, 'Come on then! Come on then, *malaka*, fight!' he takes a couple of steps towards me but I can see the fear coming over him and with a final '*Gamisou—tha se páro yia aftó!*' ('Fuck you—I'll get you for this!') he slinks away into the shadows. I should have gone straight back into the tavern but I couldn't resist chasing him down the quay to make sure he cleared right off. When I get back Heidi and the company she was with have gone, to my great dismay.

My victory is short lived however. For this evening, stepping over the threshold of the Lyraki I'm pushed back outside by the scumbag of last night who's gathered four or five of his mates together and have been lying in wait for me. Shouting oaths at me they set about me viciously punching me in the stomach, which takes my wind away, and thumping me round the head, I reel and stagger to the edge of the quay trying desperately to fend them off and would run if I could but I'd never get away—they'd beat me to the ground and batter me senseless. The little weasel of last night wants revenge, he wants blood. My only chance of getting away from them is to jump into the harbour, into the black water ten feet down. Seeing what I intend to do, one of them grabs my sleeve but I pull free, ripping the sleeve off and falling backwards into the water, and getting tangled up in the mooring ropes I have to fight free of them and duck below, resurfacing the other side of the barnacle-covered hull of a trawler. I start skirting round behind it, scraping the flesh off my arms which bleed into the water as I frantically struggle to keep myself from being dragged down underneath the gigantic, heaving hull by unseen currents. I can hear shouts and whistling and footsteps running along the quay, '*Einai ekei, piso to varca!*' They haven't gone away, they might swarm onto the trawler and batter me with poles or pelt me with some of those loose harbour stones you find in small piles along the quay. I ease my way along to the stern and with the aid of the propeller duck beneath the surface and swim the two yards or so to the next vessel, hopefully unseen by anyone that might be waiting to catch me as I traverse the gap. This boat's easier to move along as there are ropes hanging in loops from the deck, and so with increased speed and confidence I move rapidly along it to the next vessel and then to the next and soon the voices seem far away. I feel like a fox that throws the hounds off the scent by ducking under water and swimming downstream. I bide my time until I deem it safe to clamber back onto the quay. By now I'm shivering with cold and my teeth are chattering uncontrollably. Holding onto the rusty iron hoops which protrude from the harbour wall and serve as a ladder, I cling on until the voices and shouting die away and haul myself up to the top of the wall and lie out for a few minutes on the cobbled stones at the quay's edge. It's taken it out of me, this little escapade, and I don't feel I have much strength left. Then I struggle to my feet and in the shadows of the warehouses I stealthily make my way back to the taverna – dripping wet, soaked in blood and brine. I am greeted with: '*Bravo philé, palikari!*' from the musicians as I step over the threshold whilst the landlord pours me a large glass of raki. 'Don't worry 'he says they won't be coming back here.'

A few days later, sitting on the terrace of one of the restaurants which line the waterfront, drinking my morning coffee, Heidi passes by, her face lighting up when she sees me and comes over and sits at my table, calling for a coffee as she does so.

'I'm sorry I had to leave the other night, the company I was in sensed trouble and wanted to get out of there – I should have stayed but they insisted I go with them. I've been wondering, wondering how you were.'

I tell her what happened when we went outside and that I regretted not coming straight back in after the bloke had backed off because she'd gone by the time I got back. And then I told her what had happened the following night and my narrow escape from having my head kicked in.

'I'm so glad you escaped them,' she breathed, visibly shaken upon hearing the tale, 'that guy was horrible and he was a coward – he couldn't fight you alone, he had to get his friends – typical coward's behaviour. And look at your arm,' she said, 'all scratched and bruised. I will bring you something to put on it. Listen, I have to go now, but if you like you could meet me this evening at the bar I work in, one of those late night bars, up in the backstreets above the harbour,' and she tells me the name, 'I'll be there from nine o'clock on.'

I know the one she's talking about, it's one of those chat-up bars that a number of tourist girls get jobs in and which enables them to live in Greece. It's strictly chat, to get the customers to buy drinks, nothing more – unless they want to.

'It would be a pleasure,' I say.

It's getting on for ten by the time I get there as I'd been catching the evening volta on the promenade and it being a Friday evening I drummed up a fair bit of loot, after which I'd had a couple of beers on the sea-front before heading up here. I was met by a thick fog of cigarette smoke as I stepped through the door and a barrage of bouzouki from the juke box. It was a pretty seedy place.

She broke away from the customer who'd been chatting to her, he didn't look too pleased about that, and she led me to a table where we sat down. She looked ravishing in a simple, knee-length summer dress and a light touch of lipstick and mascara.

Between her entertaining customers we manage to chat a little, although the boss doesn't like her talking to me, he can see that I've got no money. She's brought me some ointment for my arm and she starts to tell me her story.

'I worked in a travel agent's in Zürich – I suppose it was the closest I could get to travelling myself. Of course, being Switzerland, we mainly dealt with skiing holidays and renting chalets in the Alps; but we also sold packages to the Mediterranean, you know, Italy, Spain, the South of France and Greece – and it was those posters of Greece especially which hung on the walls . . . white houses, blue sea, islands . . . they got into my soul. So I left and came to Greece.'

'You followed your heart.'

'Yes, like you.'

She goes on to tell me, rather coyly, that she's started painting.

'Water colours,' she says, 'there are so many things to paint here in Hania, the harbour, the cafés with their gaily coloured awnings, the old Venetian buildings, some of them crumbling, the fishing boats and the fishermen mending their nets . . . and when I have time I go out into the surrounding countryside and the little villages in the folds of the mountains. So many things everywhere: goats, donkeys, flocks of sheep, cedar trees, little wooded groves . . . '

Her enraptured descriptions have already painted a fabulous picture of Crete in my mind. She tells me her dreams, about her childhood in a little mountain village – 'I'll take you there one day,' she says, 'you'd love it, I know.'

Around two in the morning, the bar's closing up and she asks me to walk her home. It's dark outside and she takes my arm as we stumble down the precarious side street towards the harbour. We are happy and laugh as we walk along side by side, her warm body pressed close to mine. We haven't gone far when suddenly, out of the shadows, four men pounce on us, pulling her away from me and then beating me with batons and fists. All went black, and Heidi screaming is the last thing I remember. I come to just as dawn's breaking, lying in the gutter, sticky with blood and teeth broken.

What became of Heidi I'll never know. I've been looking for her ever since. She doesn't show up at the Lyraki where I wait for her in the evenings hoping she'll walk through the door. I bump into one of her companions on the harbour front, they are all wondering where she's gone and are leaving for Switzerland in a day or two and would like to say goodbye. I pluck up courage to go up to the chat up bar. As I walk in the landlord glares at me and I ask him about her: 'den 'xero,' he says gruffly, 'den doulevi edo tora,' he doesn't know, she doesn't work here now.

Dejectedly, I walk back to the harbour with the feeling that I'll never see her again and fearing the worst.

I've been reading *The Magus*, that extraordinary novel by John Fowles. Set in Spetsai, which in the book he calls Phraxos, he conjures up a world of illusion and enchantment where the hidden workings of the unconscious come into play and into which, un-

wittingly, a naive young Englishman steps and is caught up in a
series of trials, of a moral kind and highly erotic. Unable to resist his
sensual nature he fails at every turn, proving that he is incapable of
real love, which all along has been calling to him. It is painfully near
to the bone in my case, in respect to my own duplicity and inability
to truly love. And it foreshadows what is to come: the final meeting
in Paris when the truth comes out, in a dismal pizzeria and over a
bottle of wine. The crumpling of her face and the stifled cry and her
running out the door and my pursuit over the bridge to the other
side where she disappears, swallowed by the darkness.

And now, two months on and summer drawing to a close, the
scorching heat is abating, making it easier to move. I'm going to
set out around the western part of Crete and see a little of it before
the autumn rains start. What I really want to do is to walk around
the coast and into the almost impenetrable mountainous region of
Sfakia, renowned for its resistance to invaders, with its fierce fighting men, *pallikari*, who fought off both Turks and Germans, and
before those, the Venetians, none of whom were ever able to subdue
the region. Nevertheless, after the gallant capture of the German
general, Kreipe, by Patrick Leigh Fermor and members of the resistance, who were hiding out and operating from their hideouts in the
mountains, and who successfully spirited the general away to Cairo,
there were terrible reprisals, the Germans coming down heavily on
the region, burning villages and shooting the men, those that remained, the old and the very young, who were not in Albania. One
café owner took me round the back to show me the bullet holes in
the wall where the killing had been carried out.

Roaming in the hills above Kolimbari (where one day I shall begin the writing of my book), darkness is falling and it's beginning
to rain. I take shelter in the doorway of an abandoned house; it's a
fleeting storm, I'll wait for it to pass. Two boys come along, '*Yeia
sou,*' they greet me, '*Ela na spiti mas,*' and they're waving for me to go
with them to their house, just up the road, to get in out of the rain.
Not wanting to impose myself on the family I refrain; they insist.
We walk alongside one another, heads bowed down against the wind

and rain. There is a wave of warmth as we step down into the firelit kitchen of the little stone dwelling. The family rises in welcome to grasp my hand and motion me to the best seat by the fire. I am at ease, perfect peace, amongst the open, smiling faces and their excited scrutiny of me. I'm poured a glass of *tsikoudia* and in the glowing circle one by one the family is introduced – Aristo, the father, tough, weather-beaten and wise, Maria, mother of this brood of three boys, Vangelli, Petro and Sotiri and two girls, Anna and Dimitra – '*Yeia sou, mister Lala,*' they say. The fire crackles, my jacket steams as I begin to dry out. The rain comes down heavily on the roof.

'It's raining,' says Aristo, taking me quite by surprise, as he's said it in almost faultless English.

'You speak English,' I exclaim, with no little surprise,

'A little,' he says modestly

'But how?'

'Ships . . . '

Ships, *carávia,* the merchant navy is the usual reason for any linguistic abilities found in rural areas. Liverpool, Newcastle, Glasgow – he knows these places; he also knows the ports of Bombay, Hong Kong, Marseille, San Francisco, Melbourne, Reykjavík, Rio . . . the list goes on. He was at sea for some eight or nine years, joining his first ship when he was just sixteen. It was good to see the world when young, he tells me but then he got a longing to be back in his native land, his beloved Crete, and so he came back, met the girl he was to marry and now he has a few olive trees, a few vines, a few sheep, goats and a family.

'I am a *voscos,* a shepherd now, leading a simple life like my ancestors,'

'Simple perhaps, but a rich life,' I say

'A hard life,' he corrects me, 'with almost more children than I have sheep. But we all eat and we have a roof over our heads.'

The table is pulled up by the fire and supper laid on it: eggs, potatoes, bread olives and wine and, as we eat, I sense how poor this family is, how precious the food is, and I sense the dignity, the nobility in their poverty. I ask Aristo about the origin of his name for it sounds to me like an abbreviation of Aristotelous and I am curious about that, to come across an Aristotle in the remote hills of Crete.

'I think you have something very philosophical about you,' I say, 'the name fits you.'

'Not me, I am as thick as this wall,' he says, tapping it.

'All the greatest philosophers said that sort of thing about themselves, but you know many things: you know how to make a living off the land, how to till and sow it and when to harvest it, you know how to tend sheep and goats, you know how to make cheese, to grow vines, make wine . . . and I dare say, you know how to rig and steer a ship, how to navigate by the stars, you know the habits of the people of faraway coastal towns, you know how to predict the weather, tell the signs of a coming storm, you know the phases of the moon and when to sow and when to reap.'

Aristo listens with pleasure to my rapturous summing up of his knowledge and skills, as he leans on his stick stroking his flowing moustache, so characteristic of the Cretan, with the black bandanna round his head and knee-length, black leather boots.

It's a wonderful evening, with my glass constantly filled and re-filled with the fiery, home-made *tsikoudia*, the warm glow of the fire, the kindness which is almost tangible, the simplicity which makes me feel that nothing could be added to it, so perfect it is—not all the money in the world could match the wealth of an evening like this. The girls make me up a bed by the fire and I sleep like the king of Ithaca, snug and warm between sheep's fleeces, whilst the rain thunders down on the tin roof.

This is a dark road and it leads to where I know not. It winds steadily upwards towards summits silhouetted against the sky, through crags and ravines and shadows. At my side a river runs swiftly, thunderously, filling the air with a roar, with the thud of rocks and stones shifting, displaced by the torrent. I shudder at an unexpected sound or a flitting shadow—I am jumpy, inflicted with a primordial terror at this vastness, this blackness, and I have to goad myself on. And then a dog appears and trots along at my side, and my fear evaporates. Overhead, between towering peaks and sheer crags I can see stars, constellations turning. I like to think that they can see me, tiny mortal in a ravine, and that they're setting me my course, steering me somehow out of the darkness into the light, and that it's not for nothing this wandering, so aimless seeming some-times, and that there *is* some rhyme, some reason to it and that there is some great sea I'm going to, just as there is for this river which thunders along at my side. Well, whether they are or not, and whether there is some great sea I'm going to, I know that this wan-dering is not for nothing and that I'm harvesting the precious mo-ments of my life and enriching my soul with the sights and sounds and tastes of life – and with the meeting of strangers, who are not really strangers, on the road I journey along. This is my life, and any other way would be death.

Chapter 35
Jail

All good things come to an end – and who's to say but it's not ordained when they do? Perhaps it was time for me to leave Athens. It was a hot sticky night in July. I'd had a few beers in the bars around Omonia, I'd wet my whistle and whet my thirst for more, the money for which I was raising in the corridors beneath the square, when two black-clad cops were upon me.

'What are you doing?' they snapped

'I'm playing music.'

'You're begging – come with us.'

"No,' I said defiantly – I'd had a drop to drink, remember.

Furious, one of them grabbed my sleeve, 'You're coming with us you mother-fucker!'

He spoke English with a New York accent. He'd probably had some training over there and had picked up a foul vocabulary. His eyes burned with hatred. I refused to budge; he tried shoving me towards the exit, his colleague looking around uneasily. I sank to the ground and played dead. At this his fury knew no bounds: he would have kicked me to death right here on the flag stones if it wasn't for the public which had started to gather round. Outraged and protesting, the voice of Athens, like the chorus in a Greek play, 'It's injustice, it's unlawful, shoving people around like that. He's only trying to get himself a meal (even though it's a liquid one, well why not on a baking hot evening such as this!) since when was music beggary? We give him something in return for what he gives.'

Dear Greeks! Not afraid to speak their minds, they are giving me their passionate support. The crowd has swelled out of all proportion and the police are being harangued. But I know that I'm done for, I'm in for it and, laid out at the feet of the throng, I'm trembling with fear and rage. Sweeping down and grabbing me by the arms and legs, my infuriated captors drag me up the steps and out into the pandemonium of Omonia where I'm pushed into the back of a police car. A cop on either side of me pummels me with his fists, as we speed off at break-neck speed through the Athenian night. We encircle the square and hurtle down a side street where the car screeches to a halt. I'm dragged out and pushed through the doors of a grim-looking building, kicked, punched and dragged by the hair up the stairs to the second floor. I'm scared now, and utterly helpless, at the mercy of these brutes who throw me into a cell and rush at me, their fists flailing, 'We'll show you, you motherfucker! I kill you motherfucker!'

My despair increases throughout the night as I pace the cell, bound at the wrists with handcuffs. The two sadistic figures in black keep bursting through the door and setting about me with an undiluted hatred that I never wish to see again. Between these interruptions I'm left to contemplate my fate. It's a filthy, hellish place, everything is stark, cold and hard. On the walls is the congealed blood of previous victims, interposed amongst the graffiti – names, dates, curses and signals of despair. At one end of the cell high above my head is a tiny window with a grill over it. It looks out on the street. The sound from a juke box, bursts of laughter, women's voices, drift up from a café below. So maddeningly close the street seems. Some time in the very centre of the night my tormentors burst in, *'Ela do pusté!'*

They kick me through the door and along the corridor to a grim office where I'm shoved down into a chair and interrogated by a thin-lipped old geezer with spectacles:

'Why were you begging?'

'I wasn't begging, I was playing music.'

'Begging! – What are you doing in Greece without any money? Why did you call the police motherfuckers?'

'I did not.'

'Shut up. Sign this,' a piece of paper he's been writing on is pushed over to me – I try to read it, to make head or tail of it.

'Sign it, quickly,' my interrogator snaps.

'No, I want to understand it,' and a cop standing behind me brings a rubber truncheon down hard on my neck.

'Sign it *malaka!*'

'But it's not true what you've written. They're lies, lies. . . *psemata!*'

He gets furious at this, leaps up and smacks my face, and the cop standing behind me brings his truncheon down again on my neck.

'Sign it motherfucker, sign it!' they scream – I sign it, I know that I won't get out of here until I do, and then I'm wrenched from my seat, shoved up some stairs to the top of the building and thrown into a dark cell. The door slams behind me, the footsteps retreat along the corridor. It's dark in here and it smells; my eyes, gradually accustoming themselves to the darkness, make out the shape of a mattress in one corner. I sense there is someone else in here besides me.

'Hello, friend,' I jump, a human being propped up on his elbow is watching me.

'English? You English?'

He's from Tunis, been here for days on end; he tries to make an advance as I lay down on the mattress and I jump as far away from him as I can. From down below comes the sound of shouting and abuse and a woman screaming.

As the dawn light filters in through the window slit, an eye looks down on us from a peephole in the door. The key grates in the lock, the door's flung open and I'm told to follow the guard who stands on the threshold. I'm led handcuffed to the building in the *Odos Socratous,* Socrates Street, where fingerprints and photographs are taken – perhaps Socrates had his fingerprints taken here when he was arrested! – and sitting in an upright iron chair, numbers are lined up on metal chips in front of me and I'm swivelled round by a man who pulls levers, taking shots of my mug as he does so, 'Nice holiday snaps to send to my mother,' I joke, but he doesn't find it funny.

Whilst I was waiting my turn outside the door, a journalist came along and, asking me if I would put my whistle to my mouth, snapped a couple of photographs, 'Thank you,' he said, 'you'll be in the papers tomorrow.'

And now, having been through all that palaver, I'm being marched up to the courthouse through the crowds in Omonia and along the busy shopping streets, chained like a common criminal with my wrists in handcuffs behind my back. Everything seems so much more serious than the time this happened before. That was the time the officer who escorted me to the court house had actually been apologetic about my having to undergo the humiliation of wearing handcuffs in public and had removed them in a café where he took me for a coffee and a cake whilst we awaited my trial. He told me he didn't consider it a crime to play music in the streets, 'In Greece we love music.'

Released from our roles, during that brief time we spent together as man to man, we struck up a friendship with one another and I'll never forget his winking and smiling over to me in the courtroom as I was finally acquitted, for during the trial, I actually made the whole courtroom laugh and the judge, a very warm and sympathetic man, told me he'd passed me in the street a few days previously and told me I played very beautifully and then, with a smile, dismissed the case, telling me I was free to go. This time, though, the very atmosphere seems to conspire against me as I'm brought into the courtroom. The jury looks at me grimly, as if from a stage set up for a single purpose – that of despatching me to the dark underworld.

'Come forward,' the judge orders me and an accusation of vagrancy, beggary, resisting arrest and insulting behaviour and language towards the police is read out to me. Vagrancy's a charge I cannot challenge but begging, no, I was playing music.

'You were begging,' the judge snaps and that's that. 'Why did you call the police,' and here he lowers his voice, 'motherfuckers?'

'I did not.'

'It says that you did.'

'But it's not true. I swear. . .' and, putting my hand on the Bible before me, 'I swear, on the Bible, it's not true.'

'I will send for the policeman who arrested you and he will tell us if it's true or not, you may sit down now.'

Ask the cop who arrested me? But he'll lie through his teeth, of course he will, he hates me. I stand no chance now and shudder at the thought of seeing that violent man again. As he comes through the door into the court room he glances at me and goes up and stands in front of the panel. From beginning to end his tale's loaded against me. Oh yes, my language had been foul, no mistake that I'd called him and his colleague motherfuckers, no mistake there.

'Thank you, please sit down. Come forward mister Mackenzie Brown Ashford Alastair,' a fine jumble of my names they have made on that paper; lucky they don't know my real one.

'The officer that arrested you has confirmed that you insulted the police.'

'it's not true,' I put my hand on the Bible again, 'It's not true, I swear.'

'He is an officer of the law and I am obliged to believe him – you understand that this is a very serious offence – now sit down.'

I turn to go towards my place, passing my tormentor on the way he looks at me triumphantly with those vicious eyes I'll never forget, 'I told you I'd get you, you motherfucker,' he hisses. Meanwhile, there's a deadly hush in the courtroom as the prosecutor whispers to the judge behind a book he's held up to prevent us seeing their faces or hear what they say. The judge looks up and pronounces his sentence, 'You have been found guilty by the Greek law and you will serve a nine month prison sentence.' Nine months! I'm struck dumb, the courtroom seems to gasp too. He continues, 'You have a choice, either to serve nine months in prison or pay a fine,' he mentions a figure – God knows how many thousands of drachmas – certainly it's unpayable by me. I think of my father, could I possibly expect him to bail me out of this fix his worthless son has got himself into? And I feel worthless as I say: 'I will pay.'

I know that my good-hearted father will help me out. I just want to get away, escape from this nightmare; I can't stomach the thought of last night's ordeal being repeated.

'So, that's settled,' says the judge, bringing his hammer down on the desk and the court gets up to leave.

But, if I thought that by paying off my sentence with a fine was going to spell immediate release, I was mistaken.

'Hey, what's this?'

'We're going back to where we came from,' says my guard, clamping the handcuffs back around my wrists and leading me out of the courtroom.

'But, I'm free. . .'

'Not yet you ain't,' he says with a leer, 'money come first.'

The corridor is filled with the crowd which has filed out from the courtroom. Upon seeing me a Gypsy youth rushes up and thrusts two thousand drachma notes in my palm.

'*Pare Phile,*' he says, with a look of deep sympathy in his eyes, 'for cigarettes,' and he dashes away into the sunlit street.

Back in the police station I'm locked in a cell and left; they're not beating me this time, thank God, but the night is interminable as I pace up and down at the mercy of my thoughts which rush at me full of self-reproach. I chickened out in the face of the sentence, took the easy option – where is my pride? And for all that, here I am, still in the clutches of the law. Music drifts up from the street below and a woman's laughing could well be in mockery of me.

I'm awoken by the singing of a bird near the window, such sweetness amidst all this ugliness. The dawn is filtering through the window bars, lighting me up where I lie on the filthy mattress on which I'd finally laid down exhausted. I look around: the same mess on the walls of graffiti, blood and the stench of piss and shit. Well, what's in store for me today, I wonder. I stare up at the ceiling; this sleep's done me good, I feel much better about things, can even partly justify myself for taking the easy way out – anyone would have done it, surely, if they could – it's not as though I've betrayed anyone, except myself, I suppose, my pride. I console myself with the thought that I'll pay my father back one day. Footsteps are approaching, and an eye appears in the peephole, a key grates loudly in the lock and the door swings open.

'Get up and come with me,' says the cop on the on the threshold.

'Coffee time?' I joke, trying to lighten the mood.

'Moving time,' he says, snapping handcuffs around my wrists.

'Where are we going?'

'You'll see.'

A car's waiting outside. We drive off across Athens and out beyond the suburbs where we pull up in a courtyard, a large gate swings
open and I'm pushed into a dismal dungeon. As my eyes become accustomed to the darkness I make out other figures, perhaps as many
as fifty, languishing in this filthy place.

'Don't worry, friend, you won't have to stay here too long, a day
or two at the most, before you're moved to one of the prisons, and
they'll seem like paradise after this. Hey you play a pipe, huh? says a
cheery young chap suddenly recognising me, 'I've seen you playing
all over the place in Athens. What are you doing here?' He doesn't
look surprised when I tell him it's precisely for that, piping in the
streets.

'Well, small wonder, you're sticking your neck out, *philé*–you
should just go up and ask people for money.'

I haven't eaten all day and am ravenous now evening's come.
Sleep's the best remedy for hunger as you can become oblivious to
it and so I unroll my sleeping bag on a bunk and am just about to
slip into it when I hear the unmistakeable, high-pitched voice of my
friend Jean-Michel in the yard. Bounding over to the bars I come
face to face with my companion of many a wine-sodden night. With
him's Mari-Lena, the daughter of a Greek ambassador and who'd
long been one of our company in the rounds of the taverns; she'd
often accompanies Jean-Michel on his guitar as she has a wonderful voice, singing in both Greek and English; they've brought with
them another woman, a lawyer, who begins, 'I read about your arrest in the papers, they have no right to be holding you–I shall work
for your release, it will not cost you anything, it's important that
your case is exposed.'

Very touched, I thank her from the bottom of my heart, but have
to confess that, shamelessly, I'd already agreed to pay the fine.

'But they still have you, don't they. If you're not released within
a few days I shall come out to see you. I believe that you're destined
for the prison at Amfissa.'

'We've brought you some food and money,' says Mari-Lena, handing me a huge bag of goodies and six thousand drachmas–golly,
what with the money the Gypsy gave me, I'll be richer than ever.
They'd been out all day yesterday, playing in the cafes to raise the

money – bless 'em. They'd seen the write up in the papers and had gone straight along to the police station to demand what was going on and where I'd been taken – they've done all this for me. A flood of warmth surges through my heart.

'We'll keep ourselves informed of your whereabouts,' they called, as they climbed into the taxi which had brought them.

At dawn a vehicle pulls up outside; there's a commotion as names are being called out, mine is one of them. Thirteen of us are bundled into a black mariah and locked into a cage, with two guards, machine guns on their laps, watching over us. We take the road north, towards Thessaloniki. Through the slit windows Attica is flashing by, the ripe corn golden in the sunlight under a deep blue sky with not a cloud in it. Oh to be out there, wandering free on the high summer roads and to be dropping into a wayside café for a coffee or a cool beer. I look around my companions; a mixed bag of all ages, sizes, and walks of life; no doubt there's a mixed bag of crimes committed too. That one ark features and eyes rivetted to the floor, looks like he's done some dastardly deeds indeed, murdered his mother in law or something or one of the prostitutes on Athinas street. And that crafty looking bugger there looks like he's been picking pockets on the underground, whilst this one sitting right in front of me with the huge, bald cranium looks like he's straight out of a Dickens novel, from the tale of David Copperfield, perhaps, pouncing on the young Copperfield in the graveyard and frightening the life out of him; but he turned out to be not such a bad chap at all, if I remember rightly. He's looking straight ahead of him, unflinching, silent, devoid of expression, as he slowly chews gum. Is he staring at me? Crikey, I hope not, he might be thinking of pouncing on me in the prison and frightening the life out of *me*. Relax, he's not even *seeing* me – he's staring through the walls of the vehicle and out beyond. There's something about him that commands the respect of everyone present; on the rare occasions that he speaks everyone listens. His name's Angelo, and he's going to turn out to be some kind of guardian angel to me – whilst right now he's impatient to be back inside a proper prison, not those damned dungeons, to see his old mates again, to get some decent food, sleep in a proper bed and to be treated like a human being. All of a sudden, after a couple of hours' steady driving, the vehicle pulls off the road and stops in front of a restaurant.

'No loitering about outside now,' the guards warn us sternly as they unlock the cage, remove our handcuffs and escort us to the restaurant their guns trained on us, should anyone try to make a break for it. And here we are, a motley band of villains en route for prison, filing into a restaurant to mingle at large with the public and to eat and to drink as if there were no tomorrow. We sit at a large table, with our guards, machine guns on their laps beneath the tablecloth, surveying us from an adjoining table. We can order whatever we like: food, beer, wine, a final blow out before the austerities ahead.

As we swing back onto the highway there's a burst of singing and merriment. 'Play your flute for us,' demand my companions and so, to the wailing of my whistle, we speed towards our prisons. At around three o'clock, in the height of the afternoo heat, the van gone quiet with everybody drowsy and dropped into sleep, we're awoken by the sudden stopping of the vehicle and, looking through the window slits, I see that we're in the middle of some town.

'Lamia,' says someone. Everything looks white hot in the savage heat.

'You and you,' a guard points at Angelo and me, 'you get out here,' and we are led out into the fierce glare of the sun which hits us in scorching waves and into the cool dinginess of a police station, whilst the van disappears on the shimmering, burning road to Thessaloniki. We are to await here until transport's available to take us to the jail in Amfissa.

'And how long will that be?' Angelo demands to know.

'About two days.'

'*What?*' Angelo shouts, 'Two days here because it takes you all that time to find transport, you incompetent morons.'

I can see that the cops are rather intimidated by this raging bull of a man and are tip-toeing around him deferentially as they try to placate him. We're led down into a dungeon with no windows and three tiny cells with mattresses on the floor with one rough, prickly blanket—at least the place is relatively clean compared to the other dungeon. Although I never get to know the slightest thing about my companion – for he's inscrutable – an understanding grows between us, a sort of unspoken respect.

'Amfissa is not so bad,' he tells me, 'one of the best in Greece; I usually manage to get myself there.'

I wonder how the wily old fellow arranges that. 'My friends are there too,' he goes on' 'good to see one's friends again.'

He sits in his cell most of the time, cross legged on his mattress, looking not unlike the Buddha. He's a quiet man. But at the police he unleashes a hellish fury. 'How much longer here?' he demands, rattling the iron gate at the top of the stairs.

'Maybe tomorrow,' a guard timidly begins.

'What do you mean *maybe*? Maybe tomorrow, tomorrow always tomorrow! I want to know when we can get out of here.'

'Please be patient, there is nothing going that way yet.'

'Then when *is* something going that way?'

'Soon, as soon as possible.'

'*Christo*!' he roars, 'we're in the hands of morons.'

Now, on the second night here, another fellow's brought in, cursing, shouting, crying out, 'Katerina! Katerina! Katerina!' and banging his head on the bars in a frenzy. The guards come down, 'Shut up! Be quiet!'

They try to placate him – how much gentler these country cops are; they don't resort to violence like they'd have done immediately in Athens. He goes on shouting throughout the night; rattling at the bars banging his head, hard, in a blind rage. Who in Hell's Katerina and what's he done to her or she to him? Has he killed her in a fit of jealousy? Has she gone off with another man? Has *he* betrayed *her*, and now's in the depths of remorse? At last, and I think it's because he's finally knocked himself senseless, silence reigns. Angelo looks far from happy about the state of affairs in the morning. He storms up the stairs and bellows at the top of his voice. '*You lot!*' there's going to be no more nonsense now – '*You lot!*' he bellows; a guard appears, looking sheepish; from the bottom of the stairs I can see the great angry frame of my comrade shaking his fists and clutching at the bars, looking just like those depictions of the Minotaur you see on old frescos from Knossos, 'I want to go to Amfissa and I want to go *today.*'

He's tired, he's had no sleep for all the commotion in this stinking dungeon overnight – do they think he's some animal they can put in a cage and forget about? Well, they can think again because he's a human being entitled to a bit of respect – they have no right to detain him any further in this stinking humiliating hole! If there's no transport coming through: *'Panagia,' he roars,* 'are you so stupid that you can't arrange for some.' There's a consultation amongst the guards and then one of them begins speaking to Angelo meekly; I hear Angelo responding, *'Kala! Kala! Endaxi!'* (Good, good! Okay!) he turns to me smiling with a wink and then to the guards, *'Kai o philosmou, endaxi?'* (and my friend, okay?)

He comes down to me and says: 'Those jackasses have at last worked something intelligent out. We can go to Amfissa by taxi. *Fevgoume simera. . .* ' 'We go today.' Ha, to prison by taxi. Oh yes, how sublimely, supremely, ludicrous – to go to prison by taxi. This has to be done, if just to make life's tapestry complete.

Angelo and I sit at the back. A guard, a big cheery chap, with a flowing moustache, who could just as well be a tourist guide on a coach trip if it wasn't for the uniform and the machine gun on his lap, sits next to the driver. We could well be two tourists, with our bodyguard to fend off bandits just in case we're attacked as we're driven through the magnificent landscape that surrounds Delphi, centre of the Earth. The morning mist still lies in the valleys whilst overhead a deep blue sky encircles the mountain tops which tower above us. Here and there we're brought to a halt by a herd of goats, their bells tinkling, as they leisurely graze the scant, dry, foliage at the sides of the roads, our driver hooting his horn frantically. Overhead an eagle looks down on us mere mortals, as it circles the crests of the mountain range.

'You like Greece?' enquires our guard, turning to me with a benevolent smile.

'I *love* it!' I exclaim, returning his smile.

A clarinet, played in swirling Epirus-style, wails on the cassette player, sounding sometimes like a bull and sometimes like a screeching bird as it drops and ascends through the registers like the voice of the landscape and all the horizon shimmers and trembles, like a mirage in the heat. I look through the window and smile: yes truly, it's all part of life's rich tapestry, and perhaps, in Greece, this tapestry's woven with the finest colours and richest textures in all the world.

How incongruous that this picturesque, remote, little town should have a prison. We climb up steep winding streets, the driver constantly taking the wrong turning; it doesn't matter, none of us are in any particular hurry, except perhaps Angelo, sitting in silence all the way, a deep serenity in his face, looking more than ever like the Buddha. He's fidgeting now, excited, he's going to be with old pals soon. The driver stops and asks an old man the way, who gesticulates with his arms and speaks in a strong mountain accent; all the time peering curiously at the guard with the machine gun and at us prisoners in the backseat. We pull up outside the prison gates, the iron grille slides open, as though they were the gates of Hades, and inside we're stripped, searched, questioned, 'Where have you been in prison before?' they ask me, looking at the tattoos on my arm – tattoos are an insignia of jails in Greece and anyone bearing them is looked upon with suspicion out on the street.

'Nowhere,' I reply. I'm sent through into the main part of the prison and shown to a bed in a dormitory of a dozen or so beds. It's just like Marlborough, with its iron beds and wooden floors and high sash windows. Hey, what's this? – A cutting from a newspaper has been selotaped to the wall at the head of my bed, a picture of me playing the whistle; it must be the one the journalist took in the finger printing place. Several prisoners have gathered around me, curious and smiling, 'We heard you were coming and so we put your picture above your bed, welcome *philé!*' one by one shaking my hand. They're kind to me, showing me the ropes: where the showers and lavatories are, where to get coffee, where the kitchen is which we go to and line up for food when the bell rings, telling me the whole routine of the day here. I wander out into the courtyard where we're allowed out at any time except during the siesta and after nine o'clock at night. Well that strikes me as being very reasonable, it's a pleasant place in which you can stroll about or sit on the stone benches in the sun. A high wall surrounds it, with armed guards looking down on us, a reminder that this is a prison and not some kind of luxury hotel or health resort, which it could well be with its peaceful atmosphere, its deep-blue unclouded sky above and its crisp clean mountain air. Groups of prisoners are standing or sitting, whiling away the time. It's not too hard for me to see them dressed in the garb of ancient Greece, togas and sandals, discussing Plato's ideas in his Academy. . . but of course, they're more likely on the subject of crime, be it big or small, for that's the nature of *this* academy.

I fall into conversation with a fellow called Yanni – fifteen years he's done so far for holding up a bank single-handed. It's a heroic story, at least, the way he tells it to me. He'd gone into a bank in Athens with a gun in his pocket and, drawing it on one of the cashiers, he'd demanded money and she, terrified, had filled up a sack and handed it to him, it all seemed too easy – but one of the others, seeing the transaction had grabbed hold of him. 'Damn him,' says Yanni, spitting, 'in fighting free of him all the money, millions of drachmas in big juicy notes, covered the floor of the bank like a carpet. I had to climb up a column to get away from this bloody clerk who was so insistent. For some minutes I was helpless, clinging like a monkey to the pillar just below the ceiling. Then I could hold on no longer and fell, twisted my leg under me, it hurt like hell and this fellow again latched onto me – what could I do? He wouldn't let go – I warned him what I'd do if he didn't let me go; I was fair, I'd warned him,' Yanni impresses this point on me, 'I had to get away – alright I'd leave the money, I just wanted to get away but this damned clerk was preventing that, so I drew my gun on him and shot him in the stomach, he fell back and I limped to the door, tried to get onto the street but fell, and when I looked up a policeman was standing above me. Fifteen years,' he went on, 'I'd done nine years, nine years of this – can you imagine what that's like? No you can't – a long time, you say – it's a fucking lifetime. I escaped I got to Amsterdam where I started dealing drugs and lived like never before but always in fear. Then one day I was arrested by Interpol, someone had grassed, I was sent back here with another billion years added to my sentence.'

There's the most delicious supper this evening, stuffed aubergines, swimming in oil and herbs and fat, juicy *patatas*, fried in garlic – I go back for more and the cooks are very pleased with my appraisal of their culinary skills. I've won them over already, as I always aim to do with the kitchen staff wherever I happen to be, be it school, hotel or prison; and as I had done at the barracks at Colchester, where I spent some days in the officers' mess of the Black Watch as a guest of my old friend Nick, but I preferred the company in the kitchen; besides, I'd fallen foul of the colonel, having announced at dinner one evening, on my being questioned about my life on the road and having told them that I'd lived with the Gypsies – at which a few derogatory remarks had been made about them – that they were my good friends and that they were far quicker-witted than any of the company here and then going on to say, exagerrating slightly to make my point, that, before anyone realised what was happening, one of them could cause to vanish all the mess silver which lined the table whilst their heads were turned the other way, caused by a distraction at the door by his accomplice. It obviously didn't go down too well and, from then on, Nick's batman would bring me supper in my quarters. But the kitchen staff relished this interaction, and from then on would have sent up with the batman the tastiest morsels only the colonel would be served – and on the finest silver platter.

After a superbly refreshing night's sleep on my Marlborough iron bed, I'm sitting in the sunny yard of the prison drinking a big bowl of hot, milky coffee and soaking up the warm sun. Life really isn't bad here, I muse, not perhaps for a billion years like Yanni, but for a while at least, until the money comes through and, if it doesn't and I have to do the nine months, I'll have plenty of time for reading, I'll perfect my Greek whist holding discourse with my fellow in-mates, whilst writing down some of their stories and yes, with so much time on my hands, I might even begin to write my book. And, by the time I'm released it'll be spring and I can go off travelling again, having solved the problem of eking out a living through the winter. My musings are interrupted by the approach of a guard summoning me through to the guards' room. I have mixed feelings as I'm told the vice-consul's here and that I'm being released. On one hand I'm overjoyed but on the other rather dismayed: all the things I'd been excitedly planning abruptly come to an end.

'I came out myself to release you; people have been ringing me from all over Greece, asking me what I was going to do about getting you out of jail, which you shouldn't be in in the first place, as far as they were concerned – it appears you have many friends here in Greece, and they'd read about your arrest in the papers, as well as being talked about on the wireless. Greece is a small country, you know, news travels fast. I have to admit I was curious to meet you. So, although today is really my day off, I came out here myself, rather than let you wait until Monday to come back to Athens with a police escort.'

The consul turns out to be a kind, friendly, man and we chat amicably as we drive back through the stunning landscape we'd driven through yesterday in the taxi, this time in his soft-purring Mercedes, taking the mountainous, twisting, roads effortlessly, the fresh mountain air bathing my face as we speed along. My companion's not much older than myself; half Greek, half Irish, and very human.

'Your father's been on the phone to me, he's paid for your release,' for a moment the feeling of shame comes over me and I tell him that I feel I've taken the easy way out and that I should never have let my father bail me out.

'I understand you feeling that way,' he says, 'you are a proud man and you are angry at yourself, but anyone would have done that in your situation – it's true that you are in a privileged position, you have a father who can afford and is willing to bail you out, something not everyone has, but that is your luck, it's just the way things are and, in my experience, anyone will try to get someone to bail them out if they can – I think your feeling guilt about it is misplaced.'

He turns to me and says, confidentially, 'personally I don't think you should ever have been there in the first place; and besides, your parents are very worried about you, they wouldn't have it any other way. I'm taking you to Athens and putting you on a flight to Lon-

don at six-thirty this evening – but we have time enough for lunch
on the way, let's stop in Delphi, you'll be my guest.'

We sit at a table by one of the big panoramic windows looking
out over the deep valley running down to the sea and up to the towering mountains, Mount Parnassus and the Muses. They say that,
if you spend a night alone up there, by morning you'll be either a
madman or a poet, or both – I think the two go hand in hand and
that a little madness is indispensable to poetry. Bottles of ice-cold
beer arrive and along with it, *horiatiki*, the sumptious salad that
tourists call 'Greek salad', with fresh herbs and oil – no doubt from
the olive groves, dense in the valleys and climbing up the sides of the
mountains – *omeleta, patatas, skordalia, tsatsiki,* a feast indeed, followed by a typical sweet delicacy, *loukoumi*, which is what we'd call
Turkish Delight, with black Turkish – sorry, Greek! – coffee. We talk
at length on the journey to Athens; he really is a most sympathetic
man.

'It's strange the police should've been so rough with you, just for
playing music, I have always found the Athenian police so coopera-
tive. But then I am in rather a different business from you. He turns
to me and smiles it's all good material for your book, isn't it?'

I wave him goodbye at the customs control at the airport and, as
we lift into the air, I look down with the deepest love on the earth
receding from me, and out over the oyster-grey sea speckled with
islands, floating in the mauve and purple twilight. It's goodbye for
now, my eyes fill with tears at the emotion this parting brings, all
which this land has instilled in me, like the ferment in an exquisite
wine which has delighted my heart and transformed my soul.

Chapter 36
Sylvie

It's across a crowded room in Paris that I first set eyes on her. She catches my gaze and comes straight over to me and chinks my glass.

'You are the first thing that's made me smile all day; it's been such a terrible day . . . driving all the way up from the south, without exchanging a single word with my husband.'

She's a little below average height, slim, and dusky, as someone from the south might be; her hair, deep chestnut, was swept behind her ears and hung down to her shoulders, her face made me think of a forest elf, quick and alive and with lines on her forehead which told of sorrow and anxiety. I was oblivious to all else that evening and so was she, and I knew that she was the one I'd been looking for all along.

Standing at the top of the entrance to the underground in Piccadilly, I'm holding a bouquet of freesias, when she emerges, with a black knee-length skirt and jacket buttoned up to her throat against the nippy spring wind. She looks more desirable than ever as she glances around for a moment or two to see if I'm here, and here I am, striding over to her with great elation in my heart.

'Thank you, they're lovely,' she breathes, holding the flowers in her slightly trembling hand, 'how did you know that they're my favourite flowers?'

It's lunchtime and I take her hand as we walk, laughing with joy, to the Salisbury, an old mahogany pub full of mirrors, in St. Martin's

Lane. Over the second or third pint, we kiss, properly kiss, for the first time.

It's a summer of love and laughter, stealing moments, whole days and nights sometimes, to be together and doing the rounds of the pubs around Hampstead and Belsize Park, where she lives. To be in her company is sweet and exhilarating and fun, fun to a degree I'd never imagined possible with a woman, in that she gets as drunk as I do and she absolutely delights to see me get drunk as a sausage, as she puts it, and stagger about, a thing which is very unusual for a woman to find in any way funny.

Her quick wit and lewd sense of humour keep me endlessly amused, along with the impish, mischievous pranks she plays on me, which sometimes leave me in embarrassing, often awkward, situations. She's a writer too and somewhat of a Bohemian, loving the unusual, the outrageous, the preposterous, the outlandish, and she has the kind of mind that can always see beneath the surface of things and ferret out the hidden motives behind people's actions, and empathise on one hand or be sharply critical on the other. And she's uncannily perceptive of my feelings and is right there with me when I feel down in the dumps–which isn't very often when I'm in her company, but sometimes I get to thinking of the future . . . Ah, future be damned, it will sort itself out–the present is what's impor-tant, so let's make the most of it–it could hardly be better:

> Ah we drink in the London pubs
> we do, we do
> by the light of the silvery moon
> and we kiss in the alleys
> we kiss, we kiss
> that run round Hampstead town
> and we haven't a care in the world
> the world, the world
> 'cept one
> have we enough for one last drink
> at the pub in Hollybush Lane

After taking her home, late at night, I retire to St. John's grave-yard where I sleep on a tomb between a butcher and a captain of the dragoons. In the mornings, whenever she can, she brings me break-fast, a flask of coffee and a bowl of strawberries. This lasts until one morning I'm rudely awakened by a bobby standing over me telling me to get up.

'Have you been in trouble with the law before?' he demands to know.

'No.' I reply, lying.

He has a gadget on which he pushes a few buttons before telling me I've been 'telling porkie pies'. Well, alright, I was busted for pos-session of cannabis some seven or eight years ago – but I'd been to court and paid the fine for it.

He accepts that but tells me I'm not to sleep here anymore, and he's about to walk away when he suddenly smiles and, pointing to a tomb down at the bottom of the path, says, 'You're in good com-pany here, the painter, John Constable, is buried just down there.'

I was down in Wiltshire towards the end of July. It was good to be out of London and roaming again on my native hills. It was a time of reflection, trying to resolve certain issues in myself and wondering which direction my life was going to take; I was madly in love with Sylvie, but I couldn't see how it was going to work – not without terrible disruption for her and her marriage and a total realignment of my own life – for once in my life I would have to make a commit-ment and, if the whole thing led to the break-up of her marriage I'd have to be there to pick up the pieces. I was in a bit of a quandary: I wanted to be with her but at the same time I wanted to be off on my travels again. I couldn't settle down, I was thirty-two, still relatively young and still the road called, louder than ever. Whichever way I took I knew was going to be selfish but at the same time the whole situation would have to be resolved. Nevertheless, I set off for Paris at the beginning of August, leaving things in the air as far as Sylvie was concerned. I'd been in Paris a couple of days, when a letter ar-rived and my heart missed a beat when I saw her hand-writing on the envelope. I tore it open and started to read:

'I'm going to be in the south of France visiting my mother in her village. (And she scribbled down directions of how to get there.) If you've nothing better to do, perhaps we could meet there – but be discreet! – and then walk along the coast for a few days.'

With a great shout of joy and without further ado, I bade farewell to Ashley and Inês, and raced for the Porte d'Orléans where I stuck out my thumb on the southbound highway.

She was having lunch with her mother on the terrace of a café when I arrived in the square. She went a little pale when she saw me, a little panic had gripped her, but she quickly rallied to and signalled to me to come over, feigning surprise at seeing me, and introduced me to her mother as a wine connoisseur who wrote reviews on French wines for a magazine in London. We cordially shook hands and she invited me to sit at the table whilst calling to the waiter to bring me a glass of the best wine from the area. Sylvie smiled to see how I primly sipped the delicious wine that had been put down in front of me – she was used to me picking up the bottle and pouring half of it down in one gulp. We exchanged pleasantries and I could see that Sylvie was happy that I'd come. I could detect a kind of suppressed excitement in her voice and gestures, though she must have wondered how this was all going to pan out. Following some signals she was discreetly making to me, that we would rendezvous in the evening by the fountain, I turned down another glass her mother was offering me and got up and took my leave.

Having procured the items for a picnic at a little supermarket, I took a track out of the village which led to the vineyards which surrounded the village on all sides; here I got in under the vines and took advantage of the shade they afforded me from the sizzling August sun. The earth was parched and hard and so I spread out my sleeping bag to sit on and tucked in to a sumptuous feast of brie, olives, juicy, voluptuous tomatoes, a tin of chickpeas and a crispy baguette still warm from the bakery. With a full belly I stretched out on my back, looking up through the translucent green leaves through which patches of blue sky could be glimpsed when the soft breeze parted them and made them rustle against each other – otherwise there was almost complete silence; the cicadas with their incessant clacking were also stunned into silence by the fierce afternoon sun and I started drifting off into a half-sleep, somewhere on the edge of reality and you don't know if you're adream or awake – neither, perhaps, and strange things happen, Pan appears . . .

> Sometimes you really do afright me
> when out of nowhere you are here
> And you screech your pipe in my ear
> And out of my skin I start with fear
> And you jut your goat face into mine
> In the hush of noon when nothing stirs
> But the heart beat of the heart beat
> In the inner ear
> And when even the breeze is stilled
> in the vine leaves you are here
> Disrupting the planets on their courses
> The world spinning on its hinges
> Bringing chaos out of order
> And from that chaos order . . .

As the clock in the tower of the little church struck eight, she was beside me at the splashing stone fountain and, taking me by the hand led me out into the vineyard in which I'd spent the afternoon. I laid my sleeping bag out and we flung ourselves on it, tearing the clothes off each other, biting into one another's flesh.

'Meet me here, in the morning, exactly here,' she said, before getting up and leaving, I've told my mother I'm going to spend a few days walking by myself, "Don't worry, mama, I shall be alright," I assured her. Listen for the clock, I shall be here at seven. I'll walk back to the village alone now, better not too many people see us, you understand.'

She had brought me out a bottle of wine, a really fine one, saying as she gave it to me, 'Write about this one in your next piece in your wine magazine – what's it called? *The Wino's Guide to Wine* or something? – and say that it was a gift from your muse, but don't mention her name.'

I'd told her on many occasions that she was my muse, embodied in earthly guise, flesh and blood and all, for everything about her seemed to fit that exalted role, so essential in activating a poet's purpose and she seemed tailor-made for me, having everything I deemed essential for invoking poetry and, who knows, perhaps even a book – beguiling beauty, wit, mischievous humour, pathos . . .

Sitting up, half in and half out of my sleeping bag, I open the bottle and look up at the stars, listening to the night all around me; the gentle rustling of the vine leaves, the clicking of crickets, the scratching of a mouse or some small creature in the dry warm earth under a vine stump, the distant barking of a dog from a far-off lonely farm house. Up above the stars pierce the dome, stretching into its depths and into eternity, every now and then one breaking away and shooting across the sky – it being August, the sky's full of them – and I try to make a wish before it disappears, burns out, or whatever it is a shooting star does. And here in this vineyard the stars are mirrored in the fireflies which flit about on the dark earth.

After a reviving breakfast of coffee and croissants with which Sylvie wakes me, we tiptoe out of the village and onto the road leading south to the sea, some twenty odd kilometres away.

At last, at last we're together on a Mediterranean road, alone, just the two of us, – wonderfully, miraculously alone. Our lean bodies, fragrant from the sun and the salt water, reaching out, aching for each other. I cup her imp-like face in my hands and look into her brown eyes, flecked with luminous shards of emerald green, like the stars of last night in the immensity of space, dilated beneath the fringe of her dark, copper-tinted hair, her face etched with its laughing, crying, lines and with its constant animation which I could gaze upon throughout eternity. Freckles have blossomed like mushrooms over her cheeks and the bridge of her nose and beads of sweat, like freshly fallen dew have broken out on her forehead, which I kiss, gently at first, inhaling the fragrance of her skin, and then passionately, pulling her down and sinking into her, and knowing that these moments are forever ours, and will remain with us forever, even after time and circumstance so mercilessly tear us apart – as they will.

Chapter 37

On the Streets of Lisbon

Turning off the Rua das Portas de Santo Antão and into a sinister alley, the Travessa do Forno, I come upon a drinking establishment with huge barn-like doors through which I enter into a dim musky-smelling interior filled with a murmur of discordant voices. My eyes, slowly accustoming themselves to the dark interior, begin to make out my surroundings which are slowly emerging as though from a thick fog. Massive barrels adorn the walls and, as I shuffle through spit, sawdust, bones, blood and dog-ends, I gradually begin to discern an assortment of half-animated, mumbling faces arrayed along a zinc counter, each with a more ghastly pallor than the next, faintly illuminated by the lunar-like glow of a flickering neon strip which runs the length of the bar. Each of these apparitions has a vial of some murky potion before it. The landlord, grim as Hades, presides over this dismal realm dispensing the concoction which dispatches its imbiber to oblivion. I feel like Odysseus must have felt when he entered the realm of the dead, but I don't have any blood to pour for them so as to animate them and make them human again for a while.

Instead, I order one of these vials myself, the landlord staring suspiciously at me as he pours it into my glass as though I've appeared from another world – I have, one in which the sun still shines and where there are colours and living things. This place could best be described as a pit, into which the barely animated, mumbling, dead have been thrown – the 'Pit' would be an appropriate name for it.

As I stand at the counter partaking of this lethal liquid I become increasingly aware of the silent fellow, standing like a tomb, next to me. I start observing him out of the corner of my eye. At first glance he would pass for being well-dressed, even elegantly so, with a suit and tie held in place with what appears to be a golden tie-pin which glints in the neon light. He's holding himself proudly erect, in stark contrast to the other denizens of this establishment who are slouched over the bar, some of them clutching onto it as though they might topple over at any moment. On closer scrutiny the finer details of his attire become apparent: the missing buttons, the grimy collar, the frayed ends of his tie, the tie-pin no more gold than one you might get from a Christmas cracker, the lace missing from his left shoe replaced by a piece of string.

He's swarthy, perhaps Indian, and would not look out of place in a turban; what language would he speak, I wonder, if he opened his mouth and started muttering like the rest of them? He's staring blankly at the wall but I feel there are a million words in him just waiting to tumble off his tongue and, once started, would turn into an avalanche. His glass, meanwhile, has stood, full to the brim before him and untouched ever since I've been standing next to him. An amusing thought crosses my mind that he might be employing some kind of Yogi trick to transfer the alcohol content, though not the liquid for it remained in situ, by some kind of psychic means into his being – or perhaps he's exercising his will to refrain from drinking it as long as is humanly possible – or perhaps he's a fakir and he's never going to drink it, thereby inflicting a twisted kind of torture on himself. But suddenly his hand, trembling violently as though executing some kind of dance to an unseen rhythm, seizes the vial and with one tip dispenses it down his throat – I can hear it gurgle as it circumvents his Adam's apple and then he breaks his silence by declaring, 'This is not good for you.'

I turn to him bemused – he's delivered this extraordinary indictment in faultless English.

'Why not?' I query him.

'It's made from potatoes.'

'Potatoes, what on earth do you mean?'

'I mean *potatoes,*' he almost snaps my head off.

'I see,' I say, somewhat taken aback by his outburst and not seeing at all – it seems to me that, however rough the wine they're dishing up here, it's made from grapes and couldn't conceivably be derived from potatoes. I tell him so.

'If it was made from grapes I'd have a clear head and wouldn't feel as though I was drunk all the time,' and he glares at me with such ferocity that I drop the subject.

'You speak very good English,' I say, eager to change the subject, 'where are you from?'

'From Goa.'

'Ah, you're Indian.'

'No, I am not a bloody Indian – I am Portuguese,' he shouts.

'Alright, keep your shirt on,' (fortunately I don't think he understands that expression) 'so you're Portuguese,' and I look at him dubiously.

'Goa is a Portuguese colony: I was born there, I have a Portuguese identification – look,' and he thrusts a tatty ID card before my face with a photograph of himself stuck on it with a chef's hat on, more Indian looking than the maharaja with a turban. Underneath is written:

William Domingos
Birthplace: Panjim
Profession: Cook

'I was a colonel in the Goan army, then the bloody Indians came and we had to flee away. Yes Colonel William Domingos – that's who I am,' and, with sudden vehemence, he makes a sweeping gesture around the Pit, 'none of these bums know how to show any respect – they're low bums and beggars.'

'I've been working all my life to avoid working,' I spin round to see who's the owner of this raspy voice that's growled right into my ear and I come face to face with a pallid, emaciated-looking specimen with vulture-like eyes and a pencil-thin moustache, the type all my instincts tell me to steer well clear of.

'It's a waste of time watching these fools,' and he nods his head over towards the unemployed people marching through Rossio square demanding bread and work.

C'mon, it's healthier to be having a drink in the bar round the corner.'

'Okay,' I laugh and off we go.

'Mike's my name,' he begins in a quasi-American drawl, as we sit at a table in a lively dive called the Palmeira, 'At least it's the one I've been using so long I forget what my original one was – better that way, better to have no name at all in my line of business; but if ya gotta have one, best to change it to some other thing as fast as ya can. Ya see, I live by cheating.'

'Oh?'

'Yeah, by telling stories, very elaborate lies – and lies work in this world, if I told the truth I'd be more likely to get a crack on the jaw. People wouldn't like to hear the truth about me – nor about themselves, for that matter,' he adds, with a wry grin, 'and so I string a few lies together and make them into a story, a convincing one; it's an art really and sometimes I think I should be a writer, but that doesn't pay. Now, I can see that you would see straight through me if I told you, for instance, that I was a Lufthansa pilot or an officer in the army, the merchant navy or whatever, had had my drinks spiked whilst out on the town, had come round lying in the gutter of some dark alley, having been beaten and robbed of everything I had – papers, wallet, everything, and had missed ship, plane, or whatever, home – but there are others, yeah, believe me, there are others who swallow every word of it and, when I ask if it would be too much to ask for a little loan – enough for a meal and the fare home – they dig into their pockets only too glad to be able to render service to a service man in distress. I impress upon them most emphatically that it's in the nature of a loan and I'll return it just as soon as I'm home and out of this mess. "And please look me up if ever you find yourself my way, so that I may return your generosity with some lavish hospitality." And I scribble my "home" address on a piece of paper – it's the address of a cemetery in Bavaria,' his frame rattles with laughter and he emits a hissing sound through closed teeth.

'I'm German, you probably guessed that, but I try to keep quiet about my origins, except when I seize upon some German tourist with one of my stories: then the more German I am the better it pays. Anyway, I'm a "damned kraut"; I was brought up in Poland just after the war. There was nothing but poverty, real goddamn poverty that I never want to see again in all the days that I live: bread for breakfast, bread for lunch, bread for supper, cabbage soup to wash it down with. I didn't know what clothes were: but I knew all about rags—goddamn rags—the scarecrows were dressed better than I was. Would you believe that I even robbed the clothes off those scarecrows? and you know what I spent my days doing? I was watching over pigs. Yeah, I was a swineherd, chasing pigs around in the mud all day long with a stick. Christ, look at me—do I look the type that would appreciate life in the countryside, in god-forsaken hills, miles from the city? Well, I used to have a lot of dreams as I sat there, day after day, looking at pigs, 'one day, I'm gonna change all this—live in a castle,' I vowed to myself. I was well versed in fairytales, you see—castles, princesses and gold. I didn't care if I had to borrow, rob, lie, beg or cheat I was gonna get my fair share of gold. So one day I stole some money from my father—all the money he had in fact—and set out west in the search for fortune and a civilised life. I resolved never to find myself poor again. I was gonna eat caviar and drink champagne, live in a castle and have plenty of gold. That was what I'd always dreamt of and somehow—I didn't care how—I was gonna make my dreams come true,' he swills the wine around his mouth and swallows. 'Hey, let's refill our glasses, they're drained—*Oi! faz favor*,' he calls out in a most arrogant tone to the barman, '*dois coppos do vinho.*'

'So I got to Munich and it didn't take long before I got a job working side by side with American G.I.s so, as well as earning a bit of decent money for the first time in my life, I learnt American, and that would prove to be a very useful thing to learn in what was to become my trade. I stuck to that for a while, but the work I was doing was lowly, futile and boring—I won't go into the details of it, it would depress you as they depress me, cleaning up pig shit was nothing compared to some of the tasks I had to perform in those barracks. Enough of that, I was gonna get to Paris, I could already see myself there, strolling along the boulevards, dressed in fine clothes, a woman of flawless beauty and impeccable chic on my arm.'

'At first it was hard, like any city can be hard. It glittered all right, glittered like nowhere else on earth, but the glitter was not for me, not yet; this was when I first started passing myself off as an American – a Hollywood film star, a Transylvanian count . . . I don't know if you happen to know Paris – you do, huh? Well, I fell in with some beggars around St. Michel, around the fountain there . . . You know it? You've been there, huh? Well, I was broke, needed some money so I started asking the passers-by, like the rest of them were, "*T'as pas cent balles, s'il vous plait?*"

'It worked, goddammit, people gave me money. Why work when all I had to do was ask and the people gave? after all, didn't the good Lord Jesus say, "Ask, and thou shalt be given?" Never mind a few knockbacks I was gonna make an art of this. Well, I started off on the streets and then I moved into the cafés. There were plenty of rich tourists around, whatever time of the year, and hordes of Germans with more money, a lot more, than sense. I began to make money and I started to live and to dress in the manner I'd always planned to. It was then that I ran into my wife, in a bar in St. Germain, La Rhumerie where anybody who's anybody whiles away their evenings, it was an evening in spring, and right before me here was the woman, the fairy princess, if you like, with all the gold I'd been looking for. I could have lived in comfort for the rest of my life – she was a smasher to look at too, but the reason I married her was that she was rich.'

There's a commotion at the door, a lot of shouting and a drunkard being thrown out into the street.

'So, what became of your fortunes?' I ask, pointedly, glancing at his present attire: a grubby, zip-up, brown jacket, trousers once white but now grey and splattered with wine stains and shoes that look as though they're held together with nothing more than the frayed laces that tie them.

'Oh yeah, well, you know "fortune", Lady Luck they call her, and just like a goddamn woman she is, unpredictable, always up and down – not natural for her to stay steady for any length of time,' he starts philosophically, 'for a time life was good – a bed of roses, you could say – but you can have every comfort and all the money in the world, and you can still get bored – especially *then* can you get bored – and that's what happened to me. I loved my wife and all that, well sort of – I was a good husband I tell you – when we got married, I swear to god, I had every intention of staying the rest of my life with her, after all she was a gold mine. But then I met this young whore – it was not on "professional business" that I met her,' he assures me quickly. 'We met at a party – it was disastrous for my marriage – the scar you see on my face my wife put there when she found out.' A thin scar runs down from below his left ear to his chin.

'A razor blade – I was shaving before dinner one evening. She'd found a note in my pocket – ach! I don't want to talk about it – anyway, this whore and I (she was English by the way and a stunner to look at), we went down south together, down to the Côte d'Azur, Cannes, St. Tropez, Juan Les Pins – you know that area I guess – the greatest play-ground in Europe, if you've got money of course, which I had – yeah, I managed to lay my hands on several hundred thousand francs before my wife could put a stop to it.'

'Crikey.'

'Yes, a lot of money,' he chuckled, 'Enough for a little holiday, a little luxury, down there, with my younger, newer model – for a while.'

'And then?'

'Then . . . well, she was a whore wasn't she, so,' Mike drains the last of the wine in his glass, 'I became a pimp.'

We both chuckle. 'You organise your holidays well.'

'Well, that went well for a while: she'd work the cafés and the lobbies of the grand hotels and I'd wait for her, whilst doing what I most like doing – drinking. *La belle vie pour quelque temps.*' Then she fell in love with one of her "clients" and it was the street again for me. Would you believe it that a hard-hearted, heartless, son of a bitch like me could break down and cry? Well, I did. I kind of loved her you see, that English whore, and I'd thought she felt the same about me. I just drifted about for a while after that, begging, selling empty bottles (would you believe it?) – oh yes, getting them off the beaches, out of the dustbins and taking them to the shops for a goddamn twenty or thirty centimes. Christ, to think I'd been living in the best hotels in St. Tropez and here I was – bang, right up against poverty again. Goddamn poverty,' a frightened, hunted look

comes into his eyes, 'it's a predator, a ruthless mother-fucking predator that catches me every time by the tail, as I'm climbing up the
ladder.' A barely suppressed fury's come into Mike's demeanour; his
hand shakes as he lifts the glass to his lips and dispenses the contents
down his neck in one tip, 'You won't find me,' he continues, wiping
the wine off his moustache with the back of his hand, 'being haugh-
ty to a tramp or a beggar or a wino sitting on a street with his hand
out – 'cause I know too much about those twists of that bitch fate.
Yeah, tomorrow I might be sitting down right next to him. Christ,
have we got enough for another round of drinks? I'm cleaned out.'

I run into the Colonel all over the place; he's invariably full of
oaths and curses about this or that bloody bastard – a businessman,
a Scandinavian sailor perhaps, to whom he's given a guided tour
around town, taking in the grubbiest dives and the most infested
brothels, 'The bloody ill-mannered bastard!' fumes William, 'Wait
here until I finish with this girl,' he says to me, 'and then I'll pay for
you to have a fuck with her,' but the bloody bastard slips out of the
back door without leaving me even enough for a wine.'

I'm not averse to spending time in the Colonel's company. I enjoy
his stories for one thing, preposterous as they are they're reality itself,
to him.

But the bits and pieces he tells me about his past do you have a
certain credibility about them underneath the mythological trim-
mings. And he does have the air of someone fallen from a hither-to
elevated social station; in fact there's a sort of faded elegance about
him which goes with some of his gestures, haughtiness and the tie,
the tiepin and his futile attempts to keep up appearances and keep
from sinking to the level of those low bums and beggars he sees
all around him. So I'm not altogether surprised when he tells me
his father had been a doctor and he grew up in the affluent part
of Panjim. And, what's more, he does have a Portuguese surname
which he may have inherited by adoption, it being quite common
for well-to-do Goans to assume a Portuguese surname or perhaps his
father really was Portuguese. And he tells me also that at some point
in his career he'd been an accountant and I can see traces of that in
the way he tots up on his gnarled fingers, and never loses count, of

the exact number of wines he has consumed throughout the day and exactly how much, down to the last escudo, he's managed to come by and every penny he's spent. He'd told me of how his doctor had said to him his blood was forty percent alcohol and perhaps this counting of every wine he has drunk is his way of convincing himself his drinking's under control. As for being the colonel of some regiment, well this really would be a difficult one to swallow, were it not for the fact that his English really is good and he seems familiar with the kind of things they might reminisce about in the mess. So who knows. Perhaps it was just one or two gin and tonics too many which put him on the path of his slippery descent.

Here he is approaching, the morning sun glinting off his tiepin and the heel of his left shoe going clip clop, 'Hello William.'

'You bloody bastard,' he looks up startled, 'I would not have known you were here if I had not seen you.'

'I suppose you wouldn't. What are you up to?'

'I'm going for a wine–look,' he pulls out of his pocket a bank note, 'five hundred escudos. Come along I'll buy you a drink,' he says magnaminously–well I'll take up his offer I suppose, even though it's a bit early for a glass of wine–he looks as though he's just longing to tell me something: one of his outlandish stories I expect. Hah, I knew he'd choose this filthy little dive.

'*Dois coppos do vinho,*' he calls out arrogantly, clicking his fingers at the barman.

'Thank you, William. Well, what's your news, I haven't seen . . . '

'I've been at the palace had lunch with the Prince.'

'Who?'

'The bloody Prince of Portugal, you fool.'

'Ah, I see.'

'The Prince and I are old friends–"William Domingos, I invite you to lunch at the palace today," he told me over the phone at my hotel,'–his doss house, he means–'oh yes, the Prince and I are very old friends,' he announces importantly.

'Oh really, how extraordinary.'

'Extraordinary? Why extraordinary? It's quite natural that we should be.'

'Yes, naturally, but of course.'

'You know what we had for lunch? We had roast duck and soup. Soup, yes we had really good soup – hot soup and a duck – I think it was a duck, it must've been a duck for the wine we drank with it is only ever drunk with ducks. I chose the wine – the Prince said, "William Domingos you have a fine palate – I am going to ask you to go down to the cellar with my butler and select whatever you think fit." I chose the best wine that I could find, I forget the name of it but as we were eating the Prince said, "William Domingos, you've chosen the right wine," and do you know what was written on it in very small print which I couldn't see until I put my spectacles on?'

'No, what?'

'This wine should only be drunk with ducks.'

'Golly William, you know your wines then.'

'I do indeed. That's why I tell you I haven't much time for this bloody rotten potato wine,' and his trembling hand reaches out for his vial, which has been sitting on the counter untouched since he began his monologue, and, with one twist of the wrist, tips the contents down his neck.

'Then the Prince and I talked of the old days . . . reminiscing, that's what it's called: I remember the word from India, all the chaps in the mess were forever reminiscing about the good old days. That's what the Prince and I were doing all afternoon, you know, how we went shooting tigers until the cocktail hour and then we drank gin and tonic. "William Domingos," he said to me, "We have had a thoroughly good day." Then he brought me back to my hotel in his Rolls Royce – he paid my rent for a week and gave me enough money for ten wines and a bowl of soup.'

Up until now I've been lodging at the Stella Maris, the Seaman's Mission, for sailors who have got marooned in Lisbon. I heard about it from Amadou, a black fellow from the Sudan with whom I'd been drinking down near the port. He's been stranded in Lisbon for well over a year since he lost his ship whilst he was on a mammoth bender which had lasted five days, at the end of which all his wages were gone and so was his ship and he'd had to take to panhandling at which, apparently, he was quite successful, for, as he told me, he always managed to get a square meal every day and to get very drunk. He also had his Seaman's card which enabled him to lodge almost permanently at the Stella Maris. He took me back there very late that night and managed to persuade them that I'd been an old mate on the crew of the good ship something-or-other. I don't know whether they quite believed him or not but they gave me the benefit of the doubt and let me in. It was warm and friendly and clean but, staying in a room with four beds, I never knew who was going to stumble in during the night, usually in an advanced state of drunkenness, crashing and banging about, cussing and swearing, farting and belching. None of this would normally bother me too much as I was well sodden myself and I just slept through it. But after a while I began to crave some privacy and, dare I even entertain the idea, a room of my own to which I could retreat when life on the streets and in the bars became too wearying.

And now I have found it. It lies halfway up the Escadinhas do Duque, a long flight of stairs which winds all the way up from the heart of the metropolis to the Largo da Trindade and the quiet heights of the Bairro Alto. I am in a little room of the Pensão Duque where I can bolt the door and shut the street outside and whose window opens out over the winding stairway. Everything's at a tilt: the wooden floor, the door lintel, the basin which I have to fill by hand from a big enamel jug, the curtain rail, the picture on the marzipan wall and the ceiling itself, from which a bare light bulb dangles and sways about making the whole room dance with shadows when the storms blow in from the Atlantic. It's all just perfect for me and it's not unlike van Gogh's room in Arles, with the wicker chair pulled up close to the bed on which perhaps an angel would sit at night when he was asleep, to sew into the tapestry of his dreams the visions of swirling stars and suns and moons and white crested waves on the sea, and then from those dreams onto the canvas.

Just up the steps from here, as I said, is the Bairro Alto whose labyrinthine streets at night I love to wander dropping into a little bar, Sabina's, on the rua da Atalaia, to get drunk on fado and further drunk on wine. I love this place, just a simple little bar with two steps down, a stone floor and some seven or eight tables around which the working people of the area sit and suddenly one of them will stand up in hob-nailed boots and flat cap and burst into song, accompanied by two or three musicians on the marvellous, twanging, Portuguese guitar and cavacinho, a kind of small ukulele, the man singing his heart out with the intense emotion contorting his lined face and then a woman springing to her feet on one of the other tables and answering his plaintive lament or joyful lilting rendition of a song old as the coastlines and the sea-faring folk who haul their livelihoods from the rough, often treacherous swell. I usually find myself letting fall a tear or two into the 'wine-dark sea' in my glass. Fado means 'fate' and it originates from the songs of longing and lament, of hope and despair, the wives of the fishermen sang as they mended nets on the beaches, whilst keeping vigil through the nights whilst their husbands, sons and fathers were out at sea—many of whom never returned.

No mar obscuro
uma noite de tristeza . . .

Ha! There's that lottery seller who cries out down below my window in the Pensão Duque, in a voice like a farmyard cock, 'Strike it rich! Strike it rich! Buy a strip! *Cinco mil escudos! Amanha!*

Purple in the face, unshaven, unkempt, specs lopsided on his snout, tatty raincoat, he's bolting down that alley, the Travessa de Forno to top himself up at the Pit, that infamous tavern in its murky depths. May as well do the same myself, it's wet out here on the streets.

The clientele—let's call them denizens, it would be more fitting—are as bedraggled as ever today, lined up along the zinc counter, being doled out their vials by surly old Manuel—Hades I like to call him, for he really is lord of this underworld and the wine he dispenses has a similar effect to the blood Odysseus poured for the shades: it animates them almost to the point where they come back from the dead, their mumbling increasing in volume and incoherence and from time to time one of them sinks to the floor and is dragged through the sawdust to the street.

'Ha, *Pifero*, Pied Piper,' cries one of them emerging from the depths and wringing my hand, 'play *Pifero*, just for me,' It's Carlos the pimp, with all his gold rings and oozing sleaze, who controls the destinies of the two pathetic wretches he forever has his hands over, extracting banknotes they've concealed in their stocking tops and bras.

'*Pifero*, wine,' and he calls to Hades to fill me a glass, 'Piper, business no good for you today, business no good for me today my girls get wet Piper, wet, you understand *Pifero*, and not only between their legs but all over their bodies,' and he gives me a lecherous wink, 'Play me one song, *Pifero.*'

I'm loath to play him 'one song' but now with the wine he's paid me pouring down my throat I'm somewhat obliged. I manage an uninspired lament of some kind, his grinning monkey face in front of me and clapping his podgy hands, dripping with Spanish gold, as I bring it to a close, 'Bravo *Pifero*. More wine Manuel, wine for the piper,' and I'm brought another vial of *vinho*, my reward for being a good dog. I down it quick and take my leave just as one of his pathetic creatures is coming in dripping wet from the street. Carlos's forced merriment changes, just like that, to a mean, rapacious look as he looks her over and asks why she's back so soon. I've got my eyes on a table over there in the corner, but can I get to it before that drunkard, who's lurching over towards it? Yes, my luck's in, he's settled for the floor.

'*Fora! Fora,*' Manuel drags the old sot by the feet through the sawdust and deposits him on the street in the rain. I do not weep for him but I do for the canary in the cage swinging from the ceiling, a benighted soul that sees no end, no way out, lost in the darkness and the clouds of cigarette smoke, its song is of the most exquisite sweetness, like the singing I heard in a garden, long, long ago.

I don't think there's anything, apart from the prospect of free food, that makes Bob tick. If you look into his eyes you meet death. I would avoid doing that. His voice is the most lifeless I've ever heard, and the words he employs to convey to you his dreary communications curl up and die in the telling of them. When I ask him why he's come to Lisbon he replies, 'Because I couldn't think of anywhere else to go.'

We were waiting, with a dozen others, outside a shop just off the Rua do Carmo, which at the end of the day hands out the pies and sandwiches it hasn't managed to sell. He's always first in the queue and would quite happily grab the lot for himself, if the shop assistant didn't intervene. The moment the door opens is when Bob truly comes alive, like a man rising from a tomb, his face flushed with a kind of loathsome greed. If he hasn't managed to arrive before everyone else he elbows his way to the front and grabs as much as he can, stuffing a filthy old bag as full as he can and then disappearing.

He hails from Ohio, is short, stocky, grubby, and he smells. He's been in Lisbon for quite some time doing absolutely nothing apart from getting his hands on as much free grub as he can. This is literally the only thing which makes him tick. He told me how he'd joined a Hare Krishna group a while back because he'd heard that you can get free food every day and sleep gratis in the temple. He railed against the fact that it was all vegetarian and they looked at you disapprovingly if you piled your plate too high or went back for second or third helpings; being so thick-skinned and out of touch emotionally I was surprised he'd noticed that. His sojourn there ended abruptly; with his lifeless voice and without a trace of humour, he explained to me, 'There was a whole goddamn day and night of fasting in honour of the god they revered, Krishna I suppose it was, who was draped with flowers, and offerings of fruit and cakes were put before him, masses of bananas and grapes and cakes dripping with honey,' his voice had a way of dying off at the end of a sentence. I envisaged him drooling and looking at all this with lustful greed as the others were singing mantras and prostrating themselves before the cherished god.

'It was all too goddamn much. I got into the sanctuary in the middle of the night and stuffed as much into my mouth and my bag as I could, yeah, but one of the motherfuckers disturbed me and they threw me out in the morning.'

The last I saw of Bob was one evening when I was hurrying along the street towards the shop, the clock had already struck six and I was late, but just in time to see him laden down with two bulging bags of pies scuttling up a side street. I hailed him. 'Quick,' he called back, 'they're just closing up.'

'Oh sorry,' said the shop assistant who was pulling down the shutters as I got there, 'we just gave everything to that friend of yours.'

Mike and I have become drinking buddies. the 'Pit', as we've come to call that gloomy hell-hole down the *Travessa do Forno*, has become our headquarters where we drink whole days through if our fortunes allow, letting the streets, the world, time itself carry on outside without us. Sometimes we're joined by Wino Willy, though he and Mike – 'Mike the Swindler', let's call him – don't see eye to eye: William branding Mike an arrogant cheat and Mike branding William a bum.

But most days we have our trades to ply, I on the shopping streets with my penny whistle and Mike in the notorious Picnic café in Rossio, where pickpockets rub shoulders with tourists, and I think would more aptly be called 'Picpoc' – this is where Mike operates. As often as not, I'm playing by the Arco de Bandeira in the morning, to get some lunch money made and, just as often as not, up comes Mike – if I'm lucky just asking me for the price of a coffee so that he can install himself in the Picnic, if I'm unlucky he's jingling some coins of his own in his pocket and insisting I go for a drink with him. It's fatal to start so early, one never knows where one's going to be by nightfall, or in what state. Once I have the rent money in my pocket and some grub in my belly I'm ready for anything, anything.

I tell Mike about this old fellow dressed like a priest, in robes and a skull-cap, in fact like the very Pope himself, who'd approached me with some story about how he hadn't been able to get to the bank and could I lend him some money.

'Yeah, the Pope, he's good,' says Mike when I tell him about this old rogue, 'he tried it on me, but it takes one to know one and I told him outright I didn't believe a word he said, even if he swore it was true on the Bible,' here Mike hisses with laughter, 'but if it was the price of a drink he was after, c'mon, I said to him, I'll take you for a beer round the corner. Turns out he's Brazilian and highly educated, speaks seven languages – German being one of them – and he preys mostly upon old women of a religious bent, he does well with those,' Mike is interested from a professional point of view and is obviously impressed, 'Only he drinks too much and gives the game away.'

Not long after this I'm walking through the red light district, a stone's throw from the Pit, late one night when I hear shouting, cursing and swearing coming from the street outside one of the

brothels – and there, shaking his fist up at one of the windows, in all
his disheveled robes, is the raging, spluttering Pope, shouting all hell
and brimstone and to give him back his hat.

There's a tiny *ginjinha* on the Rua de Barros Queiros, which itself is no bigger than a passageway, where an elderly woman sits
on a stool at the bar smoking; a thick layer of make-up, mascara,
rouge and smudged lipstick try to conceal her pale, puffy face whilst
a short leather skirt, totally inappropriate for her age, exposes her
thin white thighs and a low-cut blouse of black lace barely covers
her shrivelled breasts so that all in all she perfectly illustrates the
expression 'mutton dressed as lamb'. She seems to be lost in her
own world, her eyes, looking up to the ceiling, seem faraway as she
watches the smoke curl up from her cigarette. I didn't realise she was
even aware of my presence, sitting inconspicuously as I was drinking my morning coffee in the corner. But then she swivels on her
stool and addresses me in French, 'Ah, *mon cherie*, I long to return
to Paris – thirty years I spent there, ah monsieur, Paris is life. I lived
near the lion of Denfert-Rochereau. I came back to Lisbon to be
near my children and now my son drugs me and hits me – look,' and
she shows me swellings on her wrists and her neck

But why should he attack his mother like this?

'*Jalousie, monsieur, jalousie . . .* '

But jealousy of what, why would a son be jealous of his mother?
'Ah, if I only knew that, *chérie*, but how can a mother understand
everything about her children?'

She suddenly throws back her head and starts singing *Fado;* apart
from the slurring, it's a sweet and rather touching rendition – it's
about love being found in hidden places in Lisbon.

'I was famous once, monsieur, I sang in Montmartre . . . '

With winter on the way it's becoming more and more difficult to
get a living off the streets and I'm just managing to tick over; November is always a sticky month but I know that things will pick up
towards Christmas. For Mike things are going from bad to worse.
The supply of tourists has practically dried up and won't start flowing in again until just before Christmas and so he's spending many

a night on the benches in the square unable to pay for a pension, or even one of the doss houses in which William is staying, which cost a mere seventy escudos a night. He's getting gaunter and more bedraggled than ever, every penny he has being spent on wine and he's becoming more and more cooped up like a vulture deprived of prey. One day his luck changes; I'm sitting in the Pit, over a bottle of 'potato wine' when in he struts and, sitting down at my table, calls for a glass and a bottle which Manuel brings, in his surly manner, slamming it down in front of him.

Manuel regards Mike with the utmost suspicion, '*Quanto é Manuel?*' Mike asks, pointing to the bottle and pulling out a wad of notes, putting one in Manuel's enormously fat hand which grabs it, stuffs it in a pocket and slams the change down on the table.

'C'mon,' he says to me, 'I'll take you to the Come Bebe for dinner, I had a spot of luck today,' and here comes the chuckling, his fragile frame rattling with laughter, then he pulls himself together and, tweaking his pencil-thin moustache with his fingers, eyes narrowing, he starts, 'there must be one, just one, German tourist arriving in Lisbon today, I said to myself as I sat in the Picnic this morning – not a single tourist inside just those other goddamn bums that hang around there spoiling business for me. So, I thought, I've gotta do something about this, and so I went to meet the afternoon train that arrives direct from Munich – hah! – there's a blonde-haired motherfucker, straight from his mother's apron strings, more money than sense. I made a beeline for him – started to introduce myself, but to my astonishment he told me to go to hell. *He told me to go to hell!*' Mike looks at me most aggrieved that anyone should address him like this, 'Christ, I was going up to welcome him to Portugal.'

'Yes, I can see that you'd be the most marvellous specimen for anyone to meet upon arriving in the country for the first time, Mike, you ought to get hired by the tourist board to welcome German tourists and make them spend money.'

He goes on, in his quasi-American drawl, 'I told him he shouldn't get into the habit of banishing people to hell, especially people he didn't know – that he'd do better to keep his mouth *shut*. Christ, I hadn't done anything to get that kind of abuse.'

'No, of course you hadn't Mike, not yet.'

'He said he was sorry, that he was tired, that he'd had all his luggage and most of the money he was carrying stolen coming through Spain. Oh shit. How much money has he got left then? I wondered, and looking at his face which was so completely confused I almost hadn't the heart to tell him my story. But I had to, even if it was only for a cup of coffee – it's in my nature. C'mon, let's go and eat something, I'll tell you the rest of the story over dinner.'

Round the corner is the Come Bebe – literally, the 'Eat Drink' – a greasy spoon with bright neon lighting, sawdust on the floor and a continual turnover of customers, mainly young men doing their military service or in town looking for work, or in town on the town – no doubt some of them just crawled out of one of the brothels in the vicinity. It's cheap and you can be dolloped up a meal and gulp it down in two minutes flat if you sit at the chromium counter on one of the high stools. Mike isn't going to be hurried, he can afford not to be. We sit down at one of the tables and are waited upon in a civilised manner. 'Here's to you, Hans,' Mike lifts his glass of ale and, chuckling, resumes his tale, 'Hans is his name – blonde haired Prussian, you know the type, never been out of Germany, never even been in a city, I shouldn't think.'

He looks at me with glee all over his face, 'This Prussian's heaven-sent.'

The food arrives and two more jugs of *Sagres* with which to wash it down. Mike's ordered a whole chicken for himself, roast potatoes and a little green salad which looks quite absurd sitting before him, as out of place as it would be in front of a wolf.

'You can have the salad, too healthy for me. That kind of thing's for rabbits.'

'So I told this Hans my story, that I'd come to Portugal for a holiday, got a bit drunk on the first night here in Lisbon, got attacked by some louts in the Bairro Alto and had had all my money stolen.'

'He believed you?'

'Listen, this fellow doesn't know what a lie is. How can you disbelieve somebody when you're unaware of even the existence of lies? Anyway, he could see the cut here on my cheek, that was proof enough that I really had been set upon by thieves,' he chuckles, knowing full well that I know how he got that a couple of nights back falling over in the Pit and scraping his cheek on the corner of the table. Manuel had advised me to take him home. 'He hasn't got a home, Manuel,' I said, 'then take him to the street,' replied Manuel, a quiver of a smile on his lips, and obviously delighted to see this arrogant German fellow in such a state.

Mike went on, 'I told him I'd telegraphed to my mother in Germany to send some money but, because of the bloody public holidays and holy days, one after another, one saint or another, they have here in this goddamn country, the money was taking a long time to get to me. So, when I told him I'd repay him when it came and if he could lend, just *lend*, me some, he peeled off two hundred marks from the wad he had in his pocket – as easy as that, two hundred marks. "If you need some more," he said, "here is the address I will be staying at, come to my room and I will give you some more." So eat, drink, money no problem, I'll be around to get some more from Hans in the morning.'

'Christ, there's William – hey William,' he bellows through the doorway to the street where old Willy can be espied sloping along in the shadows. He stops, looking like a hunched up old crow, looks from left to right around him unsure if he is imagining things – as he so often is – and then just as he is about, with a shrug of the shoulders, to continue his wary way Mike shouts again, 'William!'

The waiter rushes over, finger on lips, to stop him shouting, when Willy realises that someone really is calling his name and that it's coming from the direction of the Come Bebe – he comes up to the door and peers in.

'Over here, William,' I can see by William's expression that it's most distasteful to be hailed in this undignified manner and, now that he sees that it's Mike doing the shouting he's not going to come in, but when he sees me he comes shuffling over to the table, 'Sit down William. Wine?' demands Mike.

'Yes, but I pay,' he just cannot stoop to accepting a drink from Mike.

'Don't be insane William – with what?' and boy, does that ruffle the Colonel's feathers.

The waiter arrives with the wine and Willy fumbling with some coins tries to hand them to him, but Mike's handed a big note to the waiter saying, '*Eu pago tudo,* and keep the change.'

It won't be long before Mike really *is* paying for everything.

It's a cold, bleak evening, a fine rain making life on the streets very unpleasant and I've been making my way along the Rua das Portas de Santo Antão towards the Pit, having made just enough for a bottle of potato wine when I become aware of a voice calling out my name, it sounds urgent and pathetic. I stop, trying to make out where it's coming coming from. I can just make out an emaciated form in the shadow of a doorway.

'Mike, what are you doing there?'

'Have you seen Hans?'

'Not today, perhaps he's in the Pit.'

'Yeah, probably looking for me.'

'What do you mean Mike?'

'He's after me, he's got a knife.'

Mike, true to his nature, has been several times to Hans's hotel to get money off him, assuring him that as soon as the money arrives from his mother he'll be straight round and will repay him fully. But Hans is beginning to smell a rat – and besides, he's running out of money himself. And for the likes of Hans, as wet behind the ears as I was that first time I arrived in Paris, to run out of money in a strange city far from home is serious, a little bit terrifying. So he has started to pin Mike down about the debt, started to trail him around town and, one fine day, he inevitably appears with him in the Pit, with Mike looking subdued, even cowed, and Hans is just as I'd pictured him from Mike's description: blond hair, blue eyes, disarmingly naïve and open with a natural simplicity and kindness about him that had of course moved him to open his hand to Mike on first hearing his story.

This is the last I'll see of Mike for a long, long, time: cooped up in a doorway like a bedraggled vulture.

I've begun to like Hans, who's generous and big-hearted, the very antithesis of Mike. He has begun to frequent the Pit and is welcome at our table and, boy, can he shift that wine. The last of his savings are going on it and he's getting into that slippery descent so many of us have found ourselves on in Lisbon. He gets steaming drunk and it's evident to all that he's highly displeased with my mate Mike who no longer appears at the Pit, as he knows Hans will be there and realises he's not leaving Lisbon until he's got his money back, every single damned *pfenig* of it.

I myself nearly drank myself into an early grave over the course of that winter. I had Sylvie on my mind, Sylvie who was far away in London and I longed, I ached, to be with her. At Christmas she came out to see me – with her husband. It just made me more unhappy, seeing her but not being able to be with her and, when they went down to the Algarve for a few days, I hit the bottle as never before, from morning till evening, and most of that time's a haze. When they returned to Lisbon on new year's day they found me in a pool of blood on the rainswept street outside the Pit. I have no recollection of how I got there, of what had happened. They picked me up and took me to the emergency department at the hospital, where I had the gash on my forehead stitched up. They left for London the following day. I felt as though I'd reached the nadir of my existence and that I must pick myself up, before I slid any further, before it was too late. A few days later I went to the *poste restante* where there was a letter waiting for me from Sylvie and money, enough to get at least to Paris, hidden between the pages of a book.

Chapter 39
Gurdjieff

I returned to England to spend a few months back home in Wiltshire to reflect on things and address certain issues in myself. It was during this time I discovered the teachings of George Ivanovitch Gurdjieff. I'd awoken one bright spring morning and, after a quick breakfast, got on my bike and rode into Devizes, my local town, some six miles away. I headed straight for D'Arcy Books, a marvellous second-hand bookshop which occupied two floors and had thousands of books. I was in search of any works of C.G. Jung I didn't already have; his insights and exploration of the unconscious helped me make sense of myself and opened a world which I felt must always exist, a forgotten world which something in me dimly remembered which had all the elements of myth and magic and *meaning,* which I'd so long sought – a world beyond the mundane we take for the sole reality.

I went up the creaking wooden stairs to the first floor where the philosophical and esoteric books were and where the owner of the shop, Colin, had his office on the first floor and who would emerge from time to time to offer you a glass of wine. I ran my eye along the shelves but drew a blank as far as Jung was concerned, except for *Memories, Dreams and Reflections* which I already had. Not seeing anything else of particular interest, I was about to leave when my eye alighted on a great dark-blue tome, whose title had faded with age, on the top shelf and which seemed to me to be compelling me to reach up and take down. As I held it in my hands and looked at it, it struck me it was not unlike the book I'd seen in that vision in the cornfield in France all those years ago. Inside the cover was the title: *Psychological Commentaries on the Teaching of G.I.Gurdjieff and P.D.Ouspensky* by Maurice Nicoll and opening the book at random I read, 'Until a man realises he's asleep, nothing else can happen . . .' And I read on, 'Real inner change is a development of essence – that is, of what is the most real and the deepest part of you.' That was it, I had to have it.

It was quite expensive at twelve pounds, I looked in my pocket and found that I had but nine quid and a little change – what to do? I was not going to leave it here, it might have gone the next time I came to town – it was in my hand now and I wasn't going to let it go. Colin was not in his office so I went down to the cash desk on the ground floor, where his wife, Jenny, was sitting reading. I explained the situation to her and asked if I could put down the nine quid in my pocket and bring in the other three on the morrow.

'Of course,' she said, handing it back to me, 'it looks like an interesting book.'

I walked out of the shop with it clutched to my breast, as though it was the most precious thing in the world – and so it would prove to be. I went round the corner to the tea shop where I sat down, ordered a cup of tea and opened the book. It had previously belonged to the author's wife, Catherine Nicoll, whose name was inside the cover and who had made copious notes throughout the text. Maurice Nicoll was a doctor and psychologist who had studied under Jung in Switzerland and then had come into contact with Gurdjieff, a Greek-Armenian mystic who had first started imparting the knowledge he had gleaned, from extensive travels in the East and training in various monasteries, to small circles of students in Russia, principally Moscow and St. Petersburg. Nicoll became his student at the Prieuré, a château at Fontainebleau in France where Gurdjieff had set up a retreat for his students to work on themselves, intellectually, emotionally and by means of hard physical work, in the extensive grounds which surrounded the Prieuré. Long ago, when I was twenty or so, I had spent a night in the woods of Fontainebleau and had had a vivid dream in which a snake had shed its skin and emerged vibrant and glowing like an emerald.

The cup of tea arrived and, fishing out the change in my pocket, found to my embarrassment that I was three pence short of the price.

'I'm terribly sorry,' I stammered as I explained to the waitress my predicament and asked if I could bring in the missing three pence on the morrow.

'Of course,' she said, smiling. Everything about that day seemed to be smiling.

The main tenet of Gurdjieff's teaching was that man is asleep and does not remember himself and that if he did he would remember who he was, where he'd come from and why he was here – he would know the meaning and purpose of his life. This is what I was hungry for – a change, a redirection, a reaffirming of what I'd originally set out to do: to find romance and adventure and some kind of meaning and purpose to my life – my life in which I'd begun to stray so far from the path I'd set for my soul and feared I might never regain it. But then, I was heartened by the words of Teresa of Ávila, 'To reach something good it is very useful to have gone astray and thus acquire experience.'

They say that when a man is ready the teacher will appear – well I could not have been more ready for it seemed at this point that I had strayed so very far from myself and the meaning and purpose of my life eluded me wherever I sought it. I was at the midpoint of my life, the point at which Dante found himself in a dark wood and I needed to find my way out of it. When I first set out at the age of eighteen I had a definite purpose and that was to find romance and adventure, and certainly I found both, in abundance, with lots of despair thrown in. Well now, at the age of thirty three, I knew that time had run its course and now was the time to harvest all that I had sown, both the good and the bad, and that if I was to continue as I had up until then I would surely squander all that I had gathered along the way and would likely end up as a tramp. So now it was imperative to change, to re-direct myself, to remember why I'd come and to set my sails accordingly.

I came down one morning to find my mother having coffee in the kitchen with an old woman whose name was Vega and who had recently moved with her husband from London to Chirton, a village which lay a mile away over the fields. I could see there was something rather unusual in her and she started asking me questions. She wanted to know what I read and so I told her that I was completely engrossed in a book I'd come across about the teachings of a man called Gurdjieff.

"Gurdjieff?' she exclaimed almost jumping from her seat, "I was a pupil of Gurdjieff at his château in Fontainebleau, which book are you reading?'

'I'll show you,' and I rushed upstairs to get the precious dark blue tome.

'Maurice Nicoll, I knew him well,' she said, taking the book in her hands, opening it and seeing that it had belonged to his wife Catherine, 'my goodness and this book found its way to you – it means something you know,' she went on with rather a mysterious tone to her voice, 'where did it find you, please tell me.' And I recounted the events of that morning in Devizes.

'You see," she said, there are certain things that are set in motion when you encounter the Work – things start happening which seem like coincidences but really they're not – there's a conscious force behind them and it's as though your life from then on is being arranged by a hidden hand, chance meetings, unexpected occurrences and things happening that seem like coincidences – perhaps you've already begun to glimpse something of that from your reading of Maurice Nicoll, he'd been a student of Jung before coming over to Gurdjieff and synchronicity was a big thing with him.'

As she was leaving Vega invited me over to further our conversation with her and her husband, which I eagerly did and over the course of several evenings, and hearing from personal experience about life at the Prieuré in Fontainebleau truly brought the teachings alive and became not just words written in a book. I think they were sounding me out in these conversations we had, seeing if I had the right understanding and was ready in a practical sense for these teachings for shortly before my departure for Portugal they told me they'd tried to make contact with the director of the school in Paris which had carried on after Gurdjieff's death; but he'd been away and the people they'd spoken to were unsure of the date of his return, but they thought it wouldn't be before a month or two as he had some personal matters to take care of in the south of France and said it had been hard to get hold of him.

Now with the spring well advanced Vega knew that I was impatient to be off on my travels and her parting words were: 'All your journeying will in the end lead home, ponder that deeply.'

May is here and under a new moon, most auspicious for beginning a journey, I'm setting off again for Portugal; this time via the northern coast of Spain, and the verdant coast of Galicia, crossing the Bay of Biscay by ship from Southampton to Santander. I've got the book in my rucksack and I pore over it at any opportunity as I trudge the roads and footpaths of Galicia, this Celtic land with dolmens and villages made entirely of stone and slate from the rugged landscape. I stop to listen to the sound of the *gaida*, a small shepherd's bagpipe made of goat's bladder and with one drone, sweeter than the highland pipes I'm familiar with and haunting as I linger outside a lamplit barn.

I'm not drinking, and this is a bit of a test of the will as the people here drink a lot of cider and the bars are full of merriment and frothing vessels of this sparkling, refreshing, thirst-quenching nectar; but I'm determined to stick to my resolve and address that part of myself which had allowed my consumption of alcohol to get out of hand – it had been a great teacher, taking me to places and putting me into situations where angels had truly dreaded my treading and some of which I'd never have found my way out of had it not been for my lucky star, my guardian angel who doggedly stayed at my side through thick and thin. It was when the booze began to become my master that I knew it must be taken in hand, at least for a while. And so I've resolved not to drink for a year, which of course is going to a bit of a challenge in Lisbon when I run into the likes of Mike and Wino Willy.

Chapter 40

Lisbon Again

'Yes your old room is free,' says Luis at reception handing me the key, 'welcome back to Lisbon.'

As I flop down on the bed and listen to the familiar sounds coming through the window – the bell from the Misericordia striking the hour, the pitter-patter of feet ascending and descending the steps, the distant sound of traffic from Rossio, the screech of the tramlines on the Largo da Trindade, I stare up at the ceiling and start to take stock of myself and of everything which has conspired to bring me to this point – 'the days which have had to happen to me.' There can be no doubt that I've had all the luck in the world.

If there was any logical pattern to chance I'd not be here now: I'd have ceased to exist a long time ago. As it is, I feel that I am experiencing a resurgence of the spirit, new growth, as though this life were a womb and I am being reborn in a birth at which I myself am the midwife; rebuilding, reconstructing, restructuring, with new and vital material, an edifice which has been in danger of tumbling to the ground. I am having to rethink myself, redefine my purpose: my angel must be prompting me, nudging me in the direction which, in a seemingly miraculous fashion, I've started moving – there are forces at work in us which we cannot see nor even conceive of; they are just waiting for a signal, a command, to pull them all together so that no longer will they tear me apart with strife and contradiction but rally to the cause to which an inner voice has been calling, unheard through the din of myself.

My angel has had a busy time pulling me out of places, most perilous in many more ways than one, into which, perhaps, I should never have ventured. Or should I? Is it not, after all, absolutely essential that I do everything that I did – even the blackest things – and that I should fall in the face of many temptations, to burn my fingers in the fire, that I may learn, so that I might to my roots, enriched, return? Or, in the words of the great Alexandrian poet Kavafi, 'wealthy with all you've gained on the way.'

I am having to remember myself, who I really am, and why I came here and how I have made use of my allotted time. Is there not a reason for everything even when it seems there is no reason? Is it not perhaps the whole purpose of this life here on earth to pit ourselves against ourselves so that we might eventually become masters of our own fate – we otherwise helpless victims of it?

Wino Willy starts off immediately about the number of wines he's drunk so far today and then starts complaining about some Moroccan fellow who'd wasted his time, only paying him three beers and a *bifana* when he could have been down in Cascais and made at least a thousand escudos. He's now behind in his rent, he moans, and he goes on to tell me how he was no longer in the pension where he'd been thrown out of his cupboard, leaving behind an unpaid bill of twelve thousand escudos, and that he's now in another place where he pays only a hundred and sixty a night, a *casa do doss* opposite the Stella Maris – I know the place, I used to pass it often enough, it was just like a Victorian doss house, dark and gloomy and most certainly infested with all kinds of wildlife. All this time William's scratching himself like mad, standing at the bar, his hand in his trouser pocket. I don't need to ask him why, I guess it's fleas or more probably crabs, but he comes out with the explanation himself in great detail and I'm glad I'm not eating at the time.

'It's rat poison, he says, 'some bastard put rat poison in my wine.'

'Rat poison in your wine William?'

'Yes, some bloody junkie put it there, just for fun. Look, I've lost weight.' It's true he has, he looks quite skeletal.

'That's what it does to you, that and boils under the armpits and here where I'm scratching,' he's really going at it now.

'I have holes in my pockets so that I can scratch better,' he's saying this with a straight face and lifting his wine with his free hand and throwing it down his throat and then, in furious indignation, he blurts out, 'the bloody fucking bastards could have killed me.'

I'm amused by his story but he is going a little bit too far with his demonstrations of discomfort caused by the crabs – after all we're in a rather respectable bar and his scratching is becoming evident to all. And then to my horror he pulls his hand out of his pocket with a triumphant cry, so that all heads turn in our direction, 'I've got one of the buggers, look,' and between his two thumbnails he's popping a crab. I suggest to him that we leave after that; I am at the point where I'd gladly have pretended to have nothing to do with him. Out on the street I get him talking again and he embarks upon a story about a Japanese businessman he'd guided around Lisbon one evening, showing him the bars and getting plenty of beers and wine in return. Apparently this fellow was something to do with the Nippon Cultural Society and, according to William, was loaded.

'He had a wad of money like this,' and he indicated with a significant space between index finger and thumb. Somehow my Goan friend had managed to get six thousand escudos into his own pocket, not from dishonest means because William is never like that, but with his woeful tales of bad luck and general misfortune and was about to work on the businessman to fork out the twelve thousand escudos he owed the pension, so settling his debt and thus being able to move back into his cupboard, which he was extremely fond of.

'He would have given it to me he was drunk. We were in the Trindade – I'd gone up to the bar to get the beers and, when I came back with them he was talking to this girl – of course he was more interested in her than me and the story I was going to tell him so I just had to wait, dammit.'

I chuckle. I can just picture William sitting in front of his beer, the pained expression of one whose plans are being forestalled; he'd have been at great pains to appear not to be listening to their conversation, but listening just the same. Hopefully he hadn't yet contracted these crabs and wasn't busy in the same way he was this evening. And then he went on to tell me that no sooner had she gone – William says the Japanese man had scared her away because he spoke in a high pitched voice like a eunuch—and he was just starting to recount his tale of woe when the Jap got into a dispute with some drunks hanging about the bar and the next thing William knew a fight was about to break out and William was off. His master payoff plan had been thwarted.

'Damn bloody bad luck all evening—first the girl and then these bloody fucking drunken bastards.'

'What about the six thousand escudos you had in your pocket William?'

'I went to see the girls.'

'What girls?'

'Well, The whores of course—I had four of them.'

'Four of them, all at the same time?'

'No, one after the other. In between I ordered food and whisky—I was busy until eleven in the morning,' he laughs with a satisfied, lecherous smirk on his face as he preens his moustache.

'You dirty old goat,' I roar with laughter and, I have to say, disbelief, 'but how did you keep it up?'

'Ha, when it doesn't come up I use a carrot, I normally have one in my pocket, the girls like that, I think that they are glad when I can't come up, they like the carrot.'

Willy's infestation of crabs reminds me of a time in London when I contracted a swarm of crabs myself. Yes, it led to a lot of scratching and, desperate to get rid of them, I'd gone to a chemist in the East End in search of a cure. At the cash desk was a fellow as swarthy as William, probably of Pakistani origin.

Discreetly and in a low voice I asked him if he had anything for crabs.

'Crabs? What crabs?' he blurted out loudly.

Pointing down at my groin and making a scratching motion with my fingers, I said, almost in a whisper, 'Crabs.'

He looked at me in astonishment at my graphic demonstration and then, looking up, cried out 'CRABS!' as though by doing so he'd exorcise the demon which was obviously assailing me. And then he stared at me as if his mind had gone blank. At a loss what to do and by now acutely embarrassed I was about to run out of the shop when I espied an attractive brunette in a white coat who appeared to be arranging shelves. I went over to her and discreetly asked if she had anything for crabs.

'I don't know,' came her reply, 'I don't work here.'

This morning I took the ferry over to the other side of the estuary. The sun was shining and I knew that the Costa da Caparica would be full of people strolling on the promenade and that in a couple of hours playing I'd pick up enough to pay the rent and fill my belly for a couple of days, and that would mean a couple of days off. Half the population of Lisbon would be there, taking the air and eating in the many little tavernas which line the promenade as is habitual on a bright sunny day at the weekend. I love Caparica with its holiday atmosphere and its beach which stretches for fifty miles of uninterrupted sand, broken only by the wooden caiques, gaily coloured and curved like moons pulled up above the breakwater. Walking along this great thunderous beach I've often watched the fishermen at work, twenty or thirty of them pulling on a seemingly endless rope that leads far out into the ocean. It looks like some kind of tug-of-war with only one side visible, the other sunk in the depths. The first time I'd seen them I'd wondered what on earth was at the end of this seemingly endless line. Suddenly from the water emerged an enormous box-shaped net bursting with tens of thousands of squirming fish, sardines, mullet, tuna, mackerel, sea bass, squid and countless more, as well as a host of jellyfish, Portuguese men-of-war. Once landed, the men threw themselves on it and cut open the netting with knives; they then started to throw the jellyfish back into the sea, while women and girls rushed for boxes to load them in. I watched as all these people, busy as the bees in a hive in spring, buzzed about this strange creature that had emerged from the sea, over which swarms of seagulls swirled and screeched. Traders from the markets and restaurants of Lisbon would also be there, bargaining for lots and arguing over the prices. The rest would be traded on makeshift stalls along the promenade.

Busking was going well this morning, people smiling and throwing coins my way, sometimes giving them to their children to come

over and put them in the hat. I was facing the sea which was dancing with ripples of sunlight all the way to the horizon. As the people
passed before me like a pageant, I could see light surrounding them
and shooting like columns from their heads and into the sky, their
auras I suppose which became visible to me, probably because they
were walking in front of the sun and because of the purity of the air
flooding into my lungs as I blew. O people you are the world, with
your sorrows, your joys, your passions and your dreams – never again
shall I distance myself from you, for in our innermost beings we are
joined like stars and are one, where your sorrows are my sorrows,
your joys mine, deep down where we are all connected, all striving
for the light through the shadows – we are the flow of humanity.

I was just thinking these thoughts when a fellow, rather incongruous looking in a brightly-coloured striped blazer and straw hat,
looking like he'd stepped out of a painting by Renoir, and who'd
been standing a little way away listening to my playing and looking
at me curiously suddenly came over and put a thousand escudos
into the hat. Straightening up and stretching his hand to me, he
said, in an American drawl, 'Can I invite you for lunch, I'd like to
talk with you.'

We went to one of the little fish taverns, which are little more
than shacks that stretch along the length of the promenade, and
where they grill the fish on a charcoal brazier in front of you. We
took a table just outside the door with the immense expanse of the
ocean before us, the rolling lines of the waves like white horses gal-
loping through the green fields of the sea breaking on the shore with
a roar and flying spray.

'My name's Bernie,' my companion started as soon as we sat
down, 'I wanted to talk to you because I'm interested in the way
you live, or the way I imagine you live, that is, carefree and happy-
go-lucky, something I'd so like to be. . .' he broke off as the waiter
came over and took our order. As soon as he'd gone Bernie, a very
intense-looking individual with a distorted, sort of twisted face and
a nervous tic which made him wince every so often as though every
now and then he was haunted by some memory, resumed where he
left off and launched into a monologue:

'Yes, carefree, happy-go-lucky, not living just to make money as I did whilst frantically heaping up the things which money can buy, always more, more, more, getting richer and richer but never satisfied, like a hungry man eating and eating but getting hungrier and hungrier as he does so; it's a disease, I tell you – it's true poverty, sickness of the soul. And it's how I'd spend every waking moment of my life, working in the financial district of New York with other soulless creatures like myself, jostling for promotion, for power, for the big break which would set him above all the rest in wealth and status and constantly, constantly, grubbing for money. This was a living death!'

He looked at me with a kind of twisted grin, 'I don't think you can quite understand that, it must seem so remote, alien, from anything you've known, so utterly incomprehensible to you that someone could live their life in such a way, huh?' he looked at me, tilting his head in a way that didn't need an answer, and went on, 'I was making pots of money; big car, big modern house in the most affluent part of town, glamorous wife like a movie star. . . but the more I acquired the emptier I felt inside, to the point where it made no sense anymore and I began to have dreams in which all the gold I'd made turned to lead which weighed me down and started to crush me. My wife left me, I neglected her you see, emotionally I mean, though I'd heaped on her all the riches, fineries and gadgets a woman could possibly want, thinking that and that alone was what made a woman happy. I guess it was my upbringing that made me think that way, it had been drilled into me by my father you see, he was a banker and a heartless son of a bitch, treating my mother like a piece of shit whilst trying to make up for it by decorating her in gold and pearls, thinking this would make her happy, or at least placate her in the face of his many sordid affairs. She ended up in a psychiatric institution where she eventually withered away, isolated and betrayed. I never visited her and I didn't even go to her funeral! I guess I was following in my father's footsteps, with money my god and, my wife gone, other women, after my money of course, and I would have gone on living this soulless existence indefinitely – but then I had a burn out, contracted something similar to multiple sclerosis which paralysed me, had me in a wheelchair in utter goddam despair – when you shit and piss in your pants because you can't move to get yourself to the bathroom, you can wave goodbye to any dignity or self-respect you might once have had. I was a hopeless case in the opinion of the doctors, nothing they could do for me but put me on pills which did nothing but deaden my mind. There's no cure for your condition they told me, but we might be able to keep you alive. Alive! I was more in mind of putting an end to it all, and might have done had I not, quite by chance, come upon in a local paper which my carer had left behind, a short account of this man who'd been cured of a hitherto incurable disease by a laying on of hands by a woman who lived just a few blocks from me and whose phone number he'd included as a footnote. I didn't have any credence in things like that but I was ready to try anything – it was that or kill myself – and so I called the number.

It just took one session with her. She could see what was wrong with me the moment she walked through the door, she could see it in my aura, she told me, which was discoloured, murky, and on which she immediately set to work. It seemed as if she was wrestling with it with her hands which was very strange and from her hands I felt a warmth emanating and my whole body infused with a kind of light which, as it moved through my body I could feel cleansing it, dispelling something dark and heavy as though the healing process had begun. And then in the ensuing days, despite all the doctors' gloomy predictions, I started to get better; it was nothing short of miraculous and I couldn't help thinking I had unseen helpers out there somewhere and that the whole thing, I mean the experience of being helpless, was to show me that I was dead inside and that their helping me was literally to bring me back to life. From then on I resolved to change completely, life's too short to spend making money at the expense of life itself. I wanted to live from then on. I sold everything I had and moved to Europe where, I felt, the people and the culture was more in touch with the natural cycles of life and the earth, especially here in the south. I had always felt a kind of nostalgia which I couldn't explain when I saw the great paintings of these lands in museums and galleries – yes, I always had a kind of latent interest in art and it was nothing to do with what their monetary value might be, as you might expect from someone in my profession, no it was as if they stirred a deep memory in my soul, a glimmer of light in a soul which was all but dead. Art, I felt, was the way to rekindle the life in me and so I determined to learn to paint myself and I came to Portugal and rented a studio down in the Algarve. I applied myself diligently to painting landscapes and the sea, if only for myself.'

As we crossed over the Tagus back to Lisbon this evening he talked to me of literature and some of the great writers he'd begun to read when he was laid up in a wheelchair, especially the Russians who were so profound in their understanding of suffering and their ability to transform it. "My immersion in literature got me through many things then, it spoke to me from a place so alien to anything I knew or could even dream of.'

As we parted company in Rossio, he gave me his calling card, 'look me up if you're ever down in the Algarve, I've got to catch my train now.'

I popped into the Picnic for a coffee, stood at the counter and took his card out of my pocket; on it was written:

Bernard Levinson
Artist
'Life should be a new adventure every day and not dulled by routine.'

Passing by Rossio station, I was distracted by hundreds of people feasting around tables set up in the station forecourt. Curious, I approached and before I knew what was what, I was being greeted by lots of familiar faces and handed a great bowl of rice and beans.

I am being told it's a free feast for the down and outs of the city and that, right now, includes me. The tables are laden with all kinds of goodies: soup, cakes, bread, sausages, cheese, fish, olives, cucumbers, tomatoes . . . I chomp away merrily and it really warms my heart the way these people look after me, the way that only the poor really know how; amongst them a dear old lady who never lets my plate get empty or a dish go by without making sure I get some of it.

There's Francisco the shoeshine boy I last saw polishing Mike's Italian shoes at one of the shoeshine stands and who Mike had kicked off his stool when the poor boy had inadvertently got some polish on Mike's immaculate white trousers. There are young mothers and urchins galore and there's a fair few of the liquefied customers of the Pit, tucking in as they squabble and dribble and belch, dismayed no doubt that there's no wine to be had. And over there's João, the black fellow from Mozambique who often sings *fado* up at Sabina's, three sheets to the wind and swaying about. At the moment he's busy munching a huge chunk of *Bolo de Rei*, traditional Christmas cake made in the form of a crown, hence its name King's Cake, but I can see he'll be bursting into song in a moment or two as he's moving towards the chair which others have started to stand on and sing. He's being cheered as he gets up onto it; he's a bit of a legend and when he sings he sings with his whole heart. Someone holds the chair as he starts as it's wobbling like mad under João who, as usual, is like a floundering ship on a rough sea. His passionate rendition of *fado* brings to mind Alfredo Marceneiro, who epitomised the working man and would give performances in a working man's cap and a rag tied round his neck. And now João, swaying, almost toppling over, and spluttering out crumbs of the cake as he twists his huge blubbery lips around the song, '*O amor é água que corre,*' 'Love is water which runs away,' and getting louder and louder and somewhat off-key the more he throws himself into it. Suddenly he spots me and signals to me to step up beside him and play my whistle which I do with gusto, he improvising with words he makes up on the spot.

I met an interesting fellow at the Picnic the other evening. I'd passed him the other day on the street and wondered what the hell had happened to him, for his face was horribly disfigured as though by fire in some terrible accident.

'It was a car accident,' he told me, 'the car became a blazing inferno.' He didn't need to say more.

He's American, his name's Cyril and he's a kind of magician.

'I could be a millionaire several times over if I was unscrupulous, but I'm not – I always give the things back to them.'

What things, I wondered.

'I can remove wallets from pockets, purses from bags, watches from around wrists, necklaces from around necks – literally anything, and the wearer has no idea that I've done it, until I point it out to him or her and give it back. You see, it seems like magic but it's really just the eye is not seeing things – half the mind is asleep.'

I'm intrigued by the things he's telling me, about so much of what we think of as magic as being merely suggestion, a kind of hypnosis, the art of distraction and the manipulation of attention.

'It's like life itself,' he says, 'or what we think of as life – it's little more than a conjuring trick, the art of deception played out before our eyes, and I tell you, there are those in high places who have mastered these skills to a high degree, and usually not with the best of intentions – just look at the world around us and try to see what you're not meant to see – you might be surprised. There is real magic though, but that's something else altogether.'

Because of the way he's speaking, which is very quiet and his words a little distorted due to his disfigurement, I find it difficult to catch everything he says, the Picnic is crowded and getting noisier and noisier. So I suggest we look for a quieter place. There's one just across the square, not as lively as the Picnic by any means but one I occasionally drink my morning coffee in, it's rather upmarket and has a waitress service. We sit at a quiet table in a corner and a waitress comes to take our order. When she comes back, bringing two cups of coffee, Cyril asks her if she's missing anything – she looks at him looking rather puzzled, '*Nao*,' she says.

'Not this?' he asks, giving her silver wristwatch back to her.

'*Meu Deus*,' she gasps, cupping her hand to her mouth.

> For in and out, above, about, below,
> There's nothing but a Magic Shadow-show,
> Played in a box whose candle is the Sun,
> Round which we Phantom Figures come and go.

> Omar Khayyam

It's from Willy's mouth I have news of Mike's fortunes.

'Hah, your friend Mike,' I can tell by Willy's tone that he's got something to relate about him and he begins with relish, 'Yes, he's been back here – once he had heard that Hans had gone.'

'Oh, has he?'

'He was taken to hospital – too much of that potato wine, he couldn't take it.'

'What happened? Did you see?'

'Yes, I saw him go. I told the bugger the stuff was no good for him.'

'And that he could end up like you, William?' I couldn't resist that but immediately regret it for the Colonel glares at me furiously.

'Just a joke William, just a joke – you're looking very well,' I lie, to pacify him and smooth those ruffled feathers.

'So what happened to Hans?'

'He went to hospital, I told you,' snaps Willy impatiently, I can see that he wants to get onto the fate that had befallen Mike.

'Yes, but why did he go, what . . . '

'Wine,' says Willy, 'he drank too much of it – I tried to stop him, I said, "Look at me, I keep count of every glass of wine I have and so I never have too many."'

I chuckle at this because he does always know exactly how many glasses of wine he's had. 'This,' for instance, he will say, 'is my seventeenth wine today – the first I drank at six forty-four this morning in the Praça de Camoës,' but the thing is although he knows exactly how many he's imbibed he never sets a limit on the number, and so his advising Hans to follow his example and count them is quite futile, and his stating that he never has too many is a load of bollocks: he's perpetually in the state of having had too many, in fact he's permanently pickled.

'So you looked after him a bit, William?'

'The silly bugger wouldn't listen to me, every penny he had he drank. He never ate, he just drank. Every bloody penny he had he drank.'

'Like you,' whoops, I hope he didn't hear that, and hurry on, 'so he did still have some money?'

'No, I told you, he'd spent all his money so he was in the streets begging, and I think he was trying to cheat the tourists like your friend Mike, and he tried to be a guide like me, taking filthy businessmen and sailors to the brothels, but he was always getting into fights and coming in weeping and covered in blood.'

'Into where Willy, into the Pit?'

'Yes, the Pit, and then Manuel threw him out onto the street and he lay there in the rain until an ambulance came and took him to the hospital.'

Willy was telling me all this quite heartlessly and without a grain of pity for poor old Hans.

'I didn't see him again,' he concluded with a dismissive wave of the hand.

'But you saw Mike?'

'Oh Mike, that bloody bugger, yes, I saw him,' his face is lit up with glee now as we cross the square in the direction of the Ginjinha Rubi.

'It was in August,' Willy began, 'I'd just been having lunch with the chief of police, an old friend of mine . . . '

We are standing at the counter of the Rubi. An old woman is singing *fado* in a cracked voice on the street outside. Evening's falling. The air is full of the smell of roasting chestnuts.

Willy goes on, 'We'd had good wine – I chose it – and roast rabbit. The chief of police said, "William Damingos, rabbit is my favourite dish – do you know why?" Well, I knew why, I guessed immediately and I told him why, "because it reminds you of the villains who run like rabbits when you come along." "Exactly, Colonel," he said.'

'And so you were full of wines and roast rabbits when you met Mike?'

'Yes, I didn't want to speak to him, but he spoke to me – do you know what he asked me?'

'Can't imagine . . . '

'For money. He wanted money, for food he said.'

'And did you give him some?'

'Of course I didn't, I knew that he'd only spend it on drink, I am not a fool,'

I have to step out onto the street and explode with laughter.

'So William,' I say, recovering, 'what then?'

'Well, then he started to tell me a story.'

'What kind of story, Willy, a fairy story?'

'He'd been up in the Bairro Alto the night before, been mugged by a gang of louts, had had all his money taken and his clothes ripped off him.'

'And did you believe him?'

'Of course I didn't. He tells everyone that.'

'So you thought he was crying wolf, even though he'd got no clothes on?'

'Of course he had clothes on, though they looked like he'd got them out of the dustbin. When he saw that I didn't believe his story he pointed to a gash on his forehead, 'Look William, you see, I was attacked.''

'And then did you believe him?'

'No, I've never believed a word that cheat has said, he lives by lies and he'll die by them. That cut on his forehead he probably got falling over drunk, like he did that other time.'

Later in the evening I run into Romão, who sometimes plays the *cavacinho* at Sabina's who, after his initial delight at seeing me back, tells me that he'd run into Mike back in August, 'You should have seen him. He'd been making a lot of money up in Porto – don't ask me how – and here he was dressed like an English Lord with a cloak, white gloves and a cane. He even had those spectacles with one glass, what is it called?'

'A monocle.'

Well, well, well, and as Mike himself would say: up and down that bitch Fate.

It's a while before I run into Mike but then, all of a sudden, he's standing before me, dressed to the nines.

'I'm living up at the castle now, just outside the gates,' he says, and he starts to recount his fortunes, 'I've been up in a campsite near Porto, operating from the bar, plenty of tourists passing through, staying just long enough for me to screw the dollars out of them before they head off for the coasts, behaving as I like them to behave, not hanging around expecting a refund! So I was getting rich – and then I bumped into my wife.'

'Your wife?'

'Yeah, well, she's gonna be my wife soon – I'm getting married. She's got a house up there at the castle and . . . '

'And gold?'

'Yeah . . . credit cards galore, her father's a bank manager.'

'Dreams come true . . . you've well and truly hit the jackpot this time Mike.'

'Yeah, and this time that bitch Fate can fuck right off!' and his eyes swivel to a beautiful woman alighting from a tram.

The clock chimes another quarter – Dong! Dong! Dong! – an insomniac's nightmare. You can lie awake and count every quarter all through the night until dawn – nobody's idea of fun. We're in the middle of the night, the Swindler, no doubt, is still up mixing cocktails in his own armchair bar up at the castle, scheming. Wino Willy in his dosshouse, counting wines, conversing with princes, reminiscing with chaps in the mess about the good old days, hunting tigers, roaming the brothels with his carrot, grunting, snoring and dreaming. All's well with the world – we've all got through another day, by hook or by crook, by hustle and tussle, by guile, by smile, by chance, with Lady Luck's blessing. No doubt we shall get through tomorrow too.

Tomorrow . . . tomorrow I'm leaving; spring is here, and the old restlessness – but it's not just the road that's calling, not just the physical road beneath my feet, but a road leading into the depths of me which is calling to my soul.

Chapter 41
Early Spring, Spain

My homesickness, my longing, my *saudades*, for Portugal and the thought of the biting cold night outside, which sooner or later I shall have to step outside into, has driven me to seize pen and enter these pages with grim grin and cackle. Having thus spoken I'll be hard pushed to muster the energy to recount the moments, the moods of the long long day, for my eyes blur with sleep at the sight of the page and I long for a bed and ten hours unbroken oblivion. I was lucky to get four last night after stepping off the train in Salamanca at three in the morning and, after much wandering around the suburbs in search of a building site, unfenced, and un-dog-guarded, and finally making do on the steps of a church exposed to the view of the street and a hundred windows towering over ominously. And there was no lying in as the street was stirring and the shutters of shops were being slid up with their infernal clank and rattle, though it was barely light. I hung about doing a bit of half-hearted sightseeing and standing inside a church, until the banks opened at nine. I brought a good fistful of escudos with me that seemed impressive until they dwindled in size in the exchange. But no matter, I had enough for coffee in the station canteen and the world woke up with me. By noon I'm plying my trade on one of the pedestrian streets that leads towards the magnificent central square, the Plaza Mayor, built in the traditional Spanish Baroque style in the early eighteenth century and which was also used as a bull ring. It's a Saturday morning crowd, strolling leisurely in the warm spring sunshine and much loose change is being tossed my way. I'm astonished to count over two thousand pesetas in my hat after barely an hour's playing. Okay, I needn't bother about work for a few days.

I don't know the name of the town I'm in this evening. I stuck my thumb out after walking some twelve or thirteen miles out of Salamanca on the road to Madrid. I'd resolved to walk all the way but the road was uninspiring and it was bleak out there; a bitter wind coming over the Sierras which are white with snow and half hidden by low cloud. Far too cold, ill-equipped as I am, to be up there, for up there I'd like to be and I'm cold enough on this monotonous road down here to say sod it and stick my thumb out. I'm in a bar with a lot of noisy yokels. Not one of them has spoken to me, though they've all stared hard enough, except one drunkard who comes up speaking and spluttering right into my face, his breath all garlic and wine, and then bursting into tears. And another, a young fellow feasting at the nearby table with his loutish mates shouting, drinking, stuffing their faces with delicacies of which not a morsel is offered me despite the fellows insistent questions as to whether I believe in God and his frequent reminder that he belongs to an evangelical church, in fact he's a preacher and he shows me an identification card with the sign of a cross and blah blah blah. He won't let me get on with my reading and I am obliged to listen to his drunken drivel and to stare into a pair of obtuse unenlightened eyes. There is no comparison between the Spanish and the Portuguese. One always feels very much a stranger here, an outsider. Well it's midnight and I'm thinking of Sylvie. Time to step out into that cruel wind and face snarling, emaciated, dogs with teeth as sharp as the wind. Good God grant that I may meet no evangelist preachers tomorrow.

Just an hour or so ago I was a hundred odd kilometres from here out in the biting wind, in the bleak hills with the abandoned, crumbling villages, a score of footsore leagues this side of Avila. Now I'm in a busy café drinking *café con leche*—my oh my, does it go down well, but it's a hundred pesetas a shot And I'm sure the waiter put the price up in my honour—so I think I'd better hold my tongue rather than shout for another. Looking out on a rushing street, the din of traffic in my ears and a confounded one-armed-bandit grinds out the Blue Danube on a mechanical tongue. Cut off his arm, tie down his tongue, stop that infernal racket.

Avila was beautiful, truly beautiful. A perfect walled citadel, striking to the eyes with its contrast of shadow and light as I approached it yesterday evening coming over the rise of a mountain road as the sun was sinking pink behind it. Built between the tenth and the twelfth century, I read, it was known as the Town of Stones and Saints. Saint Teresa, the great mystic and poet, lived here, 'All things must come to the soul from its roots, from where it is planted,' she wrote. She also said, 'To reach something good it is very useful to have gone astray, and thus acquire experience.'

I walked out along the battlements atop the massive granite walls; I felt as though I was walking amongst the stars, so close they seemed, so brilliant in the dome of the sky which was like an inverted bowl. The last trace of pink was fading over the distant mountain range and the valleys spread out below were twinkling with the lights of villages. As I descended into the town a bitter wind swept down every street, but there were plenty of people strolling about and I positioned myself in a main conduit of the Sunday evening promenading population and raked in well over a thousand pesetas in barely half an hour. My fingers began to seize up with the cold and I had to call it a day. I realised that I was wealthy enough to get a room for the night and not have to face another building site night struggling to keep warm. But the town was desperately short of accommodation and the few hotels I found were all full up – *completo*. So, after a fruitless search, midnight found me in the station canteen where it was warm and there was a coffee machine which I could pump with all my small change. I drank a multitude of cups to keep alert and warm and sat there until two when I made the long postponed step into the icy outdoors to look for somewhere to doss down. Passing along a small street at the bottom end of town I espied an open door into a block of flats. I crept in and found a small alcove under the stairs, blocked by bikes behind which I could conceal myself; I was unlikely to be disturbed at this time of night and I would leave at the crack of dawn. But that damned caffeine had my thoughts turning all night long, turning and turning, so that I didn't get a wink of sleep.

No one can tell me otherwise: life is a series of disconnected happenings and constant changing landscapes as in a dream. Why do I say this, why do I always say this, and why have I reiterated it now? I'd tell you, but I've been thrown off my mental stride by a grim-faced *Guardia Civil* who's approaching me at my table and barking at me to show my passport. Because some of the numbers are worn and faded from use and exposure to the sun and rain he tells me I've been defacing them and, for a moment, it seems to be reason enough to arrest me, which I really thought he was going to do, but then he threw the passport down on the table and stormed off. Any way, back to what I was saying.

Little did I dream as I woke at first light in the dark recesses of a shopfront in Madrid this morning, rapidly rising and dressing before the light crept in and showed me up, little did I dream that the day would see me thousands of feet in the sky looking down on the landscape from the window of an Iberian Airlines aeroplane en route for Zaragoza.

I was cold, feeling grimy and in need of a wash when I got up this morning, trying to warm up in a bleak barrack-like café. It was lucky to find something open at such an unearthly hour and I gulped down the coffee greedily in an effort to warm my blood up. I thought I'd seek out the station to have my second cup and, whilst there, look at timetables and things to see if I could make at least a part of the journey to Zaragoza by train. There were plenty of local trains of course and I looked up at the enormous map of Spain on the wall of the main hall of the station and saw all the little towns dotted along the length of the line and imagined myself arriving at one of them – there perhaps, I thought, or that one a little further along. Zaragoza itself seemed so far away, nestled under the Pyrenees. I wondered, just wondered, how much it would cost to get there by train – it would be at least two to three thousand, I reckoned, beyond my resources and would wipe out the savings I'd made. Anyway, there was no harm in just enquiring about the price; so I stepped into the ticket office.

'Now, the bus will leave from here for the airport at eleven o'clock,' the woman explained to me as she handed me the change from the fifteen hundred pesetas I'd given her, along with a ticket for Zaragoza.

'Airport?' I hear you say, 'but I thought you were taking the train.'

I was, but Basque separatists have blown up the lines between here and Zaragoza, so this means I must fly. This is excellent, I think to myself at this unexpected turn of events. You see it's all as unpredictable and unforeseen as a dream, in which anything can happen, without any logic and right out of the blue.

Out on the highway beyond Zaragoza I pick up a lift heading for the frontier. It's a Polish lorry, a huge 'artic' towing two trailers. Due to its size and weight it has taken fifty or sixty yards to slow down and stop up ahead of me and I have to run the intervening distance. Climbing up into the cab I take a seat beside the driver. He's from Warsaw, a tough-looking fellow with cropped blonde hair and piercing blue eyes. I thank him profusely for his stopping, I'd had my thumb out for ages and I'd begun to think nothing was ever going to stop on that busy rushing road. He shrugs his shoulders, as if to say 'It's nothing,' and then tells me it's good to have company sometimes on these long journeys with no one to talk to but oneself. He has come all the way from Santiago de Compostela on the northwest tip of Galicia, and that, believe me, is a long way. I ask him about Poland, one of those eastern European countries I've always been curious about but never been able to go, due to the Iron Curtain.

'Don't worry,' he smiles, 'you soon will,' and he tells me about how, thanks to Lech Walesa and his *Solidarnosc* movement, the walls will soon be coming down between east and west.

Yes, I've long had the desire to go to those Eastern European countries, such as Poland, Hungary, Romania but, above all, I want to go to Russia, that immense, mysterious land which Rilke called 'the land of God'. The land that had produced the finest writers and poets: Dostoyevsky, Chekov, Gogol, Tolstoy, Pasternak, Bulgakov, Nabokov, Pushkin, Akhmatova, Tsvetaeva, Mandelstam. There must be something about Russia that engenders such genius, that nourishes the soul – and one day I know that I'll get there.

'It's all fucking politics,' he says, 'without politicians the world would be a better place.' I think if anyone would know a thing or two about 'fucking politics' it would be a Pole. Look at the history of that land, right central in the path of invading armies from both east and west, a perpetual battle ground, fought over, plundered, ravaged, sometimes even erased from the map.

'During the war Warsaw was razed to the ground,' he tells me, 'it didn't exist anymore, apart from a pile of rubble – today's Warsaw is what has arisen out of the ashes, the old part is beautiful again. But Krakow is the real gem of Poland, the old capital, which was left largely intact by the Germans.'

I tell him how the Polish had been the backbone of the RAF during the war and had it not been for them, we'd likely have lost the war in the sky, the Battle of Britain.

'Polish people know how to resist,' he says.

It's good sitting high up here in the cabin, the radiating warmth of the throbbing engine and the wise talk of this kind, thoughtful, man. How like a wanderer he too is, through the endless days and nights far from home – how self-contained, how wise with the experience he has gleaned along the way. We fall into silence and I begin to ruminate about what lies ahead; the light is gradually fading and through the purple of twilight the stars are appearing one by one. I feel things are going to be different from now on and that everything's going to fall into place – how exactly I don't know, but everything's written in the stars, which are like a map spread out before me, joined up by the paths I have wandered and those I am yet to wander. Tomorrow I shall take the road to Pau and look for the Gypsies, who I haven't seen for thirteen years.

He drops me off at the Spanish side of the frontier where his lorry has to halt up and have its cargo inspected. This can take hours, especially so for anything coming or going from behind the Iron Curtain. I cross on foot and am waved through without any hassle, despite the frontiers being on high alert after the terrorist incident. The Spanish and French posts are fourteen kilometres apart, so I have miles of no-man's land to trudge. It's bitterly cold but the walking keeps me warm and I'm exhilarated by the crisp mountain air and the whisper of the pines towering against the backdrop of majestic snow-capped mountains.

I could be in for a long session with the French frontier guards, who look upon me with suspicion, crossing on foot and at this time of night, and who could well send me back the way I've come, for lack of sufficient funds – it just depends on their mood, and whether they like the look of me, which they probably won't. I'm called into the office, paraded before them like a prime suspect, a potential criminal, an enemy of the state. They're bored, not much entertainment for them here and at this time of night – on top of that, the one I quickly size up as the boss is drinking and could get nasty. Questions are fired at me, the usual ones, 'Where are you going? What's your business in France? How much money have you got?' and so on and so forth. I answer in a casual manner, well-rehearsed over the years, and am surprised at my lack of attachment, almost as though the outcome of this little interview is of little importance. Everything's in the hand of fate, after all – fate at the moment being this half-cut cop before me who's ordered them to frisk me and search my bag. Everything depends on him and it looks like he's going to find some reason to refuse me entry into France. The only way I may be able to alter the course of things is to somehow make them laugh. Looking at them as they rifle through my rucksack for weapons, bombs or hashish, a tale of Nasruddin, *Hodja*, comes to mind.

This particular tale involved a frontier post much like this one and I begin to recount it to the guards on whom it's beginning to dawn I have nothing of any import on me or, if I have, it's very well concealed. The story goes that *Hodja* would frequently, almost daily, cross the border with a donkey, on both sides of which were strapped baskets full of straw. The guards, thinking something must be concealed underneath it, would rummage about in it but never find anything other than straw; nonplussed and, scratching their heads, they'd have to wave him through. One day, many years later, the chief of the guard post, who was retired now, bumped into *Hod-*

ja in the market of some provincial town and pleaded with him to divulge what he'd been smuggling all those years.

'Donkeys,' said he.

This does the trick, the stony faces of my inquisitors light up with laughter. The chief hands me my passport saying, *'Bienvenue en France, monsieur,'* I sling my rucksack over my shoulder and step out into the night and, with a wink at the moon, majestic in her fullness and sailing over the craggy mountain crests, I descend into France, the thunderous torrents of mountain streams, swollen by the thawing snow, filling my ears with their roar, along with the chatter and calls, screeches and songs of sleepless birds maddened by the spring night.

And I think to myself, if ever I should run into that chief of the guard post in some faraway town and he should ask me what I'd been smuggling all these years ago, I'd reply, 'The treasures of all my days which were stored up in my soul and which, even if you could have found them, you could never have taken from me.'

It's a long winding way down but my feet are light and I'm invigorated by the mountain air, the smell of the earth, the whispering of the pines and the rushing torrents which accompany me and are the music, the song, of the awakening earth. Eventually I come to the first signs of habitation, a little village through whose shuttered street I walk, the smell of horses and the ferocious barking of dogs at garden gates which make me jump out of my skin as I slip by, trying to keep the sound of my footsteps quiet, like a fugitive might. No lights from the houses, luckily no one has stirred despite the commotion of the dogs, only a solitary street lamp lights the little square where there's a little church with a porch. Great, I can take refuge in it, lay out my sleeping bag and get some sleep for what remains of the night.

The clock strikes eight and an old caretaker has come to open the door of the church. *'Bonjour, monsieur,'* I say, startled awake out my deep refreshing sleep.

'*Bonjour,*' he smiles awkwardly, a little unsure of what to make of me being here. And then the voice of a woman calling out to him, 'Is he awake?'

'Yes.'

'*Alors,* is he up?' her voice is shrill, shrill as a concierge's might be.

'*Non,*' he replies, a little obstinately.

'*Alors,* make him get up.'

'It's alright, madame, I'll get up myself.' I call out to the bossy old busybody, and I leap from my sack. The poor old fellow seems a little bewildered by it all and apologetically explains that the woman is nervous because of recent terrorist activity and sometimes fugitives escape this way into France.

I step out into the sunlit square just as the shutters of the café are being slid up. I order a café crème and sit at a table outside, soaking in the warmth of the morning sun. The *patron* tells me Pau is some seventy kilometres distant.

It's taken me a long time to find my way back to the camp, it's been so long since I've been here and I'd forgotten the path. And also wasn't sure that it would still be there – it's a Gypsy encampment, after all, and Gypsies have a way of vanishing. But now, at last, late afternoon I see the white roofs of caravans nestled amongst the fresh green trees, just as I remembered it and the sight of which always made my heart skip a beat, and I have to contain the trembling rippling through my whole body. As I round the edge of the wood I see three men standing talking at the entrance gate up ahead who turn in my direction to see who it is approaching along the path. As I get closer a flash of recognition comes into their eyes, of astonishment at what must have seemed like a ghost from the past. I raise my hand, saying, '*Jarla,*' And one of them breaks away from the group and strides towards me, his hand outstretched, saying in something near to disbelief, 'Lala, you have come back.'

It's Madjini.

He leads me into the camp, excitedly explaining who I am to all those curious faces gathering round.

'It's been a long time – we wondered what had become of you, we wondered if you were still alive.'

Madjini has aged, he'd been just a youth when I'd been here last and now he looks old, lined and scarred. The encampment's just as it had always been and the new generation of children milling around me are just like those before, these children of nature, these whirling spirals of life – it's strange to think that I'd been here before them in their encampment, their home, used their tongue and learnt their ways long before they'd even been conceived. Madjini steers me towards his caravan, 'Come and meet my wife,' he said, 'she's a *gadjine*, but she is like us'.

And curiously she is, in fact I'd not have known she wasn't a Gypsy if Madjini hadn't told me; she's small and swarthy and has all the mannerisms of a *Romani chai* and she talks to Madjini in his tongue. She starts busying around and before long there's a scrumptious supper on the table before us.

'Tatta's in hospital in Bordeaux,' Madjini tells me, 'with heart problems, and all the rest of the family are up there, camped around the hospital – you've come at the wrong time and Tatta will be so sad to miss you, he speaks of you so often.'

I'm proud to hear that, happy that he thinks of me. 'You are like a son to him – you see, you are our brother,' says Madjini. He goes on to tell me Tatta will probably come back in a few days, so you will see him then.'

He's dismayed when I tell him my plan is to go to Toulouse and then onto St. Gaudens on the morrow, where Tim's staying for a few weeks in an old mill owned by Ursula, an old friend of his, and I do feel very torn between carrying out my plan and staying on to see Tatta and the rest of the family, Dzingo, Bella, Touroute . . . all of them. But I do want to see Tim and I know that if I stay on here waiting for Tatta's return I have a good chance of missing him. Madjini asks me how I'm going to get there and when I tell him I'll stick my thumb out he shakes his head and says, 'In the morning I'll take you to the station and buy you a ticket, but tonight you stay here,' and he points to the dinky little caravan drawn up close to his.

I awake with the sun streaming in through the window and outside the cries and giggles of children come to take a peek at the funny-looking *gadjo* who's sleeping in the little caravan and whose head, probably snoring blissfully on the luxury of pillows, they could no doubt see through the window.

'*Jovek, jovek,*' I hear Madjini admonishing them and driving them away and then appears at the door with a steaming mug of milky coffee with some bread to dunk in it, a typical Gypsy breakfast.

Shortly afterwards we're on the way into town in his Mercedes.

'I've got three of these,' he says, 'good money in cars, not a bad business as long as you're prepared to pay the price – I did two years in jail, not easy for a Gypsy to be caged like a bird.'

As I lean from the window of the hissing train that suddenly had appeared from the distance and slid between the platforms, ticket for Toulouse in my pocket, Madjini reaches up, clasping my hand,

'*Latcho drom, pral,*' and, with a sudden jolt, the train moves off into the future.

Chapter 42
Hedges, Ditches and Dreams

What is to come will be created within you and from you.
Carl Jung

On my way through Athens I'd gone up to the Sanctuary of the Muses where I set myself to invoking them by reading some poems and inducing a trance-like state in order to converse with them in an altered state of mind. I spent a long time there, soaking up the atmosphere, soaking it into my blood, whispering to the Muses–the unhewn rock, the surrounding pine and olive trees and the deciduous tree with bright sunlit leaves, whose luminosity gave it the appearance of a lamp, in the central court and whose leaves ever so gently fluttered in the soft breeze and, to my listening ear, sighed with little fragments of poems which seemed to cohere into one long, epic poem, whose meaning I could barely discern but nevertheless sent shivers up my spine and to the very roots of my hair. And it put me in mind of the opening verse of the Odyssey:

> Sing to me of the man, Muse, the man of twists and turns
> driven time and again off course, once he had plundered
> the hallowed heights of Troy.
> Many cities of men he saw and learned their minds,
> many pains he suffered, heartsick on the open sea . . .

It is perhaps a little presumptuous of me to identify myself with wily Odysseus, but I too, in my own fashion, have seen many cities of men and suffered many pains on the open sea my soul has journeyed.

And what with the lulling drone of bees collecting nectar from yellow, blue and red flowers and the herbs growing in the fissures of the rocks, the rosemary, the thyme and the saffron, and the cicadas clattering ceaselessly all around, it seemed as though the Muses were joined in chorus, in a dance in the scorching afternoon sun.

Nine maidens that warm the cauldron – Muses! Come, wrap me in your arms beautiful nymphs, goddesses! Give me to drink from your potion, that I may sing sweet as the nightingale. From the dark pine woods bring me your song, gather herbs, fresh-cut, and poppies, mandrake, deadly night shade into your cauldron. Breathe on it with your honey-sweet breaths that it may seethe, and by its seething soothe me and restore me – and inspire me to sing, sing of the past and of things yet to come.

I'd taken the night boat, the good ship Kitho, to Hania and from there a bus to Kolimbari, the little fishing village I'd passed through the last time I was on Crete and where, sleeping the night on its pebbly beach and looking up at the stars, the stars were all seemingly joined up as I'd seen them once before on the island of Ibiza. Perhaps because of the dark of the moon, the sea was full of fishing boats. I'd seen them going out at dusk while sitting on the harbour wall. Engines were starting up and things made ready to put to sea for the night. I love to watch the colourful little boats cutting through the waves, bows high, midships close to the water, the skipper with his hand on the long-handled tiller at the stern. And behind, the white wake ever widening towards the shore.

Every time I woke during the night I saw lights out on the sea and could hear the engines of those close to the shore. And then, just before dawn, I was awoken to the haunting sound of the lyra coming over the still water from a boat which was lit up as in a dream for a minute or two and then suddenly vanished, into thin air it seemed, as though it was a phantom passing in the night. My head fell back on the pillow and I fell asleep and when I awoke the sky had turned maroon on the eastern horizon and then, as though emerging through a mist from the rim of the sea, a trembling, wobbling, ball, its outline not yet fixed, like the yolk of an egg before its shell hardens and becomes solid. And like a new-born baby, heralded by ribbons of colours which unfurled in the sky over this silent drama which was unfolding, the sun started out on its journey across the sky, and one by one, like sheep returning to the fold, the boats came chugging into the harbour. All the signs were there and I knew that this was where I was going to write my book.

In the market in Hania I bought a sturdy pair of home-made leather boots from the old fellow who made them and in these I arrived in Kolimbari and walked down the street towards the harbour which was lined with fishermen and their wives mending nets. Apart from the murmuring of the sea just down below everything was very quiet, as it being autumn the few tourists which come here (mass tourism had not yet spoilt this part of the island) have all gone home. So amidst this otherwise silent scene I felt not a little self-conscious and ridiculous at the loud creaking of the heels of my brand new boots from Hania which had everyone glancing up curiously to see what kind of gawky being was passing by.

Kolimbari has a gem of a little circular harbour surrounded by thick stone walls which, when a storm blows up, bear their shoulders to the gigantic waves which crash against them. There are frequent storms here, it being that time of year, late September and I've taken a room in a hotel right on the harbour for a very reasonable out-of-season price. I've had a little 'windfall' so no need to worry about money for a while and I can devote my time to writing – everything comes at the right time.

I set up a strict routine for myself, getting up at seven and ready at my desk, pen drawn, at eight – on the dot. I shall work through until noon, even if nothing comes and I write nothing. But everything will come eventually, for it's all there in my memory – and I just have to know where to start – at the beginning perhaps.

And if it happens that I find myself in front of the empty page waiting for something to come and it won't – I don't run away but stay there watching the page like a cat watches a mouse hole. Something will appear and I will catch it. I will not get distracted, I will not leave my post, not pick up a book and start reading, not get up and make another cup of coffee which I don't need, not turn on the radio. I just keep sitting there, something will eventually appear; it might be a phrase or a sentence or an image or just a single word. I pounce. It will have a string of other things in its train and like a magician pulling a seemingly endless ribbon from out of his hat, I keep pulling, it's all in there being created as it comes out, the hat is bottomless, like the legendary Grail, the cauldron of plenty, the alchemical Stone, and I keep pulling it out. The book is in there, complete to the very last full stop, along with all the books and poems I'll ever write. They'll take on their own momentum and will cascade into the air like a fountain. I'll no longer have to pull, all I will have to do is move my hand and the words will tumble onto the page.

So I keep my hand moving over the page, despite distractions, despite that fiend whispering in my ear that I've got nothing to say and may as well give it up for it's not going to get me anywhere, anyway. There, I've flicked him off my shoulder, nasty wretch, he's not welcome here. How many times has he appeared and poured his poison into my ear just as I've sat down to write – and then, dispirited, I've got up and done something else, something which really got me nowhere. No, I declare war on that accursed fiend. How many books and poems has he, over the years, prevented me from writing? That's not a rhetorical question and I'll tell you the answer to that: he has prevented me from writing all the books and poems I'd have written had he not deflated me, dampened my ardour, like oil poured on a frothing sea, like a fire extinguisher on a raging fire. Oh, and when my Muse sees him squatting there in her rightful place she doesn't come near – she who is so hard to entice and such a delight when she alights unexpectedly, unannounced, on my shoulder and breathes into my ear and a tremour runs along my spine and my hair stands on end – and I seize my pen and make what I can of the shards, the fragments, she gives me to work on . . . and out of seemingly nowhere the words appear.

I was on the island of Skyros a while back, that lovely island which rises sheer out of the sea, a great craggy escarpment whose crest is crowned with the white houses of the main town with its steep streets which twist and turn in higgledy-piggledy fashion, so as to deter the pirates who constantly tried to sack it. I had sailed there from the island of Evia on reading that it was here Rupert Brooke was buried, having died of a fever on a ship on his way to Gallipoli, and making his famous lines

> If I should die think only this of me
> That there's some corner of a foreign field
> Which is forever England . . .

words almost prophetic. And I'd written in my diary as I sat in the white square, slowly turning pink with the going down of the sun, one evening, 'What am I going to do with the words I write? Will they one day become a book? At the moment they fall higgledy-piggledy onto the page in a rough notebook and they must be worked on, hewn, like the stones which became this fabulous town, some fine cut, some rough and unhewn, and fitted together as in the building of a stone wall – like the walls I repaired on the farm on Exmoor, every stone of which I fitted into place with my bare hands – how I loved that work – and just so the book, my little town, will be built with the words which well up into the workshop of my mind to be sorted out, weighed up, chiselled and hewn as they issue forth from my right hand and fitted together on the page. And having built this little town, with whom shall I people it, who will stroll in its streets and converse in its squares? Why, with those I've encountered on the road and their stories will be the stories, along with mine, that will be told – for they are all part of the tapestry of my life, and each with his or her own story, which briefly coincided with mine.

A little girl will cartwheel over the marble square of the town; like the one who has reeled out of nowhere spinning like a disc and catching the last rays of the setting sun in her hands and her feet and her hair. A bell will ring from the little chapel over on the far hill; just like the one that is right now filling the air. A man with a funny hat and a broad open smile will laugh at nothing and at everything;

like the one I see heading towards me and is about to tell me about everything I want to know. A woman will beckon me to enter her house and I will dissolve into the twilight. There will be wine pouring in the taverns and there will be music and dancing. And all this will issue forth from my right hand and set in ink and stone.'

I stand out on the deck of the night ship to Athens, my manuscript clutched to my breast and, as the ship ploughs the heaving black Aegean, the stars which have watched over me are trailing phosphorescent in our wake.

Milton Keynes UK
Ingram Content Group UK Ltd.
UKHW021012010524
441979UK00005B/122

9 781906 834470